W9-CIE-057

CHRISTOTHERAPY II

Paulist Press/New York • Ramsey

CHRISTOTHERAPY II

The Fasting and Feasting Heart

by

Bernard J. Tyrrell, S.J.

Acknowledgement
The Publisher gratefully acknowledges the use of excerpts from the *Bulletin* of the National Guild of Catholic Psychiatrists, 120 Hill Street., Whitinsville, Massachusetts 01588, © 1977 by the National Guild of Catholic Psychiatrists.

Library of Congress
Catalog Card Number: 82-60597

ISBN: 0-8091-2482-3 (paper)
0-8091-0332-X (cloth)

Published by Paulist Press
545 Island Road, Ramsey, N.J. 07446

Printed and bound in the
United States of America

Contents

SECTION TWO: (2) THE PROCESS
The Healing and Education of Feelings

APPENDIX

to
Kay and Ron Dodson
and
my nieces,
Cathi, Sue, Margi, Teri and Jenni

Preface

This very brief preface has only one purpose and it is to thank the persons who have helped me make this book a reality. I am immensely grateful to counseling psychologist, Dr. David Fleiger of Edmonton, Canada for his unflagging encouragement and painstaking reading and critical evaluation of my manuscript. I thank him also very much for his Foreword to the book. I am also deeply indebted to Ms. Phyllis Pobst for the many stylistic improvements she made in the original draft. Her corrections were invaluable to me as I did my final draft. I owe very special thanks to theologians Robert Doran, S.J. of Regis College, J.J. Mueller, S.J. of Gonzaga University, Donald Gelpi, S.J. of the Jesuit School of Theology at Berkeley; to clinical psychologists, Dr. John Evoy, S.J. of Gonzaga University, and Mr. Michael Garrett; and to philosopher and expert in the *Spiritual Exercises* Edmund Morton, S.J. of Gonzaga University, for reading my manuscript in whole or in part and for offering many suggestions for improvement. I wish also to express my deepest appreciation to Sister Honor Mounteer, S.N.J.M. for the help and encouragement she gave me at all stages in my work and especially for her preparation of the index. Finally, I want to express in a special way my thanks to the many students I have had here at Gonzaga University and also at the Jesuit School of Theology at Berkeley, Regis College of the University of Toronto, the University of San Francisco, Newman College in Edmonton and Seattle University. I have learned much from these students through their papers and comments in class but above all through my personal contacts with them and the witness they have given and continue to give of how powerfully the healing and life-giving Christ is at work in their lives.

Note on Scriptural references: All quotations from Holy Scripture are taken from the *Jerusalem Bible* except where another version is explicitly mentioned. The other versions quoted at times are the following:

N.A.B. = *New American Bible* R.S.V. = *Revised Standard Version* T.E.V. = *Today's English Version*

Foreword

Sensitive readers and Christian practitioners like myself have already met Bernard Tyrrell in his earlier text, *Christotherapy: Healing Through Enlightenment*, finding in it a rich source of healing truth and helpful insight—a true guide for living a more authentic Christian existence. I myself am especially grateful for the existential aids of "mind-fasting" and "spirit feasting" which time and again have proven so beneficial to my own growth and developmental processes, aiding me to realize higher levels of psychic wholeness, richer forms of spiritual growth.

Christotherapy II: A New Horizon for Counselors, Spiritual Directors and Seekers of Healing and Growth in Christ continues in this same rich tradition, yet with such an expanded horizon of contents and principles, concepts and methods, techniques and illustrative examples that one can truly describe it as a *new science*, a holistic system of healing and growth of inestimable benefit to counselors and spiritual directors and to lay men and women of good will who seek to realize higher levels of psychological integrity and spiritual maturity.

Professional practitioners will find in *Christotherapy II* elements of the familiar and tried, yet what is singularly unique is the author's genuine gift of being able to demonstrate how the approaches of counseling and spiritual directing with their differing emphases in goals and methods can truly complement and enrich each other in a new synthetic "Christopsychological" response to human suffering, whether that suffering be primarily psychological, moral or spiritual in nature. The author's creative "breakthrough" into a more holistic approach transcends profoundly in effectiveness the strictly compartmentalized, separate specialization approaches which sometimes leave the individual sufferers spiritually rich but psychologically poor or vice versa.

As a counseling psychologist "schooled" in the more conventional separate specialization model of psychological counseling, it has been my experience to observe "first-hand" the fuller benefits and gains attained by clients who in seeking a more holistic and integrated approach in their struggles with such feelings as anger, depression, anxiety and guilt ended up not only psychologically healed but also at a higher plane of spiritual maturity.

Further, over the past five years I have had the privilege of leading several groups of Christian believers in introductory-type studies of Christotherapy, acquainting them with its truly holistic and catholic character, its unitive syntheses of psychological and spiritual principles and practices, its validity and practicality as a "path of enlightenment" for ordinary men and women seeking to appropriate higher levels of psychic and spiritual wholeness and maturation. And although these programs are of relatively brief duration (for the most part six weeks in length), it is abundantly clear to me (reinforced by the many comments of members attending the sessions) that such practical adaptations are possible, desired, and very beneficial. Accordingly, I invite professionals—e.g., psychologists, psychiatrists, physicians, pastors, ministers, and spiritual directors—critically to examine the wisdom and practice of *Christotherapy II*, and I urge them to make collaborative group adaptations and applications for the good of the many who aspire to higher levels of psychological and spiritual well-being.

As originator and practitioner of Christotherapy and most especially as a "wounded healer" who has done battle with his own "demons" of addiction and neurosis, Bernard Tyrrell is one who speaks from the heart, graciously sharing the fruits of his own labors in his new, highly nuanced development of the science of Christotherapy. We are indeed most fortunate to accompany the author on his scholarly, yet deeply personal in-depth journeys into the various domains of philosophy, theology, psychology and spirituality, and in his respectful searchings of sacred and secular sources and traditions of both East and West.

The author's insightful commentaries on the character and qualities that all would-be practitioners of authentic Christian counseling and spiritual directing and, in particular, of Christotherapy should possess provide a meaningful set of guidelines and safeguards to protect against such potential hazards for therapists as "burn-out," drug abuse or even suicide—phenomena unfortunately well-known among practitioners of the healing arts. The author's own reference to the words of Jesus, "If one blind man leads another, both will fall into a pit" (Mt 5:14), embodies both an assured truth and an enlightened guide to professionals and non-professionals alike.

In the new science of Christotherapy in its pure form, with

prayerful invocations of the Holy Spirit permeating its basic methods of loving, discerning and clarifying, we see at once the vital importance of the Christotherapist's own inner state of being as far as his or her effectiveness in aiding others is concerned.

Truly a book for today's Christian believers and, indeed, for anyone who finds in Jesus Christ a source of inspiration and meaning, *Christotherapy II* is a veritable "storehouse of treasures" that teach, guide, heal and nourish the minds and hearts of all authentic seekers of healing and spiritual maturity. We are indeed most fortunate and grateful for the gift of this work.

Dr. David Fleiger
Edmonton, Alberta
Canada

1

Introduction: Passages and Conversions

"Passing over" is an inward journeying with sympathetic understanding into another culture, way of life, or religion. "Coming back" is an interior return to the starting point with a transformed insight into one's own culture, way of life, or religion.[1] The present book is the fruit of one man's passages. In my case the adventures of passing over and coming back have centered on the quest for healing, growth and wholeness in Christ. I am writing this book out of my desire to comfort others with the same consolations with which I have been comforted (2 Cor. 1: 1–4) in my journeying.

In a previous book, *Christotherapy,*[2] I tried to share the first fruits of my passing over to the healing way of Dr. Thomas Hora's spiritual psychotherapy[3] and my coming back to my Catholic Christian heritage by writing of my deepened insight into Christ as healer of the whole person. As I look back I am happy with that first effort to share the results of my spiritual journeying. But in the interval since I completed *Christotherapy* I have learned that the processes of passing over and coming back can be diverse, ongoing and expansive; and I have learned in many other ways as well.

In *Christotherapy* I spoke of the healing and growth process as an ascent of the "spiral of transcendence."[4] I used the image of a spiral since in a spiral it is possible to *re-cover* the same ground but at successively higher levels. I spoke of transcendence because the human being with the help of God is called constantly to move beyond and upward. In the years that have passed I have moved around my own spiral a number of times; I hope more often forward and upward than downward and backward. I have passed over again and again into the way of Hora's spiritual psychiatry and to other ways and paths of living—in greater or lesser intensity. Each time I come back with deeper insight into the inexhaustible riches of the healing and life-giving Christ.

Apart from these passages, I have learned in other ways. Reviewers have proven very helpful. They have served as a catalyst for growth in knowledge and needed humility.

Likewise, the many questions posed to me in my lectures and workshops in the United States and Canada have forced me to consider many new problems and to rethink old views. Above all, I have learned priceless lessons from the hundreds of people I have had the privilege to direct spiritually and to aid in their struggles to come to grips with neurosis and addiction. There is no substitute for the experience and wisdom that come to the "wounded healer." There is growth, not only in knowledge, but also in the ongoing inner healing from which deeper wisdom springs. If I might dare express this insight in the form of a beatitude: "Blessed are healers for they shall be healed."

From *Christotherapy* to *Christotherapy II*

When I wrote *Christotherapy* my aim was to sketch a theology of Christ as healer of the whole person—beginning in this life and realized fully in the life of final resurrection. One of my specific goals was to work out the rudiments of a Christian approach to counseling and psychotherapy.[5] I used key insights of such psychotherapists as Drs. Thomas Hora, Viktor Frankl, William Glasser, Kazimierz Dabrowski, and others as well, as lenses through which I could meditatively look at Scripture and Christian teachings in a new way. I tried to highlight and at times make explicit psychotherapeutic elements present in the revelation of Jesus Christ.

One reviewer[6] suggested that what I seemed to be attempting in *Christotherapy* was a contemporary reevaluation of the basics of the Christian spiritual life. In *Christotherapy* I do try to deal with the undergirding principles of Christian existence. I do strive to show how true Christian spirituality impacts the human person in all the dimensions of his or her existence, the psychological and bodily, as well as the spiritual. In fact, it is just as valid to look upon my book *Christotherapy* as an initiation to an holistic type of spiritual direction which explicitly uses tools and insights of psychology and psychotherapy, as it is to view it as an introduction to a new form of counseling or psychotherapy which makes prayer, God and Christ central to its structure.

I hope to suggest in the present book how *Christotherapy* in its *ideal* form is a new "holy science" which goes beyond the contemporary "sciences" of spiritual directing and counseling by integrating the theory and practice of the latter into a higher synthesis, a "new wisdom." Ideally, the Christotherapist as a practitioner of this "new wisdom" is equally competent in knowledge of the healing and growth principles of spirituality and psychology and performs in an integrated fashion the practices previously exercised separately by spiritual directors and counselors. The Christotherapist in this perspective is able as an instrument of Christ to guide a person, whether deeply wounded psychologically or a mystic at a very high level, toward the ideal of holistic psycho-spiritual wholeness and holiness.

I have just stated my view of the "holy science" of Christotherapy in its *ideal* form. But I realize that today the general practice is to specialize either in spiritual directing or (in its most enlightened form) a Christ-centered form of counseling or psychotherapy. For this reason a chief aim in this present book is to show how the principles and methods of Christotherapy can be utilized *in an adapted form* by spiritual directors, Christian counselors and lay persons who seek with God's help healing and growth for themselves and others. Although I conceive of Christotherapy in its ideal form as beyond the proposed compartmentalized practices of spiritual directing and counseling, I believe that it is great progress for individuals to grasp that a Christian psychotherapy is possible and desirable,[7] and that spiritual direction in our complex culture requires deep knowledge of the natural workings of the human psyche as well as of the subtle workings of grace in the human spirit.

"New Wisdom"

A principal breakthrough insight which helped me to develop my own example of the new wisdom is the understanding that there exists a powerful analogy and relationship between four key conversion processes which human beings can experience. The four conversion processes are: religious conversion, moral conversion, psychological conversion, and the conversion from addiction.[8] All of these processes involve two fundamental stages: radical conversion and ongoing conversion. Further, radical conversion and ongoing conversion each divide into two basic movements.

In radical conversion an individual *turns away* from a fundamentally destructive type of being and acting and *turns toward* a basically constructive and life-fulfilling way of existing and functioning. In ongoing conversion the individual *confirms* the first turning of radical conversion by practicing an ever deeper rejection of remaining destructive tendencies. The individual likewise *transforms* the second turning of radical conversion by embracing ever more intensely life-enriching values.

The Holy Spirit and the gifts of the Spirit are active in each of these conversion processes in an appropriate way. Human freedom and decision also play a critical role in the unfolding of these conversions.

Another key insight that grounds my particular development of the new wisdom is the understanding that one of the most effective ways to relate the mystery of Christ to each of the conversions is to use in a creatively adaptive fashion the dynamic movement present in the *Spiritual Exercises* of St. Ignatius.[9] Gaston Fessard, in his brilliant studies of the *Spiritual Exercises,*[10] showed me that there is a fourfold "symphonic" movement present in the processes of religious and moral conversion. Reflections on my own experiences as a "recovered and recovering"[11] neurotic and addict, and as a wounded healer seeking to help others in similar difficulties, helped me to see that this same fourfold movement is *analogously* at work in psychological conversion and in conversion from addiction.

Mine is not the first attempt to relate the *Spiritual Exercises* to the healing and growth of the psyche. Carl Jung, one of the great founders of modern psychology, in a series of lectures commented at length on these *Exercises* and their implications for the development of psychic integration.[12] Moreover, in his work *Aion*[13] Jung creatively paraphrased the first sentence of the famous "First Principle and Foundation" with which Ignatius begins the *Exercises*. The original sentence reads: "Man is created to praise, reverence, and serve God our Lord, and by this means to save his soul."[14] Jung's paraphrase is:

> Man's consciousness was created to the end that it may (1) recognize . . . its descent from a higher unity. . . ; (2) pay due and careful regard to this source. . . ; (3) execute its commands intelligently and responsibly. . . ; and (4) thereby afford the psyche as a whole the optimum degree of life and development. . . .[15]

Jung's avowed aim in this paraphrase was to salvage and show the relevance of the deep psychological insight in the Ignatian statement by putting it in more secular terms. Jung felt that the modern mind had largely lost the ability spontaneously to appreciate and understand in a fruitful way the theological language of the last two thousand years.

While Jung sought to save the valid psychological insight in the theological text of Ignatius by expressing it in secular language, I seek, as one of my goals, to use valid insights of secular psychology and therapy as a means of making explicit authentic psychotherapeutic dimensions present in Christ's revelation. I did this in *Christotherapy* by showing how Christians can see Christ in a new way with the aid of Viktor Frankl's more "secular" insight into the healing that comes through the discovery of meaning in life and existence; with the help of the Spirit, the Christian may discover Christ as revealer of both human and divine meaning, and as source of psychic as well as spiritual healing and transformation.[16] In a similar way I hope to show how contemporary insights of psychology can shed light on the psychotherapeutic relevance of the Ignatian *Exercises*.

Jung found it necessary to "demythologize" the theological language of Ignatius in order to speak to contemporaries antagonistic or indifferent to religion. My work, on the other hand, is addressed primarily to a readership sympathetic both to religion and to the legitimate insights of science. The aim of the new wisdom is to bring together these two spheres which have often been subject to rigid separation and compartmentalization. My goal is an integration in theory and practice of the principles of healing and growth present in Christian revelation, the Ignatian *Exercises,* and the secular fields of psychology and psychotherapy. This new science respects the real distinctions between the sacred and the profane, revelation and nature; but it transcends the radical separation of the two spheres.

As a Christian who acknowledges that Christ's redemptive activity has universal significance and impact, I believe that Christ, through the power of his Spirit, is at work at least in a hidden fashion in the hearts of all human beings everywhere. This means that Christ, through his Holy Spirit, is at work at least "anonymously" in the healing and growth processes of all individuals who are anywhere struggling with sin, neurosis or addiction and with the summons to move toward higher levels of wholeness and holiness. My most pressing concern here however, is to see that *at least* Christians who search for radical and ongoing healing and growth become aware of the tremendous power available to them in the healing and life-giving Christ. But this book should also be of interest and aid to anyone who acknowledges in Christ a unique source of wisdom and insight, if not of total salvation.

Although I use the Scriptural image of "turning" throughout this book as a basic metaphor for the four movements of the conversions, I also at times use the image of "ascending a spiral" to represent the fact that individuals and communities can prayerfully reenact the turnings of radical conversion and can intensify the turnings of ongoing conversion at ever higher levels. Thus, for example, at times during spiritual retreats and at certain points in the liturgical cycle, individuals and groups recall and renew in mind, heart, memory and imagination their radical renunciation of Satan and evil and their equally radical commitment to Christ and his Kingdom. This is spiritually re-covering at a higher level in the upward spiral of transcendence ground already covered in radical conversion. Dante, John of the Cross, and many others have used the image of a constant ascent of a mountain to describe ongoing conversion. Dante depicts the ascent of the Mount of Purgatory as involving many purifications and movements to higher levels. John of the Cross describes the ascent of Mount Carmel as a succession of inner detachments, dark nights, leading toward ever richer encounters with God. The lesson of the saints is that the turnings-from and turnings-toward of ongoing conversion, the daily dying and rising, take place at ever higher levels in the ascent of the spiral that leads to the top of the mountain where at last God speaks to his chosen ones with his Face unveiled. This is the deeper meaning of the words of the Psalmist: "Send out your light and your truth, let these be my guide, to lead me to your holy mountain, and to the place where you live" (Ps. 43:3).

Passages

It was the sharpness of personal pain that drove me into the series of passages through which I learned what rich relationships and affinities there are among the various conversions.

Acute neurotic pain first goaded me into passing over into the psychotherapeutic world of Dr. Thomas Hora. His emphasis on the centrality of God and prayer in the process of therapy stunned and perplexed me. Somewhat desperately I looked around for some living flesh and blood example of a neurotic who had found healing in an appeal to God and his Christ. Providentially, I found what I was looking for in Maurice Nesbitt's powerful account of his own healing in *Where No Fear Was*.[17] At once I felt a strong personal bond with Nesbitt; fear was also my special demon. He told of his having a nervous breakdown as a young man of twenty and again as a middle-aged man of fifty. After his search he began to think he had learned nothing in thirty years and that he faced no future except misery and despair. In search of psychological emancipation he turned to Scripture and discovered that Jesus in his words and parables had a psychological and spiritual teaching which could free him from his neurotic chains. Nesbitt's discovery led to his own liberation. In turn it gave me hope, although he also taught me at the same time that the healing of neurosis can be a "bloody" and often lengthy process.

Neurotic pain was the catalyst for my passing over into the worlds of Hora and Nesbitt. The agony of active addiction, alcoholism, drove me to pass over into the world of Guest House, a treatment center for alcoholic priests and religious brothers.[18] At Guest House I read the "Big Book" which is the basic text for *Alcoholics Anonymous* and bears that latter name as its official title.[19] In my comments here I write as a non-member of *Alcoholics Anonymous,* but as one who has passed over deeply and empathetically into the basic horizon and worldview of *Alcoholics Anonymous*.

In my meditative reading of the "Big Book" I first learned that the *Alcoholics Anonymous* movement had its roots in the powerful conversion experience of its co-founder, Bill Wilson. My reading of the "Big Book" also gave me the opportunity to pass over into the lives of a whole series of anonymous individuals, pioneers of the *Alcoholics Anonymous* movement, who found healing and spiritual growth by living the principles of *Alcoholics Anonymous*. Their stories heightened my awareness that the healing of an addict requires conversion; that it is a dynamic process with stages, and that God-given enlightened personal decision is vital to it.

What struck me most forcefully in my various quests for healing was that I inevitably found myself propelled into a headlong encounter with God. Francis Thompson's daring description of God as the *Hound of Heaven* was verified for me again and again as I sought various forms of healing. At each passage I was confronted with the relentless Lord and I came back to my particular Christian traditions and roots with a transformed understanding, a renewed commitment and a grateful heart.

A more recent passage is my encounter with the world of "charismatic renewal." In the fall of 1976 I was one of some two hundred people who participated in a "Healing of Memories" day under the direction of Dennis and Matthew Linn, priests who work in the spiritual healing ministry. It was an inspiring and healing experience. Later I spoke with them at length about the ministry of healing and celebrated the liturgy with them. They had read *Christotherapy*. I had read their book, *Healing of Memories*,[20] and had also experienced their healing ministry first-hand. We found that we shared much in common, though our approaches to psychological and spiritual healing differ somewhat. This meeting with the Linns gave me great encouragement and consolation and it awakened in me a more intense desire to pray for deeper experiences of living in the Holy Spirit.

A year and a half later I came across Msgr. David Rosage's book, *Discovering Pathways to Prayer.*[21] This beautiful book awakened in me the memories of the Spirit-filled meeting with the Linn brothers and I prayed with more zeal for those gifts the Holy Spirit intended for me. I was further blessed by meeting with Sister Mary Jane Linn, C.S.J., a cousin of Dennis and Matt, who had dedicated her life to praying for the healing ministry of her cousins and others. We talked of my prayer to the Holy Spirit and later Sister Linn wrote me that she and another sister were making a special novena of prayers that I might receive "baptism of the Holy Spirit." I understood this to mean a richer experience of the graces of the sacraments of baptism and confirmation[22] and I joined them in this prayer. As a result I did come to experience a change in the way I prayed. More than before I wanted to praise, bless and thank God continually for his gifts and to be more open to the work of the Spirit.

My new experience of the gifts of the Spirit did not awaken in me the desire to become a member of a charismatic group. My experience confirms, I believe, Cardinal Leo Joseph Suenens' view that the deepest calling of the "charismatic movement" is not to draw all others into the official movement, but to inspire all Christians to desire the gifts of the Holy Spirit and to live a fuller life in Christ.[23]

I recount my charismatic passage out of a sense of gratitude to Matt and Dennis Linn, to Msgr. Rosage, and especially to Sister

Mary Jane Linn who was killed in an automobile accident in the late spring of 1979 and is now face-to-face with the God she loves so much. I also tell of this particular passage because I am so often asked at workshops and lectures where I stand in regard to the official charismatic movement and how Christotherapy relates to the diverse charismatic approaches to inner healing.

It is my view that the worldwide charismatic movement springs from the Holy Spirit. I think a Catholic charismatic group is authentic when (1) it deepens the private and communal prayers of the individuals involved; (2) its members are led to a richer participation in the sacramental life of the Church; (3) it fosters enlightened obedience to legitimate church authorities; and (4) it blossoms in ever richer service of the poor, the sick, the hungry, the persecuted, and the exploited. Where such fruits are present in any Christian movement there is little doubt that the finger of God is there.

Gradually my experience of these passages awoke in me a desire to return with my new vision to my spiritual roots as a Jesuit, a follower of Saint Ignatius of Loyola, my special father in Christ. At the beginning of my passing over adventures I had become quite cool toward the Ignatian *Spiritual Exercises*. They had formed the basis of thirty-day retreats and many eight-day retreats, but had not brought healing for my neurosis or addiction. Through the spiritual lenses of Hora and Nesbitt, of the people at Guest House, the pioneers of *Alcoholics Anonymous* and many others, I began to look at the *Exercises* in a new way. I was amazed at the power for spiritual reformation and transformation I now saw there. In making the *Spiritual Exercises* with this renewed outlook I have grown yearly in my appreciation for the great gift of the Spirit they are.

Four Conversion Processes

For this book to become a reality I needed more than the adventures of passing over into the psychotherapeutic worlds of Hora and the Guest House, coupled with my charismatic experience and transformed participation in the *Spiritual Exercises*. I also needed to grasp the analogy among these diverse forms of conversion. An enthusiastic assimilation of Bernard Lonergan's highly rewarding method of doing philosophy and theology gave me a good start in my quest for a unified understanding of my conversion experiences. Lonergan taught me much about the nature of religious and moral conversion. Further encounters with the famous *Twelve Steps* of *Alcoholics Anonymous,* the writings of Gaston Fessard and Andras Angyal[24] provided me with the pivotal insight needed. There exists a powerful analogy and relationship between the four basic conversion processes I mentioned.

Religious Conversion

Webster's New Collegiate Dictionary (1980) gives the verb "to convert" and the noun "conversion" primarily religious meanings. "To convert" is "to bring over from one belief . . . to another," and "conversion" basically means "an experience associated with a definite and decisive adoption of religion." Religious conversion provides the paradigm for understanding all other forms of conversion.

In the Christian tradition there are many modes of Christian conversion. There is the case of the infant who is baptized and then dies. There is the instance of the person baptized in infancy who reaches an appropriate level of psychological and moral development, ratifies the gift received in baptism and never deviates afterwards from the path of righteousness. There is the complex situation of an adult Christian who shifts allegiance from one Christian denomination to another. In each instance the reality of Christian conversion is involved in some manner. I use, however, as my basic example of Christian religious conversion the adult who is converted *from* a root-level denial of God in mind, heart and actions *to* a state of basic commitment to Jesus Christ in mind, heart, loving and acting.

Saint Augustine gives eloquent, moving witness to this "turning-from" and "turning-toward" of radical religious conversion and to the initiating, transforming and consummating role of God in the process. He tells how in a period of great crisis and inner struggle, "I cast myself down I know not how, under a certain fig tree, giving full vent to my tears."[25] He adds:

> And, not indeed in these words, yet to this purpose, spake I much unto Thee: "And Thou, O Lord, how long?" . . . "How long, Lord, wilt Thou be angry, for ever? Remember not our former iniquities," for I felt that I was held by them. I sent up these sorrowful words: "How long? How long? Tomorrow and tomorrow? Why not now? Why not is there this hour an end to my uncleanness?"[26]

Augustine continues:

> So was I speaking and weeping in the most bitter contrition of my heart, when, lo! I heard from a neighbouring house a voice as of boy or girl, I know not, chanting and oft repeating, "Take up and read; take up and read."[27]

Augustine's glance fell on a volume of the writings of Paul the Apostle. He opened it and read this section: "Let us live decently as people do in the daytime: no drunken orgies, no promiscuity or licentiousness, and no wrangling or jealousy. Let your armour be the Lord Jesus Christ; forget about satisfying your bodies with all their cravings" (Rm. 13:13–14). Augustine then recounts: "No further would I read; nor needed I: for instantly at the end of this sentence, by a light as it were of serenity infused into my heart, all the darkness of doubt vanished."[28]

Augustine's dramatic description of his conversion experience in the garden reflects central elements of the radical conversion process spoken of in the Hebrew and New Testaments. In an early address to the people of Israel the Apostle Peter reminded them that it is God who takes the initiative in turning them from the path of evil: "God raised up his servant and sent him to bless you by turning every one of you from your wicked ways" (Ac. 3:26). Augustine experienced God's initiative at work in the voice of the child who chanted: "Take and read." The Lord Jesus told Paul on the way to Damascus that he was sending him to the Gentiles "to open their eyes, so that they may turn from darkness to light, from the dominion of Satan to God" (Ac. 26:18). In the same way, over three hundred years later, God used the words of Paul to let Augustine know that he had to renounce the works of the flesh and turn from them once and for all. At the same moment Augustine was told to let his "armour be the Lord Jesus Christ."

Ezechiel, one of the great prophets of the Hebrew Testament, spoke often of the need for conversion; he described the core moment of radical conversion by putting these words on God's lips: "I will give them a single heart, and I will put a new spirit in them; I will remove the heart of stone from their bodies and give them a heart of flesh" (Ezk. 11:19). Paul depicted this same moment when he wrote to the Romans that "the love of God has been poured into our hearts by the Holy Spirit which has been given us" (Rm. 5:5). When Augustine wrote that darkness vanished as a light of serenity was infused into his heart, he touched the same reality, the core of religious conversion.

I have described the two movements of religious conversion respectively as a turning from darkness and a turning toward light. Thomas Aquinas, however, analyzes the process in a different way. He names four elements in what he considers to be their natural and proper order: "The infusion of grace, the movement of free choice toward God by faith, the movement of free choice against sin, and the remission of guilt."[29] Aquinas' order of elements appears to contradict my own since he indicates that in a person's response to God's justifying action there is first a turning of free will to God in faith and then a turning from sin. This seeming contradiction between our approaches can be cleared up by distinguishing between the instant or core moment of radical conversion and the movement which leads up to it and culminates in it. I agree with Aquinas' analysis of the instant of justification or radical religious conversion. There is no question but that the "turning-toward" enjoys a natural priority over the "turning-from." As Aquinas succinctly argues: "He who is being justified detests sin because it is against God, and thus the movement of free choice towards God naturally precedes the movement of free choice against sin, since it is its cause and reason."[30] But Aquinas insists that there is no temporal succession of elements in the core moment of justification. Aquinas also teaches that in the adult who is justified preparatory phases occur. Aquinas writes that "before justification, a man must detest each sin he remembers to have committed."[31] This harmonizes with the general Roman Catholic belief solemnly professed at the Council of Trent that a person can dispose and prepare himself for the grace of justification by assenting to God's initial calls and awakening graces.

In the case of sinners in need of radical religious conversion, God must often begin to move a person toward the core moment of radical conversion or justification by such graces as arousing in him or her a sense of disgust with the self-destructive effects of immoral living, a fear of punishment for continued rejection of God, a growing feeling of guilt and shame, an experience of moral impotence and powerlessness, and similar graces. Apart from God's healing grace these experiences could lead to despair and even suicide; but when these experiences are enlightened by God's healing grace they become occasions for a person to begin to turn away from a destructive, idolatrous, self-centered type of existence and to turn toward the true source of life.

In the Hebrew Testament we read how God sought again and again to bring his wayward people back to himself by letting them experience the harshness of life apart from him. In the book of Hosea, the prophet's unfaithful wife Gomer is a symbol of Israel in her infidelity to the Lord. And how does the Lord act to bring his spouse back?

> I am going to block her way with thorns, and wall her in so that she cannot find her way; she will chase after her lovers and never catch up with them, she will search for them and never find them. Then she will say, "I will go back to my first husband, I was happier then than I am today" (Ho. 2:6–7).

Notice the parallel in Gomer's experience and that of the prodigal son in the celebrated Lucan parable. Luke writes that after the son squandered his inheritance in loose living and found himself in the midst of a famine,

> . . . he hired himself out to one of the local inhabitants who put him on his farm to feed the pigs. And he would willingly have filled his belly with the husks the pigs were eating but no one offered him anything. Then he came to his senses and said, "How many of my father's paid servants have more food than they want, and here am I dying of hunger! I will leave this place and go to my father . . ." (Lk. 15:15–18).

The examples of Gomer and the prodigal son graphically portray the beginnings of the process of radical conversion as a painful turning away from what is destructive. It is true, of course, that in the New Testament conversion is seen primarily as a joyous happening. "Aversion from the sinful past and the return of the whole man to God is a joyful event for God and men."[32] There is no contradiction in stressing the joy at the core of radical conversion while remembering that the initial stage of turning away from what is evil can be quite painful.

The process of Christian religious conversion is not finished at the core moment when God replaces the heart of stone with the heart of flesh and pours forth his love through the gift of the Holy Spirit. There must follow a daily battle against the world, the flesh and the devil; justification should be the beginning of sanctification. This is the ongoing phase of religious conversion, which continuously confirms and deepens the turning-from and transforms the turning-toward of radical conversion. The inescapable summons is to an ever-growing love of God and neighbor.

The author of the epistle to the Hebrews exhorts his fellow Christians in words which capture very well the ever intensifying turning-from and turning-towards of ongoing religious conversion:

> With so many witnesses in a great cloud on every side of us, we too, then, should throw off everything that hinders us, especially the sin that clings so easily, and keep running steadily in the race we have started. Let us not lose sight of Jesus, who leads us in our faith and brings it to perfection: for the sake of the joy which was still in the future, he endured the cross . . . and *from now on has taken his place at the right* of God's throne (Heb. 12:1–2).

The writer of Hebrews is here reminding his readers of the need to turn away more completely from whatever weight and sin still encumber them, and above all, to turn with fixed gaze towards Jesus who is now enthroned at God's right hand. The metaphor of the race used here echoes the words Paul wrote to the Philippians:

> Not that I have become perfect yet: I have not yet won, but I am still running, trying to capture the prize for which Christ Jesus has captured me. I can assure you . . . I am far from thinking I have already won. All I can say is that I forget the past and I strain ahead for what is still to come; I am racing for the finish, for the prize to which God calls us upward to receive in Christ Jesus (Ph. 3:12–15).

Radically converted Christians must take up the cross daily in ongoing imitation of Christ and of his disciple Paul (Ph. 3:17); they must seek to share ever more richly, even in this life, in Christ's resurrection by seeking "the things that are in heaven, where Christ is, sitting at God's right hand" (Col. 3:1). This ongoing conversion, this daily dying and rising with Christ, this continuous turning-from and turning-toward, is repeated at higher and higher levels in the spiral of transcendence. The reality of the ongoing nature of religious conversion is clearly manifested in the life and writings of such an early Christian saint as Ignatius of Antioch and of such towering Christian mystics as Teresa of

Avila and John of the Cross, who speak respectively of ever richer interior mansions, and of a succession of dark nights and ever more luminous dawns.

Moral Conversion

Religious conversion and moral conversion are clearly interrelated. Yet, there are grounds both in ordinary experience, and in philosophy and theology as well, for considering moral conversion in its own right instead of just as an aspect of religious conversion. There are countless examples of non-believers and of self-acknowledged atheists who live highly upright, moral lives. It is a fact of life that the human community finds it possible in everyday affairs, in professional discussions (e.g. at the United Nations), to consider moral issues without reference to religion. People can consider morality from the viewpoint of experience and reason alone. This is why, for example, Bernard Lonergan is able to offer a definition of moral conversion which is intelligible to theists and atheists alike. He defines moral conversion as deciding to act responsibly and to be governed fundamentally in one's ethical activities by the criterion of what is truly good and worthwhile, instead of by what merely satisfies one's immediate demands for self-gratification.[33]

Moral conversion, like religious conversion, consists in radical and ongoing stages. In radical moral conversion, a person makes a fundamental about-face in which he or she turns from a basically destructive set of values and way of acting, and turns toward authentic values and forms of behavior. In ongoing moral conversion the individual turns away ever more firmly from temptation arising from old corrosive allegiances, and turns ever more fully towards the new world of values and practices embraced in moral conversion.

Roman Catholics and many other Christians believe that the effects of original and personal sin so interfere with a person's natural moral functioning that apart from the gift of God's transforming love and his healing and enlightening graces, no radical or sustained ongoing moral conversion is possible. Bernard Lonergan cogently argues that only basic and ongoing religious conversion makes conversion in the moral sphere effective.[34]

Yet, we must remember that the presence of the Holy Spirit of Christ may be effectively working and transforming, even though unrecognized. Most Catholic theologians hold, especially in the light of the teachings of Vatican II, that the Holy Spirit is powerfully and transformatively at work in all humans, at least in an invisible, hidden, interior fashion. Consequently, wherever radical and sustained ongoing moral conversion takes place, this is due to the presence of an inner religious conversion effected by the Holy Spirit. This is so even if the inwardly converted person is not an explicit Christian believer or reflectively aware of the true inner source of his or her conversions. As Karl Rahner has put it:

> Where a man is detached from self . . . loves his neighbor unselfishly, trustingly accepts his existence in its incomprehensibility. . . ; where he succeeds in renouncing the idols of his mortal fear and hunger for life, there the kingdom of God, God himself . . . is accepted and known, even if this occurs quite unreflectingly. In this way the conversion remains implicit and "anonymous" and in certain circumstances Christ is not expressly known (though attained in his "Spirit").[35]

The dark side of the truth about the anonymous work of the Holy Spirit of Christ in human hearts is sin. I have chosen to dodge the issue of sin temporarily because it is a theological notion and I wanted to look at moral conversion from a nontheological point of view. But, the position of Rahner, Lonergan, and other theologians on the anonymous working of the Holy Spirit in the hearts of all human beings equally implies that when a person says a radical *No* rather than *Yes* to authentic demands of life and of existence, this person is also saying a radical *No* to God and to Christ, even though perhaps not in a reflectively conscious manner.

Ladislas Orsy has described the person who says *No* to the authentic demands of existence through the exercise of a radical, fundamental moral option as "*given to evil.*"[36] Orsy and others sharply distinguish between the type of *No* whereby a person disposes of himself or herself as a whole in a destructive way and so "sins unto death,"[37] and the type of *No* which merely weakens the person's fundamental commitment to what is truly good. Classical Roman Catholic theology spoke of "mortal" and "venial" sin. Many moral theologians today prefer to speak in more personalist terms of a fundamental moral option as opposed to the more limited exercise of human freedom. These writers also put more emphasis on basic inner orientations and moral stances than on isolated moral acts. Despite this trend, however, Orsy does not hesitate to give examples of individual moral acts which he says tend to betray in a person the presence of a radical option against God, and therefore of "internal death."[38]

> Coolly calculated homicide, the denial of faith for temporal advantages, the contempt of the marriage covenant through adultery, the ruining of someone through perjury, the misuse of funds given for the support of orphans and widows.[39]

In these cases there is often enough a need for radical religious and moral conversion.

One final point in considering moral conversion is that those who are radically converted to a new moral life know through bitter experience the particular idol or group of idols they are prone to worship. This sadly won self-knowledge serves to tip-off these persons about the particular form of turning-from and turning-toward which their ongoing moral conversion should take. Divine providence in this way turns the weapons of the Evil One against himself by utilizing the very character weaknesses and foibles of individuals as a means of drawing them to ever higher levels in the spiral of ongoing moral and religious conversion.

Psychological Conversion

What is psychological conversion?[40] The expression "psychological conversion" is my own. By it I mean a shift from a basically neurotic way of existing and functioning to a dominantly healthy state. Like religious and moral conversion, psychological conversion is a process with two basic stages: radical and ongoing. In each stage there is a turning from what is neurotically destructive and a turning toward what is truly healthy. Unlike religious and moral conversion, the idea of a psychological conversion is recent. To understand it requires a precise grasp of the meaning of neurosis and the best methods for healing it. Later in this book I will offer my own view of the causes and meaning of neurosis and some basic methods for dealing with it, together with concrete examples of the healing process in action. Here I wish simply to present two modern psychological models dealing respectively with the healing of neurosis and personality development. These models of Drs. Andras Angyal and Kazimierz Dabrowski have in part inspired and lent support to the model of psychological conversion I am developing.

Andras Angyal

Dr. Andras Angyal, a Hungarian psychiatrist, in *Neurosis and Its Treatment: A Holistic Theory,*[41] offers an explanation of the stages in the healing of neurosis which analogously parallels my own model of the stages of religious and moral conversion. He first speaks in global terms of the initial and final phases of the neurotic's healing and growth. There is the beginning, when the neurotic pattern of living is dominant; and there is the culmination when the health pattern has gained ascendency. Between the two stages occurs what Angyal calls "the struggle for decision."

As the personal drama of the struggle for decision unfolds, with the aid of the therapist the sufferer starts to recognize in a deeply felt way the destructiveness of his or her neurotic way of existing and through a kind of therapeutically-facilitated "demolition process," begins to turn away from it. Likewise the sufferer begins to experience an awakening of the drive for mental and emotional health and wholeness. Again, through the instrumentality of the therapist a type of "reconstruction process" is effected in the person through which he or she moves toward a truly healthy way of living in the world. The struggle for decision manifests itself in one, or most often, a series of enlightened decisions and turning points which eventually lead to the dominance of the health pattern.

Yet, even when the healthy pattern is firmly established, the process is not over. Relapses are a real possibility; vigilance and ongoing resistance against temptations are vital. Even late in therapy there can be a sharp resurgence of negative symptoms. A potentiality for malfunctioning remains and is immediately activated "when the patient succumbs to conceit, pride, or self-centeredness, and retreats into his angry, anxious isolation."[42] Still, though the need remains to turn away ever more firmly from destructive tendencies, the person at this stage, above all, turns ever more fully toward the cultivation of healthy patterns of living.

It is easy to see the similarity between the stages of Angyal's model for the healing of neurosis and the stages of religious and moral conversion. In all three there is a radical turning away from a basically destructive way of existing and acting, and a turning toward a way of life which is basically good. Similarly, once this radical shift occurs, in all three cases there likewise occurs an ongoing turning away from negative inclinations and seductive tendencies and an ever fuller embracing of life-producing values and patterns of living.

Kazimierz Dabrowski

It is with caution that I use Dabrowski's model[43] as an aid in building up my own model of psychological conversion. As I read Dabrowski, I see that his primary focus is on personality development and the process by which a person moves from a primitive level of personality integration to the highest level. Dabrowski contends that many so-called "neurotic" and even some "psychotic" symptoms are not really pathological. Rather, they are signs of the occurrence of a positive disintegration of the lower level of personality and the creation of a higher one. I myself, however, would tend at times to see a true healing of pathology, a real psychological conversion, where Dabrowski would see a form of personality development. Yet, despite some disagreements about what symptoms are pathological and which are not, I find Dabrowski's model highly useful.

Dabrowski's model is helpful for a number of reasons. It is concerned in part with symptoms classically called neurotic. It effectively demonstrates how a person with the help of certain inner psychic and spiritual resources can make a creative use of so-called "neurotic" and at times "psychotic" symptoms to move toward a new and higher level of personality development. Although Dabrowski focuses on development rather than on conversion, his model consists of a series of stages and movements which parallel in a number of ways the dynamic phases and "turnings" of psychological conversion as I am developing it.

Central to Dabrowski's model is the insight that the disintegration of the low level of personality structure is required for a higher level to be born. For example, where a primitive habit of angry reaction is dominant in a person, there is need for a breaking up of this habit so that a more mature form of controlled anger-response can emerge. This is an example of a positive disintegration since it results in a new and richer way of being.

In the process of positive disintegration, the person first begins to feel that his or her present level of development is inadequate or constrictive. There is often an outbreak of so-called "neurotic" or even "psychotic" symptoms. Feelings such as shame, guilt, fear, anxiety, disquietude, dissatisfaction and astonishment at oneself emerge. These experiences trigger in the person a struggle to free oneself from primitive, stereotyped, repetitious types of personality organization. At the same time, the individual begins to be drawn by new values and goals. These dawning attractions motivate a person to reach out toward a richer level of existing. To the extent that the person deals with difficulties he or she is experiencing in a positive rather than a negative fashion, growth takes place. Through a series of insight-directed decisions the individual rejects what is primitive and immature, and embraces authentically fulfilling values. Ideally, there comes into being a new and harmonious organization of all one's psychic, aesthetic, intellectual, emotional and spiritual functions. Concretely, however, the process of growth through positive disintegration is a gradual one, and the individual moves toward the highest level of personality development by realizing successively higher partial integrations.

It is easy to see certain parallels between the stages of Dabrowski's process of positive disintegration and the stages of religious, moral, and psychological conversion. There is the initial stage of radical dissatisfaction and turning away from the inadequate or destructive. There is the increasing attraction of new values and the ideal of a novel personality integration. This radical turning away from the negative and turning toward the positive is effectively consolidated and actualized in a decision, or generally in a series of enlightened decisions. There is further the ongoing process in which the movement toward the ideal of high level personality integration is gradually intensified and successfully realized through further rejection of immature or actually destructive elements, and the adoption of higher values more in harmony with total personality integration. Dabrowski's overall concern with personality development is a comprehensive one and envisages an integration of the human person which is at once psychological, cognitive, affective, social, aesthetic, moral and spiritual. His greatest contribution to Christotherapy lies in his insights into the forms of healing and growth which parallel the upward spiralings of ongoing conversion in all its forms.

Conversion from Addiction

The notion of the healing of addiction as a conversion[44] is also comparatively recent. Hopefully, its meaning will become clear as the book unfolds. In later chapters I will offer a theory of addiction and suggest key methods for the healing of addiction, together with concrete examples. For the moment I presuppose on the part of the reader at least a common sense understanding of the term addiction. My aim here is to introduce a model for the healing of addiction which has partly inspired my idea of the healing of addiction as a conversion process consisting of radical and ongoing stages, each of which involves a turning away from the addictive object and a turning toward life and true freedom. The model I am speaking of is the famous *Twelve Steps* of *Alcoholics Anonymous*.

The first of the *Twelve Steps* reads: "We admitted we were powerless over alcohol—that our lives had become unmanageable." This admission of personal powerlessness is the first dynamic step that enables the actively addicted person to begin to turn away from the addictive object. The second step is: "[We] came to believe that a Power greater than ourselves could restore us to sanity." This is followed by the third vital step: "[We] made a decision to turn our will and our lives over to the care of God as we understood Him." In these second and third steps the addict makes a radical turn toward the value of sobriety and the Power that can bring it about.

Nine more steps follow. Step four: "[We] made a searching and fearless moral inventory of ourselves"; step five: "Admitted to God, to ourselves, and to another human being, the exact nature of our wrongs"; step six: "Were entirely ready to have God remove all these defects of character"; step seven: "Humbly asked Him to remove our shortcomings"; step eight: "Made a list of all persons we had harmed, and became willing to make amends to them all"; step nine: "Made direct amends to such people wherever possible, except when to do so would injure them or others"; step ten: "Continued to take personal inventory and when we were wrong promptly admitted it"; step eleven: "Sought through prayer and meditation to improve our conscious contact with God as we understood Him, praying only for knowledge of His will for us and the power to carry that out"; step twelve: "Having had a spiritual awakening as the result of these steps, we tried to carry this message to alcoholics, and to practice these principles in all our affairs."[45] In steps four through ten we see an ongoing attempt to turn ever more fully from remaining addictive tendencies and temptations; and especially in steps eleven and twelve we see manifest a transforming cultivation of life-enhancing values, the seeking of ever richer contact with God, and a growing commitment to the service of others, especially those suffering from active addiction.

Certainly these *Twelve Steps* express a deep conversion, touching the human being at his or her psychological, moral and spiritual core. Clearly, there is also a striking parallel between the movement of the *Twelve Steps* offered by *Alcoholics Anonymous* for the healing of addiction and the stages we have seen at work in religious, moral and psychological conversion.

The group called *Emotions Anonymous*[46] is grounded on the same *Twelve Steps* which are the cornerstone of *Alcoholics Anonymous*. The members of *Emotions Anonymous* acknowledge that they are powerless over their emotions rather than over alcohol, but the dynamic stages of the healing process are exactly the same in both groups. The basic stages of radical and ongoing conversion with their respective turnings are at the heart of both healing processes. The use of the *Twelve Steps* by *Emotions Anonymous* thus provides added support for my model of psychological conversion with its particular stages and turnings. Finally, the *Twelve Steps* are used by individuals addicted to such widely diverse objects as food and gambling. This justifies my appeal to the *Twelve Steps* as an appropriate instrument for healing all types of addiction.

Why is there such a similarity in the basic structure and movements of religious, moral, and psychological conversion and conversion from addiction? Of course, this entire book seeks to answer that question. But an initial response is that all four conversions touch the human being in a holistic way. All four involve massive shifts from evil or grossly inadequate ways of living to ways of existing and acting which are truly life-enriching and abundant with life. All four bring reformations and transformations on the levels of meaning and value. All four are touched by the grace of God and require the exercise of freedom at certain stages.

Although there are many similarities between the four conversion processes, it is important to distinguish between them. I do not hold that all forms of addiction are reducible to neurosis.

Nor do I hold—and most psychologists agree on this—that neurosis is a type of addiction. Further, although elements of religious and moral conversion are inevitably at work in the healing processes of neurosis and addiction, the latter are not (apart from striking exceptions) simply the same thing as undergoing a religious and moral conversion. I hold that it is possible to be radically neurotic—even psychotic—and at the same time to be a very holy person.[47] I likewise hold that it is possible to be actively addicted and yet to be in a significant stage of ongoing religious and moral conversion.

Generally speaking, neurotics and addicts are not such by free choice. And, for the most part, *severely* neurotic and *severely* addicted individuals need very special assistance from other human beings in order to reach the point where they become capable of taking a firm stand in freedom toward their neurosis and addiction. There are, of course, exceptions. God does at times intervene in a very dramatic way to heal the neurotic or the addict. But in his providence God seems most often to use human beings as his instruments in bringing about the healing of radical neurosis and addiction.

Religious conversion (at least anonymous) and moral conversion of a radical and/or ongoing nature are necessary, but generally not sufficient conditions for a high level, holistic healing of neurosis and addiction. As a rule, the healing of neurosis and addiction requires a subtle combination of psychological and spiritual elements. This is why I do not consider it valid simply to reduce psychological conversion or conversion from addiction to forms of religious-moral conversion. Further, there is great danger in this type of reduction. It gives the severely neurotic or addicted individual the impression that he or she remains sick simply because of a lack of good will and faith. This can cause great inner anguish and even the temptation to despair when healing does not come despite much prayer on the part of the sick person and others.

The Spiritual Exercises and Conversion

In *Christotherapy* I took a first step toward relating the mystery of Christ in its manifold dimensions to the healing and growth of those who are spiritually, morally and neurotically troubled. At that point I did not focus specifically on the highly nuanced stages involved in the healing of neurosis and the other conversions.

Gaston Fessard provided me with the *catalyst* for two insights which are basic to this book: (1) religious and moral conversion are dynamic processes involving radical and ongoing stages with movements of turning-from and turning-toward; (2) the *Spiritual Exercises* are a dynamic representation of the stages and turnings of religious and moral conversion and relate the mystery of Christ to each of the stages and turnings in a dynamic, methodical, and progressive fashion. I use the word *catalyst* to describe Fessard's influence in my development of these key insights because I make use of Fessard in a highly creative and adaptive fashion, and do not attempt to adhere strictly to his highly subtle philosophical and theological interpretation of the *Exercises*.

It was not my reading of Fessard, but the study of the writings of Andras Angyal and my encounter with the Twelve Steps of *Alcoholics Anonymous* which triggered in me the insight that the healing processes of neurosis and addiction are conversion processes with radical and ongoing stages. But once I saw the similarity between the stages of religious and moral conversion and those of the processes of the healing of neurosis and addiction, I was able, with the help of Fessard's work, to discover a potentially rich link between the *Spiritual Exercises* and the stages of healing neurosis and addiction and to see how Ignatius and his *Exercises* might provide a key for relating the mystery of Christ powerfully and effectively to these conversions.

I wish to show more in detail how Fessard's analysis of the *Spiritual Exercises* provides basic inspiration and underpinnings for my models of religious and moral conversion, but first I think a few introductory comments about the *Spiritual Exercises* are in order.

What are the *Spiritual Exercises*? There is no simple answer. In a real sense, only the person who has made them knows what the *Spiritual Exercises* are. The text of the *Exercises*[48] itself is the product of the conversion and prayer experiences of St. Ignatius of Loyola. It provides in a kind of telegraphese code a model and set of instructions for one form of prolonged Christian prayer, and for guiding others to participate in that form of prayer. A well-known psychiatrist, on reading the text of the *Exercises,* remarked that he found the work quite dull and uninspiring. This reaction is understandable enough since Ignatius did not intend the manual of the *Exercises* as a book to be read, but rather as a heuristic set of instructions for entry into a dynamic form of prayer experience.

In its ideal form, the process of making the *Exercises* takes about a month. Ignatius divides the *Exercises* into four periods which he refers to as "Weeks." These "Weeks" do not necessarily last seven days each, but taken together in the full so-called "long" retreat, they add up to thirty days. The director can expand or contract the number of days spent in a particular Week according to the spiritual movements in the mind, heart, imagination and feelings of the retreatant. An expert spiritual guide is needed who acts as an instrument of the Holy Spirit in leading the retreatant through the interrelated meditations, contemplations, and other exercises. This guide, in the ideal retreat, does not "preach" the *Exercises,* though this does occur in certain adaptations of the *Exercises*. Rather, the guide meets with the retreatant each day for a period not to exceed an hour, and offers certain suggestions regarding the subject matter for prayer, guided by the text of the *Exercises,* but not slavishly so. The director is also available to discuss the various interior movements of mind, heart, imagination and feelings which the retreatant may experience.

Commentators on the *Spiritual Exercises* disagree to some extent about the basic practical goal Saint Ignatius intends for individuals making the *Exercises*. All agree, however, that one valid reason for entering the long retreat is to seek to make what Ignatius spoke of as an "election."

In an "election-centered" retreat, the individual seeks to discern God's will about a particular concrete issue so that he or she can make a specific choice or "election." The election is not between an obvious moral evil and an obvious good since the person entering into the thirty day retreat is generally presupposed to be in a state of ongoing religious and moral conversion. Rather, the election is a matter of choosing what is "better" among two or more morally good possibilities open to the person. A person may be seeking to know, for instance, whether it is God's will (and so better) for him or her to marry or to serve God in a single life. Clearly, what is better for one is not always better for another. At its core the election is at once the work of God and the free response of the retreatant, as the Christian, by prayer, comes to know God's choice, and simultaneously assents to the divine election.

I will try to show briefly how Fessard depicts the *Exercises* as helping a person to make and confirm an election by a powerful reenactment in mind, heart, and imagination of the basic "turnings" of radical and ongoing religious and moral conversion.

Gaston Fessard and the Process of the Spiritual Exercises

The person who enters into the thirty day retreat is presumed to be radically converted religiously and morally and to be in good psychological and physical condition. The retreatant, before entering the First Week of the *Exercises,* prayerfully meditates on God as the creative Source and Goal of the human heart—the One to be loved, revered and served for himself, in one's neighbor and through the proper use of created things. This preliminary prayer-exercise is called the meditation on "The First Principle and Foundation." Through this prayer the retreatant hopefully enters the four Weeks of the *Exercises* permeated and alive with a sense of the intimate presence of divine, creative Love.

In the First Week, sustained and empowered by the presence of Christ the Redeemer, the retreatant meditates on such radical sins (fundamental options against God) as those of the fallen angels, of Adam and Eve, and of some human being who is imagined to have died in a state of radical alienation from God. The retreatant also considers his or her own personal sinfulness and lasting need of the redemptive grace of Christ. In these meditations, with the help of healing and enlightening grace, the true "reality" of sin unfolds; sin is revealed in its absurdity, as a self-destruction ending in the reality of eternal hell. A deep personal realization of what sin is brings loathing for sin, and the retreatant turns away from it through renewed repentance and contrition. These humble, interior activities are due to the ever-present, redeeming love and grace of Christ. The Christian is never asked to face the negative apart from the powerful, sustaining presence of Christ the Redeemer.

The experience of the initiative of divine mercy and love opens the retreatant to a vision of Christ the King; through the meditations and contemplations of the Second Week the retreatant is drawn to renew his or her radical turning toward Christ and his Kingdom of Life and Love by a deeper resolve to follow him poor, suffering, and humiliated wherever he may lead.

The prayerful experience of the first two Weeks in which the turning-from and turning-toward of radical religious and moral conversion are renewed at a higher level in the spiral of transcendence disposes the retreatant for an authentic discernment of God's will regarding the specific election he or she is seeking to make.

But, making the election does not end the retreat; for if the election is to be a vital reality in the person's life, he or she must confirm it by a more complete rejection of any remaining sinful attachments. Likewise the retreatant, with God's help, must transform the election by a powerful, prayerful, deeper turning toward authentic value.

The Third Week of the *Exercises* begins with a contemplation of Christ in his covenantal self-offering at the Last Supper, and the retreatant unites his or her particular self-offering made in the election to this sacrificial act of Christ. Contemplations follow on Christ in the various mysteries of his passion and death, inspiring in the retreatant an ever deeper turning away from sin because of what it does to Christ and to the members of his mystical body here on earth in which he still suffers: "Saul, Saul, why do you persecute me?" (Ac. 9:4). These contemplations also move the retreatant toward an ever stronger confirmation of the election. This Third Week is a powerful expression of the turning-from of ongoing religious and moral conversion.

At this point in the retreat, the Father's initiative in raising up his Son enables the retreatant to turn from contemplating the Crucified to a blessed beholding of the risen and glorified Christ, who sends forth his Spirit. The joy-filled contemplations of the Fourth Week consolidate the election and transform it into stronger commitment, deepening the turning-toward of ongoing religious and moral conversion by a transfiguring experience of the glorified Christ.

Finally, just as the consideration of God as Source and Goal began the retreat, so a "contemplation to attain love" crowns it. The retreatant prayerfully beholds God laboring at the heart of his creation for the good of all.

It is not necessary for the reader of this book to have made the *Exercises* in order to understand and profitably utilize the applications I will make of them to the healing of neurosis and addiction and to spiritual direction of an elementary and more advanced nature. Of course, a person who does have an experiential knowledge of the *Exercises* will be able to appreciate certain implications of my approach which might elude some others.

In Part One of this book I consider, in a first section, the human subject who individually and as a member of the human community undergoes religious and moral conversion and is subject to various types of development and possible deformation. In a second section, I present my particular model of the "new wisdom." I offer an integrated set of spiritual and psychological principles; I relate the principles and methods of Christotherapy *in an adapted fashion* to the distinct practices of spiritual directing and counseling. Finally, I sketch the qualities and methods of the Christotherapist.

In Part Two I show how the principles and methods of Christotherapy are applicable to the healing of sin, neurosis and addiction, to the facilitating of ongoing growth in key areas of human development, and to the healing and education of feelings.

In the first section of Part Two, I focus on each of the four Weeks of the *Exercises* and I show concretely how the Christotherapist uses key elements of each of the Weeks as a means for relating the mystery of Christ in a particularly appropriate way to the distinct stages and turnings of the four conversion processes. I also demonstrate through many concrete examples how the movement of the *Exercises,* the *Twelve Steps* of *Alcoholics Anonymous* and related groups, and central methods of Drs. Angyal, Assagioli, and others mutually illuminate one another and deeply enrich and confirm the validity of the key principles and methods of Christotherapy.

In the second section of Part Two, I show in a very practical way how it is possible for persons using the approach of Christotherapy to effect in themselves and others the healing and education of the basic feelings of anxiety, fear, anger, guilt, sadness and depression. I do not have a special chapter on the feeling of love because I deal with it throughout the book, and in a special way in my chapters on the four Weeks.

SECTION ONE

The Human Subject: Development and Deformations

1

FOUNDATIONS

2

The Self and Self-Image

Every human being has a unique set of fingerprints and voiceprint. At a deeper level of participation in the gift of creation each person has a unique core of individual existence—his or her identity. Identity in this deeper sense is what makes me to be this particular *existing* individual, and nobody else.[1] The ultimate subject named when the word "I" is used is the unique identity which I am, this particular existing human individual. Tolstoy, for example, was an infant, a child, a youth, a young man, a middle-aged man and an old man. But Tolstoy retained his identity as this particular existing human being throughout all the developments and sufferings he underwent in his long career. It is true that the human subject grows and develops in many ways. But without a lasting identity as this particular existing individual it would not be one's own self but another self which would be realized.

Self and Anti-Self

The term "self," as I use it, refers to the human person created with a unique identity and endowed with all the natural properties and dimensions which properly belong to a human being. The self is an incarnate subject, a natural unity in one person of body and soul; it has physical, chemical, biological, psychic, intellectual and volitional dimensions. The self is a distinct, individual being but it is by nature social. It is endowed with intelligence and freedom, created good but capable of doing evil.

In his *Purgatorio* Dante poetically captures the shift from a vision of the self as it comes forth fresh from God's creative hands to a view of the self as concretely involved in the event of human becoming, with its joys, dangers and corruptions:

> From the hand of God, whose love shines like a ray upon it, even before birth, comes forth the simple soul which, like a child at play,
> cries, laughs, and ignorant of every measure but the glad impulse of its joyous Maker, turns eagerly to all that gives it pleasure.
> It tastes small pleasures first. To these it clings, deceived, and seeks no others, unless someone curb it, or guide its love to higher things.[2]

The self as concretely engaged in human history is subject to the effects of the original sinfulness of humanity and open to many deformations. I use the term anti-self to include every phantasy, image, thought, choice, belief, action, habit, error, illusion, or form of ignorance which impedes, distorts, or prevents authentic development and results instead in deformations with all their destructive somatic, psychic, spiritual consequences. The self is created in the image and likeness of God and experiences the inner imperatives: Be attentive! Be understanding! Be reasonable! Be responsible! Be loving![3] The anti-self is the sum of all failures, conscious and unconscious, compulsive and free, to be obedient to these God-given drives of the human self.

Christ-self and Antichrist-self

The New Testament describes as an adopted child of God (Ep. 1:5; Rm. 8:15) the person who has accepted Christ in faith and undergone baptism in his Name. The person the Father adopts as his child in Christ through the power of the Holy Spirit does not lose his or her identity as this particular existing individual, but begins to live at a new and incomparably higher level of existence. Indeed, the Holy Spirit of the Father and the Son becomes the transformative principle of new life in the person. For this reason Holy Scripture describes the believer as one who has put on Christ (Ga. 3:27) and who can now say: "I live now not with my own life but with the life of Christ who lives in me. The life I now live in this body I live in faith: faith in the Son of God" (Ga. 2:20). By the Christ-self, then, I mean the self as it is transformed and made a sharer in the divine nature through the power of the Holy Spirit of Christ (2 P. 1:4). The Christ-self is present and alive in the person who has received Jesus Christ as Lord and walks according to his Spirit (Col. 2:6).

Yet, Holy Scripture speaks not only of the adopted children of God but also of antichrists. The author of the first letter of John writes to his flock that "many antichrists have come" (1 Jn. 2:18 R.S.V.) and that an antichrist is "he who denies the Father and the Son" (1 Jn. 2:22 R.S.V.). I adopt the expression antichrist from Scripture and speak of the antichrist-self. The antichrist-self means anything in a person which is opposed to Christ, his Kingdom, his commandments. The person who says a radical "No" to God, the person who "sins unto death," is ruled by the antichrist-self, just as the person who says a radical "Yes" to God is ruled by the Spirit of the Christ. And anytime a person fails in some degree to walk according to the Spirit of Christ, he or she is succumbing to certain antichrist tendencies.

The True Self

Religious and psychological literature is full of reflections about the nature of the "true self." I use this term to describe the self at any stage of *authentic* existence or development. The true self, then, is the self as initially endowed by God with dynamic orientations toward meaning, truth, goodness, value and the divine and it is the self insofar as its potentialities for authentic existence are, in fact, realized.

I disagree fundamentally with materialistic theories of true selfhood, such as those of Freud and Marx, because I hold that the self is created in God's own image and possesses an intrinsic spiritual dimension. I also have problems with interpretations of the self which in my opinion overstress the spirituality of the true self at the expense of its material dimensions. Both Drs. Roberto Assagioli, the founder of *Psychosynthesis,*[4] and Thomas Hora, who has had such a profound influence on my development of Christotherapy, fall into an exaggerated emphasis on the spirituality of the true self.

Assagioli distinguishes between the empirical ego and the real or higher Self. His higher Self is above and basically unaffected by bodily conditions and the thoughts of the conscious ego. In fact, he sees the conscious ego as a reflection or projection of the higher Self in the realm of personality.[5] Hora, in a similar, though more radical way, distinguishes between the ego or personal self, which belongs to the realm of appearances, and the individual as a spiritual emanation of God,[6] which is always loving, intelligent and good[7] and is a perfect reflection of a perfect God.[8]

My basic difference with Drs. Assagioli and Hora lies in my emphasis on the bodily as a real and permanent dimension of *true* selfhood. The true self is an incarnate subject, a unity of body and spirit in one person; this unity remains such even when the perfect Christ-self is realized in the final resurrection from the dead. Assagioli's language makes me uneasy insofar as he describes the real Self as above and unaffected by mind and bodily conditions. Likewise, Hora's reduction of the bodily to the realm of mere appearances does not fit into my particular Christian perspective. I believe that incarnation and resurrection are at the core of Christian belief and both testify to the reality, goodness and lastingness of matter. Significantly, Hora has recently called the ascension of Jesus an "excarnation."[9] This dovetails neatly with another recent comment of Hora that "if we knew what we really are, we would disappear."[10] For Hora, perfect enlightenment means complete transcendence of the world of appearances and the realization that we are perfect, individual spiritual emanations from the perfect God, from whom only the perfect can proceed. All else is illusion and error.

Self-image and Self-concept

Dr. Andras Angyal uses the expression "the symbolic self" to signify the whole of a person's conscious self-perceptions and self-evaluations.[11] I believe that the symbolic self is at the core of a person's self-image. But I also hold that the self-image consists of unconscious as well as conscious materials. I use the term *self-concept* to indicate that concepts and ideas as well as images are involved in a person's self-symbolization and self-perception.

The self-image and self-concept are multidimensional. Among the most significant dimensions are: body image, interpersonal image, self-esteem—image and religious self-image.[12] The body image is a person's condensed representation, both conscious and unconscious, of past, present and fantasied experiences of his or her own body. The interpersonal self-image is an individual's internalized perception of himself or herself, based on the expectations of others—parents, peers, teachers, employers. The self-esteem image is a person's basic feelings of being lovable or not lovable, worthwhile or not worthwhile, significant or insignificant. The religious self-image is the believer's conscious and unconscious, perceiving, symbolizing and imagining of how God sees him or her.

An individual's self-image and self-concept realize varying degrees of accuracy and inaccuracy, truth and falsity. The self-image and concept can be constructive and life-enriching or destructive and life-denying. If a person's self-image and concept are generally inaccurate and negative, the individual will often be tempted to give up or else to yield to an endless striving for total perfection in a futile attempt to use success as a substitute for the internal perception of an adequate and worthwhile self.

Consciousness, Twilight Consciousness and the Unconscious

The self-image and the self-concept involve conscious and unconscious elements. What then is consciousness? What is the unconscious? Is there an intermediate or twilight state between high level conscious functioning and the strictly unconscious? These are thorny issues which are sharply disputed in philosophy and psychology. I did not address these issues in *Christotherapy*. Here I intend to present my own views while dodging as far as possible the web of controversies touching on these matters.

What does it mean to be conscious? A common mistake is to think of consciousness as self-reflection or introspection of some sort. But consciousness is not this bending back upon oneself in reflection, but a simple internal experience of oneself and one's activities of sensing, feeling, thinking, judging, reflecting, deciding, acting. To be conscious is not the same thing as to know an object. When the master calls his dog he does so consciously—he obviously cannot call his dog when he is knocked unconscious. But though the master is conscious of himself calling the dog his consciousness is not reflective or self-conscious. His whole attention is on the dog. Basically, then, consciousness is not the presence of an object to a subject but the simple presence in non-reflective awareness of the subject to himself or herself. Thus, when I say to another person, "I love you," I say it with my whole attention focused on that person and not on myself. Yet, when I say "I love you" to that person, I do it consciously, not unconsciously. I am present to myself as an acting subject, even though I am not thinking about myself.

There are different levels of conscious functioning.[13] At the lowest level of conscious or at least semi-conscious functioning dreaming occurs. Next comes the level of sense experience, of seeing, hearing, touching, tasting, smelling. There follows the level of understanding, of insight, of theory, of hypothesis, of conceptualizing. Beyond this level there occurs the level of reflection, of weighing evidence, of judging. The three levels of experiencing, understanding and judging comprise the basic stages of the knowing process. But the human person's conscious activities are not limited to the level of knowing. Beyond the level of knowing there is the level of deliberation, of feeling, of conscious response to values, of decision, and of action. Finally, at the peak of the levels of conscious human functioning there is the graced level of being in love with God. This level embraces ordinary, conscious, God-inspired acts of faith, hope and love as well as the many mansions of mystical experience. Assagioli refers to the supreme level of spiritual Self-realization as the sphere of the "Higher Unconscious or Superconscious."[14] I co-opt his word "superconscious" because, though the mystic in ecstasy is transported beyond narrow ego-concerns and becomes spiritually intoxicated with God, this holy drunkenness is not unconsciousness, but a very high and most intense consciousness: a super-consciousness.

Twilight Consciousness

In conversing with someone a person may be commenting on the weather but at the same time there can be various imaginings, feelings, thoughts, phantasies "flashing off and on" in the background or lower recesses of his or her mind and psyche. The speaker can also be experiencing various surges of psychic need, e.g., a need for succorance or for dominating the other person.[15] These imaginings and other mental occurrences are at work in the conscious experience of the speaker but most often he or she does not reflectively advert to these phenomena or focus attention on them. These non-focal psychic and mental happenings are taking place in what I refer to as the zone of twilight consciousness.[16]

Dr. Wilhelm Stekel has written that "our thinking is a polyphony. There are always several thoughts working simultaneously, one of which is the bearer of the leading voice. The other thoughts represent medium and low voices."[17] Stekel's medium and low voices are occurring in the zone of twilight consciousness. He suggests that psychoanalysis must come to grips with the medium and low voices in the polyphony of our thinking. These medium and low voices are conscious, that is, they are experienced. But it can require the work of a therapist to get an individual to advert to and reflect upon these psychic events which are transpiring in the lower recesses of his or her mental and psychic center.

Recently, in developing a cognitive approach to therapy Dr. Aaron Beck has recounted his advertence to the recurrence in his patients of what he names "automatic thoughts."[18] He found that apart from the wishes, thoughts, feelings and imaginings which the patient spontaneously expresses in the free association process there is a flow of thoughts running parallel to the patient's explicitly recounted thoughts to which he or she does not advert. Beck discovered that the more hidden stream of thoughts and images is characterized by a number of significant features: these thoughts and images are self-referential and self-critical; they occur rapidly and tend to emerge automatically; they possess a certain autonomy and in more disturbed individuals are very difficult to turn off; they take imagistic as well as verbal form; they tend to involve more distortions of reality than do other forms of thought; they are specific and discrete and occur in a kind of telegraphic style or shorthand. Individuals in therapy do not tend to report these thoughts and images when they are encouraged to speak freely about whatever comes to them. Beck suggests that this is due to the fact that individuals have the habit of talking to themselves in one way and to the rest of the world in a different manner. He sees these automatic thoughts and images as the most crucial and significant data for utilization in effective therapy. His automatic mental and psychic phenomena provide yet another example of events belonging to the zone of twilight consciousness.

The Unconscious

My reading of a wide variety of psychologists and therapists leads me to the conclusion that many authorities who use the term unconscious are, in fact, referring to the realm of twilight consciousness.[19] Various modern psychologists hold that such defense mechanisms as repression, denial, rationalization and other "strategies of self-deception"[20] occur consciously, though non-reflectively, as well as unconsciously in the strict sense. In the classical Freudian tradition the unconscious in the strictest sense names the psychic zone containing repressed images, memories, thoughts and other materials which cannot be recalled at will or brought to a level of even twilight consciousness without special therapeutic help or the occurrence of special healing events which trigger their release. Throughout this book I will use the term "unconscious" broadly to refer to events in twilight consciousness as well as to psychic happenings in the zone of the strict unconscious in the Freudian sense. When I refer to the latter zone exclusively I will speak of the *strictly* unconscious or the *deep* unconscious.[21]

Finally, although Carl Jung's theory and therapy are not central to my development of *Christotherapy* I do draw upon various Jungian notions and I believe that psychologists and therapists of a Jungian orientation will find more complementarity than conflict between the two approaches. For this reason, I round off my discussion of the self, consciousness and the unconscious with a reflection on Jung's theory of the "collective unconscious."

Dr. Jung suggests that images which constantly recur in dreams, myths, stories and many other cultural forms suggest that there exist at the deepest level of the unconscious—the collective unconscious—inherited predispositions to respond to given situations and stimuli in a determinate fashion. He calls these strictly unconscious predispositions "archetypes." Some of the principal archetypes are the *persona,* concretely revealed in one's public personality; the *shadow,* symbolized in the repugnant, undeveloped personal characteristics we hide from ourselves; the *anima* and the *animus,* expressed in our idealized images of the opposite sex; and the *Self,* the human person's basic drive for unity and wholeness, revealed historically in such symbols as the Buddha and the Christ.

Without subscribing to all the nuances of Jung's theory, I do agree that the types of spontaneous images Jung roots in archetypal dispositions do recur widely in the experience of individuals and groups of highly diverse cultures and epochs. Further, psychological analysis tends to confirm that each person's self-image, self-concept and process of development are influenced by factors similar to those Jung attributes to his archetypes and those concrete expressions. Finally, Jung's theory of the archetype of the *Self* as an inner drive toward wholeness complements my stress on the vocation of each person to realize ever more deeply the potentialities of the natural self and of the Christ-self. I presuppose, however, an interpretation of Jung's *Self* which allows for the reality of a transcendent God, the truly redemptive work of Jesus Christ who died and rose for our salvation and the activity of the Holy Spirit of Christ deep within the human person.[22]

3

The Developing Self

The first stage in the development of the self takes place within the mother's womb. After birth the infant exists for some time in an oceanic world where he or she does not distinguish between self and world, between self and other persons or between the body and its parts. After four or five months the infant begins to recognize the mothering figure as a source of pleasure, warmth and sustenance. Gradually the baby comes to recognize other elements in its world as possessing a certain permanence—persons, toys. But the sense of self as a distinct, conscious, personal center comes only around the eighteenth month. From this point on the child begins to emerge from a basically passive kind of existence; he or she begins to exercise initiative and to oppose actively and resist persons and objects in the environment. Parents need to understand that the resistance of the two year old is not disobedience in the adult sense, but part of the child's attempt to discover and constitute himself or herself as a distinct, autonomous individual.[1]

Psychologist Dr. David Ausubel[2] holds that in a healthy development the child initially experiences that his or her basic needs are met as they arise: hunger is experienced; the child cries and is fed. This is the "omnipotence" phase of development. Whatever the child wants, the child gets. But the child gradually comes to experience that he or she is completely dependent on others for the fulfillment of basic needs. This dawning experience of dependence roughly coincides with the emergence in the child of a sense of himself or herself as a distinct individual.

Ausubel recognizes the child's growing sense of dependence as healthy so long as it does not lead to a radical devaluation of the child's self-esteem, self-worth and personal feelings of adequacy. He holds that if the parents or parental substitutes love and value the child for himself or herself the child will be able to identify with the parental figures. The child becomes a "satellite" of the parents who are the all-powerful figures in the child's mini-world. Because the child is loved and accepted for himself or herself it is possible for the child to bask in the warmth and security of the parents' love and to grow in a sense of basic worth and well-being. But, if the parents do not love the child but instead reject him or her or value the child in terms of what he or she can do or become, then the child cannot "satellize" and is incapable of deriving a sense of basic inner worth and lovableness from parents with whom it is impossible to identify.

Psychiatrist Dr. Conrad Baars confirms Ausubel's emphasis on the child's need for acceptance by saying that it is not enough for parents to bring a child into the world physically; they must also bestow on the child the gift of "psychic birth." Psychic birth is the child's deep experience of being loved and accepted for himself or herself with no conditions attached. In Baars' words, "*psychic birth* through authentic affirmation is an absolute necessity for man to be capable of finding true happiness in this life."[3]

According to Dr. Abraham Maslow the earliest stages of human growth are radically *receptive* in character and this further confirms the theories of Ausubel and Baars. Maslow has outlined a hierarchy of human needs, beginning with the needs for food, drink and basic sustenance.[4] The infant is absolutely dependent on others for the fulfillment of these basic physical needs as well as for the next need in Maslow's hierarchy, the need for safety and fundamental security. Yet, the child cannot thrive, or perhaps even at times survive, if only these most basic needs are met. The studies of Rene Spitz show that children raised in prison by mothers who loved them were far less subject to early death, disease, psychosis and neurosis than those brought up in institutions with excellent hygienic conditions and physical care but in an absence of mothering love.[5] Next in Maslow's ladder of human needs are those for love, affection and a sense of belonging. Immediately following are the needs for a sense of self-esteem, self-worth and self-respect. The child in his or her earlier stages of development is radically dependent on others for the fulfillment of these natural longings for love and a sense of individual worth and self-esteem.

As the growing human being passes from the radical receptivity of infancy through childhood and adolescence into young and mature adulthood he or she can develop in a variety of ways, including those forms of development which are processes of conversion. I distinguish between certain forms of development and conversion because, although every authentic conversion is a form of development, it does not follow that every type of development is a conversion. In my usage, at least, both radical and ongoing forms of conversion involve a turning from what is destructive and a turning toward what is life-giving. A development, on the other hand, can simply involve a movement from a more primitive to a higher phase in the growth process, e.g., from adolescence to young adulthood. Of course, in the unfolding of the concrete life-process of the individual developments and conversions are often identical or at least tightly interwoven.

Forms and Stages of Development

There are many forms of human development. A person is able to develop cognitively,[6] psychologically, socially, morally, aesthetically, spiritually[7]—to name but a few principal developmental areas. But there are not only many forms of development. There are also sequential stages at work in many of these spheres of development.

Erik Erikson proposes an eight-stage model of growth or deterioration.[8] In this model the positive stages of psycho-social development are basic trust, autonomy, initiative, industry, identity, intimacy, generativity, and ego integrity. The negative counterparts to this series of healthy developments are mistrust, shame and doubt, guilt, inferiority, role confusion, isolation, stagnation and despair. In Erikson's analysis, the later stages depend to some extent on the earlier, but there is no rigid, unalterable determinism to it: new crises may undo earlier developments. Throughout life there is a deepening or weakening of various stages.

Lawrence Kohlberg has worked out a six-stage model of cognitive-moral development, based on the different reasons individuals give for why a particular moral choice is right or wrong.[9] In the first two stages the physical consequences of an action, i.e., reward or punishment, constitute the standard for judging an action right or wrong. In the next two stages the requirements of peers and of society constitute the criteria for judging the moral quality of an action. In the final two stages, contractual agreement, the demands of justice, and personal conscience, operating according to responsibly chosen moral standards, provide the standard for judging the ethical quality of particular moral decisions.

Bernard Boelen, using an approach based on existential philosophy as well as psychology, traces the development of the human individual from infancy through childhood and adolescence into the highest phase of human maturation.[10] His focus is on the unfolding of the healthy, whole individual. In his model each developmental stage involves certain crisis experiences which, if handled properly, lead to the emergence of a higher level of personality integration. Boelen is excellent in his treatment of the worlds and crises of the adolescent and young adult. But where he is most unique is in his treatment of adult maturation. His model stands out in its stress on the need to measure the quality of a person's maturation in terms of his or her response to the gift of existence and to the transcendent mystery of Being or God.

Kazimierz Dabrowski, like Boelen, is interested in the holistic development of the human person. He proposes that the two *key* factors which determine the developmental potential of an individual are: (1) the intensity of presence in him or her of five forms of "overexcitability" and (2) the number and quality of psychic "dynamisms" he or she possesses.

Dabrowski's five forms of "overexcitability"[11] are: psychomotor, sensual, imaginational, intellectual and emotional. Psychomotor overexcitability is an intensified excitability of the neuro-muscular system. It is manifested in violent play, impetuous actions, rapid talk, gesticulations and similar overflows of organic energy. Sensual overexcitability is basically a heightened experiencing of sensory pleasure; it is revealed in a need for comfort, a variety of sexual experiences, attention-seeking, delight in superficial fashion and beauty, overindulgence in food and drink. Imaginational overexcitability involves a pure and a less pure form. In its pure form it involves inventiveness, vivid, animated visualization, the use of metaphor and image in verbal expression, an associating of images and impressions. In its less pure form it manifests itself in nightmares, fears of the unknown, a mixing of fiction and truth. Intellectual overexcitability reveals itself in a love of analysis, a persistence in asking questions, an eagerness for knowledge, theoretical analysis. Emotional overexcitability in its more positive form is a quality of deeply experienced emotional relationships. These deeply felt relationships can involve strong attachments to persons, animals and other living creatures and places. Emotions important for development on this level are timidity, enthusiasm, care for others, concern about death, anxiety, exclusive friendship relationships. In a person with a variety of forms of overexcitability there is usually a dominant form accompanied by the other forms in various strengths. It is only in persons locked into the most primitive form of personality integration that there is little manifestation of the forms of overexcitability or solely the psychomotor or sensual forms.

Besides the five forms of overexcitability there are Dabrowski's psychic dynamisms.[12] These are psychological dispositional traits which shape development. A partial list of these dynamisms are: empathy, creative instinct, a recognition of a hierarchy of values, dissatisfaction with oneself, disquietude and astonishment with oneself, a sense of inferiority toward oneself (perceived gap between the self I am and the self I desire to become), feelings of shame and guilt, capacity for self-criticism, self-control, self-education, self-therapy, confidence in one's development, freedom from factors that constrict personality development, attraction felt toward high level personality ideals. These dynamisms vary in quality and importance. Some are relevant to early personality development; they tend to disappear as the movement toward higher level personality integration takes place through a series of positive disintegrations of inadequate personality structures and habits.

Although for Dabrowski the developmental potential of an individual is determined according to the type, number and intensity of forms of overexcitability and of psychic dynamisms a person possesses, environmental factors can impede development. It is possible that an individual can remain at a very low level of personality integration throughout his or her life.[13] But when a person is not too deprived in early childhood and is endowed with intense forms of imaginational, intellectual and emotional overexcitability and a high number of psychic dynamisms then the possibility of moving toward a very high level of personality integration is quite good.

Dabrowski, like Boelen, is open in his model of personality development to the transcendent. His dynamisms cover the entire range of human orientations, including an openness to the cosmic, the mystical and the divine. But I would like to add to Dabrowski's equation for developmental potential the presence to the individual of the inner grace, light, strength and inspiration of the Holy Spirit and the quality of the person's response to the graces offered. For a truly holistic approach to human development must acknowledge the vital role both of the grace of God and of the free human response to the gift of this grace. The highest form of personal maturation and development involves a belief encounter with Jesus Christ in word, sacrament and prayer, mediated through the Christian community. At this level the human person with the aid of grace puts on the mind and heart of Christ and the natural self is transformed into the Christ-self.

Feelings and Human Development

"The whole mass and momentum of living is in feeling."[14] Development in the area of feelings or emotions affects every other form of human growth in a profound way. Even the process of knowing with its stages of experiencing, understanding and judging "is paper-thin" without feelings.[15]

Contemporary studies suggest that feelings or emotions emerge in a certain order in infants and become more complex as the baby and then the child develops his or her capacity to imagine, remember, think and interpret.

Carroll Izard in his massive work *Human Emotions* proposes that emotions involve neurophysiological, expressive and experiential components.[16] By expressive he means the ability to manifest emotions in facial expressions and in other bodily ways. By experiential he refers to external perception and to internal elements such as memory and imagination. He agrees that the child only begins to discriminate his or her mother from others in the fourth or fifth month. But, he says that from birth the child experiences and expresses emotions of distress,[17] interest, excitement[18] and, likely, joy.[19] The sound of a voice and the sight of a face evoke smiles in the infant in the first few weeks after birth.[20] But, these early smiles are not the social smiles of the child who in the fourth or fifth month begins to recognize and distinguish the mother from others.[21]

Izard sees the emotion of fear[22] appearing in the second half of the child's first year, while anger[23] and the more reflective emotions of shame[24] and guilt[25] come later in the developmental process. Erik Erikson agrees, since in his model of development shame and guilt only make a dominant appearance respectively in the second and third stages of the eight-stage model.[26]

As the child develops the capacity to imagine, to remember, to talk, to think, and to interpret experiences, his or her emotional responses to what goes on externally and internally are mediated by an ever-growing collection of memories, images and interpretations. Ausubel believes that the first step in responding emotionally is the interpretation of an event as either enhancing or threatening one's basic ego needs, goals and values. In fact, Ausubel holds that the individual's interpretation of the stimulus to which he or she is responding emotionally is more determinative of the nature and quality of the feeling response than is the object of the response itself.[27] I believe that this can, in fact, often be the case. A simple example bears this out. It is easy to notice what different emotional responses two different persons can have when they meet a snake. One may experience interest and fascination, the other may feel fear, loathing, terror. Lonergan remarks that such factors as education, temperament, sex, age and existential concern can explain why different people may not have the same feelings about the same object.[28]

Dr. Abraham Low, the founder of *Recovery Incorporated,* largely agrees with Ausubel and Lonergan that feeling responses are mediated by factors other than the object itself to which the feelings are responding. He states that most feelings are "overlaid and modified and taken captive by a thought."[29] In fact, Low wonders whether "pure" feeling responses which are completely unmediated by the filter of thought ever occur.[30] The central text for members of *Emotions Anonymous* also states that negative thought patterns underlie emotional illness.[31]

Basically, there are two classes of feelings.[32] There are general feeling states such as anxiety and fatigue which arise independently of our perception of certain objects. There is a much broader class of feelings which arise as responses to perceiving, imagining, representing or knowing certain objects. Examples of this latter type of feeling include fear, delight, hate, envy. This latter category of feelings can also be divided according to the type of objects the feelings respond to. There is one type of objects to which both brute animals and human beings respond. These are objects on the sense level and evoke feelings of pleasure and pain, of desire and fear. The second type of objects include the whole realm of values, moving from the simple value of bodily vigor to the highest mystical values. Here there is a hierarchy of feeling responses. There are feeling responses to the vital values of health and strength, to the social values of order and community, to the cultural values of art and literature, to the unique value of another living human being, to the religious values revealed in Christ. One of the most significant achievements of human living is the education of feeling responses to authentic human and divine values.

Christian Parenting

It is easy to see how parents or their substitutes play a dramatic role in the education of the emotional responses of their child. Through the intersubjective means of facial expression, touch and tone of voice they first communicate to their child a sense of being loved, cherished and valued. They form a child's initial body and social self-image. They mediate his or her first encounter with life and the world. They use symbols, words, stories, art, and actions to educate their children's feeling responses to many types of human and spiritual values.

For the Apostle Paul the Christian community at its best is the ideal place where the child can be sheltered from the destructive influences of the world enslaved by sin, and nurtured and educated in the true wisdom that comes from Christ and is Christ. Jerome Murphy-O'Connor suggests that the reason Paul told the Corinthians that their children were not "unclean . . . but holy" (1 Cor. 7:14 R.S.V.) was because Paul believed that children imbibe the basic attitudes of their parents and for Paul these children were born into freedom and a milieu of authentic living.[33] These children ideally "had never been subject to the value system of the 'world' " and hence "even prior to the age of adult decision, they had participated in the freedom of those who had chosen authenticity."[34]

Murphy-O'Connor's interpretation of Paul's view of the community as protecting and sanctifying children leads us to a deeper and richer understanding of infant baptism. When Christian parents have their baby baptized, it symbolizes their pledge to raise the child in the world, but not as a child of the world. Ideally, they cherish their faith in Christ so deeply that they know it would be impossible not to communicate to the child in every way "the breadth and the length, the height and the depth" of the mystery of Jesus Christ (Ep. 3:18). From the very beginning authentic Christian parents speak of the riches of Christ's love implicitly through smiles, touches, tone of voice. As the child grows they pass on his meanings and values through their words, through the symbols and art forms they use and stories they teach. Paul believed that just as the authentic example of a Christian husband or wife would save the unbelieving spouse (1 Cor. 7:14) so too the lives of truly Christian parents would affect their children, making them "not unclean, but holy."

Paul urged his congregations to be imitators of him as he was of Christ (1 Cor. 11:1). Christian parents too, sustained by the wider Christian community in which they live and from which they draw needed sustenance and support, are to represent Christ to their children and to imitate Christ so that their children, by imitating them in turn, may learn how to be "fully human, fully alive"[35] and how to live as God's most dear children and as brothers and sisters of their elder brother Jesus.

The Law of Decrease-Increase

John the Baptist announced when Jesus appeared, "He must increase, but I must decrease" (Jn. 3:30 RSV). This law of "decrease-increase" has an analogy in the parents' influence on the developing child, adolescent and young adult. Parents have the awesome calling not only to confer the gifts of self-esteem, self-worth and a participation in the world of authentic human-Christian values on their child but also, as he or she grows, to allow greater freedom in which the child can develop internal capacities for self-development, self-direction, self-transcendence. Parents must be willing to decrease their control gradually so that their child can take risks and exercise a growing initiative. Erikson and Boelen teach that parents must encourage the growing young person to develop autonomy, self-direction, initiative, industry and a creative use of tools and things.

Yet, parents must decrease their degree of control without permitting their child to be seriously endangered and without allowing her or him to lose a sense of limits or a proper respect for other persons and for the legitimate demands of life and the world. The secret is to learn how to avoid the extremes of a radical permissiveness which leaves the child confused and directionless and a rigid authoritarianism which prevents the blossoming of a proper self-concept, a growing sense of personal autonomy and an openness to the exercise of initiative and industry.

The law of "decrease-increase" affects families more intensely as children become teenagers and move into young adulthood. Parents must decrease their control by encouraging the young person to enter wider social spheres and to experiment with different kinds of work and different interests. They must resist the strong temptation to manipulate the vocational choices of their children, yet not abdicate their responsibility to give wise counsel when it is needed or asked for. It is through expanding interpersonal meetings and tackling jobs that young people develop their sense of personal identity and their direction in life, and learn to relate to members of the other sex in authentic intimacy.

The law of "decrease-increase" reaches its high point when the young person leaves home to take a job and perhaps to choose a spouse. Parents must exercise a high degree of "letting be" at this point. But this loving allowing the offspring to control their own lives is never a matter of abandonment or of leaving alone. There is an analogy here with Jesus' teaching that "anyone who wants to save his life will lose it; but anyone who loses his life for my sake, that man will save it" (Lk. 9:24). The parents who refuse to decrease, who cling tenaciously to their children, can harm their development and often find themselves in the end abandoned by their children. But those who are willing to let go of their children and let them lead their own lives will, in turn, receive greater love and concern from them and not find themselves alone in their declining years.

My stress on the role of parents in the authentic education and development of their children needs to be balanced with the truth that children as they grow become subject to wider and wider spheres of influence. Also, as the human being develops he or she plays an increasingly greater role in determining the course of his or her development. This means that it is by no means the parents or parental substitutes alone who bear responsibility for the authentic development of their offspring.

Self-Realization through Self-Transcendence

The ideal goal of parents and educators is to foster in young people intense processes of self-direction and self-transcendence. The expression "self-realization through self-transcendence" is Lonergan's[36] but can also be found in almost the same words in Viktor Frankl's writings.[37] Both men see the process of self-transcendence as the key to high level, holistic maturity.

Transcendence is going-beyond; in the act of knowing, for instance, we transcend ourselves by entering a world of meaning, truth and reality greater than ourselves. We find ourselves to be only one element in the universe of being. In the act of loving we transcend ourselves by delighting in values—natural beauty, works of art, above all other persons—which are beyond ourselves and lift us out of ourselves. Frankl writes, "Consider the eye. . . . A healthy eye sees nothing of itself . . . it is self-transcendent."[38] Self-realization, self-actualization, self-development are in their richest forms the effects of self-transcendence.

Frankl says it eloquently:

> Being human is being always directed, and pointing, to something or someone other than oneself: to a meaning to fulfill or another human being to encounter, a cause to serve or a person to love. Only to the extent that someone is living out this self-transcendence of human existence is he truly human or does he become his true self.[39]

There is, of course, a valid kind of self-love and of seeking to fulfill one's own needs. Scripture speaks of loving our neighbors *as ourselves* (Lk. 10:27). If I am hungry or thirsty, I seek food or drink for myself; if I need shelter, I seek a place of rest and security. Maslow points out that we have important needs for food, security and the like, and it is legitimate to fulfill these needs as long as we do not do it at the expense of others. Focusing on ourselves and our own needs is sometimes valid within limits. But, as we move beyond basic physical needs to the inner needs of the mind and heart for meaning and value, self-realization comes more and more from self-transcendence. The artist who loses himself in the creation of a work of art is the one who most realizes himself as an artist. The philosopher who is more interested in truth than in herself as the one who possesses it is the true philosopher, the true "lover of wisdom." The lover who forgets himself, delighting in his beloved, is the most self-actualized as a lover. It is in this realm of what Maslow calls "metaneeds,"[40] the needs for beauty, truth, goodness, value, that the dynamic of self-realization through self-transcendence is most fully at work.

Operating and Integrating

In human growth there is need not only for operating, for moving beyond, for transcending but also for consolidating, for deepening, for integrating. It is not enough just to discover new ways of thinking, feeling, acting. It is equally important to form good habits, to develop consistency in one's self-concept and personality, to integrate in a truly holistic and complementary fashion the different areas in one's development, to effect a harmony between the levels of the deep unconscious, twilight consciousness and the different forms of conscious striving and acting.

Lonergan calls the dynamisms in us which move us from lower to higher levels of activity and transcendence "operators." He names the conserving, sustaining, consolidating principles in us "integrators."[41] Among these operators is the "quasi-operator" that makes unrecognized or depressed psychic needs manifest in dreams or in the bizarre images that pop into consciousness unexpectedly.[42] It also shapes the images that lead to insight and recalls evidence that was ignored or overlooked. At a higher level the operators are manifested in the questions: What does it mean? Is it true? Is it truly worthwhile?[43] The integrators are familiarly known as acquired habits;[44] they are the conserving forces that provide continuity, consistency, reliability.

At the heart of created reality there is a basic tension between limitation and transcendence, between what is and what can be, between maintaining a level of development and moving beyond it. In persons this tension appears in the interplay between the integrators and operators of human development. Lonergan speaks of defective habits and routines which must be relentlessly opposed and transformed by the operators. Dabrowski writes of a very primitive integration which is narrow and rigid, characterized by selfish egocentrism; the person may be dominated by ambition, craving for security, lack of concern for others.[45] What is needed is the action of developmental dynamisms like dissatisfaction with oneself, a sense of guilt, of shame, astonishment with oneself. These can bring about a positive disintegration, breaking up the primary or primitive level of integration and leading to a higher level of personality functioning and integration.

"Seasons" and "Passages"

Besides these movements which Lonergan calls operators and Dabrowski names developmental dynamisms, there are other catalysts of change. Some are external accidents: the death of a parent or a friend, natural or civil disasters. They may cause massive shakeups in a person's life and trigger new growth or worse decline, higher integration or despair. There are also internal catalysts like illness, which can be the occasions of rich inner development or severe deterioration.

There are likewise key chronological psycho-social stages in ordinary human life which tend to bring on change, reformation or recommitment, positive or negative disintegration. Other chronological psycho-social stages favor quiet consolidation, conservation and the deepening of integration.

Daniel Levinson in *The Seasons of a Man's Life,*[46] Gail Sheehy in *Passages,*[47] and Bernard Boelen all propose that there are critical periods in the growth of men and women when change, uprooting, radical reevaluations, new or renewed commitments and decisions are to be expected, and other periods in psycho-social development when the mood and movement is toward stability, deeper rooting, consolidating and settling down. They agree that the shift from adolescence to young adulthood, coming roughly at ages 17–22 for men and two years earlier for women, and the mid-life transition occurring around 40–45 for men and a little earlier for women, are normally times of transition, change and operating. They consider the period of young adulthood leading to the mid-life crisis, and the period afterwards ending in the late adult years around 60 to 65 for men and a few years earlier for women, as basically given to consolidation and integration. Of course, they acknowledge that there is a fluidity in the suggested chronology and that each person varies. They also point out that failures to develop authentically can delay or prevent the occurrence of the later states with their different tasks, risks and opportunities.

Jung, Assagioli and Boelen have all stressed that in ideal development there is a significant turning-toward the spiritual and transcendent during the mid-life transition. This harmonizes with my belief in an ongoing deepening of moral and religious conversion, as a person ascends to higher levels in the spiral of transcendence. Certainly this does not preclude the possibility that a person may make God the radical focal center of his or her life at an earlier age. The book of Wisdom reminds us that "length of days is not what makes age honorable, nor number of years the true measure of life" (4:8). Wisdom teaches that "understanding . . . is man's gray hairs" (4:9) and speaks of the death of the young and virtuous: "Coming to perfection in so short a while, he achieved long life; his soul being pleasing to the Lord, he has taken him quickly from the wickedness around him" (4:13). The growing number of young Christian martyrs and saints like Agnes, Maria Goretti, Stanislaus, Therese of Lisieux, and Dominic Savio is proof of the lasting truth of these words.

A holistic Christian approach to the movements of operating and integrating includes the action of the Holy Spirit at all stages in all the seasons and passages of life. The person who actively cooperates with the grace of the Spirit moves gradually to a level of self-transcendence and integration, an ever deeper realization of the richest dimensions of the Christ-self, which immeasurably surpasses all purely natural forms of self-realization.

We discern in the writings of a variety of modern and contemporary psychologists and thinkers an attempt to depict the vocation of the human being as a call to the highest levels of psychological and spiritual wholeness and holiness. We see this in Erikson's explanation of the eighth stage of authentic development, ego integrity, in which death loses its bitter sting and wisdom is born. We see it in Jung's paraphrase of St. Ignatius, where he acknowledges that the deepest calling of human consciousness is to recognize its descent from a higher unity and to surrender to this source. We see it in Assagioli's description of that synthesis of spirit and psyche in which the Higher Self, the True Self, is realized. Dabrowski depicts it in the higher level secondary integration with its cultural and spiritual excellence. Boelen describes it in his existential language as the final yet ongoing integration which is a holy, creative surrender to Being. All these wise adventurers in the realm of psyche and spirit are pointing in their own fashion toward that spiritual state of integration which is the mystical presence in a human person of the Christ-self in its most radiant possible manifestation in this life.

4

The Self in Deformation

In Leviticus Yahweh urges his people to "reform" (26:23) and live according to his way. To be in need of reformation implies a deformed condition in those needing reform. I choose the word "deformation" to describe the condition of the sinner alienated from God. I also use the term deformation to describe the condition of the neurotic and the addict but I do so in these latter instances without necessarily implying that personal sin or immorality is the cause of the individual's neurosis or addiction. I prefer to speak of neurosis and addiction as deformations rather than disorders because the word deformation has more of a dynamic, progressive connotation than does the word disorder. And I tend to view both neurosis and addiction as illnesses of a progressive character.

Neurotic Deformation

Initially, it may prove helpful to compare neurosis as a psychological deformation with the condition of physical deformity. A baby can be born with a physical defect, or can be deformed physically through disease or an accident. It makes little sense, however, unless one believes that the sole cause of neurosis is some genetic or chemical defect, to speak of a baby as born with a neurotic deformity. There is some possibility that pre-natal experiences or the birth-experience itself can begin the process of neurotic deformation. But I hold that neurosis generally unfolds in the early years of the child's growth period. With many authorities I agree that the first six years of a child's life are extremely significant as far as the occurrence of neurotic deformation is concerned. But I also acknowledge that traumatic experiences, severe rejection, and miseducation about basic psychological needs and the way to fulfill them can cause neurosis of varying intensity even in the teenage and later periods. Psychological deformation, accordingly, can occur in initially healthy individuals due to negative interpersonal experiences or miseducation just as, analogously, physical deformity can result from illnesses or accidents which befall individuals who were born physically healthy and whole.

Experts in psychology distinguish between neurotic and psychotic abnormality; the principal differences lie in the severity of the deformation and the degree of loss of contact with reality. The radically neurotically wounded person suffers from severe psychic discomforts such as massive anxiety, exaggerated fears, deep hostility, paralyzing guilt, unrecognized or unacknowledged anger, depression, debilitating tension, a sense of partial loss of control of the self and of life, and other symptoms. Yet the neurotic knows who he or she is, is aware that something is very wrong, and knows what is going on in the world around. This person does not hear strange voices of non-existent people or claim to be Napoleon or Christ. The psychotic, in contrast, suffers from radical personality disintegration and loss of contact with reality. Psychosis is marked by major thought disturbances, delusions, hallucinations, severe mood alterations in rapid succession, and other symptoms. Many theorists argue for a genetic factor in some or all psychotic disturbances.

As a basic definition I propose that neurotic deformation consists in either or both of the following states: (1) a person's deeply-felt sense of being unlovable and worthless, and accompanying destructive, largely unrecognized attitudes and self-defeating strategies for dealing with this negative self-image; (2) severe repression in a person and/or other destructive effects and expressions of miseducation which cause great psychic discomfort, and impair the ability to function well in the give-and-take of everyday life.

I should explain my two-fold definition of the nature of neurosis. In the classical approaches of Freud and Jung, repression is given a dominant, if not exclusive, role as the cause of neurosis. Contemporary psychologists such as Drs. David Ausubel, William Glasser[1] and many others suggest that a sense of rejection, a feeling of being worthless and unlovable as a person is at the root of neurotic deformation. Dr. Conrad Baars, however, theorizes that repression or a lack of acceptance or both of these factors together can underlie neurosis.[2] I agree with Baars that it is not possible to reduce the cause of all neurosis to one single factor.

Rejection and Neurotic Deformation

One principal type of neurotic deformation is the existence in a person of a sense of rejection, of being unlovable and worthless. In Ausubel's terms we are dealing with a person who has experienced rejection or who has only been valued extrinsically for what he or she could become or achieve. This individual, if rejected or extrinsically valued by his or her parent(s) at a very early age, was unable to identify with the parent(s) or parental substitute(s) and to derive from these "omnipotent" ones a sense of personal worth, lovableness and acceptance.

Dr. John Evoy, author of the very recent *The Rejected,*[3] develops the theme of rejection by describing it from the point of view of rejected individuals. Basically, the latter will speak of rejection as "*their emotionally toned knowledge that they were not loved and wanted, for themselves, by one or both parents.*"[4] In Baars' rather striking expression, these individuals had failed to experience the gift of "psychic birth." The rejected individuals understandably feel inferior, inadequate, uncertain, and insecure.[5]

Are there degrees in the experience and effects of rejection or of extrinsic valuation? Spitz indicates that in some cases when a child is radically deprived of a loving, caring environment, the child may die. Angyal remarks that the neurotic is lucky because things could have been much worse. He says, "There are no neurotics whose early childhood did not contain some constructive elements, some substantial gratifications, some sources of affection."[6] If all constructive elements are absent, psychosis, not neurosis, will result.[7] Erikson also makes the point that when a person does not develop basic trust, schizophrenia can result.[8] Kayla Bernheim and Richard Lewin in their recent book *Schizophrenia* also acknowledge that "early results of family studies indicate the presence of conflict or disorganization in the families of those children who go on to become schizophrenic."[9]

Augustine, Pascal, Lonergan and many others have spoken poetically of a "knowledge born of love" and "reasons of the heart" which only lovers know.[10] The opposite of this knowledge is an existential ignorance and error of the heart, born of a failure to be loved and valued in oneself, which only the rejected suffer. This "anti-knowledge" of the heart is *ignorance* because it is the absence of appreciation and insight into one's inherent value and excellence. This anti-knowledge is *error* because the inner sense of unlovableness and worthlessness it causes is a lie. It is *existential* because it touches the core of a person's existence, questioning the very worth of that existence. This anti-knowledge of the heart is at the center of the neurotic deformation I have described, belonging to the dark realm of the anti-self and the anti-self-image.

There is the further difficulty of the presence in the unloved of destructive, largely unrecognized attitudes and self-defeating strategies for dealing with his or her negative self-image. In his long years of therapeutic work, Evoy found that persons who had a negative self-image, rooted in rejection or extrinsic valuation, possessed destructive attitudes about the criteria for personal acceptance,[11] and developed self-defeating strategies for disproving their low self-evaluations.[12]

Evoy discovered that the parents or parent-substitutes were the main source of the neurotic's criteria for acceptance. Some parents made demands for even minimal or token acceptance or tolerance, and the child unconsciously accepted these demands as the yardstick of personal worth and acceptance.[13] Some children, for instance, were led to believe that acceptance had to be earned; others tied acceptability to behavior that was demanded or forbidden; still others played a role—a boy might act like a girl to please his mother, who had wanted a daughter.[14]

Evoy found that the rejected ones zeroed in on two areas in their endless striving to disprove their low self-esteem: the attempt to gain love and affection from others, and the attempt to achieve.[15] From his counseling experience he generalized that women tended to be affection-hunters whereas men strove for achievement. But he observed that in the last few years, a growing number of rejected or extrinsically-valued women expressed the driving, all-consuming need to achieve.[16]

The strategies of the rejected to gain affection or achievement and in this way to disprove their low self-esteem proved self-defeating. Those individuals driven by affection-hunger often used hostile or sexual behavior which they themselves found morally unacceptable. This confirmed their feelings of worthlessness.[17] Those who tried to prove their self-worth through various achievements showed an exaggerated competitiveness, and remained unimpressed, no matter how well they did.[18] The rejected sufferers also used tactics like flattery, bragging and exaggerating, which are self-defeating; they were often possessed by a spirit of intense jealousy and resentment.[19]

Andras Angyal confirms that persons who lack a sense of being lovable and worthwhile unconsciously develop destructive attitudes and self-defeating habits to deal with their feelings of worthlessness. He notes that some love-deprived people seek "fame, prestige, a reputation, titles" as a weak substitute for the self-worth they do not feel.[20] Others impose all sorts of obligations on themselves, and "life becomes a set of hated demands one . . . tries to fulfill."[21] Still others set up for themselves an impossible ideal of absolute perfection; a neurotic says to himself, for example, that "if he were perfect, and only then, he could not doubt his worth."[22]

Angyal has observed that some neurotics force themselves on other people or feign helplessness to get some response, some attention. In his therapeutic work with those individuals he tries to show them that they are not wrong in wanting affection and a basic feeling of worth, but that they have wrong attitudes and assumptions about what it means to be worthwhile, and are using "methods that are doomed to failure."[23]

I mentioned earlier that the neurotic's destructive attitudes and self-defeating strategies are largely unrecognized. This may be for various reasons: they are totally or partially repressed; they are consciously felt but not understood or named; they are "lower voices" in the background or twilight zone of consciousness. These attitudes and strategies may also go unrecognized because they are errors which have "become lodged in the habitual background whence spring our . . . insights."[24] But some concrete examples will help us. Albert Ellis holds that irrational beliefs such as "it is a dire necessity for an adult human being to be loved or approved by virtually every significant other person in his community"[25] are the basic causes of neurotic deformation but that individuals do not generally advert to these beliefs, even though they are not unconscious in the deep sense. Ellis' irrational beliefs belong to the lower voices in the polyphony of thoughts in human consciousness. Evoy in similar fashion observes that very few of the rejected recognize that their striving for affection or achievement is an attempt to compensate their feeling of worthlessness.[26] Finally, psychiatrist James Gill offers the example of a young man who lacked love as a child and who now as an ordained priest is ostensibly dedicated to the selfless love of others but who in fact is unconsciously manipulating and using others to fulfill his unmet affective needs. The priest is not aware of the true meaning of his activities or of the conflict which exists between his ideal of selfless service and his actual strategies for dealing with others.[27] The neurotic, in fact, is so prone to misinterpret his or her life experiences that one psychiatrist has defined neurosis as "cumulatively misinterpreted experience."[28]

The form of neurosis I have been describing up to this point is a deformation that is total in its impact. It touches the whole person in his or her basic self-image, feelings, beliefs, actions. Angyal somewhere compares neurosis to a cancer which has metastasized and my own counseling experience bears this out. This first form of neurosis is not limited to the mind or the heart, to the imagination or the feelings. It is a whole way of being in the world.

I do suggest, however, that just as there are degrees in the experience and effects of being unloved and unaffirmed, so there are degrees of distortion in the destructive attitudes and self-defeating strategies of the neurotic. At one extreme the distortions are so severe that the suffering person is in need of a radical healing. At the other extreme there is the minimal type of neurotic discomfort that at some point becomes indistinguishable from the sufferings of the everyday person in his or her everyday world, the sufferings of the type of person Eugene Kennedy somewhere refers to as "normally abnormal."

Repression and Neurotic Deformation

The strictest form of repression is a totally unconscious process of excluding even from the zone of twilight consciousness certain impulses, instincts, and desires which are totally unacceptable at any level of consciousness. In the Freudian tradition repression is especially related to the sexual instinct. But this latter instinct must not be understood in too limited a fashion; it includes not only the explicitly genital but the entire orientation of the body toward pleasure. In the Jungian tradition repression is expanded to include such psychic functions as thinking and feeling, sensation and intuition. If, for example, a person tries to meet the demands of existence mainly through thinking, his or her feeling function becomes repressed. In both the Freudian and Jungian psychotherapeutic traditions where repression is too severe neurosis results. It tends to manifest itself in psychic disruptions such as hysteria, phobias, hypochondriasis, strange bodily sensations and other similar phenomena.

Psychologists and therapists such as Drs. O. Hobart Mowrer and Viktor Frankl extended the field of possible objects of repression still further. It is Mowrer's theory that neurotic disturbances are the result of the repression of guilt which is real and deserved and should be admitted and atoned.[29] Frankl, too, holds that neurosis can be due to a repression of conscience,[30] although he agrees with Freud that neurosis can be due to repression in the area of the sexual instinct. He goes still further in his view that there can also be a repression of the will to meaning[31] and of the religious instinct.[32] These latter forms of repression can result in what Frankl calls "noögenic neurosis."[33] This kind of neurosis expresses itself in a sense of meaninglessness and can lead to addiction, despair and even suicide.[34]

I hold that there do exist repressive activities in the areas of sexuality, personality orientations and functions, conscience, will to meaning, values and the drive to religion. I believe, however, that repression *can* initially involve a semi-deliberate excluding from awareness of certain impulses, drives or personality orientations. Later the individual is no longer conscious at all or only dimly so of the repressed impulse, drive or orientation. In fact, he or she can come to the point of actually denying any experience, even incipient, of the presence of the repressed element.

Repression, I think, is largely caused by existential miseducation. For example, some parents may have a puritanical attitude toward sex, and so teach their children to see even the experience of sexual desire, or any feelings of interest in sex, as evil. It can also result from falsely believing that acknowledging or expressing some impulses will cause severe illness or even insanity.

Repression in the young also often results from the fear of the loss of parental love or at least the diminishment of this love. If, for example, a parent teaches it is always wrong to express anger, the child may refrain from expressing anger for fear of losing the parent's love. Rejected or extrinsically valued children are especially prone to severe repressive activity as they are to various other destructive psychological activities.

Repression is not the only effect of existential miseducation. Well-meaning parents who know little about mental health and the laws of growth can cause real damage without intending to do so. Angyal gives the example of parents who try to protect their children from all danger to such an extent that they prevent the child's development of initiative and sense of autonomy and industry.[35] Such a child may grow up mistrusting the world, life and existence. Parents can also cause their children to develop a pattern of non-commitment by being inconsistent in their treatment, by making conflicting demands, or by failing to practice what they preach.[36] These are just a few examples of the miseducation which can lead to diverse forms of neurosis as individuals grow up.

Society, Sin and Neurosis

Phil Brown, the author of *Toward a Marxist Psychology,* indicts capitalist society as the chief source of alienation from true selfhood and of neurotic deformations.[37] He is not alone in believing that society, with its corrupt ideology, is the chief culprit in the case of neurosis. For years Thomas Szasz[38] and Ronald Laing[39] have argued that the ideological and behavioral "straitjacket" which society imposes on each person is the root of so-called "mental illness." The argument is sometimes heard that the mentally ill are really healthy and it is society which is sick.

There are deep roots in the Christian tradition which lend support to the view that society is a major, if not exclusive, cause of neurotic disturbance. In *Foundations of Christian Faith,* Karl Rahner, discussing original sin, states that a radical "no" to God at the beginning of human history changed the whole course of history for the worse. He says that "toil, ignorance, sickness, pain and death as we encounter them" are the result of the false decision of "Adam" and would not be present "*in the same way* we actually experience them" if it were not for original sin.[40] Murphy-O'Connor writes in a similar vein that "Sin is the 'world' in the false orientation given humankind by the sin of Adam" and that "this orientation is ratified and intensified by the attitudes of his (Adam's) descendants."[41] These writers both offer support to the theory that societal forces beyond the control of any one person are at least partly responsible for such sicknesses as neurosis. Of course they don't exclude the possibility that individuals actively cooperate in their own and others' deformation.

Dr. Karen Horney in her classic work *The Neurotic Personality of Our Time*[42] and Viktor Frankl in *The Unheard Cry for Meaning*[43] both indict society for its role in causing neurotic deformation. Horney points out the many contradictory messages given by society which cause conflict in people: for instance, the American stress on competition and the need to succeed versus the importance of brotherly love.[44] She also notes the contradiction in American society between the push for "conspicuous consumption" and the inability of many people to satisfy these so-called needs.[45] The person who is likely to become neurotic, she believes, is the one who has experienced these cultural contradictions intensely in childhood and has been unable to resolve them.[46] Frankl cites the hedonistic stress on self-realization and the widespread denial of transcendence and the will to meaning as key sources of noögenic neurosis, addiction, crime and increasing violence in America and elsewhere.[47]

Lonergan, too, puts great emphasis on the role of society for good or ill in human formation. People are born and brought up in communities, and the individual's potentialities for self-transcendence are limited by the common beliefs and assumptions of his or her community.[48] For example, if the community shares a bias like racism or a basically materialistic outlook, it will be very difficult for a person to resist the corruption of that bias. In this context Hora writes that "contemporary man lives in an increasingly polluted atmosphere, in . . . a mental climate that is more or less overcharged and harmful."[49] The mental atmosphere families live in, as Hora and others see it, is filled with false values, assumptions, beliefs and ideas about what it really means to be happy and fulfilled human beings. Often in trying to live according to these destructive norms of happiness, parents try to fulfill their so-called needs at the expense of the authentic needs of their children—and the result is children who feel unloved and are seriously miseducated about life.

A holistic Christian approach to the problem of neurosis must take account not only of the intersubjective sphere of the family but also of the broader context of society and human history to understand the underlying, ultimate causes of this major source of human suffering.

Addictive Deformation

The term addiction has traditionally referred to a compulsive, physiological need for a drug, such as heroin. In recent literature the term addiction is used to designate a compulsive physiological and/or psychological need for objects as varied as alcohol, food, cigarettes, gambling and even persons or groups.

Addiction as a chemical dependency manifests itself when the presence of the addictive substance in the body becomes a necessity for the maintenance of normal cellular activity; once the drug is withdrawn various distortions of physiological processes tend to occur such as the withdrawal symptoms of convulsions and hallucinations. The chemically dependent individual is characterized by an inability to control the beginning or termination of intake of the addictive substance. The craving for the substance takes on a compulsive, overpowering character and there is a tendency to make use of the substance in continually increasing amounts.

Dr. George Mann in his *Recovery of Reality*[50] indicates that addiction is a highly complex matter and must not be oversimplified. He provides an index in which substances are listed according to their potential for creating addiction and dependency. At the bottom of the list in an ascending order are caffeine, marijuana, hashish. At the very top of the list is heroin. Alcohol is in the upper third section of the list.[51]

My aim so far has been to provide a basic view of the nature of chemical dependency. I would like to focus now on the cause or causes of the deformation of addiction. But at once we are involved in an area of controversy. Is addiction to drugs basically a matter of moral depravity? Is it due principally to a habit-forming quality present in some chemical substances? Is addiction to chemicals due to a psychological deformation? Most experts today do not hold that the major cause of addiction is to be located in moral depravity. It could, of course, be a disposing factor. Also, the moral dimension certainly enters into the healing process at some point. But the basic key to the meaning of addiction does not seem to lie simply in a failure to be moral. There is greater dispute, however, when it comes to a discussion of the other possible causes of addiction.

Mann distinguishes between four types of chemically-addictive people.[52] The first group consists of those who have a very low tolerance for emotional pain and stress, and whose major coping device is medication. The second class comprises those who in their lives develop adequate ways of coping, but whose stress-tolerance is rather low, and who buckle under too heavy stress, resorting to mood-altering chemicals to relieve their pain and anxiety. In the third group are people whose basal metabolism differs from the average. Mann contends that research supports the view that some persons have a metabolic predisposition to abuse certain kinds of drugs. These people have brain and liver enzymes different from those of the average person. His fourth group is made up of those people who are predisposed to depend on certain chemicals by their heredity: the physical make-up of these persons simply does not permit their using drugs like alcohol for pleasure or relaxation. He writes that this last group constitutes a very small percentage of the total population of addicts.

Unlike Mann, Dr. William Glasser in his book *Positive Addiction*[53] argues that chemical and other forms of addiction are all due to a lack of fulfillment of the basic needs to be loved and to love and to feel worthwhile to oneself and others. I myself hold that the initial cause of chemical addiction can be any one or a particular combination of the causes of chemical addiction which Dr. Mann suggests. An individual could conceivably have metabolic, hereditary and psychological causes of his or her addiction. I do agree, however, with Dr. James Royce that in the chemical addiction of alcoholism and, I believe, in varying degrees in other chemical addictions as well, whatever the cause, the habit acquires its own functional autonomy; that is, it becomes its own motive for action. Alcoholics eventually drink because they are alcoholic, regardless of why they originally started drinking. The compulsion to drink is now rooted "in [a] . . . whole complex of mental and biological changes. . . ."[54]

Non-Chemical Addictive Deformations

Dr. Stanton Peele, author of *Love and Addiction,*[55] argues that individuals can become addicted to an object, to a sensation, and even to a person. He states that an addiction exists when a person's attachment to the sensation, object or person in question is such that it "lessens his appreciation of and ability to deal with other things in his environment or in himself" and when he "becomes increasingly dependent on that experience as his only source of gratification."[56]

Peele speaks about becoming addicted to a sensation. I think that this can occur in the area of masturbation.[57] In my Christotherapeutic work I have encountered individuals who led exemplary Christian lives except that they experienced a seemingly endless battle in their struggle with masturbation. They prayed and prayed for relief; they got endless advice and tried all sorts of tactics. But in spite of everything they continued to fail in this area. Clearly in these cases a true compulsion existed; there was a sense of powerlessness just as real as there is in the case of alcoholism. Also, in many cases this problem caused great inner suffering and impeded the sufferers in their prayers and in their attempts to live, love and work in a happy fashion. Certainly all the earmarks of true addiction are manifest in this situation. I believe that the acknowledgement of the possibility of true addiction in the area of masturbation can aid immeasurably in helping individuals to come to some understanding of their sense of powerlessness in this area. It can also open the way for a new exploration of therapeutic possibilities in an area where there has been much pain and frustration.[58]

Addiction to gambling is an example of addiction to an activity or object in the broad sense. Gambling addiction resembles alcoholism in its compulsivity and its tendency to produce a basic lack of manageability in the addict's life. As for its cause, Dr. Robert Custer, an expert in the area of compulsive gambling, suggests that in most instances "the man or woman who becomes a compulsive gambler suffered from a lack of affection in childhood. The excitement of gambling is used to blot out the feeling of rejection."[59] This explanation harmonizes with that of Glasser who holds that all forms of addiction are rooted in the failure to have love and worth needs fulfilled. I have also heard it suggested, however, that the ritual and excitement of gambling causes a certain flow of adrenalin and the individual becomes addicted to this sensation.

Peele also speaks of becoming addicted to persons. There are recurrent phenomena such as the Jim Jones affair which suggest the possibility that individuals can become addicted to certain personalities and/or groups with their rituals and beliefs. Often people who become "addicted" to individuals like Jim Jones are psychologically deformed individuals.

I have been speaking of addiction to a cult leader and/or group but Peele also suggests that one person can become addicted to another in the one-to-one relationships which exist between lovers or even in marriage. He indicates that when a lover or spouse becomes so dependent on the other person that there is a loss of appreciation of other values, a growing dependence on the other person as the sole source of gratification and a lessening in the ability to manage one's own life that an addiction exists.[60] But I am willing to acknowledge that this may be using addiction in a very analogous sense. There is nonetheless a real problem present and approaching it as a type of addiction can shed real light on the problem and perhaps open up new possibilities of therapeutic assistance.

SECTION TWO

The New Wisdom

1

FOUNDATIONS

5

Principles and Methods of a Spiritual-Psychological Synthesis

Viktor Frankl in 1938 coined the expression "height psychology."[1] He did not intend to deny the validity of Freud's discovery of "depth psychology" with its unconscious instinctual drives but to affirm the coexistence in the human being of an openness to meaning, to value, to self-transcendence. Frankl, like Roberto Assagioli,[2] was a pioneer in the attempt to relate the sphere of psychology and psychotherapy to the higher dimensions, orientations and aspirations of men and women. Without the seminal efforts of these highly creative thinkers to expand the boundaries of psychology, contemporary attempts to bring about a synthesis of spiritual and psychological principles of healing and growth would be completely unthinkable.

Four contemporary approaches to effecting healing and growth in the human psyche are the exclusively spiritual, the materialist, separate specialization and the spiritual-psychological. A brief sketch of these four approaches will serve as a very helpful means of clarifying and highlighting the meaning of the spiritual-psychological synthetic approach.

The exclusively spiritual approach holds that the only valid avenue to wholeness is the spiritual. Mary Baker Eddy's[3] Christian Science religion appears to embody this viewpoint. Also, faith healers who on principle exclude *any* recourse to a physician or a person knowledgeable in psychology or psychiatry fall under this classification.

The materialist approach denies the existence of God; it holds that the human being is ultimately reducible to purely material components; it views religion in principle as error and even as a source of neurosis and moral, cognitive and cultural negative disintegration. It holds that a strictly secular, materialistic psychology and psychotherapy offers the only valid way for effecting psychological healing and growth in persons.

The separate specialization approach holds that it is primarily the task of the psychologist or the psychiatrist to deal with the healing of psychological deformations and it is principally the function of the priest, minister or other specialist in the realm of religion to handle problems of a spiritual or religious nature. Proponents of this approach do not, on principle, view religion and psychiatry as either at war with each other or even as indifferent toward one another. In fact, there is often a practice of enlightened referral. A priest, for example, who discovers that the complaint of his parishioner is basically psychological in nature will send the suffering individual to a psychologist or psychiatrist. Likewise, a psychiatrist who finds that his or her patient is basically troubled with a religious rather than a psychological difficulty will recommend consultation with a rabbi, priest, or minister, as the situation suggests. Practitioners of this third approach also engage in mutual consultation when they are both dealing with the same person but from their diverse perspectives. I believe that presently most Christian psychologists, psychiatrists and ministers of religion operate out of this third option.

The spiritual-psychological synthetic approach seeks to integrate the principles and healing methods of psychology and psychiatry with those of a particular religion or spirituality, into a higher synthesis which is both theoretical and practical. In both the theory and the practice of such a synthesis there is a distinction but no separation between the principles and methods used by psychology and those used by the religion or spiritual way. Ideally, the therapist who takes the synthetic approach uses spiritual/religious principles and methods as well as psychological and psychotherapeutic ones to facilitate the healing of deformations and addictions and holistic growth. He or she also uses psychological insights and tools along with spiritual ones to help a person grow spiritually, in prayer and other ways, in order to reach, with the help of God's grace, higher levels of holiness.

The synthetic approach transcends the traditional separation between psychology/psychotherapy, on the one hand, and spiritual direction on the other. It does not deny, however, that a secular psychologist or psychotherapist can be an effective agent in the healing of psychological deformation. It also acknowledges that the spiritual director who knows enough psychology to recognize the presence of psychological deformations and various growth crises when they occur and who is enlightened enough to make referrals at the appropriate time can be an effective spiritual guide. But the synthetic approach does maintain that the ideal lies beyond the separate specialization option. Finally, the synthetic approach insists that this spiritual-psychological synthesis should be available to those who actively seek out this particular way of healing and growing; but it should never be imposed on anyone.

There are a growing number of therapists who, in their theory and practice, are seeking in varying degrees to synthesize spiritual and psychological principles and methods in order to facilitate healing and growth. Some concrete examples of individuals who have inspired or are presently engaged in this synthetic approach are Roberto Assagioli, John Sanford, Alphonse Calabrese, Dennis and Matthew Linn and Lawrence Crabb, Jr.

Roberto Assagioli

My expression "spiritual-psychological synthesis" is inspired by Dr. Assagioli's description in his book *Psychosynthesis* of a higher type of psychosynthesis which he refers to as a "Spiritual Psychosynthesis."[4] He distinguishes his spiritual psychosynthesis from a personal psychosynthesis. The latter precedes the former and is concerned with helping persons become psychologically well adjusted and capable of working in harmony with others.[5] The aim of spiritual psychosynthesis is to help the person develop dimensions and release energies of what Assagioli refers to as the spiritual Self.[6]

The work of Assagioli did not influence me in my initial elaborating of Christotherapy. But I have come to see many affinities between psychosynthesis and Christotherapy. There is also a growing impact of Assagioli's insights in my more recent nuancing of Christotherapy as a spiritual-psychological synthesis. For these reasons I will comment briefly here on Assagioli's overall psychosynthetic approach and I will refer later to more specific aspects of psychosynthesis to the extent that they serve to illuminate or enrich Christotherapy.

Assagioli defines psychosynthesis as the "conscious attempt to *cooperate* with the natural process of personal development."[7] For authentic cooperation, "a conceptual understanding, a framework, and a range of practical techniques"[8] are required.

Psychosynthesis "integrates the best available concepts and methods into an inclusive but growing framework, so as to facilitate the natural human drive toward development."[9]

Assagioli was one of the pioneers of Freudian psychoanalysis in Italy, but became convinced very early in his career that Freud did not give significant recognition to the higher dimensions of the human person. Unlike Freud, Assagioli acknowledged the primacy of the spiritual in human existence. But he maintained that his method was neutral toward the diverse philosophical systems and religions. Appealing to the "direct experience"[10] of spiritual realities, his stated aim was to work from the direct spiritual experience and toward the deepening of it. In his personal psychosynthesis, Assagioli made use of insights and methods of Freud, Adler, Jung and others. In his spiritual psychosynthesis Assagioli elaborated exercises for the realization of the true or spiritual Self, based on such works as the *Legend of the Grail* and Dante's *Divine Comedy*. Assagioli drew on a wide number of Eastern and Western techniques for spiritual development without explicitly espousing any particular religious doctrinal view. I believe, however, that Assagioli's interpretation of the nature of the ego, of the spiritual Self, of the will and of other basic realities does, in fact, imply a particular metaphysical view of the ultimate nature of reality.

John Sanford

John Sanford is a Jungian analyst and an Episcopal priest. In his books, *The Kingdom Within,*[11] *Dreams and Healing,*[12] *Healing and Wholeness,*[13] and others along the same lines, he provides a striking example of a therapist who synthesizes psychological and spiritual principles of healing and growth. As a follower of Jung, Sanford lays stress on the interpretation of dreams as a means of psychological healing. For Sanford, dreams may well be the most significant and frequent way in which the "Word of God is spoken."[14] In fact, he believes that the Spirit of God is at work every night in our dreams, sending us food for our hungry souls.[15] His is a clear synthesis of classical psychology's emphasis on dream interpretation with the biblical data on God's work in our dreams.

Sanford places great importance on the practice of prayer for persons seeking psychological healing as well as deeper growth in the life of the spirit. He urges those who come to him to "pray, and to go about it in whatever way is natural"[16] to the person. In speaking of Christian prayer he remarks that "the cross, or the birth of Christ, for instance, may be the object of a contemplation in which it is hoped that the deeper meanings of the Christian images will speak to the mediator to enrich his mind and heal his spirit."[17] Here again there is a deep interweaving of the psychological and the spiritual.

Sanford describes Jesus of Nazareth as "the prototype both of the developed ego and of the Total Man."[18] In his view, through suffering and resurrection Jesus "merges forever with the human psyche and becomes the archetype of totality for all of us, transforming the destiny of mankind."[19] He looks to Jesus as the perfect exemplar of what it is to be fully human and psychologically integrated. Like other Christian theological writers of the past and present, he believes that it is only in Jesus that the meaning of what it is to be human is fully revealed. Finally, he describes his book *The Kingdom Within* as an "outline of a psychological-spiritual theory of the kingdom of God."[20] His own words clearly bear out his basic spiritual-psychological synthetic orientation.[21]

Alphonse Calabrese

Dr. Alphonse Calabrese is a psychoanalyst who experienced a charismatic renewal of his Christian commitment, and discovered how to integrate into his psychoanalytic practice key Christian principles and ways of healing. In his book *The Christian Love Treatment*[22] he makes use of Freud's insights into the importance of early child-parent relationships,[23] the role of repression,[24] the function of transference, i.e., the process whereby the patient in therapy transfers emotions felt toward his or her real parents onto the therapist[25] and other basic Freudian principles. At the same time this Christian analyst introduces prayer into the heart of the therapeutic process—prayer for and with the client.[26] He stresses the importance of developing an authentic conscience and a true sense of sin and guilt;[27] he emphasizes the exercise of responsibility.[28] In working with Christians, he does not hesitate to bring Christian values and moral principles explicitly into therapy.[29] He provides a good example of a therapist who has broken out of the separate specialization model and is seeking to effect a spiritual-psychological synthesis.

Dennis and Matthew Linn

In their books *Healing of Memories*[30] and *Healing Life's Hurts*[31] Dennis and Matthew Linn provide yet another example from the charismatic perspective of an attempt to work out a spiritual-psychological synthesis of healing and growth principles and methods. In *Healing Life's Hurts* they integrate into a spiritual framework the model of Dr. Elisabeth Kübler-Ross, who concluded after years of working with dying patients that there were definite stages through which her patients passed when faced with the real, proximate possibility of death. Kübler-Ross names these five stages denial, anger, bargaining, depression and acceptance.[32] The Linn brothers take this five-stage model and apply it to the healing of painful, traumatic, often repressed memories. In their experiences people tend to pass through these same five stages as they move from their initial reaction to a traumatic event toward the stage of full forgiveness. In adopting the Kübler-Ross model the Linns take each of the five stages and integrate them into the Christian perspective of healing and forgiveness. For example, in the case of the first stage, denial, they begin by showing how individuals initially tend to screen out hurtful interpersonal memories by denial and other defenses such as rationalizing and repression. Next they give an example of the occurrence of denial in some Scriptural incident. In a third step they look at the positive aspect of denial and show that a moderate form of denial in the face of a severe trauma can be helpful until the person is more able to deal with the wounding experience. In the final phase of dealing with denial the Linns instruct such wounded individuals to tell Christ how they feel; to behold Christ in Scripture; to contemplate him as he deals with a denial; to desire to assimilate his attitude of mind and heart; to prayerfully try to imagine what Christ would tell them to do in their particular situation and finally to seek to follow Christ's example and teaching in their own handling of denial.[33] The Linn brothers repeat this same sequence in integrating the other four stages of anger, bargaining, depression and acceptance within a Christian perspective of healing. Clearly the approach of Dennis and Matt Linn provides a striking example of a specific spiritual-psychological synthesis.

Lawrence J. Crabb, Jr.

Dr. Lawrence Crabb, Jr., a clinical psychologist and committed Christian, in his books *Basic Principles of Biblical Counseling*[34] and *Effective Biblical Counseling*[35] outlines a model of Christian counseling which combines the psychological insights of the cognitive therapy of Dr. Albert Ellis and others with basic biblical teachings, as they are received within the Presbyterian tradition. Crabb assigns a clear primacy to Holy Scripture and places all the insights and methods of psychology under the judgment of the Word of God. But he does make use of those psychological principles and methods which do not contradict the teachings of Christ.

Local Christian churches, Crabb urges, can and should take responsibility for helping in the healing of psychologically troubled Christians. He suggests that all members of a local Christian community are called to do "Counseling By Encouragement."[36] Beyond that, he proposes that certain members of each community can be sufficiently trained in basic psychological and Christian principles of counseling to be able to "meet every nonorganic counseling need within the local church."[37] He calls this latter kind of psychological help "Counseling By Enlightenment." In Crabb's plan, a layman can be trained for this kind of counseling within a year. I find Crabb overly optimistic about the time required to train a layperson to engage effectively in the type of counseling he describes. But I agree with him that local Christian churches can and should play a much more active role in helping their psychologically wounded members. When I consider the tremendous healing potential of various self-help groups it becomes eminently clear to me that the Christian churches have been greatly remiss in the use of their own rich resources for facilitating the healing of psychological and addictive deformations. There is need for much creative work to be done in this area.

Thomas Hora and Metapsychiatry

Dr. Thomas Hora is the contemporary therapist who has provided the greatest inspiration for me in my own quest for wholeness and in my development of Christotherapy as a spiritual-psychological synthesis. I do not include Hora, however, among those who are presently seeking to effect a spiritual-psychological synthesis. At an earlier stage in his development Hora did seek to effect such a synthesis but presently in his existential metapsychiatry he holds that the healing of all psychological difficulties which appear to plague human individuals comes about exclusively through spiritual enlightenment.

In *Christotherapy* I acknowledge with great gratitude the pervasive influence of Hora's insights and methods throughout my book; but I also state that "there are fundamental differences between Dr. Hora and myself in our respective understanding of the nature of the self and God, of Jesus Christ and the incarnation, of ecclesial Christianity, and of other important issues."[38] In the period since *Christotherapy* appeared in print I have been asked again and again in classes, in public lectures and at institutes to clarify Hora's positions as they relate to my development of Christotherapy and to basic Catholic Christian beliefs and practices. Since these questions continue to arise and, just as importantly, because Hora's ideas and methods continue to exercise a major influence in my present writing, I will focus attention in the immediately following pages on Hora's background, key stages in his development, central principles of his existential metapsychiatry, his view of God, the human individual, Jesus and sin, and on some key differences which exist between his ideas and Catholic Christian beliefs.

Stages of Development in Hora's Approach

Thomas Hora was born in Czechoslovakia in 1914. He received his medical and psychiatric degrees from the University of Budapest in 1942 and from Prague Charles University in 1945. He has been faculty member, lecturer and supervisor at a number of institutes and clinics in the United States and in 1959 was the winner of the Karen Horney Award for his contributions in psychiatry.

Dr. Hora is in a state of ongoing evolution in his development of what he terms "metapsychiatry."[39] His early writings, produced not too long after he completed his medical and psychiatric studies, show clearly the influence of Freud in ideas and vocabulary. Some typical titles of these early articles are: "The Problem of Negative Countertransference";[40] "The Dissocial Superego";[41] "Masochistic Use of Anxiety."[42] Hora, however, quite early in his career, like Assagioli, became dissatisfied with the failure of psychoanalysis to take account of the spiritual dimensions of the human being and began to study the writings of Martin Heidegger, Gabriel Marcel, Martin Buber and other existentialist writers. He also interested himself in the existential psychiatric approach of Ludwig Binswanger. He delved into the writings of Buddhism and other Eastern religions and studied under a Zen master for a time. Hora's articles during the 1960–1970 period show a growing influence of the Hebrew and Christian Scriptures. His latest books *Existential Metapsychiatry*[43] and *Dialogues in Metapsychiatry*[44] give a clear preeminence to the teachings of Jesus.

Hora sharply distinguishes, as does Assagioli, between religion and spirituality and, like Assagioli, Hora appeals primarily to direct spiritual experience rather than to religious traditions and doctrines as the principal source for validating principles and methods of healing and growth. Hora does not align himself with any traditional Christian denomination but claims to be Christian in the sense of remaining faithful to the deepest spiritual teaching of Jesus.

It is difficult to categorize Hora's approach because of the evolution of his thought. But reflecting on my personal contact with him and on his writings and taped lectures, I see him moving from a dominantly psychiatric emphasis, through a psychological-spiritual synthesis, toward an exclusively spiritual stress.

Existential Metapsychiatry

Thomas Hora's *meta*psychiatry is not only *meta* in the sense of moving beyond, but also in the sense of radically transcending and leaving behind. It is true that even in his most recent dialogues and lectures he continues to use classical psychiatric terms like "resistance," but he gives them a meaning which goes beyond their usage in classical psychiatry.

As I understand it, Hora's present view is that the traditional methods and ideas of psychology/psychiatry are locked into what Buddhist writers have called "cause-effect thinking." This would be characterized by questions like "Who did what to whom, where, when and how?" Cause-effect thinking, from this viewpoint, operates in the realm of appearances rather than dealing with the spiritual, the really real.

Hora distinguishes sharply between the world of phenomena—what appears to be—and the world of what really is—the spiritual, the transcendent, the divine. In the latter, human persons are seen to be emanations of the perfect God, expressing the divine qualities of love, wisdom, goodness, peace, assurance and joy. For him, the cause-effect thinking of traditional psychology and psychotherapy cannot get beyond the level of appearances to the level of the really real.

In Hora's existential metapsychiatry the two basic questions are: "What is the meaning of what seems to be? . . . What is what really *is*?"[45] The pathway to wholeness for Hora consists in the enlightened reception of an answer to these two basic questions. The answer to the question about the meaning of what seems to be consists in the existential recognition that all phenomena of disease, disharmony and the accompanying suffering are manifestations and expressions of erroneous mental perceptions of the meaning of life and of existence. The existential recognition of the relationship between the phenomena of disease, disharmony, the accompanying suffering and specific erroneous mental attitudes leads to an enlightened regretting of the error and a letting go of the deceptive attitude or belief. The process of regretting and letting go leads in turn to reformation, which consists in the discovery and cultivation of true ideas of reality. In the moment of reformation the answer to the second basic question of metapsychiatry, that is, "What is what really is?" is revealed and authentic existence is realized. This process of healing and growth through enlightenment is ongoing. There is a need for recognition of more subtle forms of error and the suffering which accompanies them and for yet more enlightened moments of regret and reformation. The ultimate goal is ascension in which the individual totally transcends the realm of appearances and enters into the purely spiritual sphere of the divine.

Hora's View of God, Man, Jesus and Sin

In his most recent works, Dr. Hora understands God as perfect life,[46] as infinite Love,[47] as Mind,[48] as omnipresent, omnipotent, omniscient, omniactive,[49] as the one Power in the universe,[50] and as Cosmic Consciousness.[51] He also insists that God is not a person[52] and that human beings do not have a personal relationship with God. He never refers to God as a Trinity and his stress on the unity and non-personal nature of God excludes this basic Christian understanding.

What is Hora's concept of the human person? At times he refers to the human individual as a creation of God: "Man is what

God has created; man is a creation of God."[53] But for the most part, he uses the language of "emanation" to describe this relationship:

> The idea of man having to reach to God in prayer is a very widespread and deeply ingrained erroneous assumption. The important thing is that we do not move toward God; we are emanating from God. When we come to understand and see ourselves as emanations of divine Principle, then it is very easy for us to understand that we are Godlike. That which emanates from God has all the qualities of God. The sunbeam emanating from the sun has all the qualities of the sun. We are all radiances of Love-Intelligence. We are always at one with God.[54]

Hora constantly emphasizes that on the level of what really is the human individual is a perfect reflection of a perfect God.[55] The human being is an expression of the divine Mind which manifests itself "through an infinite variety of individualities which are always intelligent, loving and good.[56] The human individual on the level of what really is "lives in divine reality where everything is timeless, infinite, immortal and perfect."[57]

Jesus is for Hora "the supreme teacher and greatest master"[58] because he realized the "at-one-ment" of the human being with God: "Jesus said that God and man are one, inseparable."[59] Hora does not see Jesus as divine in a way that we are not but as an individual who understood what each of us truly is in our reality beyond the realm of what seems to be. Jesus was on the cutting edge of the process of evolution. "Jesus was spearheading this process; he was and is thousands of years in advance of the rest of us in his ability to behold."[60] When Hora speaks of beholding he means seeing behind what seems to be to what really is. Jesus beheld the truth that he and all of us are even now, on the level of what really is, at one with God and his radiant expressions.

Hora maintains that there is no interdependence among human beings. "We do not depend on anyone, just as we do not make anyone depend on us. . . . Our good does not come *from* people, though it may come *through* people."[61] All interaction between human beings is an illusion.[62] There is only the omniactive power of God which each emanation manifests.[63] Human beings are not called to interact but to "jointly participate in the truth of omniactive Mind."[64]

But what of material existence and our experience of interaction? For Hora "material life is a dream, the dreamer is also a dream."[65] We dream that "we are living in interaction with other people."[66] The fact, however, is that "there is only the omnipresence of omniactive, omniscient Mind manifesting itself in an infinite variety of ways, always intelligent, always loving, always good, and always harmonious."[67]

And what of sin? Sin belongs to the realm of what seems to be. Hora writes:

> In reality there are no sinners, there are no guilty people and there is no evil. In the phenomenal world there are endless manifestations of ignorance. And these manifestations can be individual, collective, national, and international. The cataclysmic evil of the Vietnam war was a clear historical manifestation of ignorance acting itself out on an international scene.[68]

Hora holds that "there is only one problem which humankind has and that is ignorance."[69] But ignorance can be healed. And what is the remedy that heals: "Knowledge. Right knowledge. Knowledge of the truth of what really is."[70]

Hora's basic vision of the nature of God, of human existence and of evil is profoundly Oriental. But it is not possible to reduce Hora's position to any specific Buddhist or Hindu viewpoint. Hora is monistic in his doctrine that there is only One Power, One Mind in reality. But he is pluralistic in his tenet that there are a great number of individualized manifestations, expressions of the one divine Love-Intelligence.

John Cobb in his book *The Structure of Christian Existence*, in discussing Indian religions, contrasts the divergent doctrines of the Vedantist and Sankhya schools and his comments help illuminate aspects of Hora's approach.[71] In the Sankhya view individuals are not really involved in matter and contaminated by it but only believe themselves to be so out of ignorance. Cobb's description of this aspect of Sankhya belief fits Hora's approach very well:

> In reality they [the individuals] remained quite free and pure. The problem was that this reality was concealed from the busy ego. It believed itself to be constantly affected by all

> the changing world of things. The task was to still the restless activity of the mind so that the true self could become visible in its absolute imperturbability. When man recognized himself thus for what he was, wholly beyond the sphere of change and suffering, he experienced reality and was released from the illusion of actual participation in change and suffering.[72]

Hora differs, however, from the Sankhya doctrine of radical pluralism because he views individuals as emanations of the one divine Mind. In this latter emphasis Hora at times seems to approximate the Vedanta doctrine that all reality is one and all distinction mere appearance. But perhaps the Christian influence with its stress on the human individual as distinct and made in the image and likeness of God prevents Hora from yielding completely to the radical Vedanta belief that all reality is one.[73] In any case, Hora shares in common with Vedantist monism and Sankhya pluralism the conviction that the really real lies beyond the realm of appearances and that the central human problem is ignorance of what really is.[74]

The major differences which exist between the principles and assumptions of Hora's metapsychiatry and the principal beliefs of the major Christian denominations are quite clear. For Roman Catholic Christianity and for most other mainline Christian churches God is personal and indeed three Persons, Father, Son and Holy Spirit. For Hora God is non-personal and the One Who is without any interpersonal relationships. Again, for most of the major Christian Churches Christ is believed to be the unique Son of God, worthy of divine worship and sole redeemer of humankind through his death and resurrection. For Hora Christ is not divine in an absolutely unique sense and he saves us not from sin but from ignorance by demonstrating for us the truth that each of us is in our true selfhood a perfect child of God, just as Christ is. Further, in Roman Catholic Christian belief, the human person is created by God, consists of body and soul in a unity, exercises a real, though created causality, interacts with other human beings in a mutual interdependence and is the source, through his or her freely willed moral failures, of the existence of various evils in the world as we presently experience them. Hora's view clearly differs sharply from these fundamental Roman Catholic beliefs. Finally, Hora's exclusively spiritual understanding of reality means that he does not put the same value on the historical, the sacramental, and the institutional, as do the Roman Catholic and other major historical Christian churches.

In *Christotherapy* I drew on those aspects of Hora's approach which I found that I could creatively transform and adapt within a Roman Catholic Christian framework. I chose not to focus on those factors of Hora's thought and method which are incompatible with basic Roman Catholic Christian beliefs and practices. Now that I have pointed out the key areas of disagreement between the principles and assumptions of Hora's existential metapsychiatry and Catholic Christian beliefs and practices, in the remainder of my book I will once again focus mainly on those dimensions of Hora's approach which I can fruitfully utilize or reformulate so as to fit within an orthodox Roman Catholic Christian framework.

The very positive response to *Christotherapy,* which is pervaded with Hora's influence and inspiration, the book's translation into several major languages, the many healing experiences which people have had in reading the book and have written or told me about, and the gratitude which so many have felt toward Hora and expressed to me—all these felicitous happenings make it abundantly clear to me that adapting Hora's work for traditional Christians is worthwhile. With God's help I plan to continue. I personally appreciate Hora as a very wise, creative individual. I thank God for the new ecumenical climate, the understanding of the universal working of the Holy Spirit's grace in all who are of good will, which makes such an ongoing dialogue and transformative encounter possible.

Christotherapy as a Spiritual-Psychological Synthesis

Each attempt at a spiritual-psychological synthesis rests on certain basic understandings about the nature of psychology and psychotherapy, of spirituality and religion and the relationship between them. What particular understanding of these diverse spheres and their interrelationships underpins Christotherapy?

E. Mansell Pattison in a discussion of psychology, religion and psychotherapy utilizes a schema involving four basic relationships which encompass the foundational issues of a spiritual-psychological synthesis.[75] Pattison's schema consists of the following four sets of terms and relationships: (1) psychological means to psychological goals; (2) psychological means to spiritual goals; (3)

spiritual means to psychological goals; and (4) spiritual means to spiritual goals. I will take these four relational statements, adapt them to suit my own particular frame of reference and use them as a vehicle for laying out basic principles which underlie Christotherapy as a specific spiritual-psychological synthesis.

Psychological Means to Psychological Goals

There is no need for any complex discussion to explain the relationship of psychological means to psychological goals. I have already considered this relationship at length in my reflections on human development. As Maslow, Glasser and others clearly demonstrate, human beings have basic psychological needs. They have, for example, needs for a sense of being loved and valued for themselves. These basic psychological needs or goals of the human psyche are fulfilled naturally through the gifts of authentic human love and valuing bestowed by parents, parent-substitutes, relatives, teachers and friends. Here we have clear unambiguous examples of psychological goals which are met through the psychological means of authentic acts of loving and valuing.

There are also certain natural psychological means for fulfilling natural psychological goals which secular psychology affirms but which Christ also taught us as an individual who possessed a human nature with all the needs and potentialities this implies. For example, Jesus showed in word and action again and again that human love is vital for a happy life, and that we should love each other, just as we love and value ourselves. He was telling us something which natural psychological research can also, in principle, discover. Truly human as well as truly divine, he had in himself all the basic human needs, and he experienced the fulfillment of these basic needs in part through the love and friendship and care of other human beings. Christ also loved those around him, and sought to fulfill their deep natural needs in a rich human way. We have only to think of his agony in Gethsemane to know that he had a deep human need for support and love. And there are countless examples in the Gospels of Christ fulfilling the psychological needs of others for love and a sense of self-worth.

Psychological Means to Spiritual Goals

Relating psychological means to spiritual goals is a complex matter. Psychologist Paul Vitz quite recently warned about the current danger of making psychology a substitute for religion or a new religion itself.[76] Also, in a much earlier period of Christianity the Church sharply condemned the view that the human being is able in some way to achieve salvation through personal effort apart from the help of the healing and sanctifying grace of Christ.[77] To avoid error in this complex area I will indicate very precisely what I understand by spiritual in the present context and I will show through examples precisely what I mean when I speak of relating psychological means to spiritual goals.

The word spiritual is often used to refer to what is non-material. In this sense the soul is spoken of as a spiritual substance, and intellectual and volitional activities are described as spiritual activities. At times I use the word spiritual in the present book in the way I have just described. But in the present context I use the word spiritual to refer strictly to the Father's saving and reconciling work in Christ, to the work of the Holy Spirit of Christ through which God justifies and sanctifies us and leads us toward the full glorification of the final resurrection from the dead.

Earlier I distinguished between the self and the Christ-self. The self is the human person with his or her identity and natural powers and orientations. The Christ-self, on the other hand, is the self as filled with the justifying gift of God's love; it is the self as transformed by the sanctifying activity of the Holy Spirit; it is the self, adopted as a son or daughter of God and brother or sister of Jesus Christ. It is not in the power of the self in its natural endowments and potentialities to effect in any way its justification or sanctification. These latter are pure gifts of God. When I use the word spiritual, then, in the present context I refer strictly to the realm of grace which is completely beyond the self in its natural powers and orientations.

How, then, in terms of what I have just written about the distinction between the self and the Christ-self, between nature and grace,[78] does it make any sense at all to speak of psychological means to spiritual goals?

The expression "grace builds on nature" provides a key to what I mean when I speak of relating psychological means to spiritual goals. I offer, as an example, the case of a boy who has a terribly negative father-image and finds it impossible to use Scriptural passages for prayer where God is depicted as Father. Here we have an instance of a natural, psychological block which is preventing an individual from engaging in a certain form of prayerful use of Scripture. If, however, through therapy, the boy's father-image is changed and the psychological block removed, then the boy becomes capable of using certain Scriptural passages for prayer which he could not previously utilize. Now the boy is able to respond freely to the grace God offers to him as he contemplates Scriptural passages where God is depicted as Father. Here a psychological means is related to a spiritual goal, namely, the removal of a psychological block makes it possible for the boy now to respond freely to God in prayer as his Father. I am not implying that the removal of the psychological block is *the cause* of the boy's graced free response to God in prayer. But until the therapist was able to aid the boy to change his father-image, the latter was not, in fact, psychologically free to respond to God's graced invitation to call him Father.

Spiritual Means to Psychological Goals

In the book *He Touched Me,* John Powell tells of a highly neurotic woman who had been coming to him for years seeking healing.[79] It seemed that nothing could really help her. Then after he had been away from his counseling for a summer, Powell heard from her again. He expected "the same old neurotic whine, the same indecision, the same egocentricity that is born of deeply embedded pain."[80] Instead, he met a transformed woman who simply thanked him for his help in the years past, and told him that as a result of meeting Jesus Christ in a charismatic prayer situation she had been healed. Powell bears eloquent testimony to the fact that the woman really was healed, and radiated a new, radical wholeness. Here we have a clear, unambiguous example of a spiritual means—a graced encounter with Jesus Christ in a community of faith—which had the effect of healing deep neurotic deformation.

I myself have met individuals who have revealed to me that in making the *Spiritual Exercises* they experienced a personal encounter with Jesus Christ which gave them a lasting sense of being loved and of value in themselves—something which they had longed for, indeed, ached for, over the years but had never previously experienced. These personal testimonies are to me striking examples of how spiritual means can be instrumental in effecting the realization of psychological goals. Finally, any priest who has ministered for some time in bringing the sacrament of reconciliation to psychologically wounded individuals can testify to instances where the experience of the forgiveness of Jesus Christ has brought profound healing not only to the wounded spirit but also to the deformed psyche as well. Once again, we have examples of spiritual means which fulfill psychological goals.

Spiritual Means to Spiritual Goals

There is no complexity involved in the relationship of spiritual means to spiritual goals. A good example is prayer. In the prayer of petition an individual may ask the Lord in faith to grant a deepening of his or her love of God. This prayer of petition is a spiritual means because it is the Holy Spirit who inspires and sustains in us every desire to grow in loving communion with the Father and his Son. The goal is likewise spiritual since growth in the love of God is the very core of spiritual existence. Further, any authentic participation in the sacraments of the People of God is a basic instance of the use of spiritual means to realize spiritual goals.

Christotherapy and Psychosynthesis

My brief consideration of the spheres of the spiritual and of the psychological in terms of their distinctive goals, the means utilized to reach their goals and the basic relationships between them provides the necessary foundations for effecting a true Christ-centered spiritual-psychological synthesis. Although the remainder of this book consists in the concrete fleshing out of my Christotherapeutic synthesis, I would like to begin this process by drawing some initial comparisons and contrasts between Christotherapy and Assagioli's personal and spiritual psychosynthesis.

Christotherapy is a Christ-centered spiritual-psychological synthesis. This means that Christ forms the nucleus of the spiritual segment of Christotherapy as a *spiritual*-psychological synthesis. In Assagioli's spiritual psychosynthesis what he calls "the Inner Christ" is just one of a number of possible symbols used to represent or aid in the realization of the spiritual Self.[81] In Christotherapy the Jesus Christ of history and of the living tradition of the Christian churches is absolutely normative and central.

In Christotherapy Christ is normative in a certain sense even in relation to the principles and methods of psychology and therapy. I agree with Crabb that where there is a clear (and not merely apparent) irreconcilable conflict between a principle or method of psychology or psychotherapy and a basic Christian belief or practice, it is the Word of God rather than the word of a particular psychological theorist which is ultimately decisive.

Christotherapy is equally a spiritual-*psychological* synthesis, and as such it utilizes methods and insights of Hora's existential metapsychiatry and of certain other psychologists and psychotherapists as well. In the book *Christotherapy* Hora was the dominant psychotherapeutic influence, though I also made use of insights and methods of Frankl, Glasser, Ellis, Dabrowski and others. Hora remains a very strong influence in the present book but Angyal, Dabrowski, Assagioli, Beck, Baars, Evoy and others also play a very important role.

Assagioli in his personal and spiritual-psychosynthesis makes use in a methodical and consistent way of insights of Freud, Jung and a variety of other psychologists, psychotherapists and spiritual writers. In similar fashion in the present book I integrate a variety of psychological principles and methods into my Christotherapeutic synthesis. But, like Assagioli, I seek to integrate these principles and methods in a consistent and methodical way. I try to integrate psychological principles and methods which complement rather than conflict with one another and are in harmony with my overall understanding of the distinction and interrelationship between spiritual and psychological goals and means. My aim is to avoid an eclecticism and to develop my Christ-centered spiritual-psychological synthesis in a coherent and methodical manner. Like Assagioli, I am open to the incorporation of further principles and methods into my synthesis as long as they are consistent with my approach. Unlike Assagioli, I exclude on principle any insights or methods which are truly irreconcilable with my basic framework of Christian belief and practice.

Christotherapy, as a synthesis of the spiritual and the psychological, integrates the natural principles and methods of facilitating healing and growth with the spiritual principles and methods for effecting healing and growth revealed or implicitly contained in the Christ-event. For example, in *Christotherapy* I showed how Frankl's insight into the great healing power of meaning can be elevated into a Christian context in which Christ is revealed to be the way, the light, the meaning, the truth which enlightens, heals and sets human hearts free in the most radical and holistic manner.[82] In this case the truth of Frankl's psychological insight into the healing potential of newly discovered meaning is not denied. Rather it is lifted up into a new context incredibly enriched from the viewpoint of Christian belief. There takes place, if you will, a certain "transignification" of the psychological insight into the healing value of the discovery of meaning; Christ is seen to be the "super-meaning" who fulfills the natural desire for meaning in a way which completely surpasses all the natural expectations of the human mind and heart.

Christotherapy also integrates the insights and methods of psychology with revealed healing and growth-producing truths in a systematic and methodical manner. Just as Matthew and Dennis Linn integrated in a methodical fashion the stages of Kübler-Ross with forms of prayer and meditative reflection and decision, I also in my book *Christotherapy* worked out the stages of what I referred to as the process of mind-fasting in a way which integrated insights of psychology with forms of prayer and I continue to utilize this integrative approach. Christotherapy differs here from psychosynthesis in that it does not distinguish between a personal psychosynthesis and a spiritual psychosynthesis. In Christotherapy, spiritual practices such as prayer are integrated into the healing and growth processes from the earliest stages for, just as in the Twelve Steps of *Alcoholics Anonymous* and *Emotions Anonymous* there is room from the start for a spiritual dimension, for prayer, for openness to a Higher Power, so also in Christotherapy there is a spiritual invitation freely offered at every stage of the healing process.

Christotherapy, like psychosynthesis, is characterized by certain dominant emphases and unique characteristics. Thus, Christotherapy makes healing and growth *through enlightenment* a central theme. This *enlightenment* is both of the heart and the mind; it touches the psyche and the spirit, involving both love and knowledge. It is an enlightenment consisting both of natural and spiritual (graced) elements. For instance, it can involve the experience of the gift of *natural human love* and the *inward spiritual* gift of the *love* poured into our hearts by the Holy Spirit. This enlightenment at the core of Christotherapy is manifest in decisions and actions; it is holistic, transforming enlightenment. It reaches into the depths of the "unconscious," to the roots of the human psyche, and transforms even the dreams, primal imaginations and phantasms of the person.

Unlike Christotherapy, psychosynthesis makes the "act of will" central. But Assagioli does not mean by this the blind force of the old "will-power" school. Instead he sees the act of will as a process, involving stages he calls "Purpose, Deliberation, Decision, Affirmation, Planning, and the Direction of the Execution."[83] He means a will which is multi-dimensional, existential, dynamic, good, personal, transpersonal, universal and joyous. Assagioli is not locked into a narrow faculty psychology approach which imprisons intellect and will in airtight compartments; for him there is a dynamic interplay of intelligence, decision, love and freedom. In this his thought resembles that of Bernard Lonergan,[84] whose approach has had a strong influence on the development of Christotherapy. From Lonergan I have taken a dynamic vision of the relationships of intelligence, judgment, decision, freedom and love. Nonetheless, for Christotherapy, enlightenment is central; while for Assagioli's psychosynthesis it is the notion of will which plays the unifying role. Hopefully, this comparison of Christotherapy with psychosynthesis has served to clarify through contrast and complementarity the central focus of Christotherapy as a Christ-centered spiritual-psychological synthesis.

6

Christotherapy, Spiritual Directing and Counseling

Saint Ignatius in his "Rules for the Discernment of Spirits" writes that "the thoughts that spring from consolation are the opposite of those that spring from desolation."[1] Dr. Allen Wiesen, a contemporary clinical psychologist, in his book *Positive Therapy* remarks that negative emotional states tend to perdure and that they elicit "correspondingly negative thoughts."[2] Here we have an example of a contemporary psychologist confirming certain insights of a great sixteenth century saint and spiritual director. In the time of Saint Ignatius the sciences and practices of psychotherapy and counseling, as we know them today, had not yet evolved. Yet, when we read the writings of such spiritual geniuses as Saints Teresa of Avila, John of the Cross, Ignatius, Francis de Sales, and others we see that these great spiritual directors possessed keen insights into the natural propensities and workings of the human psyche as well as into the subtle activities of the Holy Spirit in the human mind and heart. In fact, these saints in their concrete practice of spiritual direction actually performed many of the functions which we today link with the practices of counseling and psychotherapy.

In the evolution of human consciousness, just as there took place a separation of the natural sciences from philosophy, so there occurred a development in which psychotherapy emerged as a healing science quite distinct from the ancient "holy healing and guidance science" of spiritual direction. Initially, there existed a state of war between Freudian inspired psychotherapy and religion with its "holy sciences." Gradually a state of neutrality and even in some cases of mutual respect developed. Certain psychotherapists found they could believe in God and yet remain psychotherapists. Likewise, lay Catholics, priests and sisters became psychotherapists and counselors. But the separate specialization mentality held sway. Presently, however, attempts at the formation of spiritual-psychological syntheses are taking place and Christotherapy represents one of these attempts.

There is no compelling reason, either theoretical or practical, why certain individuals cannot become equally competent in the knowledge and application of the healing and growth principles and practices of psychology and of spirituality. In fact, there is an ever increasing number of ministers, priests, and lay individuals who today possess equal professional competence in the areas of counseling and spirituality. It is my belief that individuals who do achieve competency in both areas and possess the necessary psychological, intellectual, religious, moral, and spiritual qualities can learn to integrate their theoretical and practical knowledge of the two areas in such a way that they can fulfill in a holistic, unified fashion the functions they previously exercised separately under the respective titles of counselor (psychiatrist) or spiritual director.

The *ideal* Christotherapist is a person who possesses equal competency in the areas of counseling (psychotherapy) and spiritual directing and has integrated the theories and methods of the two spheres in such a fashion that he or she transcends the former separation of the two areas and functions as a "Christian Integrationist." The ideal Christotherapist makes use of spiritual and psychological means in an integrative fashion, acting as an instrument of Christ and aided by the graces of the Holy Spirit, to help bring about the goals of the Christian seeking wholeness and holiness in Christ. The availability of the ideal Christotherapist makes it unnecessary for an individual suffering from neurotic and/or addictive deformation and desirous of spiritual guidance to go to a counselor (psychiatrist) for psychological help and to a spiritual director for spiritual aid. Likewise, the availability of the ideal Christotherapist obviates the need for a Christian who wishes to realize higher levels of psychological and spiritual growth to go to a psychologist (psychiatrist) for psychological assistance and to a spiritual director for spiritual guidance.

The processes of psychological and spiritual development and conversion are dynamically, symbiotically interrelated in the life process of the concrete individual. For this reason, a person who understands and who is able to apply in an integrated way the principles and methods of psychological and spiritual healing and growth will be in the best possible position to function most effectively as Christ's instrument for facilitating holistic psychological and spiritual healing and growth in a person. The ideal Christotherapist, for example, will be able to help a neurotically suffering individual to pray in a way which will facilitate his or her psychological healing; at the same time the Christotherapist with his or her understanding of the particular suffering, temperament and psychic qualities of the individual will be able to help the person to utilize a form of prayer which truly builds on nature and will prove most appropriate for the spiritual development of the person. Likewise, the ideal Christotherapist will be best able to recognize when a *seeker* (the "seeker" here and elsewhere stands for anyone seeking any aid from the Christotherapist) is suffering from distorted, destructive religious attitudes and practices; he or she will then be able gradually through the use of appropriate psychological and spiritual means to lead the person to psychological wholeness and to authentic forms of religious commitment and practice.[3] The ideal Christotherapist will understand in regard to a particular case what particular combination of psychological and spiritual means should be employed and what degree of emphasis should be placed on the employment of psychological or spiritual means at various stages in the healing and growth process.

Clearly, my position on the nature of the ideal Christotherapist and the type of functions which he or she can perform is based on a particular optic which simply transcends present views on the necessity of separating the processes of counseling and spiritual directing. I also realize that there are at present a limited, though increasing, number of individuals who possess the theoretical and practical knowledge and skills to operate fully in the way the ideal Christotherapist is called to function. For this reason I wish to show how individuals who are specialists in either spiritual directing or counseling but who wish to function in a more holistic manner can fruitfully utilize key principles and methods of Christotherapy in an adapted fashion.

In what follows I will contrast a rigid separate specialization approach to spiritual directing and counseling with what I choose to call a "Christopsychological" approach to these areas of aiding others. This Christopsychological approach represents an intermediate stage between Christotherapy in its pure, ideal form and the radically non-holistic approaches to spiritual directing and counseling which some still attempt to practice. The Christopsychological approach then is an adapted form of Christotherapy in its principles and methods but is not Christotherapy in its ideal form.

The Separate Specialization Model of Spiritual Direction

Those who hold for the strict separation model of spiritual directing consider that the goal of spiritual direction is exclusively spiritual, and that the means used must necessarily be exclusively spiritual, too. It follows that the proper candidates for spiritual direction are the psychologically healthy and spiritually advanced.

In describing the separate specialization model of spiritual direction, I am going to suggest a set of characteristics which describe it in its ideal form. It is difficult to find authors who consistently, both in theory and in practice, work according to the separate specialization model. Accordingly, those who are quoted here, directly or indirectly, should not necessarily be taken to be adherents of the separate specialization model; all that is implied is that the particular statement cited expresses and is compatible with some aspect of that model. Many statements about the goals and means of spiritual direction are acceptable to those who take the separate specialization approach and also to those open to a spiritual-psychological synthetic approach; for instance, all would agree that *a* valid goal of spiritual direction is growth in love of God.

In the separate specialization model of spiritual directing, the goals of the person seeking direction can be described in a number of ways. They might be encounter with God, growth in prayer,[4] growing in the virtues of faith and hope and love, becoming holy,[5] spiritual maturity, contemplation, discerning providential guidance in one's life,[6] discovering one's vocation, development of the likeness of Christ in the soul,[7] listening to the Word of God in Scripture and in daily living, improving one's relationship with God,[8] encounter with Mystery and the transcendent, strictly supernatural,[9] dealing with dark night experiences,[10] freedom from self-will and from self-deceit, detachment from one's ego,[11] liberation from sin and guilt, greater freedom in the experience of God's forgiveness.[12] What stands out about these goals is that they have an exclusively spiritual focus: either they involve growth in the life of the Spirit and communion with God in finding his Will, or dying to sinful impediments to union with God and the experience of his forgiveness.

In the separate specialization model of spiritual directing some of the principal means employed by the spiritual director and/or by the directee are: (1) acknowledgement that the Holy Spirit is the principal guide of the one directed in his or her movement through Christ to the Father; (2) the practice of discernment by both director and the one directed regarding the person's development of prayer; (3) conversations in which the one directed relates his or her faith experiences and is helped to discover their providential meaning; (4) the director suggesting to the one directed various ways of prayer; (5) the director indicating to the one directed some ways of objectifying and clarifying his or her spiritual progress;[13] (6) the director answering any questions about prayer, moral matters and doctrine.[14] As with the goals of spiritual direction in the separate specialization model, what stands out about the means utilized in this model is their basically spiritual character. Likewise, the person who is considered appropriate for spiritual direction under this approach is a psychologically healthy individual who wants to develop richer dimensions of a prayer life which is already basically sound and growing. The relationship between the director and the one directed is that of adult to adult.[15]

The Christopsychological Model of Spiritual Directing

How does the Christopsychological model of spiritual direction differ in its goals, means, and proper participants from this separate specialization approach?

In the Christopsychological understanding of spiritual direction, the goals of the person seeking direction include all of those mentioned in the separate specialization model, but not in an exclusive sense. Other goals which I add in the Christopsychological model are: (1) the integration of the directee's spiritual life—the life of prayer, basic beliefs and religious practices—with his or her psychological and social life, and other forms and stages of his or her development; (2) learning how to pray in ways which build on one's natural temperament and disposition; (3) for the neurotically troubled individual a goal may be to learn how to pray in ways that do not intensify neurotic preoccupation with self, but rather help him or her to become God-centered and forgetful of self; (4) for recovered-and-recovering neurotic and addiction-prone people, one goal may be the discovery of creative and prayerful ways of using suffering to build up the People of God and grow toward sanctification.

There is a spiritual element preeminently present in all of the goals of persons seeking spiritual direction which I have just listed under the Christopsychological model. Indeed, if the spiritual was not preeminently present in these goals I do not think it would be appropriate to describe them as proper goals of *spiritual* direction. Yet, what the added goals of my model contribute is basically a holistic dimension. Thus, for example, the integration of a person's spiritual life with the other forms and stages of the person's ongoing development involves an enrichment not only of the spiritual life of the person but of his or her psychic, social, and cognitive life as well. Again, learning how to pray in ways which build on one's temperament rather than war against it not only brings about a blossoming in the person's prayer life but also creates a psycho-spiritual harmony in the individual. The goals, accordingly, of spiritual direction in the Christopsychological model are preeminently, but not exclusively, spiritual. They embody the ideal of a holy wholeness, of an integral imitation of Christ and realization of the self in Christ.

The means which may be used in Christopsychological spiritual direction include all those listed for the separate specialization model, but I add the following: (1) the practice on the part of the spiritual director of diagnostic and appreciative discernment; (2) the possession and utilization on the part of the spiritual director of sound knowledge of ancient and contemporary theories and practices of spiritual direction, of basic theories and methods of psychology and of the nature of neurotic and addictive deformation; (3) the possession on the part of the spiritual director of a sound knowledge of theology, including doctrinal, moral, pastoral theology and the ability to apply this knowledge in appropriate ways in the process of spiritual directing.

What clearly stands out about a number of the means which the Christopsychological model of spiritual direction recommends is the clearly holistic character of these means. It is, according to this model, an essential task of the spiritual director to utilize at times psychological means in order to bring about spiritual goals. For instance, through the use of the psychological means of knowledge of temperament and psychic dispositions the spiritual director is able to help the directee to develop better methods and forms of prayer.

Because of my stress on the integral use of principles and methods of psychology and counseling in doing spiritual direction, I agree completely with Dr. James Gill that individuals who are called and designated to undertake the arduous task of spiritual directing should have a solid background in psychology as well as in theology.[16] The practice of spiritual directing in a professional manner requires as a key means special knowledge of the human psyche in its healthy and unhealthy inner workings because the Holy Spirit in the bestowal of gifts of prayer and other charisms as a general rule builds on and operates within the activities—conscious and unconscious—of the human psyche.

Who, finally, are the proper subjects of spiritual direction according to the Christopsychological model? Damien Isabell in his *The Spiritual Director* remarks that the one-to-one form of spiritual directing has been reserved primarily throughout the history of the spiritual direction movement for a "select group of people."[17] He argues that it is necessary to make spiritual direction available to a much wider group of individuals. I am personally convinced of the correctness of Isabell's view because of the obvious and urgent need for spiritual direction which I have encountered in laypersons as well as in priests and those with special religious vows. I have also found a great yearning and need for spiritual direction among neurotically and addictively troubled individuals who are at various stages in dealing with their illness. For these reasons, I list among the proper subjects for one or other form of spiritual direction: (1) anyone who is seeking a guided approach to healing and growth in his or her relationship with God; (2) anyone who desires to integrate his or her spiritual life with other forms and stages of his or her existence; (3) the neurotically or addictively troubled person who is in a stage of ongoing conversion in his or her struggle and who wishes to learn how to pray in ways which are in touch with and utilize for the good the particular form of suffering which he or she experiences; (4) institutionalized individuals who suffer from severe forms of psychological disorder but who have moments or lengthy periods of clarity and desire advice about how to pray or how to utilize their illness in a salvific manner.

Clearly there are and must be various levels, degrees of intensity, and forms of emphasis in spiritual direction. I agree with Damien Isabell that there is room for short-term spiritual direction which may deal with an *ad hoc* problem in prayer or some similar issue, and there is also room for long-term direction[18]—direction which aims at helping the individual in an overall development of prayer, in the quest for high levels of holy-holistic personality integration, or some other preeminently spiritual goal.

The Separate Specialization Model of Counseling

Authors differ in their definition and use of the terms counseling and psychotherapy. The general usage of Dr. Gerald Corey in *Theory and Practice of Counseling and Psychotherapy* is workable. Although he often uses the terms interchangeably, he does suggest that counseling *tends* to deal with particular crises in life, while psychotherapy aims at deep structural changes in personality.[19] There is a possible analogy here to short-term and long-term spiritual directing. For the sake of simplicity I will use the term counseling to mean both short-term advising and long-term psychotherapy. I recognize that distinctions are often drawn between spiritual directing and pastoral counseling. But I am setting up a new model in the counseling-spiritual directing area with its own distinctions and sets of terms and relations. I leave it up to others to adapt in a creative fashion my model to such areas as pastoral counseling, counseling and guidance and vocational guidance.

In the separate specialization model of counseling, the goals are psychological and and the means used to reach these goals are psychological. The proper subjects for such counseling range from severely troubled neurotics and addicts to those who need vocational guidance, or are seeking higher, richer levels of psychological maturity. The goals of the separate specialization model include: (1) healing of psychological deformations, and of addictive deformations to the extent that there are psychological factors involved in the addiction; (2) solving problems which a person is experiencing in personal relationships;[20] (3) healing of personality difficulties which are rooted in unconscious conflicts or traumatic experiences;[21] (4) overcoming of one-sided personality development—for instance, a person's thought function is overdeveloped whereas the feeling function is repressed; (5) overcoming psychological immaturity; (6) getting in touch with oneself and forming a well-integrated, realistic ego;[22] (7) learning how to meet the demands and pressures of the real world in a healthy fashion.[23] The common denominator in all these goals is their psychological nature.

The means used in the separate specialization model of counseling include: (1) therapeutic use of the relationship between counselor and the one counseled[24] (for some this involves maintaining a certain neutrality and aloofness which is believed to encourage "transference;" for others it means the expression of warmth, care, concern, radical acceptance and affirmation); (2) the use of particular therapeutic methods such as nondirective counseling, psychoanalysis, Gestalt, transactional analysis, primal scream therapy, behavior modification. The important point to keep in mind is that all these means are strictly psychological and are used to realize strictly psychological goals. Psychiatrists, of course, and counselors working in conjunction with physicians at times utilize drugs as part of therapy. Likewise, psychiatrists and counselors often recommend special diets, physical exercise, breathing exercises, and similar aids to help the counselee in his or her quest for psychological healing or maturity. But in these latter cases it is still a matter of using strictly natural (not spiritual) means to reach natural physical and psychological goals.

Adherents of the separate specialization model of counseling consider its proper subjects to be: (1) persons who suffer from psychological deformations due to psychological causes; (2) addicts, when the addiction is caused by psychological factors; (3) persons who are immature in their personal and psycho-social development; (4) "normally abnormal" people who are subject to particular intrapsychic problems like depression, or who are undergoing particular crises in their interpersonal relationships, work, or their general life situations; (5) psychologically healthy persons who want vocational, avocational, or other forms of guidance.

The Christopsychological Model of Counseling

The outstanding difference between the separate specialization model of counseling and the Christopsychological model is *Christ.* The title of my book *Christotherapy* literally means *therapy through Christ.* The central point of that book is that Christ is directly and intrinsically related to the healing, not only of sin, but of neurotic and addictive disorders and even at times of physical illness. He is the healer of the whole person, most radically through his life, death, and resurrection. "I am the resurrection. If anyone believes in me, even though he dies he will live, and whoever lives and believes in me will never die" (Jn. 11:26).

Christ definitively heals all who believe in him in the final resurrection from the dead. But Christ is available even now as healer in some way of the diseases of those who believe in him, since we are urged to pray for all of our needs and to believe that he, Jesus the healer, is "living for ever to intercede for all who come to God through him" (Heb. 7:25).

Christ is the "Tremendous Lover"[25] who can touch the hearts of the rejected and bestow on those individuals a dawning and ever increasing sense of self-worth, self-respect, self-appreciation, self-value. Christ is healer as the very Word and Truth of God made flesh, who through the life-giving meanings and values he reveals, can remove the false beliefs, destructive assumptions, existential ignorance and error of the illusion-bound human mind and heart. Christ is healer in the realm of the unconscious because through the power of his Holy Spirit he is silently and invisibly at work in the most hidden recesses of the human psyche, at the very fountainhead of the images, dreams, and phantasms of the human person. Clearly, Christ is *the* factor which most distinguishes the Christopsychological model of counseling from the separate specialization model.

The goals of the persons who seek Christopsychological counseling include all listed earlier for the separate specialization model, but to each is added a spiritual and specifically Christian dimension. I offer as examples the following cases: (1) the person in need of healing of neurotic or addictive deformation who includes elements of moral and religious conversion in his or her overall goal of healing, especially when the absence in the person of these conversions is at least in part the cause of the neurosis; (2) the individual in quest of healing in interpersonal difficulties who seeks healing as a wounded member of the People of God, and has as a goal that wholeness in interpersonal relationships which is appropriate for a member of the Body of Christ; (3) the psychologically immature individual who seeks the goal of a psychological maturity grounded in part in the lived imitation of Christ; (4) the individual desiring healing or refinement in such feeling areas as fear, anger, guilt, sadness who seeks as a goal an education and transformation of his or her feelings rooted in the imitation of Christ in his humanity and empowered by the Holy Spirit; (5) the psychologically healthy individual who desires to realize yet higher levels of psychological development rooted in part in a deeper assimilation of the human values Christ cherished in accord with the way he cherished them.

Dr. Thomas Hora provided the matrix of my insight into the subtle process of transformation of goals which takes place when the natural process of counseling is lifted up and integrated into a God-centered context. A key insight of Hora is that individuals who suffer often labor under the false belief that the aim in life is to feel good at all costs and that it is legitimate to utilize any narcotizing agent available in order to escape from pain and feel good. Hora emphasizes, however, that the very means sufferers very often use in order to feel good actually end up making them feel bad, in fact, worse than ever. What is required in Hora's view is the enlightened understanding that an authentic state of well-being can only flow from the living of a life dedicated to the cultivation of authentic, existentially valid values. In this context, "feeling good" becomes an effect of "being good" where being good is not understood in a narrow moralistic sense but rather as a condition of participating in and manifesting Christ-like qualities. In Hora's perspective, for deep, lasting healing to take place the sufferer needs to shift his or her focus from the desire to be free from all pain to a quest for the realization of God's kingdom and his righteousness. To the extent that this shift occurs and the sufferer begins to seek first God's kingdom and glory "all these other things" (Mt. 6:33), namely freedom from neurotic and/or addictive pain, will be given as well.

What are the basic means used in the Christopsychological model of counseling? In general, the counselor who is following a Christopsychological approach is open to the use of psychological means to effect psychological goals, just as in other forms of counseling. For example, a principal psychological means used in Christotherapy is the existential loving of the suffering neurotic or addict as a person who is unique, worthwhile and valuable in himself or herself. This method was mentioned before as one used by the separate specialization model of counseling. Another common means is the uncovering of irrational beliefs—such as this one listed by Dr. Albert Ellis: "the idea that one should be thoroughly competent, adequate, and achieving in all possible respects if one is to consider oneself worthwhile."[26] Here again, a psychological means of cognitive therapy is used to reach a psychological goal.

What radically divides separate specialization counseling from Christopsychological counseling is the emphasis which the second puts on using spiritual means to realize psychological goals. For example, Christopsychological counseling uses prayer, both for and at times with the counselee, as a way to bring about psychological healing. This model also makes prayer a central element in its basic counseling techniques of diagnostic and appreciative discernment and in the mind-fasting and spirit-feasting which the counselee is invited to practice.

An apt candidate for counseling under the Christotherapeutic model would be any believing Christian who seeks any of the goals I have mentioned so far, and who wants to pursue them in a Christ-centered context, using spiritual as well as psychological means.

The model of spiritual-psychological counseling which I have worked out here is articulated within the context of Roman Catholic theology, as I understand it. For this reason members of other Christian ecclesial groups will need to modify my approach in certain respects insofar as it diverges from their own beliefs and practices.

I hold that the ideal counseling situation exists—all other things being equal—where the counselor and counselee share a common background of religious beliefs and values. Of course, I am presupposing that the background of religious beliefs shared in common is existentially valid and in harmony with reality as it really is. For if a therapist holds religious beliefs which are false then the counselee will either yield to these false beliefs or will be in a constant state of spiritual resistance to the therapist. This spiritual resistance will be added to the natural resistance to healing which is always part of the therapeutic process. To be healed is a painful process and individuals who are accustomed to their old ways, no matter how painful they may be, are reticent to give up the old and to embrace the new. It is, therefore, an added burden when a counselee is placed in a position where he or she must resist false beliefs held by the therapist. For this reason I think that Dr. William Kraft is right when he argues that "a potential client or patient has the right to know about a doctor's background, value system, and, in general, the way he or she thinks and feels about life."[27] After all, Jung himself once wisely observed that the therapist's philosophy of life "guides the life of the therapist and shapes the spirit of his therapy."[28]

It is my hope that professional spiritual directors and Christian counselors who are presently working according to the separate specialization models will critically evaluate the Christopsychological models which I have presented and move toward an adoption of the Christopsychological model appropriate to their field of specialization if they find value in my approach. Likewise, it is my hope that professional spiritual directors and Christian counselors who are already, in effect, functioning according to a more holistic model will consider the possibility of moving beyond the level of Christopsychological specialization in either spiritual direction or counseling toward the practice of Christotherapy in its ideal form. Happily, my presentation of Christotherapy in this book is multileveled. This means that professionals and nonprofessionals alike are not faced with an either/or option in regard to Christotherapy as a viable approach but can accept, for example, the validity of my Christopsychological model of spiritual directing and/or counseling without necessarily accepting the model of Christotherapy as I present it in its pure, ideal form.

7

The Qualities of the Christotherapist

There are certain qualities, namely, basic ongoing conversions and forms of self-knowledge which should be present in the Christotherapist if he or she is to function as an effective instrument of the healing and life-giving Christ. The dynamic presence of these qualities in the Christotherapist is vital not only for the good of those seeking the aid of the Christotherapist but for the well-being of the Christotherapist as well.

Experts show that men and women who work with troubled or deprived clients or groups are especially prone to the phenomenon called "burnout,"[1] to the use of drugs, and even to suicide. A counselor or therapist who suffers from burnout will lose interest in the persons needing help; he or she will cease to care, and will probably feel a sense of physical, emotional and spiritual lassitude and alienation. The burned-out person will no longer be creative, and these people often give up their work completely. Others remain on their jobs, but treat those who come to them for help in an indifferent, even dehumanizing way.[2] Statistics continue to show a higher than average rate of drug abuse and suicide among doctors than in the general population—and this is especially true of psychiatrists. Factors like overwork, lack of proper consultation and dialogue with peers, poor working conditions, too little vacation or leisure time, and family troubles can contribute to the occurrence of burnout, drug abuse and even suicide. But I believe that often enough it is the absence of conversion in one or another area, a lack of certain natural or spiritual qualities and authentic self-knowledge, which lie at the root of burnout, abuse of drugs or suicide of members of the helping professions.

Hora correctly observes that "in the psychotherapeutic encounter patient and therapist are mutually affecting each other far beyond verbal and sensory stimuli." This means that "under favorable conditions the healthy phenomena of the therapist prevail over the unhealthy influence of the patient." But if the psychotherapist is not sufficiently enlightened then the therapist "may become sick for the duration of his contact with . . . [the] patient."[3] A cumulative buildup of such negative experiences can, of course, lead to a severe form of burnout or even to suicide. It follows that it is at great personal risk that counselors and spiritual directors seek to come to the aid of the troubled and deprived—especially the spiritually and psychologically deprived—when these "helpers" are themselves lacking in ongoing religious, moral and other basic types of conversion and self-knowledge which they personally need. Never were the words of the poet more applicable: "Fools rush in where angels fear to tread."[4]

If, however, an unconverted spiritual director or counselor risks personal disaster in seeking to aid the spiritually and/or emotionally troubled, an equal or even worse catastrophe awaits those who come to these so-called "healers" seeking assistance. As Jesus put it: "If one blind man leads another, both will fall into a pit" (Mt. 15:14).

Religious Conversion

The presence in the Christotherapist of ever deepening ongoing religious conversion is the *root* requirement if the Christotherapist is to be an effective instrument of Christ.

The apostle Paul made it quite clear that an individual who did not possess the Holy Spirit and the Spirit's gifts of love and wisdom was incapable of authentic spiritual discernment and understanding: "An unspiritual person is one who does not accept anything of the Spirit of God: he sees it all as nonsense; it is beyond his understanding because it can only be understood by means of the Spirit" (1 Cor. 2:14). The words of Paul lead to the necessary conclusion that, since spiritual discernment is at the core of Christotherapy, ever deepening ongoing religious conversion must be present in the Christotherapist.

The fullness of Christian conversion exists in those who not only possess the inner divine gift of being in love with God but also explicit faith in Jesus Christ as he is proclaimed through the preaching of the Gospel and at work in the historical community born at Pentecost. When I speak here accordingly of the need for the presence of ongoing religious conversion in the Christotherapist I refer *ideally* to the presence of the fullness of Christian conversion which involves not only the gift of God's love poured into the heart by the Holy Spirit (Rm. 5:5) but also an active and faithful membership in the historical church of Jesus Christ and a rich participation in the sacramental life of the Christian community.

Moral Conversion

The Christotherapist must also be in a state of ongoing, ever-deepening moral conversion if he or she is to be an authentic and effective instrument of Christ. Lonergan has defined moral conversion as "the existential decision to guide one's decisions and actions not by satisfactions but by values, by what is truly worthwhile."[5] The Christotherapist must embody a lived commitment to basic Christian moral values if he or she is to have real impact. Where the seeker of aid and guidance is in need of radical religious and moral conversion, the clear presence of ongoing religious and moral conversion in the life of the Christotherapist will be the witness which the client needs to see. Further, where the Christotherapist is dealing with individuals lacking psychic birth, and where strong resistance is encountered, a type of love is required which is selfless, persevering and undeviating, even in the face of expressions of hostility and ingratitude. But, apart from the presence in the Christotherapist of an ongoing moral conversion, grounded in ongoing religious conversion, this type of love is impossible.

Intellectual Conversion

Today there is rightly and happily a great stress laid on the interior spiritual bonds which unite all men and women of good will. There is also a beautiful ecumenical emphasis given to the common elements which, at a very deep spiritual level, bind together Christians who are still separated from each other in various ways. But it would be a real disservice to that drive toward unity which animates the ecumenical movement to say that differences in explicit beliefs are irrelevant or unimportant. It would do no good to deny that objectively false religious beliefs can cause real harm—spiritually, psychologically, socially, and in many other ways.

St. Paul was deeply concerned about the fidelity of Christian believers to the basic beliefs of the community. He sharply criticized the Galatians in his epistle to them for deciding to follow "a different version of the Good News" (1:6) and warned them that "if anyone preaches a version of the Good News different from the one we have already preached to you . . . he is to be condemned" (1:8). Paul understood from a theological perspective what modern cognitive therapists express in psychological terms: basic beliefs have a tremendous impact on our daily living and false beliefs about fundamental existential matters can cause immeasurable damage.

The Christotherapist must be able to critique both theological and psychological beliefs for the client as part of effective guidance. In order to engage in this kind of critique, the Christotherapist must experience in his or her own life not only ongoing religious and moral conversion but also a certain degree of "intellectual conversion."

Bernard Lonergan coined the expression "intellectual conversion."[6] Lonergan indicates that St. Augustine underwent a certain type of intellectual conversion when he broke through his materialistic philosophy to see that spiritual realities exist as well as material things.[7] Lonergan also suggests that the Christian believer undergoes a certain elemental form of intellectual conversion when he or she confesses that God is Spirit.[8] The Christian realizes that it is not only the material things of sense experience which are real. Lonergan refers to this type of conversion as "intellectual" because it involves an activity of the mind by which a person judges that being or reality includes both matter and spirit and is not simply reducible to one or the other.

There are, as with other forms of conversion, various degrees of intellectual conversion. In the book *Insight,*[9] Lonergan provides a guide to the fullest and most sophisticated form of intellectual conversion. Such a rigorous kind of intellectual conversion is necessary for a person who intends to work out a theory of the foundations of a spiritual-psychological synthesis, but not for someone who simply wants to practice Christotherapy. But the latter does need that intellectual conversion which consists of a critical, faith-guided use of intelligence, and which sets a person free from philosophical, theological and psycho-social errors which threaten holistic healing and growth.

The Christotherapist needs to possess a degree of intellectual conversion sufficient to critique and reject in an enlightened manner radical materialism (the belief that matter is all that exists); radical idealism (the belief that spirit or mind is all that exists); radical determinism (the belief that human freedom of choice is an illusion); psychological reductionism (the belief that psychology is a necessary, adequate and completely sufficient substitute for religion or spirituality); spiritual or religious reductionism (the belief that spirituality and religion are necessary and fully adequate replacements in all respects for psychology and psychotherapy); psychological-spiritual melding (the belief that the psychological and spiritual are so merged together in human experience that it is neither necessary nor useful to acknowledge a real distinction, though not a separation, between the psychological and spiritual dimensions of human existence).

The Christotherapist manifests an intellectually converted consciousness to the extent that she or he is capable of separating, through the use of critical intelligence, guided by faith, the "chaff" of fundamentally destructive religious and psychological beliefs and practices from the "wheat" of authentic, truly healing, life-realizing religious and psychological beliefs and practices. I must add that I am using "intellectual conversion" in a less restrictive, wider sense than Lonergan does. But I do believe that I am remaining faithful to the basic spirit of his expression.

It may seem surprising that I speak of the need for a critique of psychological *beliefs* as well as religious ones, but I am convinced that belief plays just as large a role in sciences such as psychology as it does in the area of religion.[10] In analyzing the process of knowing, it becomes clear that we can only claim to *know*, in a strict sense, those things which we have personally understood and verified for ourselves. The rest of our so-called "knowledge" is really belief. Anything we accept on the testimony of others is a matter of belief, not of knowledge in the strict sense. For example, only those who have been in Rome *know* that Rome exists. All the rest *believe* it. The Christotherapist has to be able to engage in a critique of the beliefs of psychology and psychotherapy as well as of the beliefs of religion. Of course, the *ultimate* norm for the critique of a Roman Catholic Christotherapist is the teaching of Christ as it is handed down, authentically developed and communicated in the Roman Catholic ecclesial community. Non-Roman Catholic Christotherapists will have analogous norms.

Earlier I referred to the irrational ideas which Dr. Albert Ellis (who is a professed atheist) considers to be at the root of neurotic difficulties. I agree that most of the ideas Ellis refers to as "irrational" are indeed such. But I would like to offer an example of a Christotherapeutic critique of one of the so-called irrational ideas of Ellis, namely his eighth irrational idea: "the idea that one should be dependent on others and needs someone stronger than oneself on whom to rely."[11]

From a critical psychological point of view, Ellis is certainly correct that there is a false type of dependence on others which impedes a person's mature development: for instance, a 32-year-old man or woman who is still "tied to mother's apron strings." On the other hand, spiritually-inspired self-help groups and certain fundamental truths of Christian revelation assert that there is room for forms of dependence which liberate a person, and which facilitate human and spiritual growth rather than causing stagnation. In *Alcoholics Anonymous, Emotions Anonymous* and similar groups the path to healing requires the explicit acknowledgement by the sufferers that their lives have become unmanageable, and that only reliance on a higher Power can restore them to sanity. Acknowledging dependence in this way becomes a source of freedom, rather than enslavement. And in Christian revelation, the author of the Fourth Gospel attributes these words to Christ: "Apart from me you can do nothing" (Jn. 15:5 R.S.V.). St. Paul also acknowledges that strength comes to him from his confession of personal weakness and his need to rely on Christ: "It is when I am weak that I am strong" (2 Cor. 12:10). "There is nothing I cannot master with the help of the One who gives me strength" (Ph. 4:13).

Clearly, the whole issue of a healthy and an unhealthy form of dependence is very subtle. It is necessary to make a very careful differentiation between various psychological and religious ideas of dependence, and the relationship between them. It follows that above all a person who is morally and religiously converted, who is knowledgeable in theology and psychology, and who has experienced a basic intellectual conversion, will be able to deal most adequately with such issues as destructive and constructive dependence.

Dr. Eli Chesen, in his *Religion May Be Hazardous to Your Health,*[12] gives many examples of how certain beliefs or combinations of beliefs as learned by children from their parents and church communities can be very harmful to the psychological development of the children. I do not concur with all aspects of Chesen's analysis, but I do agree with him that erroneous religious beliefs which touch our basic daily living can have a very destructive effect. The Christotherapist must definitely be able to form a critique of existentially-destructive religious beliefs.

Dr. Adrian van Kaam, who has made outstanding contributions to the development of an existential psychotherapy, has pointed out that the spiritual director, too, can be subject to erroneous attitudes. Among the destructive beliefs he lists are "the conviction that a deficient person must be straightened out before he can grow in the life of the Spirit or be initiated into its mystery"[13] and "an overestimation of the possibilities of psychological direction usually accompanied by an underevaluation of the graced possibilities of spiritual direction."[14] I agree with Dr. van Kaam about the erroneous quality of these beliefs.

I will conclude my discussion of intellectual conversion and the Christotherapist by offering a list of eleven erroneous beliefs which are held by many and which I believe become a source of spiritual and at times psychological and even physical suffering for those who cling to them. Naturally this list is not exhaustive and I do not intend to offer a commentary on these beliefs. I have already indicated, either implicitly or explictly, why I consider some of these beliefs erroneous and destructive and I will have occasion to touch on some of the others later in one fashion or another. But here I invite the reader to reflect prayerfully on these beliefs and to decide for himself or herself where he or she stands personally regarding these beliefs.

Eleven Erroneous Beliefs

1. Human beings are *alone* in the universe and are *solely* in charge of their destinies.

2. The providence of God is not intimately at work in every internal and external occurrence in the individual's life.

3. Acknowledging radical dependence on God makes it impossible for a person to realize his or her full potential as a human being.

4. The human being finds his or her authentic fulfillment by *always* subordinating the satisfaction and needs of others to the satisfaction and needs of himself or herself.

5. A person does not *immediately* and *necessarily* suffer evil consequences in some sphere of his or her being as a result of deliberately, knowingly and freely doing what he or she knows to be immoral and contrary to the will of God.

6. Physical or mental illness in a person, or the involvement of that person in an "accident," is always a sign of some religious, moral or spiritual deficiency in that person.

7. A person should *always unconditionally* seek to be rich rather than poor, to be healthy rather than sick, to be honored rather than considered unimportant, and to live a long life rather than a short life.

8. Jesus Christ *cannot* fulfill unmet psychological needs through a faith-encounter of the psychologically wounded person with him.

9. Psychological wholeness and holiness are identical in every respect.

10. If a person is not healed of physical or mental illness despite prayers for healing, it is always a sign of lack of faith, either in the ill person who prays or in those who pray for the ill person: sickness patiently accepted can never be a means of growth in holiness for the sick person or for anyone else.

11. There is no life beyond this present life: there is no final judgment in which "God will repay each one as his works deserve" (Rm. 2:6); there is no final resurrection from the dead, or eternal life with God.

Psychological Conversion, Conversion from Addiction and the Christotherapist

It is neither desirable nor helpful for a person who needs radical psychological conversion or radical conversion from addiction to function actively as a Christotherapist. An individual who is lacking in a basic sense of self-worth and self-appreciation will not be able to help others to appreciate their own inner value and worth as persons and and as children created in the image and likeness of God. Likewise, an individual whose mind is darkened with distorted beliefs and whose heart is filled with false value judgments about what real psychological and holistic human happiness is and how it is able to be realized will never be able to provide a guiding light or beacon of hope for those who are themselves rudderless in a dark sea of psychic unrest. Again, an individual who is still actively addicted in a radical fashion to a drug, an activity or a person will not be able to provide any ongoing fruitful aid to individuals seeking freedom from addiction or any other form of psychological or spiritual aid. I am not saying that the radically unconverted individuals I have been describing are completely incapable at any time of giving some momentary help or advice to others. I am also not denying that in guided or self-help groups individuals who are deeply wounded can mutually aid one another. But I am saying that these individuals who are in need of radical psychological conversion or of radical conversion from addiction are not capable of actively functioning as Christotherapists.

But if it is necessary to insist that a person who needs radical psychological conversion or radical conversion from addiction is not able to be an authentic Christotherapist, it is equally important to point out that the "wounded healer" who is in an advanced stage of ongoing conversion from these deformations *can* be an extremely effective Christotherapist. Naturally such a wounded healer should also be in an advanced stage of ongoing moral and religious conversion.

But in speaking of the need for an "advanced" stage of ongoing conversion in these individuals, I do not mean they will have achieved complete psychic wholeness or heroic holiness or exalted mysticism. What I do mean is that a person who is experiencing ongoing psychological conversion should be capable of coping adequately with psychological struggles and difficulties which will arise sometimes and should be able to love others in a healthy way, and to work effectively and creatively. Likewise, I mean that the person in a state of ongoing conversion from addiction should have concretely demonstrated a form of truly healthy sobriety—a psychic and spiritual as well as physical freedom from the addictive object—for a significant period of time and should, as in the case of the psychologically converted individual, be capable of loving and working in an effective fashion. *BUT,* and I must stress this, I do not mean that these wounded healers in states of ongoing conversion must be free from all need to struggle or from all psychic pain or from the temptations which are the lot of most humans who are striving to live good lives and generally succeed in doing so. We all know of individuals who suffered from psychological and/or addictive deformations who, after they underwent radical conversion, proceeded to become outstanding healers. Matt Talbot, Anton T. Boisen, O. Hobart Mowrer, Bill Wilson—these are but a few of a whole host of individuals who passed through severe forms of mental or addictive suffering to become powerful instruments of healing in the lives of others. Many of us also have been blessed by personal encounters with "unsung" individuals who have gone through terrible struggles with psychological or addictive "demons" and who, though perhaps still "walking wounded," have gone on to be bearers of the torch of hope in a world where there is so much darkness and pain.

Self-Knowledge

One of the most important qualities an authentic Christotherapist needs to possess is self-knowledge. Kenneth Leech in his book *Soul Friend* writes: "A guide [spiritual director] who has not encountered his own passions, his own inner conflicts, who does not truly know his darkness and light, will be of no value in the spiritual battle."[15] St. Ignatius of Loyola is a striking example of an individual who grew profoundly in self-knowledge through his interior struggles with the "angels of light and darkness." As a result he developed a set of rules for spiritual discernment which remain just as powerful, valid and useful today as they were in the sixteenth century.

Self-knowledge is multidimensional. It involves insight into the origin and meaning of one's basic feeling responses and states. It consists in an understanding of one's fundamental self-concept and self-image. It is a reflective grasp of one's basic strengths and weaknesses, of one's talents and temptations, born of deep personal experience. Self-knowledge is always only partial and incomplete for we are mysteries to ourselves. The richest forms of self-knowledge are gifts for which we should humbly pray, realizing that true inner wisdom is hidden "from the learned and the clever" but is revealed to "mere children" (Lk. 10:21).

A person comes to self-knowledge in many ways. The self-knowledge of St. Ignatius of Loyola, like that of St. Augustine, was at its richest level the fruit of radical and ongoing religious and moral conversion. The self-knowledge of Anton Boisen flowed in a special way from psychological conversion. The self-knowledge of Matt Talbot and Bill Wilson was won in the crucible of conversion from addiction. Of course, all of these individuals grew in self-knowledge through other means as well.

Certainly conversion in one or all of its forms is a principal path to self-knowledge. But there is also a profound self-knowledge which arises in the course of the *natural* unfolding from stage to stage of human developmental processes. Conversion, as I understand it, always involves either a radical or an ongoing turning away from what is destructive and death-producing, and a turning-toward what is constructive and life-enriching. Development, on the other hand, as I generally employ the term, refers to the movement from a lower to a higher stage of maturation, for example, from late adolescence to young adulthood. Luke is describing a spiritual developmental process rather than a conversion when he writes of Jesus: "Meanwhile the child grew to maturity and he was filled with wisdom" (Lk. 2:40). The grace of God is, of course, at work in distinctive ways in the developmental process as transformed by religious and moral conversion. Dabrowski is referring to a blossoming of developmental processes when he writes:

> There are people, though rarely met, whose initial integration belongs to the higher level, whose rich structure, constantly improved by life's experiences and reflections, does not undergo the process of disintegration, but harmoniously and without greater shock develops into a full personality.[16]

All growth in religious and moral self-knowledge comes from the root of religious and moral conversion in sinful human beings. But not all growth in psychological self-knowledge (for example, growth in knowledge of one's self-image and feelings) is the product of psychological conversion or conversion from addiction, because not all people are subject to serious psychological or addictive deformations. Growth in knowledge of the psyche and of the whole domain of affections can result from psychological conversion, but it may also result from a normal developmental process.

Dabrowski writes of psychic and other forms of self-knowledge which are the product of the process of positive disintegration. I believe that the knowledge of self which is the fruit of the process of positive disintegration is a knowledge born of conversion when the positive disintegration involves a breakdown of a primitive personality integration which is basically negative and the realization of a higher integration which is positive. This latter type of self-knowledge is realized, for example, by the person who through a shattering, deeply painful set of experiences discovers that the quest for sexual satisfaction with no concern for one's partner's authentic needs is a dead end and that genuine sexual fulfillment and happiness are found only in a context of love and self-sacrifice.

In a concrete individual, of course, all the diverse paths to self-knowledge (radical conversion in its diverse forms, normal personality development) are subtly intertwined. The self-knowledge which is the hard-won goal of these diverse processes is as subtle, discrete and unified as are the paths by which it is reached. It is vital that the Christotherapist grasp the intricacies of his or her own journey through the labyrinth of the self toward the goal of enlightened self-understanding if she or he is to help others making this journey to take direct routes and to avoid dead ends or endless wanderings. For individuals in interior darkness are least aware of the type of conversions and self-knowledge which they really need. These individuals are also most inclined to take every detour available in order to avoid their particular way to Golgotha—disintegration of the anti-self—which alone will lead them to the Mount of Resurrection—true selfhood in Christ. This is why a spiritual guide who knows well the diverse meanderings of the human spirit can be such a blessing for the seeker of life and wholeness who still dwells in darkness.

The presence of self-knowledge, like that of intellectual conversion, is required in the Christotherapist because of the great damage which inevitably results both for guides and seekers of aid alike when this self-knowledge or conversion is absent. Saint Teresa of Avila, for example, insisted strongly that the spiritual director should be learned—in my terminology intellectually converted—in order to avoid personal difficulties and to avoid fostering false forms of mysticism, a downgrading of the importance of the humanity of Christ and other errors. In similar fashion today psychoanalysts in certain schools are required to undergo analysis in order to become internally free from any unconscious personal difficulties which may be present and to grow in a positive understanding of the human psyche and its processes. I do not believe that it is essential for the Christotherapist to have gone through counseling but a self-knowledge rooted deeply in personal experience and self-analysis is essential.

8

Methods of the Christotherapist

The anonymous author of the fourteenth-century classic, *The Cloud of Unknowing,* tells his readers that techniques for controlling their thoughts during prayer are "better learned from God through experience than from any man in this life." But he adds at once: "All the same I will tell you a little about two techniques for handling distractions."[1] The author concludes by inviting his readers to try the techniques and improve on them if they can. I want to issue the same cautions and the same invitation before describing the methods of the Christotherapist. The anonymous mystic reminds us that God is the primary agent and teacher of prayer, but that it is legitimate for a person to reflect on his or her personal prayer experience and to try to develop techniques which might help others. Naturally it is up to the reader to evaluate these techniques in the light of Christ's teachings and the reader's own experience. But since my Christotherapeutic approach is somewhat new, readers may find the advice of the fourteenth century mystic appropriate here.

The Method of Existential Loving

The key role that love plays in therapy is receiving more attention recently, as books like *Love Therapy,*[2] *Healing Love,*[3] *When Love Is Lost,*[4] and *The Christian Love Treatment*[5] testify. But if counselors and psychotherapists are called to use love as a method, it is also true that the spiritual director "must love his directee, otherwise all his talk about God's love will be in vain."[6]

The Christotherapist is called to love existentially those who come to him or her. To love a person existentially is to value the gift of unique existence which the person possesses and incarnates. Existential loving is a holistic form of loving which is at once affective, contemplative and volitional. It involves verbal communication, but also non-verbal forms such as a smile, a gentle touch, an easy abiding with the person in silence. A truly existential, holistic love for another involves liking the person and not just a volitional love which desires good for the individual. Of course, negative affective feelings on the part of the Christotherapist or of the seeker of aid can at times be a source of an enlightened understanding which leads to healing and growth. For example, a seeker's dislike of the Christotherapist, which, in turn, makes it difficult for the Christotherapist to like the seeker, may be rooted in deep insecurity which makes the seeker fearful of manifesting or accepting affection lest rejection result. The Christotherapist, accordingly, needs to explore the possible meaning of the negative affective feelings he or she is experiencing in the presence of the seeker. But where, as the encounters proceed, the Christotherapist continues to experience dislike of the seeker and no means is found to overcome this, then the Christotherapist must find some way to discontinue the sessions and to recommend someone else. This is necessary because even if the Christotherapist does not communicate his or her dislike of the seeker in a verbal manner it will be communicated and perceived in various non-verbal ways and this will make effective Christotherapeutic aid impossible.

The holistic, existential loving of the Christotherapist should flow from the wellspring of his or her own experience of psychological and spiritual fulfillment. Only the person who has received the gift of "psychic birth," who has a basic sense of self-worth and self-appreciation, can effectively love another person for himself or herself, with no strings attached. Of course, an individual who has undergone radical psychological conversion and is in an advanced stage of ongoing psychological conversion can also love others existentially and with profound acceptance.

As Joseph Pieper has said so well, to love another is to say to that person from the core of one's being, "It's good that you exist."[7] This type of love means taking delight in the uniqueness, inner value and worth of the person. Pieper suggests that to love another person by delighting in him or her is to re-enact "the primal affirmation that took place in the Creation."[8] The Christotherapist rejoices and delights in the seeker as created in the image and likeness of God—endowed with natural gifts of intelligence and freedom, in varying degrees of development. The Christotherapist seeks prayerfully to make the seeker aware of the divine likeness or spark glowing deep within the inner self and to help the seeker to love the divine spark which he or she is.

The Christotherapist also beholds the seeker as a sister or brother of Jesus Christ, redeemed by his blood and loved deeply by him in spite of any and all defects. "What proves that God loves us is that Christ died for us while we were still sinners" (Rm. 5:7). The Christotherapist must constantly ask the Spirit of Christ to open his or her eyes in order to behold the human and God-like qualities which are at least seminally present in the person who comes seeking some kind of assistance.

With the help of the Spirit of God, the Christotherapist can seek to make love bloom where it is least apparent. John of the Cross said, "Where there is no love, put love, and you will draw out love."[9] The Christotherapist shares in a way in God's own creative activity, and his or her existential loving blends with the divine evaluation of creation: "God saw all he had made, and indeed it was very good" (Gn. 1:31). It is not that the Christotherapist denies the reality of sin, but he or she does realize that "where sin increased, grace abounded all the more" (Rm. 5:10 R.S.V.), and that "for anyone who is in Christ, there is a new creation" (2 Cor. 5:17).

Authentic existential loving is not sentimental; it can be quite tough; it involves acceptance but it does not condone the irresponsible; it can confront; also, where the Christotherapist is dealing with an individual lacking in psychic birth existential loving takes on a more intense form than in cases where the Christotherapist is working with a person who is psychologically whole and seeking deeper maturation and transformation in Christ. Finally, authentic existential loving liberates individuals from unhealthy forms of dependence; it creates a legitimate sense of autonomy and independence in individuals previously lacking in these qualities and it enriches all who experience it in their capacity to enter into creative, life-giving, loving relationships with others.

The Methods of Existential Discerning and Clarification

Along with existential loving two other key methods of the Christotherapist are existential discerning and existential clarification. All three of these processes involve truly natural, human dynamics. But they also require for holistic effectiveness the prayerful invocation of the Holy Spirit and they depend on the assistance of grace which, if granted, complements, strengthens, illumines and transfigures these natural processes in Christ. This does not mean, however, that the operation together of these natural human processes and the graces of the Holy Spirit dissolves the real distinction between the natural human processes and the spiritual elements involved or that the human is totally absorbed into the spiritual or that the spiritual is reduced simply to very perfect forms of human activity. The process of human existential loving, for example, when it is complemented and energized by the divine gift of charity (a strictly spiritual, supernatural gift) does not lose its human character. Rather, if I may borrow an analogy from the Fathers of the Church and adapt it somewhat, the process of loving, enlivened by the infusion of the gift of charity by the Spirit, retains its identity just as a piece of iron, plunged into a fire, remains iron even though it glows with the light and heat of the fire and is suffused with its splendor. The same type of analogy applies to the human processes of discerning and clarifying when they are touched by grace. These latter processes too are strengthened, illumined and transfigured by gifts of faith, wisdom and other spiritual charisms. But they are not destroyed in their natural qualities as they work together in a dynamic inward symbiosis with the graces of the Spirit. The Christotherapist, in other words, functions in a truly human way and at the same time is uplifted, enlightened, strengthened and transfigured by the gifts of the Holy Spirit of Christ.

The Method of Existential Discerning

There are two basic forms of existential discerning: existential diagnosis and existential appreciation. The Christotherapist is called to diagnose the existential meaning of whatever spiritual, psychological, somatic or external difficulties are troubling the seeker. He or she is also called to appreciate the existential, life-giving, life-enhancing qualities which are potential or actual in the seeker and to embrace, nourish, cultivate and cherish them.

I speak of *existential* diagnosis and *existential* appreciation,[10] using the adjective to mean those factors in human living which touch the human being at the very core of his or her being. Specifically, "existential" designates those basic meanings and values, those key beliefs, attitudes and assumptions, which generate either spiritual, psychological and somatic wholeness or deformation, disorder and illness.

Existential Diagnosis

In my terminology an individual is *existentially* in error who—consciously or unconsciously, freely or compulsively—is living according to false ideas or beliefs about what true fulfillment is and how it is to be realized and who, as a consequence, is suffering spiritually, psychologically, somatically or through negative external happenings. This person is also in a state of *existential* ignorance in the sense that he or she is either passively ignorant of his or her real condition and of those transformations which could bring healing and wholeness or is actively ignoring these basic realities.

One of the main tasks of the Christotherapist is to try to help the error-burdened, existentially ignorant person through existential diagnosis (provided, of course, that the person wants help). This process involves a prayerful, Spirit-guided attempt to get at and understand particular errors, false beliefs and corrosive assumptions about how to live and find fulfillment; these mistaken ideas are often unconscious, and they underlie and are manifested in the various deformations, illnesses and destructive external events which may have brought the person to the Christotherapist.

The word *diagnosis* usually has a medical meaning, but it has been used before in a pastoral context;[11] the Greek root word means to go beyond the superficial level of physical appearances and penetrate to the deeper reality, the source of the illness. Existential diagnosis in Christotherapy is understanding the underlying destructive belief or assumption which is manifested in a particular symptomatology or negative occurrence. In *Christotherapy*[12] I cited Paul's statement that "every thought is our prisoner, captured to be brought into obedience to Christ" (2 Cor. 10:5) as a basic biblical expression of the ongoing need for diagnostic discernment. To transpose Paul's exhortation into a contemporary psycho-spiritual context, the Christotherapist through diagnostic discerning is called to help to liberate the enslaved individual who is held captive by unconscious, destructive beliefs, assumptions, biases.

Existential Appreciation

A person who is existentially wise is living according to an authentic understanding of the true meaning of life and of happiness. This man or woman is living in the truth existentially, and is freely ruled by the grace of the Holy Spirit. Such a person is holy, as a result. To the extent that God grants, he or she is also whole in mind and body, and untroubled in the events of his or her daily life. I repeat, however, that illness in mind or body and the occurrence of negative external events are never in themselves necessary signs of a lack of existential wisdom in an individual. But they can be.

One of the principal tasks of the Christotherapist is to discern in the person who comes to her or him the person's good qualities, both those which give, enhance and enrich life, as well as those which the person needs to realize and cultivate. The Christotherapist seeks to behold with the "inner eye," lighted by the Spirit, the spark of the divine and whatever is humanly good and lovely in the person who comes for help. Prayerfully, with Spirit-guided imagination, the Christotherapist tries to see in needy, deficient individuals the blossoming of desirable qualities not yet present. This again is a matter of beholding the person, in prayerful desire, as actually possessing these qualities. "Where you do not find these qualities, behold them, and then you will find them there." This practice of existential appreciation always means focusing on what is rich and good.

I use the word appreciate to refer to the discerning of what is lovely, to the discriminating of what is excellent, to the understanding of what is true, to the perceiving of what is beautiful, to the savoring of what is truly delightful, to the intuiting of the deepest of spiritual and mystical values. Appreciation, like diagnosis, implies the power to penetrate below the surface but what appreciation uncovers is not the erroneous but the true, not ignorance but wisdom, not the worthless but the realm of human and divine values in all their richness. The appreciator can also behold the wounded face of the Crucified and weep with him. Saint Ignatius, after all, calls it a form of consolation when one is inspired by the Spirit to shed tears because of the sufferings of Christ the Lord.[13] Finally, existential appreciation also involves discerning the will and call of the Lord and that call at times can be to suffering and even to martyrdom. "Happy are you when people abuse you and persecute you and speak all kinds of calumny against you on my account. Rejoice and be glad" (Mt. 5:11–12).

Some Requirements for Effective Existential Discerning

This list of qualities which are important for existential discernment comes in part from the writings of Dr. Hora, and from my conversations with him.

To reach (with God's help) a correct existential diagnosis and appreciation of what is going on in the person seeking help, the Christotherapist:

1. needs to be deeply sensitive to the fact that he or she is always acting as an instrument of Christ the Healer, who bestows abundant life.

2. needs to be interiorly sober and reverently alert to the inspirations of the Spirit of God, who, like the wind, comes and goes and "blows wherever it pleases" (Jn. 3:8).

3. needs to meditate constantly on the life and mysteries of Christ, to imitate Christ and to seek to put on the mind of Christ.

4. needs to be wakefully and prayerfully receptive to what unfolds in the seeker from moment to moment.

5. needs to be a person who lives at ever-deepening levels of commitment to authentic values, and to the truths which liberate and are the source of abundant life.

6. needs to be a person who possesses a child-like humbleness of heart, and a spirit of openness, unclouded by bias.

7. needs to be capable of "paying attention" to what *is.* This "payment" is made in the coin of forgetfulness of self and self-concern, which is required in order to listen and attend fully to the presence and needs of another.

8. needs to treat the person seeking not as a specimen to be dissected or analyzed, but as a person to be understood and loved.

9. needs to try in a constant, persevering way to understand, to love and cherish, and to delight in all authentic spiritual and human values.

10. needs to avoid trespassing or intruding in the life of the seeker because this causes resistance and a sense of interior violation in those desiring aid.

11. needs to renounce mere curiosity about the life, habits and activities of the person seeking aid, and to focus on what is essentially related to the healing and guidance processes.

12. needs to avoid irresponsible speculations or the urge to leap to judgment without giving "interior space" and "psychological time" to the person, so that he or she can gradually reveal himself or herself.

13. needs to be aware of any temptations he or she experiences in working with the person seeking; paying attention to such experiences can reveal to the Christotherapist his or her own inner weaknesses, as well as disclosing the existential meaning of the particular problem or issue which brought the person to seek aid.

This list of some requirements for effective existential discernment, both diagnostic and appreciative, is not complete, but it does cover a good number of the major requirements.

The Method of Existential Clarification

Existential clarification is the process by which the Christotherapist seeks to communicate his or her diagnostic and appreciative discernment to the seeker in such a manner that the latter equally comes to participate in and personally verify for himself or herself this diagnostic and appreciative understanding. The method of existential clarification, like that of existential discerning, involves two phases.

In the first phase of existential clarification, the Christotherapist prayerfully tries to make clear for the seeker the existential meaning of whatever destructive or growth-inhibiting factors the person is experiencing. Through the use of examples, images and descriptions, the Christotherapist tries to help the seeker to grasp in a vital way the inner relationship between the problem experienced and some destructive, erroneous attitude or belief (or constellation of such attitudes and beliefs) which he or she entertains and lives by.

In the second phase of existential clarification, the Christotherapist prayerfully tries to help the seeker to discover and delight in those authentic values and truths which are especially life-giving and life-enriching for him or her. Using personal experiences, Holy Scripture, poetry and other means the Christotherapist tries to help the seeker understand, appreciate and cultivate the authentic, wholesome, integrative, humanistic and spiritual Christian truths and values which he or she needs, in order to live in a holistic, holy, and richly-abundant way.

The two phases of existential clarification are necessary complements to each other, because the person suffering from existential error needs to replace this particular error with a particular existential truth. For example, a person who wrongly believes that happiness always lies in the future, never in the present, needs to discover and cultivate the existential truth that the richness of the Kingdom of God is real here and now (Lk. 17:21), and available to anyone who opens the inner eyes of the heart to it. Existential clarification in this case would begin by helping the sufferer discover that his or her belief that happiness is *only* in the future is blocking the possibility of experiencing happiness in the present, and is a source of ongoing misery. The second phase of this clarification would involve helping the person discover the truth of the present reality of the Kingdom of God in his or her own heart.

It is important to *emphasize* that in the concrete case, where the clarification process is unfolding well, the seeker is actively, prayerfully involved. He or she is seeking *together with* the Christotherapist for a diagnostic and appreciative discernment. It is often true that in the very moment of being understood, a person understands. At times, too, the seeker, with the help of the Holy Spirit, realizes an authentic diagnostic or appreciative discernment before the Christotherapist. This is a very happy occurrence, and the sign of an accelerated pace in the person's healing and growth through enlightenment.

I must also stress that although the Christotherapist can bestow the gift of psychic birth on an individual, he or she can never bestow the gift of overcoming existential error or of discovering existential truth or value. The Christotherapist can clarify and create optimal conditions for the occurrence of existential understanding but the act of discerning itself is a spontaneous event in the seeker and it cannot be willed or effected necessarily by either the Christotherapist or the seeker. In the case where a person is trying to discern God's positive will about a vocational or avocational choice, or to make some kind of decision, the Christotherapist can try to create a proper climate for discerning or deciding—but can never do the discerning or deciding for the individual.

Some Requirements for Effective Existential Clarification

Earlier I offered a summary of some key elements which aid the process of existential discernment. Here I add a condensed, complementary list of factors which enable, constitute or facilitate the method of existential clarification.

Effective existential clarification requires that the Christotherapist:

1. Invite the seeker to join him or her in praying for an unmasking of destructive, disintegrative, pain-causing attitudes and beliefs, and in praying for the grace to discern and cultivate what is good: those truths and values which lead toward health and positive integration, which are a source of peace and gratitude, assurance, love and joy for the person.

2. Be capable of depicting for the seeker in a striking, graphic manner how his or her unhappiness flows directly from specific patterns of belief and behavior; the Christotherapist must be able to show how corrosive the erroneous attitudes are, in a way which will help the client to be most disposed toward self-understanding; the seeker must be helped to verify personally, at a "gut as well as mental" level, the self-destructiveness of these beliefs, so that he or she can choose to let go of the "inner devils" and invite "angels of light" to come in.

3. Be constantly alert to the fact that the seeker will perceive in some fashion whatever erroneous beliefs, false

"gods" the Christotherapist covertly or overtly cherishes and clings to and will either unknowingly embrace these errors and false values or will fight against them.

4. Must aid the seeker to unmask the covert desires, fears, hates, loves, false expectations, self-deceptions and hidden rationalizations which are the source of his or her suffering, and at the same time are working like a powerful undercurrent against enlightenment, healing and growth.

5. Must be alive with authentic humanistic and spiritual/Christian values; he or she must be able to depict the beauty, wholesomeness and excellence of those values in such a way that the seeker will come to delight in, cherish and love them, will personally verify their integrative, peace-generating, life-enriching qualities, and will see that they lead to wholeness and holiness.

6. Must possess a consciousness so rooted, grounded and centered in Christ and the truths and values he incarnates, exemplifies, loves and delights in, that the very being of the Christotherapist will be a key source of inspiration and value-clarification for the one seeking help.

Mind-Fasting and Spirit-Feasting

The methods of mind-fasting and spirit-feasting are central to Christotherapy. They are meant to be practiced equally by the Christotherapist in his or her daily living and by those with whom the Christotherapist works. The expression "mind-fasting" comes originally from the Taoist writer Chuang Tzu[14] and I have coined the expression "spirit-feasting" to describe the complementary process to mind-fasting.[15]

Stages of the Mind-Fasting Process

Stage One: NEGATIVE DATA: The experience of some disorder, disease, crisis; this negative experience can be bodily, psychological, spiritual, an external event or any combination of negative factors.

Stage Two: PRAYER FOR DIAGNOSTIC DISCERNMENT: The prayerful quest for a correct diagnostic understanding and evaluation of the negative element in one's experience.

Stage Three: REVELATION/RECOGNITION: The inspired (correct) diagnostic discernment of the existential meaning of the negative factor in one's experience.

Stage Four: DECISION/DEMONSTRATION: The enlightened decision to act in accord with the diagnostic understanding which has been revealed; this involves an ongoing prayer to God to remove the existentially erroneous belief, defect, behavior at work in one's life; it also involves cooperating with the Holy Spirit by freely letting go of, fasting from the erroneous attitude which underlies one's negative experiences and by actively and consciously refraining from the destructive behavior flowing from the erroneous attitude. The ongoing practice of this Spirit-inspired and grace-supported fasting results in a growing freedom from the initial negative experiences and demonstrates the fruitfulness of this process of fasting, rooted in a correct diagnostic discernment.

Stages of the Spirit-Feasting Process

Stage One: POSITIVE DATA: Finding oneself placed or placing oneself in the presence of some potential source of authentic enrichment of the whole person, e.g. Holy Scripture, a beautiful natural scene, a work of art, an interpersonal encounter.

Stage Two: PRAYER FOR APPRECIATIVE DISCERNMENT: The prayerful quest for an appreciative existential discerning and valuing of the potential source of authentic existential enrichment.

Stage Three: REVELATION/RECOGNITION: The inspired gift of an appreciative discerning and cherishing of the value revealed to one.

Stage Four: DECISION/DEMONSTRATION: The enlightened decision to act in accord with the discerning appreciation with which one has been gifted; this involves an ongoing prayer to God to deepen the revelation one has received; it involves an ongoing cooperation with the Holy Spirit by delighting in, feasting on and living in harmony with the revealed value. The ongoing practice of this inspired feasting of the mind, heart and imagination results in a growing experience of peace, love, gratitude, assurance, praise and joy and demonstrates the fruitfulness of the spirit-feasting process, rooted in an authentic appreciative discernment.

My outline of the stages of the mind-fasting and spirit-feasting processes is not intended as a straitjacket for the individual who wishes to utilize the mind-fasting and spirit-feasting processes. I believe that there is a natural, spontaneous flow in the stages of these processes, as I have described them, but I also believe that there is room for real flexibility in the concrete ways in which persons choose to make use of these processes. I must also stress that the person who practices these processes is called in his or her concrete daily living to blend them in accord with the particular life-demands and opportunities which present themselves.

The principal aim of the Christotherapist in making use of the methods of existential discerning and clarification is to aid the seeker of wholeness in Christ to engage fruitfully in the practice of the mind-fasting and spirit-feasting processes. Often the Christotherapist needs to utilize the method of existential loving in order to bring a person to the point where he or she can begin to practice mind-fasting and spirit-feasting. I would like to offer one example here of how a Christotherapist and a seeker of wholeness in Christ might interact in a quest for realizing the goal of the seeker. But it is in Part Two of this book that I will make detailed applications of the principles and methods of Christotherapy.

An Example

Let us say that a woman, Ann, is suffering very much in her relationships with others. She wants very much to enjoy close, warm friendships, but instead she is constantly rebuffed when she tries to get close to others. She finds that the more she attempts to make friends, the more people back away from her. Ann has become progressively more lonely, more isolated, more alienated from others. In her loneliness she finds herself envious, jealous, and daily more unhappy. Finally she seeks the help of Bill, a Christotherapist, because she finds the pain unbearable.

Bill receives Ann in an accepting, open-hearted , open-minded way and tries to create a climate of love, care and affirmation, just as he does for anyone who comes to him. He also encourages Ann to pray, as he does, for an understanding of the true meaning of her suffering. Bill tries to cultivate a humble heart, an attitude of "choiceless awareness"[16]—free of bias and preconceptions—letting Ann be Ann in his presence, so that with the help of the Holy Spirit he can come to a correct diagnosis of the meaning of Ann's pain.

Let us say that in the course of the Christotherapeutic relationship, Bill comes to understand and verify for himself that Ann lacks a basic sense of self-worth and self-esteem. He also comes to the correct diagnostic understanding that Ann is dominated by the false, unrecognized belief that she needs to "possess" people, to have their complete and undivided attention at all times and their exclusive allegiance, in order truly to enjoy their friendship.

As Ann's condition is revealed to Bill he continues to love and accept her in a holistic manner. Prayerfully, he seeks to appreciate Ann's good qualities, as they are revealed to him, and to point them out to Ann and to invite her to delight in them, to spirit-feast. At the same time he tries to clarify for her, using examples from her own life as they come up in therapy, how she is ruled by a "possessivist" attitude in her approach to others, and how this driving urge to "have" friends scares them off—since they do not want to be imprisoned, like butterflies in a jar. In this way Bill issues an invitation to Ann to engage in the mind-fasting process.

Bill tries to clarify for Ann the real value of letting other people be who they are without clinging to them. He helps her to appreciate that delighting in the good qualities of another without dwelling on one's own lack of these qualities, and without attempting to prevent anyone else from delighting in them, brings liberation, joy, peace, and is a matrix for the birth of true and lasting friendships. Ann gradually learns how to engage in the mind-fasting and spirit-feasting processes.

Gradually, due to her experience of Bill's acceptance and love and because of her personal diagnosis and verification of how self-destructive her possessive, envious, jealous forms of thinking, desiring and acting really are, Ann makes a decision (most often a series of decisions) to fast from what is self-destructive and to spirit-feast in the presence of the good qualities of others in a truly free, non-clinging way. Ann gradually passes from radical into ongoing psychological conversion and, if she chooses, can terminate her sessions with Bill. She has reached the point where she is capable of a certain self-therapy and spiritual self-direction, aided, of course, by the Holy Spirit. She continues to grow in her daily practice of the prayerful processes of mind-fasting and spirit-feasting. But since Bill is a Christotherapist, Ann is free to seek his continuing guidance as she moves forward in an upward spiral of ongoing religious and moral as well as psychological conversion.

Ideally, throughout the Christotherapeutic encounters Bill personally embodies and appeals to the example and teaching of Christ. He loves Ann with a Christly love and draws her to discern the great warm, accepting love which Christ has for her. He likewise seeks to let grow and shine within himself the Christ-mind and the Christ-heart. He constantly utilizes teachings of Christ as well as the wisdom of valid psychology to clarify for Ann the self-destructiveness of certain ways of thinking, desiring, phantasizing, imagining and acting and the self-enriching, self-transforming characteristics of certain other forms of thinking, desiring, etc. As a result, if Ann decides to terminate her sessions with Bill, she will not be alone but will always experience the beneficial presence, comfort and help of THE THERAPIST: JESUS CHRIST.

In my example I tried to interweave in a dynamic fashion the two processes of mind-fasting and spirit-feasting. I must emphasize that it is never helpful to encourage a person to engage in the process of mind-fasting without making certain that the person will complement this process with the spirit-feasting process. As I make clear in *Christotherapy,*[17] it is never enough just to drive out devils. The devils must be replaced with angels of light.

Thus, if a person is enslaved by the "demon" of anger, this demon must be replaced with the "angel" of serenity.

A Comparison of Methods: Dr. Lawrence Crabb

Dr. Crabb's method of counseling consists of seven principal steps:[18]

1. The counselor tries to pinpoint the particular problem-feeling which the client is experiencing, e.g., anxiety, guilt, a sense of emptiness, resentment.

2. An effort is made to uncover the particular goal-oriented behavior which is the context in which the problem-feeling arises, for example, a man experiences anxiety whenever he is involved in situations involving possible business promotion; here the feeling of anxiety is clearly connected with the goal of realizing monetary success.

3. There is a search to uncover the wrong belief—the problem-thinking—unconsciously at work in the goal-oriented striving of the person who is suffering. To continue with the example presented in step two, the counselor comes to understand that the suffering individual has identified personal significance with financial success; the trouble-producing assumption is that "significance equals money."

4. An attempt is made to convince the counselee that his or her thinking is erroneous and to show in a persuasive way the biblical route to fulfillment of the need the sufferer experiences. The fourth step is not easy; in the case we have been dealing with the counselee's belief that significance equals monetary success is charged with a strong affective component. In Crabb's view it is Christ alone who gives the gift of significance through the bestowal of justification. To help the counselee change his wrong thinking to right thinking Crabb tries to help the sufferer pick out the set of circumstances where he first learned his false belief about significance; he gives support and encouragement in order to reduce possible resistance; he also suggests to the counselee that he write

down on a small piece of paper his false belief and on another the contradictory biblical truth.

5. An attempt is made to secure commitment on the part of the counselee. It is not enough for the latter to recognize the error of his or her old assumption and to begin to recognize the new biblical truth; the counselee has to decide to act consistently with his or her new understanding; Crabb stresses that the counselee needs to be encouraged to act according to what he or she thinks and not according to his or her feelings; he suggests that confession is a very appropriate action at this step in the process.

6. An effort is made to plan and carry out appropriate biblical behavior. Crabb follows Leon Festinger's view that when a person holds two dissonant beliefs or attitudes, the one which is reinforced through consistent behavior will become stronger.[19]

7. The counselee comes to identify in his or her experience an absence of sin-related feelings and the presence of spiritual feelings; "many Christians have . . . the experience of 'feeling really good' when they are consciously abiding in Christ and the experience of feeling that 'something is wrong' when they are out of fellowship."[20]

There are a number of basic similarities between Dr. Crabb's method and the methods of Christotherapy. Both stress the importance of getting at the false beliefs which often unconsciously underlie disturbed feelings. Both emphasize the need to complement the unmasking of the erroneous assumptions with a revealing of the true views and values. Both require a decision on the part of the seeker to act in accord with the new understanding. Finally, both acknowledge that as the seeker lives in harmony with the new truth, he or she experiences an absence of the suffering which was present before and a growing experience of joy, peace, happiness and other gifts of the Holy Spirit.

There are also some differences between the methods of Crabb and those of Christotherapy. I place great importance on introducing prayer into the heart of the diagnostic and appreciative discernment processes of both the Christotherapist and the seeker. I emphasize human as well as specifically spiritual and biblical values; for example, human existential loving can bring about a person's psychic birth and foster a sense of self-worth and significance. As I understand Dr. Crabb, only a faith-encounter with Christ can give a person a true sense of worth and significance. I agree that Jesus Christ can fulfill unmet human needs through a faith-encounter. But I believe that he also uses human beings to fulfill the psychological needs of other human beings by means of love and acceptance. I also stress that a key task of the Christotherapist is to demonstrate in a graphic manner for the seeker the intrinsic connection between the pain he or she is experiencing and a particular false belief or set of false beliefs out of which he or she is living. Thomas Aquinas wrote that "we do not offend God except by doing something contrary to our own good."[21] It is consequently the task of the Christotherapist to clarify for the seeker how living in accord with a particular belief (for instance, significance equals money) is making him or her miserable. The seeker can then understand powerfully, on a gut level, that giving up the false belief is a matter of enlightened self-interest, as well as obedience to the will of God. The Christotherapist also has the task of clarifying for the seeker the intrinsic, integrative, life-enriching qualities of the new truth which is substituted for the old error.

Dr. Roberto Assagioli

Dr. Assagioli recommends the method he calls "disidentification," which in some respects resembles the process of mind-fasting.[22] He also suggests, for some, engaging in what he names "new identifications,"[23] and higher processes of spiritual self-realization. There are some parallels between these processes and aspects of spirit-feasting.

About disidentification, Assagioli says, "we are dominated by everything with which our self becomes identified. We can dominate and control everything from which we disidentify ourselves."[24] For example, if we identify ourselves with our fears, our weaknesses, our faults, harmful images, various complexes[25] (such as inferiority), we limit ourselves. In fact, we become in a certain sense paralyzed. If I say, "I am depressed," I become more and more dominated by this depression. But if I objectify my feeling of depression—if, rather than repeating inwardly, "I am depressed," I say instead, "A wave of depression is trying to overwhelm me"—then I can look critically at my feeling, try to get at its origins, see its damaging effects and its lack of foundation, and so gain greater freedom from its domination.

Assagioli warns that an *excessive* analysis and criticism can paralyze our feelings. He suggests that we should try to dissolve undesirable images, impulses, complexes and tendencies (such as the "I am a victim" complex) by unmasking and understanding these destructive elements of our experience. He urges that the best way to disintegrate harmful images, complexes and similar phenomena is through objectification, critical analysis and discrimination. By these methods we "employ cold, impersonal observation"[26] of our disturbing images or feelings; we deal with them as if they were phenomena occurring outside ourselves; we "create a 'psychological distance' between ourselves and them, keeping these images or complexes at arm's length, so to speak, and then quietly consider their origin, their nature and—their stupidity!"[27]

Assagioli suggests a set of disidentification exercises which ground the process of personal psychosynthesis, and which can protect us in advance from succumbing to negative identifications. Briefly put, he recommends that we put ourselves in a relaxed position, breathe deeply, and then make some basic affirmations slowly and thoughtfully. Some key affirmations are: "I *have* a body but I *am not* my body"; "I *have* emotions but I *am not* my emotions"; "I *have* a mind but I *am not* my mind"; "I *have* desires, but I *am not* my desires."[28] At the end comes the process of identification in which the individual makes this affirmation:

> I recognize and affirm myself as a center of pure self-awareness and of creative, dynamic energy. I realize that from this center of true identity I can learn to observe, direct, and harmonize all the psychological processes and the physical body. I will to achieve a constant awareness of this fact in the midst of my everyday life, and to use it to help me and give increasing meaning and direction to my life.[29]

Dr. Assagioli's disidentification process resembles the method of mind-fasting in its recognition of the need for freedom from the tyranny of undesirable images, problem-feelings, and complexes. Also, his stress on the need to put a certain distance between oneself and harmful images or feelings resembles the emphasis in mind-fasting on the need to cultivate a "choiceless awareness" and a mental attitude of "letting be" in the presence of the troublesome phenomenon, so that it can reveal itself as it truly is. Likewise, Assagioli's focus on the need to unmask and understand the disturbing phenomenon closely parallels the quest for existential diagnostic understanding in the mind-fasting process.

Assagioli balances the disidentification process with a positive affirming of one's true identity. In *Psychosynthesis* Assagioli indicates that there are various stages involved in the realization of personal and of spiritual psychosynthesis.[30] He suggests a method of developing "new identifications" as an intermediate stage in moving toward Self-realization. He points out that the ultimate goal is "to unite the lower with the higher Self,"[31] in other words, to unite the "I" of our everyday experience with the true Higher Self. But . . .

> men and women who [at least for the present] cannot reach their true Self in its pure essence can create a picture and an ideal of perfected personality adequate to their caliber, their stage of development and their psychological type, and therefore, can make this ideal practicable in actual life.[32]

For some, this ideal can be that of becoming a good mother or father; for others it can be becoming a good artist, teacher, philosopher, seeker after the truth. Assagioli insists that the ideal must be realistic and not neurotically perfectionistic; he notes that for some people of a rather plastic nature, the preference is not to set an ideal for themselves, but to let themselves be guided by God, and to let the Spirit of God choose what they should become. This kind of person tries to eliminate the negative factors in his or her life and to be in tune with God, or with cosmic order or universal harmony. Both those who choose their own goals and those who allow a higher power to choose their goals for them are moving toward personal psychosynthesis, and hopefully perhaps also toward the higher goal of spiritual psychosynthesis. In this stage of spiritual psychosynthesis, there is an ever-deepening realization of true spiritual Selfhood.

A stage in spiritual Self-realization can involve "the momentary or more or less temporary identification or blending of the I-consciousness with the spiritual Self, in which the former, which is the reflection of the latter, becomes reunited, blended with the spiritual Self."[33] For Assagioli there are certain symbols which can be used to evoke the spiritual Self. Among these symbols are the "Inner Christ" and the "Inner Master" or "Teacher." Through the technique of Inner Dialogue, the personal self can establish a fruitful relationship with the spiritual Self.[34] Intense experiences of bliss, spiritual ecstasy, and self-forgetfulness can occur, but this does not mean one is severed from the world or life. In fact, the person in spiritual Self-realization experiences increased creativity, improved ability to serve humankind in various ways.

There are some basic similarities and affinities between spirit-feasting and Assagioli's outline of the processes of affirmation of true identity, developing ideals of new identities, and ever-deepening personal and spiritual psychosynthesis. Affirmation of true identity, for instance, which is a positive complement to the disidentification process, parallels spirit-feasting as a complement to mind-fasting. Assagioli's stress on the development of new identities harmonizes with the emphasis in Christotherapy on the existential appreciation and cultivation of those authentic humanistic and spiritual qualities which enrich a person's life and make possible a fuller blossoming of true selfhood. In acknowledging that it is valid for some persons to let God guide them in determining their new identities, Assagioli offers a certain parallel to the emphasis in Christotherapy on a *prayerful* quest for existential appreciation. And there is some correspondence between the Christotherapist's invitation to the seeker to share in higher, more mystical forms of spirit-feasting and Assagioli's encouragement to those who feel so inclined to engage in an Inner Dialogue with the Inner Christ.

There are certain differences in terminology and *perhaps* also in psychology and metaphysics which exist between Christotherapy and psychosynthesis. For example, in psychosynthesis the individual affirms that "I have a body, a mind, emotions but I am not my body or my mind or my emotions. Rather, I am a Center of pure self-consciousness." I believe that it is very helpful both therapeutically and for psychological and spiritual maturation to affirm as a result of enlightened understanding that "I am not *reducible* to my body or to my emotions or to my mind. I am, moreover, not to be *identified* with any particular ideas or feelings which I may entertain or experience." I am, however, uncomfortable with any language which tends to suggest that the real or true or deepest self is disincarnate. I think that Assagioli does struggle to avoid spiritual reductionism and perhaps he succeeds in doing so. But I am at least ill at ease with the language of some of his affirmations about the true self or identity. I myself would prefer to utilize the following affirmation: "I am an incarnate subject, endowed with bodily, psychic, intellectual, volitional, spiritual capacities or potentialities." In this latter affirmation it is clear that the true self, the real self is the whole person—body-soul-spirit[35]—existing and functioning in an integral, authentic, holistic and holy manner.

The Method of Dream Interpretation

The interpretation of dreams is the key method of the classical approaches of Freud and Jung. The key methods of Christotherapy are existential loving, existential discerning and existential clarification. In Christotherapy, dreams are viewed as *one* source of data which can be utilized for the purposes of existential discerning and existential clarification. The Christotherapist can seek prayerfully to discover unconscious erroneous assumptions, beliefs, hidden self-destructive orientations embodied in dreams. Likewise the Christotherapist can prayerfully seek to diagnose through dreams the existence of repressed dimensions of the personality which need to be recognized, expressed and cultivated in an appropriate manner. Also, the Christotherapist can seek prayerfully to recognize through an appreciative discernment positive callings and qualities revealed in dreams. I do not believe that the Christotherapist must utilize dream analysis in order to aid a person in moving toward holistic healing and wholeness in Christ but it is one effective means of diagnostic and appreciative discernment which the Christotherapist can employ if the seeker desires this and the Christotherapist is competent in this area. I myself prefer the Jungian over the Freudian approach to the interpretation of dreams and I especially recommend the works of Dr. Robert Doran for further study in this area.[36]

In dealing with dreams, I tend to follow some rules which Dr. Ann Faraday has laid out in *The Dream Game.*[37] Some of her suggestions are:

1. A dream should be interpreted literally before it is subjected to metaphorical interpretation; for example, if you

dream that you are about to fall down your basement steps, check the steps the next morning before you look for further symbolic meaning in the dream.

2. If a dream does not make sense in a literal way, then it probably symbolizes something or someone in your life, or a dimension of your own personality; for instance, if you dream of a fascist you may have recently behaved in a fascistic manner.

3. Dreams are triggered by something in our heart or in our mind; images and characters appear in our dreams because "they represent the voices of the past which still live on in us and influence our present behavior, or to tell us that something in our present situation reminds us of a similar situation in the past."[38]

4. A dream's feeling tone often provides a clue to an element in our particular life-situation; for instance, "if the feeling tone of the dream is miserable, then the dream was sparked by some miserable situation in the dreamer's current life."[39]

5. The same dreams occurring at different periods in one's life can have different meanings according to differences in one's life-situation.

6. "A dream does not indulge in reminiscence for its own sake."[40] Dreams do not tell us what we already know, unless we are failing to do what we know we should do.

7. The occurrence of so-called dream symbols like falling, flying, and so on, can have the meanings commonly attributed to them, but in any particular instance they can have quite unique meanings related to the particular life-situation of the dreamer.

8. Dreams are given to expand, not to diminish or impoverish us.

9. "A dream is correctly interpreted when and only when it makes sense to the dreamer in terms of his present life situation and moves him to change his life constructively."[41] Dr. Robert Doran lends striking support to this last point of Faraday's when he writes:

> With the aid of an analyst, I interpret the symbols of my dreams; I affirm the meaning interpreted; I thus come to a knowledge of my present condition, situation, and possibilities, through the illumination of 'how I find myself' afforded by the symbolic images. . . . As Jung rightly insists, the image is creative. Psychotherapy aims not only at self-knowledge but also, beyond the affirmation of an interpretation as true, at the constitution and transformation of the subject and his world through authentic praxis. . . .What am I going to do about it? The interpretation of the image ought not to be affirmed as true, is not correctly so affirmed, unless it includes an interpretation of the creative possibilities revealed in the image.[42]

Faraday and Doran both insist strongly that a correct interpretation of the dream must be proven in decision and constructive self-transforming activity. This is a direct parallel to my own requirement that a correct existential diagnosis and appreciation must blossom in decision, and a demonstration of its authenticity through continuous fasting and feasting of mind, heart and spirit.

Another norm I follow in the interpretation of dreams is that the Holy Spirit of God is profoundly at work in dreams, just as in all other activities and dimensions of human existence. Consequently, I insist on approaching the interpretation of dreams prayerfully. Dr. Fredrick Crowe in an unpublished article,[43] which I found most enlightening, suggests that it is a very fruitful, psychic and spiritual practice to integrate into our early morning prayers the images and feelings still alive in us of the dream state from which we have just awakened. The psychic orientation of the dream toward the dreamer's realization of a more abundant life is then consciously integrated into prayer, which is the greatest dynamo for human self-transcendence given to a person by the power of the Holy Spirit. For those who want to read further about this rich area, I especially recommend John A. Sanford[44] and Morton Kelsey.[45]

The Method of Healing of Memories

Today, especially in official charismatic circles but not exclusively so, there is a strong emphasis on the healing of memories. Earlier I offered a sketch of the method Matthew and Dennis Linn employ in their approach to the healing of memories. In Christotherapy, along with existential loving, the principal methods involve the diagnostic unmasking of unconscious, self-destructive attitudes, the appreciative discerning of authentic values and life-giving truths and the living out of these discernments in the ongoing practices of mind-fasting and spirit-feasting. Dr. Hora cites an unnamed French psychiatrist[46] who stresses that it is not so much through remembering that healing takes place; rather, it is through the experience of healing that remembering occurs. In Christotherapy the viewpoint is that just as the experience of existential loving often allows repressed memories of rejection to emerge and to be dealt with constructively, so the healing of self-destructive attitudes and assumptions allows negative memories to surface in consciousness and enables the sufferer to handle these memories in a healing and transformative fashion. For example, if an individual understands and verifies for herself or himself that resentment is a self-destructive form of phantasizing and begins to let go of this form of negative imaging, then, as past memories, heavy with resentment, emerge in consciousness he or she will be able to free these memories of the poison of resentment and transform them.

Of course, attitudes are intertwined with memories. But attitudes are general, basic orientations whereas memories are individual. In Christotherapy in the healing through enlightenment process an attempt is made to get at the dominant self-destructive attitudes, beliefs and assumptions which determine specific responses of individuals to others in concrete situations. The basic theory of Christotherapy is that if the healing of a basic destructive attitude or assumption takes place then it will enable the sufferer not only to respond in a new way to interpersonal crises or difficulties as they arise but also to handle in a creative, positive way memories of past negative interpersonal conflicts as they surface in consciousness. The basic healing of a negative, self-destructive attitude potentially contains in itself the healing of a multitude of past negative memories where the presence of this attitude was dominantly operative. The healing of one basic negative attitude also prepares the seeker to deal with future interpersonal crises in a way which will not result in the creation of new negative traumatic memories which will then require healing.

As I remarked earlier in this book there are many paths leading to healing and wholeness. I also mentioned that I had attended a healing of memories session conducted by Matthew and Dennis Linn and found it very helpful. My present comments then are meant to shed light on the reasons why I place a primary emphasis on the healing of attitudes. They are not intended as an attack on the healing of memories approach. In fact, I find it helpful at times to utilize elements of the approach of the Linns when I am confronted with an individual struggling with an especially traumatic memory. Likewise, Dennis and Matthew Linn bring the healing of attitudes into their book *Healing Life's Hurts* and even offer a simplified version of ten of Ellis's irrational ideas with accompanying Scriptural verses.[47]

SECTION ONE

The Healing of Sin, Neurosis and Addiction

2

THE PROCESS

9

Reforming

Introduction to the Four Weeks

Religious and moral conversion are dynamic processes with diverse stages of a radical and ongoing nature. The same is true analogously of psychological conversion and of conversion from addiction. This means that the Christotherapist must apply and adapt basic principles and methods of Christotherapy in accord with the particular stage or stages of the conversions at which the seeker of aid is living. This approach is in harmony with the practice of Saint Ignatius who mirrors in the dynamic movement of his *Spiritual Exercises* the stages of radical and ongoing religious and moral conversion and who specifically adapts his forms of prayer and "rules for the discernment of spirits" to the diverse stages or "Weeks" of the *Spiritual Exercises.*

My aim in Section One of *The Process* is to focus on the four Weeks of the *Spiritual Exercises* and to show how the dynamic movements and key insights of these four Weeks provide a powerful vehicle for relating the mystery of Christ in its multiple dimensions to the distinct stages of the healing of sin, neurosis and addiction. My goal is also to demonstrate concretely how the dynamic movement of the *Spiritual Exercises,* the *Twelve Steps* of *Alcoholics Anonymous* and related groups, and central insights of Drs. Angyal, Assagioli and others mutually illuminate one another and confirm the validity and fruitfulness of the key principles and methods of Christotherapy.

A classical formulation of the goals of the four Weeks of the *Spiritual Exercises* is:

First Week: "To reform the deformed."
Second Week: "To conform the reformed."
Third Week: "To confirm the conformed."
Fourth Week: "To transform the confirmed."

Gaston Fessard recalls and makes creative use of this old formulation and I find it illuminating and helpful.[1] In the light of this classical formulation I name the four chapters of this section of the book: *Reforming, Conforming, Confirming* and *Transforming.* I begin my reflections in each of these chapters with some basic comments on the particular Week of the *Spiritual Exercises* under consideration and I use certain insights and dynamics of the Week as a vehicle for relating principles and methods of Christotherapy to the stage in the healing of neurosis and addiction which corresponds analogously to the Week in question.

In my initial reflections on each Week of the *Spiritual Exercises,* I focus attention on the healing of sin and growth in the life of grace since this is the underlying aim of the *Spiritual Exercises.* But I must add at once that my use of elements in the *Spiritual Exercises* is selective and adapted to the particular goals of this book. I am not attempting a commentary on the *Spiritual Exercises* nor am I directly seeking to provide advice about how an individual should make the *Spiritual Exercises.* Of course, my reflections on elements of the *Spiritual Exercises* will hopefully shed light on the meaning and value of these *Exercises* and provide indications of how individuals might direct or make the *Spiritual Exercises* in a richer way. But these latter effects are not my basic aim in this book.

Preliminary Observations

Before I introduce the First Week and relate it and key principles and methods of Christotherapy to the initial stage in the healing of neurosis and addiction, some preliminary observations are appropriate.

First, individuals subject to severe neurotic and/or addictive deformations should always undergo thorough medical examinations. Persons who are in a state of radical, active addiction to alcohol or drugs will often need hospitalization before any extensive spiritual-psychological therapy can be profitably utilized.

Second, in the case of addictions (in the strict sense) the best hope for recovery consists in participation by the addicted individuals in special programs, institutes set up specifically for dealing with addiction in a holistic manner. Such programs are widely available both in the United States and in many other countries as well. *Alcoholics Anonymous,* of course, for individuals who have received or are receiving whatever medical help they need, is one of the most effective programs which exists to aid individuals addicted to alcohol. In the case of neurotic deformation one-to-one therapy is very often a most effective instrument of healing. But such groups as *Emotions Anonymous* and *Recovery Incorporated* can often provide either an adequate therapeutic instrument for recovery or excellent supplementary aid to a person who is also engaged in a one-to-one therapy situation.

Third, the basic principles and methods of Christotherapy are applicable both in one-to-one counseling and in group therapy when all members of the group are explicitly open to using a Christ-centered spiritual-psychological program. Persons who are participating in groups such as *Alcoholics Anonymous, Emotions Anonymous, Recovery Incorporated,* and so on, and who are open to recognizing the presence of Christ in the healing process, can find great help in the use of principles and methods of Christotherapy.

Fourth, God is active through his providence and his healing and life-giving grace in the first and all subsequent stages of the processes of truly holistic psychological conversion and conversion from addiction. This activity of God is powerfully revealed in the story of the lasting conversion from addiction of Mr. William (Bill) Wilson and in the tremendous success of healing movements such as *Alcoholics Anonymous* and *Emotions Anonymous,* which in large measure owe their origin or at least inspiration to Mr. Wilson. In the *Big Book* Bill Wilson states unequivocally that he owed his healing from alcohol addiction to the direct intervention of God. Wilson recounts that "God comes to most men gradually, but His impact on me was sudden and profound."[2] In his surrendering to "the Father of Light who presides over us all" Wilson experienced, as he put it,

> a sense of victory, followed by such a peace and serenity as I had never known. There was utter confidence. I felt lifted up, as though the great clean wind of a mountain top blew through and through.[3]

Wilson went on to found with the help of others *Alcoholics Anonymous* and to work out the famous *Twelve Steps* which have been an effective instrument of healing for thousands upon thousands of addictively and neurotically troubled individuals.

There are certain striking similarities between the life and works of Saint Ignatius of Loyola and Bill Wilson. Both experienced radical eruptions of God in their lives. Both created powerful, lasting structures which would dispose others to participate in some fashion in the type of conversion which they had experienced. Saint Ignatius devised the *Spiritual Exercises* and Bill Wilson worked on the formation of the *Twelve Steps.*[4] Both programs in their initial stages require the persons truly desirous of reform in their lives to face basic negative factors in their lives, to acknowledge a sense of personal powerlessness and inability to save themselves. Both assign a central role to prayer and to God in the healing processes with which they are specifically concerned. In the *Twelve Steps,* of course, the notion of God is kept quite open so that individuals can relate to God as they personally experience him. But Wilson himself in his autobiographical statement speaks of God in clearly Christian terms as "the Father of Light who presides over us all."

First Week

The goals of the First Week of the *Spiritual Exercises* are many. The ultimate goal of the First Week, when it is viewed as a stage in the overall four Week process, is to put a person in the right disposition of mind and heart for making a proper "election," or, more generally, to aid the retreatant to respond more fully to the call to love the Lord with all one's heart, strength and understanding (Mk. 12:33). Saint Ignatius, however, in his introductory observations regarding the directing or making of the *Spiritual Exercises,* suggests that the immediate goals of the First Week of the *Exercises* are "contrition, sorrow and tears for sin."[5]

The meditations and prayers of petition contained in the First Week reveal the proximate goals of the Week in a very clear and concrete way. Saint Ignatius suggests as proper subjects for meditation during the First Week the sin of the angels, the sin of Adam and Eve, the sin of one human being who went to hell because of his or her sin, hell, death and judgment. He indicates that the prayers of petition which the retreatant offers during the First Week should be in accord with the subject matter of the meditations.[6] Thus, Ignatius suggests that the retreatant when meditating on sin should pray for "shame and confusion,"[7] "for a growing and intense sorrow for my sins,"[8] for "a deep knowledge of my sins and a feeling of abhorrence for them,"[9] for "an understanding of the disorder of my actions, that filled with horror of them, I may amend my life and put it in order,"[10] for "a knowledge of the world, that filled with horror, I may put away from me all that is worldly and vain."[11] In the meditation on hell Ignatius indicates that the retreatant should pray for "a deep sense of the pain which the lost suffer, that if because of my faults I forget the love of the eternal Lord, at least the fear of these punishments will keep me from falling into sin."[12]

Commenting on the classical description of the First Week, namely, "to reform the deformed," Gaston Fessard explains well the kind of meditations and petitions Ignatius is proposing. He observes that although the human being is created for obedience, for the praise, reverence and service of God, the first radical human choice was to declare complete autonomy and independence from God: "Created for obedience, the creature deforms itself by disobedience."[13] Then how can the deformed be reformed? Fessard emphasizes that for this reform, this conversion, to begin, sin must be unmasked and seen for what it really is. The person must understand that sin is a process of self-destruction, which culminates in the ultimate emptiness and horror of hell. Gerard Kirk has put it this way:

> In itself pure emptiness, sin represents to the sinner his innermost reality. How reach him, then, with an awareness of his plight, the first step to conversion? Let him see the development of this interior cancer; let him witness the growth of sin itself even to the disclosing of that lie which is its hidden essence. . . . If sin follows its course it leads personal liberty to the torments of hell.[14]

But the prayerful meditations through which the retreatant understands and experiences at a gut level that the fruit of sin is self-destruction and death and hell should not culminate in despair. They should bring a contrition which is rooted in trust and hope in the saving action of Jesus, the Redeemer. As Fessard eloquently expresses it,

> . . . suddenly aware of the self-destruction that is the term of his disobedience, the sinner wonders that he is still alive. The death which he now knows he has merited by his transgression has not come; he understands then that Love is upon him.[15]

The gift of freedom, which sin has deformed, will now be reformed by redemptive Love. This is why, at the end of the first meditation of the *Exercises,* Ignatius proposes that the retreatant place himself or herself before Christ the Lord on the cross, and speak with Christ exactly "as one friend speaks to another."[16]

Certainly deep sorrow, shame, confusion and tears for one's sins are important fruits of the meditations in the First Week. But the sorrow and contrition are pervaded with a sense of the healing presence of divine mercy, and of profound thanksgiving for the gift of forgiveness and interior reformation which the retreatant is experiencing. In this spirit the retreat director often suggests, for the final prayerful considerations of the First Week, either Psalm 51 or the parable of the prodigal son—both of which proclaim in powerful images the reality of divine forgiveness and grace.

Most often, the person making the retreat is already in a stage of ongoing religious and moral conversion. This means that the retreatant does not actually pass through the stages of radical conversion, but rather "re-enacts" these stages through prayerful meditations and imagination, in order to deepen his or her radical commitment, and to be more perfectly disposed to seek and find the will of God, and to love him more fully. It is the exception when a person participating in the *Spiritual Exercises* actually undergoes a radical religious and moral conversion.

One vital task of the spiritual guide is to offer encouragement and support to the retreatant who is suffering temptations, desolations and difficulties.[17] The corresponding role of the Christotherapist is to be a loving, strengthening, protective presence to the seeker of healing who is in the crucible of a neurotic or addictive hell. Just as Virgil, who symbolizes human agency in the *Divine Comedy,* is sent by Divine Love to be a companion to Dante and guide him in his healing journey through Hell,[18] so God in his providence gives the Christotherapist to the sufferer as a loving guide and protector. In groups such as *Alcoholics Anonymous* and *Emotions Anonymous* it is all the members of the group, together and individually, who offer refuge and firm protection to the sufferer who is tempted to despair or to return to the old ways.

Another of the guide's basic tasks, according to the *Spiritual Exercises,* is to present materials for the retreatant's meditations.[19] In the same way the Christotherapist is called to present certain matters for reflection to the seeker. But whereas the retreat guide invites the retreatant to meditate on sin and to see with the mind's eye "the vast fires"[20] which are the ultimate effect of sin, the Christotherapist suggests to the neurotic and the addict certain "meditations" on their neurotic or addictive ways of being, and on the "living hell" they are experiencing here and now because of these patterns of living.

One of the principal aims of the "meditations" proposed to the sinner, the neurotic and the addict is what I described earlier as "diagnostic discernment." But there is a difference in the order of the meditations which the retreat director proposes to the one making the retreat and the "meditations" which the Christotherapist suggests to the radically neurotic or addicted individual. Saint Ignatius begins by proposing meditations on sin and ends with meditations on hell. On the contrary, the Christotherapist begins by suggesting to the neurotic or addict that he or she seek to diagnose the meaning of the "living hell" in which he or she finds himself or herself. But the aim of the retreat director and of the Christotherapist who is working with a neurotic or addict is the same, namely, to facilitate the occurrence of a diagnostic discernment which hopefully will lead to decision, reform and ongoing fasting of the mind, heart and imagination.

In the third exercise of the First Week, Ignatius suggests that the sinner should pray for "a deep knowledge" and "an understanding" of sin and its disorder, so that feelings of "abhorrence" and "horror"[21] will lead to a reformed life. Similarly Dr. Andras Angyal writes about the need for a type of insight by which the neurotic grasps in a holistic way that his or her neurotic assumptions are invalid, that they are radically destructive, and that they cheat him or her of life and of real happiness.[22] Dr. David Stewart in *Thirst for Freedom* stresses this need for the active alcoholic to have a depth-insight, to grasp "the futility of his deceptive thinking"[23] and alcoholic pattern of living. With this insight comes surrender, in which the alcoholic acknowledges personal powerlessness over alcohol and begins a positive phase of living; "he now avoids drinking because *for him* there is greater good to be had in not drinking."[24] Angyal and Stewart, each from his unique perspective, are describing that gut-level insight (or diagnostic discernment) by which the sufferer grasps in a deep, transforming way the necessary connection between the hell he or she is experiencing and the self-defeating, self-destructive patterns of thinking, desiring and acting which have dominated him or her.

It is a major task of the Christotherapist to create the conditions in which the neurotic and addict can be optimally disposed for the occurrence of healing diagnostic insights and consequent enlightened decisions. The principal method which the Christotherapist employs to realize this goal—apart from existential loving—is the process of existential clarification. Through this process the Christotherapist continuously holds up before the sufferer examples taken from the latter's own daily life which help him or her to reach a gut-level understanding of the utter bankruptcy of the neurotic and/or addictive way of life and to unmask the false attitudes and assumptions which underlie his or her neurotic and/or addictive behavior.

In the case of severe neurosis—what I have called radical psychological deformation—Dr. Angyal insists that "a sweeping experience of bankruptcy must come if the person is to break out of his neurotic enclosure and take a chance on a different mode of existence which at first is unfamiliar and frightening."[25] What Angyal describes as the bankruptcy experience finds its exact counterpart in what is often called "hitting bottom," an experience which most addicts must undergo if they are to have an authentic conversion from their addiction. This experience of hitting bottom is tersely described in the remark made about one alcoholic: "He was licked and he both knew it and felt it."[26]

The bankruptcy experience of the neurotic and the hitting bottom phenomenon of the addict both have their counterpart on the strictly religious and moral level in the experience of the Psalmist in *Psalm* 51 where he speaks to God about "the bones you have crushed" (51:8). But nowhere is the need for a *spiritual* bankruptcy or hitting bottom experience more dramatically expressed than in John Donne's *Holy Sonnet 14* where the poet has the sinner pray in utter desperation:

> Batter my heart, three person'd God; for, you
> As yet but knocke, breathe, shine, and seeke to mend;
> That I may rise, and stand, o'erthrow me, and bend
> Your force to breake, blowe, burn and make me new.[27]

It is, of course, not possible for the Christotherapist to undergo the experience of spiritual bankruptcy in the place of a sinner who may be in need of this experience. If the sinner in question happens to be making the First Week of the *Spiritual Exercises* only he or she can actually have the searing "spiritual hitting bottom" experience. Likewise, it is not possible for the Christotherapist to undergo the bankruptcy experience for the neurotic or to have the "hitting bottom" experience for the addict. But through the use of prayerful existential clarification the Christotherapist seeks to aid the individual in need of a spiritual "hitting bottom" experience to be disposed properly for the occurrence of the needed diagnostic insight. Again, through the use of existential clarification the Christotherapist constantly seeks to dispose the neurotic for the occurrence of the searing insight that his or her neurotic ways are futile, hopeless, that they "just do not work."[28] Likewise, through the use of existential clarification the Christotherapist seeks to create the conditions whereby the addict can come to the shattering insight that the addictive way of living is, in fact, a way of dying, a gross form of self-destruction, a one-way street which ends in insanity or death.

It is true that the experience of "bankruptcy" and "hitting bottom" can, where an individual is isolated, lead to radical despair and suicide. But, with the help of God's grace and often with the support of a retreat director, a friend, therapist, or a therapeutic group such as *Alcoholics Anonymous* the experiences of "bankruptcy" and "hitting bottom" can lead the sufferers to humble acknowledgements of their powerlessness in the face of their sins, emotions or objects of addiction—acknowledgements which pave the way for openness to the help of a greater Power.

In the case of neurotics and addicts the aim of the process of existential clarification is not only to facilitate and hasten the occurrence of the bankruptcy and hitting bottom experiences and the healing acknowledgements of personal powerlessness which follow but also to help these sufferers to gain existential diagnostic insight into the "mythologies," the false attitudes and destructive assumptions which underlie their neurotic and addictive patterns of behavior. The neurotic and addictive sufferers need what Angyal calls "holistic insights," that is, "insights into attitudes which affect large areas of the person's life."[29] These attitudes, as Dr. Aaron Beck and others have clearly demonstrated, appear at times in the "lower voices" or "automatic thoughts and images" which occur in the background of consciousness. In this case, it is the task of the Christotherapist to help the neurotic and the addict: (1) to attend to these "lower voices," (2) to note how pathological feelings of fear, anger, depression, and resentment result from these automatic thoughts and images, and consequently (3) to begin to let go of these irrational beliefs and attitudes because they are seen to be irrational.

In certain cases the destructive assumptions of the neurotic and the addict are implicitly rather than explicitly at work. In this situation the Christotherapist must use existential clarification constantly to bring to the sufferer's attention the situations and times when he or she behaves *as if* certain irrational beliefs were true. As Angyal puts it, if the sufferer

> is confronted with a sufficient number of cases in which he has behaved *as if* he believed certain false things to be true, these "as ifs" gradually add up, and the patient reaches a point where he himself can discover the general pattern of his fantastic beliefs.[30]

The Christotherapist can also use such widely diverse data as dreams, journals, handwriting, bodily and facial expressions, illnesses, and even accidents to help in diagnosis, and to help the seeker unmask implicit beliefs, assumptions and attitudes which are inauthentic. Even secular therapists, for example, acknowledge that being accident-prone can be a symptom of psychic difficulties.

Groups such as *Alcoholics Anonymous, Overeaters Anonymous* and *Recovery Incorporated* can also be powerful instruments for existential clarification, and catalysts for diagnostic understanding in suffering persons. In the First Week of the *Spiritual Exercises,* Ignatius urges the retreatant to pray for a knowledge of the "world," so that he or she can come to loathe, detest and shrink away in horror from it. In groups like *Alcoholics Anonymous* a spontaneous, communal existential clarification and diagnosis occurs, through which the destructive ways of the "world" (as they are at work in neurosis and addiction) are unmasked, seen for what they really are, and, consequently, loathed and rejected with the help of God's grace.

In such groups as *Alcoholics Anonymous* there prevails a "no-nonsense" tough-mindedness, a rigorous type of contemporary asceticism which refuses to embrace or even tolerate the hedonistic, selfish disvalues of the "world of the anti-self" but instead relentlessly exposes and denounces these disvalues as auto-destructive and anti-human. Just as South American liberation theology diagnoses and "denounces"[31] enslaving, degrading, dehumanizing socio-economic and political structures and views, so, analogously, in groups such as *Alcoholics Anonymous* there is an instinctive communal exposing of the myths of the world of the anti-self for what they really are: mechanisms of auto-destruction. There occurs in these groups an ongoing "demolition," to use Dr. Angyal's expression, of false addictive and neurotic assumptions. Likewise, there takes place a process of "disidentification," such as that which Dr. Assagioli describes. In this latter process the sufferers discover that they can disidentify from certain harmful, destructive thoughts, images, ideas which are present in their consciousness. They become capable, as it were, of standing back from these ideas, images, of objectifying them, of subjecting them to critical, evaluative analysis, of transcending them.[32]

The expression "stinking thinking" is often used by members of *Alcoholics Anonymous* and related groups. It means any way of thinking, phantasizing, imagining and desiring which is negative and destructive, such as resentment, self-pity, envy, jealousy, pride, refusal to forgive and forget—all of which almost inevitably accompany active addiction and/or neurosis. It may seem odd and vulgar to refer to certain kinds of thinking as "stinking," but the use of strong images is an especially powerful means of existential clarification, and helps to trigger diagnostic understanding. St. Ignatius, for example, suggests to the person meditating that he or she perceive "with the sense of smell . . . the smoke, the sulphur, the filth, the corruption"[33] of hell. In Canto XI of *Hell,* Dante states that the "stench thrown up by the abyss so overpowered us that we drew back, cowering behind the wall."[34] A commentator remarks that "the stink is, of course, symbolic of the foulness of Hell and its sins."[35]

In groups like *Alcoholics Anonymous,* as member after member in the telling of their life stories vividly clarify, diagnose, denounce and reject diverse forms of "stinking thinking" and the hell which flowed from them, other members of the group likewise come in varying degrees to recognize, identify and diagnose in themselves the existence of these auto-destructive phenomena; these newly enlightened individuals then proceed to denounce these poisonous mind-sets and heart-sets, to demolish them, to disidentify from them, to fast from them in their mind, heart and imagination.

In the beginning "first week" meditations of the neurotic and the addict, there is most often an appeal to a very elemental form of love-of-self or enlightened self-interest. Through diagnostic discernment the sufferer grasps in a very vivid way that if he or she wants to be free from the terrible pain he or she is experiencing, the only rational thing to do is to give up certain cherished beliefs, strategies and behavior which are irrational.

Saint Bernard of Clairvaux worked out a model of four "degrees" of love, and described the first degree as "the love by which a man loves himself above all for his own sake."[36] This love "is planted in nature," since "who is there who hates his own flesh?"[37] This love is not evil in itself, but can become immoderate. In the initial meditations of the neurotic and the addict it is basically this natural love of self, the love which seeks to avoid pain, which is first awakened and becomes a motivation for renouncing neurotic and addictive patterns of thinking, desiring and living.

In harmony with the thinking of developmental psychologists such as Lawrence Kohlberg, the Catholic Christian tradition has always acknowledged that there are different levels of motivation, and that fear of punishment or the desire to escape pain can be a valid motive for avoiding some actions. St. Ignatius reflects this tradition when he states that the retreatant should pray for an imaginative experience of the pain felt by the damned, so that if he or she should ever forget the love of God, at least the fear of punishment will keep him or her from falling into sin. In the same tradition, Dante describes the first book of the *Divine Comedy* as "The Canticle of Pain,"[38] and explains the purpose of his symbolic journey into Hell by having Virgil remark: "That he [Dante] may experience all while yet alive I, who am dead, must lead him through the drear and darkened halls of Hell, from round to round."[39] Like Ignatius, Dante is appealing in his "Canticle of Pain," at least in part, to the first degree of love—the love of self through which a person abstains from evil to avoid pain. Another example of this motivation is found in the "Act of Contrition" which Christians pray:

> O my God, I am heartily sorry for having offended Thee because I dread the loss of heaven and the pains of hell, but most of all because I offend Thee Who are all good and worthy of all my love.

Of course, the Catholic Christian tradition acknowledges that it is only God's gift of his love flooding our hearts which sanctifies us and makes us his children in Christ, alive in the Holy Spirit. But the same tradition also recognizes the legitimacy of avoiding evil at least in part from fear of punishment and hope of reward. In a similar way counselors and psychotherapists generally hold that the realization of high-level, ongoing psychological conversion and conversion from addiction requires ever-deepening positive motivation, and commitment to the values of health and wholeness. But many of these therapists also maintain that there is some value in aversion therapy, through which, by psychological and chemical means, an addict is helped to develop an intense psychological and physical loathing for the object of his or her addiction.

In concluding these reflections on the "reforming" stage in the healing of sin, neurosis and addiction, I must add one caution. Even though the First Week of the *Spiritual Exercises* particularly involves confronting the negative, and emphasizes existential diagnosis, Ignatius incorporates a very positive dimension. He places the retreatant in the presence of Christ, the merciful and forgiving Redeemer, and asks the retreatant to behold his or her crucified Lover. He asks the retreatant to inquire from the heart, "What have I done for Christ? . . . What am I doing for Christ? . . . What ought I to do for Christ?"[40] Even in the First Week we find this positive dimension, a stress on trusting Christ. There is an existential discerning of authentic values, and the heart's feasting in the presence of those values. In the final colloquy, or prayer, of the second exercise of the First Week, Ignatius says:

> I will conclude with a colloquy, extolling the mercy of God our Lord, pouring out my thoughts to Him, and giving thanks to Him that up to this very moment He has granted me life. I will resolve with His grace to amend for the future.[41]

Similarly, in the "first week" of the healing of neurosis and addiction, even though there is an important focus on existential diagnosis with its dynamics of denouncing, demolishing, disidentifying and fasting of mind and heart, there is also the positive element of trusting in Christ the healer throughout the process. The neurotic and the addict, like the sinner of the First Week, are not alone in their struggle but are called to discern appreciatively the ever present reality of the love of Christ the healer and of the Christotherapist. From the very beginning of the turning-from stage of psychological conversion and of conversion from addiction the Christotherapist seeks through existential loving to remove a sense of worthlessness and to replace it with a sense of worth which the sufferer can delight in. Likewise, from the very beginning the Christotherapist is present as one who incarnates in his or her daily living the life-giving truths and values which the sufferer is called to discern appreciatively and embrace. This means that in the actual concrete order of healing the process of existential diagnosis is always accompanied by the prayerful process of existential appreciation. This is true of the First Week of the *Spiritual Exercises* and it is true of the "first week" stage in the healing of radical psychological and addictive deformation. Indeed, this is one of the chief lessons which the Christotherapist learns from the movement and meditations of the First Week. He or she then creatively applies these insights in the areas of the healing of radical neurosis and addiction.

It remains true, however, that there is a real legitimacy, both from the viewpoint of theory and of concrete living, for distinguishing a stage of turning-from or demolition from a stage of turning-toward or reconstruction in the process of radical healing of sin, neurosis and addiction. There is a clearly observable natural progression in the process of healing of neurosis and addiction from a confrontation with what is negative toward an embracing of what is life-giving. And it is this existential progression which justifies the division of the process of radical healing into the two stages of turning-from and turning-toward, of reforming and conforming.

10

Conforming

The word "conforming" is often used negatively today, to mean a slavish, external, unenlightened imitation of another. But when the Apostle Paul wrote that God the Father chose those whom he foreknew "to be conformed to the image of his Son" (Rm. 8:29 R.S.V.), Paul was describing not an external but an internal "conformation." He meant a conformation through which those who are called "become true images" (Rm. 8:29) of the Son, profoundly one with him in mind, heart, imagination and spirit. It is in this sense that I use "conforming" here.

Like a movement in a symphony, the Second Week of the *Spiritual Exercises* is part of a greater organic unity. But at the same time it has its own internal order, rhythm, dynamics and aims. As a stage in the overall process of the *Spiritual Exercises,* the Second Week has the goal of bringing about the right disposition of mind and heart in the retreatant, so that he or she can make a good election or, more generally, grow and deepen in the love of God. But the Second Week also encompasses within itself the specific goals of individual meditations and contemplations.

With the mention of meditations and contemplations, the question naturally surfaces: What is the difference for Ignatius between a meditation and a contemplation? David Stanley, an Ignatian scholar, explains the distinction in terms of the subject matter involved. He says that the meditation has as its focus matters of faith such as original sin, hell, Christ at work *today* in the Church battling with Satan. Contemplations, on the other hand, focus on the mysteries of the life of Jesus: the birth at Bethlehem, his baptism in the Jordan, the post-resurrection appearances to his disciples.[1] Thomas Green, another Ignatian scholar, defines the difference between meditation and contemplation in the light of the type of "mental activities" which the one praying engages in. For Green a person in meditation makes use of his or her understanding and reasoning, whereas in contemplation he or she utilizes the imagination, relives various events of Jesus' earthly life and imaginatively places himself or herself with Jesus in these events.[2] Both Stanley and Green reveal good insights in their explanations of the terms contemplation and meditation; I also agree with Stanley that there is a fluidity in the way Ignatius uses the two terms.[3]

In the classical formulation I mentioned earlier, the specific goal of the Second Week is "to conform the reformed." Gaston Fessard says that the meditations of the First Week graphically portray for the retreatant what happens when the creature, in an act of disobedience, tries to affirm itself as absolutely autonomous and independent of God. The result is a self-destructive process which ends in the emptiness of hell. Fessard describes the meditations and contemplations of the Second Week as placing before the retreatant the image of Jesus Christ, the one who as man is truly free in his exercise of perfect obedience to the Father. In contrast to the disobedience which led Adam and his children toward radical non-fulfillment and the hollow absurdity of hell, the obedience of Christ, the new Adam, brings true fulfillment and abundant life to those who accept him and obey the Father with and through him in the power of the Holy Spirit.

Through the meditations and contemplations of the Second Week, the retreatant turns again toward that one from whom he or she had once turned away in sin. Through these meditations and contemplations, the retreatant realizes that Christ was perfectly free in his perfect obedience, and that he or she will become truly free in wanting what Christ wants, in fighting what Christ fights, in embracing what Christ embraces.[4]

In the authentic prayer of contrition of the First Week, the repentant sinner has experienced the deep grace of "being turned-toward God," and has freely cooperated in "turning toward God." Yet the subjects of the First Week meditations are sin and its effects. It is only in the meditation on the Kingdom, and in the meditations and contemplations of the Second Week, that Christ becomes the focal subject matter. This is one reason I use the metaphor of turning-from to describe the main event of the First Week, and the metaphor of turning-toward for the basic dynamic of the Second Week, but most certainly there are elements of both "turnings" in both Weeks.

St. Ignatius indicates that it is appropriate to give some version of the First Week to anyone of good will.[5] But the spiritual director should only give the further considerations of the Kingdom, the Second Week and the following Weeks to people who show the possibility of real spiritual fruitfulness or, as John English puts it, "a magnanimity and a generosity of soul that may not be found in everybody."[6] Anyone then who enters the Second Week is presumed to be advancing in the upward spiral of ongoing religious and moral conversion. It follows that when I relate elements of the Kingdom and of Second Week meditations and contemplations to the second stage in the process of the healing of radical neurotic and addictive deformations I do so only in a highly adapted, modified fashion. I do not wish to imply, for example, that the Christotherapist in working with the neurotic or addict in the turning-toward stage of radical conversion makes use of the exact sequence of stages of development present in the Second Week. Rather, the Christotherapist is able to gain certain insights from the different meditations, contemplations and movements of the Second and following Weeks which he or she can then creatively apply and adapt (according to the circumstances and individual needs) to the healing of neurosis and addiction.

The Kingdom

In the *Spiritual Exercises,* the meditation entitled "the Kingdom of Christ" provides a link between the meditations of the First Week and the meditations and contemplations of the Second Week, and also a basic foundation for the Second Week. In the First Week the retreatant prayerfully asks: "What ought I to do for Christ?" In the Kingdom meditation, which sits astride the First and Second Weeks, Christ answers the retreatant's prayer with a dramatic summons:

> It is my will to conquer the whole world and all my enemies, and thus to enter into the glory of my Father. Therefore, whoever wishes to join me in this enterprise must be willing to labor with me, that by following me in suffering, he may follow me in glory.[7]

In the Kingdom meditation the retreatant is invited to *turn toward* Christ, to embrace his cause, to labor with him for the realization of his Kingdom.

The Preface of the Mass of Christ the King captures the core meaning of the Kingdom of Christ when it describes it as

> an eternal and universal kingdom:
> a kingdom of truth and life,
> a kingdom of holiness and grace,
> a kingdom of justice, love, and peace.[8]

The meditations and contemplations of the Second Week unveil in a brilliantly orchestrated sequence the concrete implications of the Kingdom meditation, and of a "Yes" from the retreatant to Christ's summons to join him in the realization of the Kingdom. As Edouard Pousset observes, there must be no romantic illusions about the realization of the Kingdom. Bringing about the Reign of Christ requires the follower of Christ to learn his battle strategies and fight with him against the forces of evil. And successfully battling with Christ requires from the disciple a radical and complete detachment from all idols and self-centeredness.[9] This total detachment is gradually realized as the retreatant goes through the great structural meditations and the contemplations of the Second Week. In the unfolding of this Week there is a dynamic, rhythmic interweaving of basic meditations and contemplations. The meditations focus on Christ *presently* at work in the world. The contemplations focus on the scriptural accounts of Jesus in his hidden and public life, to enable the retreatant to place himself or herself with Christ in his mysteries and to put on the mind and heart of Christ.

Neurosis, Addiction and the Kingdom

Christ calls each person to seek the realization of the Kingdom in his or her own unique situation and circumstances. Radical neurotic and addictive deformations may make this impossible, or impede a person's free, conscious quest of the Kingdom. Because of this, it is Christ's positive will that neurotic and addictively suffering people seek healing and wholeness, so that (with the help of grace) they can make real, or deepen, the quest for the Kingdom in their own lives. In effect, Christ says to the neurotic or addicted person: "I want you to seek healing through prayerful reliance on me and through the ministry of those human beings who are available to help you, so that my victory over evil may be more fully manifest."

At times, just as with physical illness, God does not grant the gift of total healing, despite the sincere efforts and prayers of the sufferer and the help and prayers of others. Yet, in this case God always gives the sufferer grace to be free in the depths of the spirit from *sinful* bondage to the illness, even though some physical and/or psychic suffering remains. Through patient endurance the suffering individuals are able to unite their pain to the passion of Christ for the good of God's people, and to say with the Apostle Paul: "It makes me happy to suffer for you, as I am suffering now, and in my own body to do what I can to make up all that has still to be undergone by Christ for the sake of his body, the Church" (Col. 1:24–25).

In the process of radical psychological conversion and of conversion from addiction, turning toward authentic life-giving meaning and values is crucial, in fact, more crucial than turning from what is destructive, if true radical healing is to result. Thomas Chalmers speaks of "the expulsive power of a new affection,"[10] and this felicitous phrase highlights the fact that it is the gift of a new attraction to life-enriching values which drives out the devils of negativity. John Donne gives poetic confirmation to Chalmers' insight in the final lines of *Holy Sonnet 14:*

> Take mee to you, imprison mee, for I,
> Except you enthrall mee, never shall be free,
> Nor ever chaste, except you ravish mee.[11]

Andras Angyal strongly endorses the importance of the moment of turning-toward in the healing of neurosis when he insists that therapists must foster the process of reconstruction as "deliberately and systematically"as they pursue the demolition process.[12] And Angyal, though himself in the psychoanalytic tradition, criticizes Freudian analysis for incorrectly assuming that when the unhealthy elements of personality and their origins are unmasked and worked through, then "the healthy forces will automatically assert themselves and take over."[13] Angyal stresses the need to cultivate the positive, healthy orientations of personality which are submerged in the neurosis, and acknowledges that in his own therapeutic work he devotes more than half the time to the work of reconstruction.[14]

More recently, Dr. Allen Wiesen in *Positive Therapy* sharply criticizes contemporary forms of therapy which put a primary, almost exclusive, emphasis on coming to grips with negative personality factors, traumas and memories.[15] Wiesen himself directs the energies of the sufferer toward the discovery, appreciation and cultivation of positive humanistic values, goals and opportunities.

I agree wholeheartedly with Drs. Angyal and Wiesen that the most important phase in the healing of neurosis is the positive work of reconstruction, in which the sufferer's healthy orientations toward existential truth, value, beauty, and wholeness are awakened and strengthened. Through holistic, existential loving the Christotherapist helps the sufferer to discover his or her value as a person; in this process of entering the kingdom of true selfhood the seeker becomes increasingly liberated from the tyranny of negative self-images and concepts which belong to the dark kingdom of the anti-self. Again, through existential clarification the Christotherapist tries to help the sufferer see the worth of the quest for mental health and other human values. The Christotherapist also tries to help the sufferer come to the momentous insight that Christ is *with* him or her in the battle for true selfhood, and that this battle is, in fact, an integral part of Christ's struggle to actualize the Kingdom of God on earth—the Kingdom of truth and of life, of holiness and wholeness, of love and of peace.

Colin Wilson offers some intriguing observations about addiction and its cure which place central importance on the value of turning toward what is positive in the healing of radical addiction.[16] Wilson's hypothesis is that the alcoholic drinks because he or she is seeking "peak-experience": experiences of ecstasy, joy, peace, serenity. Wilson holds that this is the same goal which motivates other addicts as well. Unfortunately, however, the addict is moving away from the possibility of peak-experiences "like a lost traveller walking away from the inn in which he hopes to spend the night."[17] Wilson details experiments in which alcoholics are given LSD or mescalin and then through the use of poetry or music or colors blending on a screen the alcoholics "are suddenly gripped and shaken by a sense of *meaning,* of just how incredibly interesting life can be for the undefeated."[18] While I am quite skeptical about Wilson's explanation of the nature of alcoholism and about the suggested use of drugs as a partial means for creating peak experiences, I do agree with Wilson that discovery of meaning, opening up to the incredibly rich world of true values, and turning toward the kingdom of life and its beauty is vital in the healing of addiction.

In *Alcoholics Anonymous* and related groups there is a turning-toward which consists in trusting in a higher Power and participating in a communal process of existential clarification and discernment in which the values of health, wholeness and sobriety are gradually discovered, appreciated and embraced. The Second Step of *Alcoholics Anonymous* reads: "We came to believe that a Power greater than ourselves could restore us to sanity." This Second Step involves breaking out of the shell of a self-deceptive sense of radical autonomy, and engaging in a self-transcending activity which confesses the need for the help of a greater Power. For some it is the *Alcoholics Anonymous* group which is the greater Power. For others the greater Power is the God of one of the world religions. For all, the particular group which they join provides the unique matrix in which sobriety is realized. By participating in the group, addicts learn from the life stories of others how defeat can be transformed into victory. Hearing recovered and recovering addicts speak glowingly and thankfully of sobriety, of emotional stability, of newfound life-interests, fledgling members come to discern and gradually verify for themselves the excellence of an addiction-free life. What Christotherapy adds to the many benefits of participation in groups such as *Alcoholics Anonymous* is a therapeutic stress on the value of explicitly trusting Christ, and on discerning and delighting in the values of the Kingdom of God which Christ proclaims.

The Healing and Life-Giving Trinity

Saint Ignatius reveals in his *Spiritual Diary*[19] that he was profoundly graced with mystical experiences of God as Trinity. Ignatius recounts that he was inspired to pray to each of the Three Divine Persons individually and also to pray to them together as the Trinity which is the One God. In the *Spiritual Exercises* Ignatius often suggests to the retreatant that he or she pray to "God our Lord" and seek to do all things to the praise of the "Divine Majesty." Ignatius generally intends these titles to refer to the Trinity of Father, Son and Holy Spirit, except where he expressly applies them to one or other of the Divine Persons.[20] In light of Ignatius' rich Trinitarian spirituality it is not surprising that in the first contemplation of the Second Week, the contemplation of the mystery of the Annunciation, Ignatius invites the retreatant to behold the Three Divine Persons in their loving decision that the Second Person should become man for the salvation of the human race. Because Ignatius himself was often inspired to pray to the Three Persons who are the One God he concludes his remarks on the first contemplation of the Second Week by suggesting to the retreatant that he or she "think over what I ought to say to the Three Divine Persons."[21]

Ignatius' emphasis on the central role of the Three Divine Persons in the salvation process, and on the value of praying to the Three Persons individually and as Trinity, is in deepest accord with the most central beliefs and practices of the Christian community. In the sacred liturgy the People of God address special prayers and hymns to each of the Three Divine Persons. This practice finds its doctrinal grounds implicitly in Holy Scripture and explicitly in such ancient professions of faith as the Nicene Creed. In this confession of belief Christians are instructed to adore and glorify the Father, the Son and the Holy Spirit. Bernard Lonergan makes it quite clear in his various talks and writings that we can only properly offer adoration and glory to *Persons:* to conscious divine subjects who in the unity of their nature understand, love and act.[22]

The Three Divine Persons are intimately at work in the religious and moral conversion processes, and in the dynamic unfolding of psychological conversion and of conversion from addiction. In accord with the free, eternal decision of the Three Who are the One God, the Father sends the Eternal Son to become man so that we human beings can be saved from our sins and delivered from all evils. As a result of the death and resurrection of Jesus Christ, the Father and the Son, in a *real*[23] but invisible way, send the Holy Spirit into our hearts so that we are able to cry out "Jesus is Lord" (1 Cor. 12:3). In being transformed into the image of the Son we are able to call God "Abba, Father" (Rm. 8:16) and to return through Jesus to the Father.

The Holy Spirit

Although it is the Father who begins the work of salvation by sending the Son, it is by the action within us of the Holy Spirit—the Gift of the Father and the Son—that we are empowered to return to the Father through the Son. The Holy Spirit is at work in us as the Gift who pours forth love into our hearts (Rm. 5:5). Through the light and power of the love poured into our hearts by the Holy Spirit we become capable of loving and delighting in ourselves as beloved children of the Father. Simultaneously we are enabled to love and affirm others as sharing in (or called to share in) the divine nature as God's most dear children (2 P. 1:4).

This gift of love also helps us in our struggle to deal with what is negative and wounded in ourselves and others. The Holy Spirit is active in the surge of inner strength which leads the neurotic and the addict to acknowledge their sense of powerlessness over their neurotic and/or addictive enslavement, and to begin to trust the Higher Power which can restore them to sanity and wholeness. The Holy Spirit works in us as the Consoler and Strengthener who helps us oust resentment, and dispel irrational rebellion, violence and selfishness.[24] The Church expresses her confidence in the healing role of the Holy Spirit when she prays to this Spirit on Pentecost:

> Wash clean the sinful soul, rain down your grace on the parched soul and heal the injured soul. Soften the hard heart, cherish and warm the ice-cold heart, and give direction to the wayward.[25]

The Holy Spirit is at work in us not only as Healer but as Giver of countless charisms and blessings. In the magnificent twelfth chapter of the First Epistle to the Corinthians, Paul lists a wide variety of gifts which the Holy Spirit gives:

> One may have the gift of preaching with wisdom given him by the Spirit; another may have the gift of preaching instruction given him by the same Spirit; and another the gift of faith given by the same Spirit; another again the gift of healing, through this one Spirit; one, the power of miracles, another, prophecy; another the gift of recognizing spirits; another the gift of tongues and another the ability to interpret them. All these are the work of one and the same Spirit, who distributes different gifts to different people just as he chooses (1 Cor. 12:8–14).

But above all, it is the role of the Holy Spirit to lead us to the Son, to bring to our minds and hearts all the things that Jesus said and did (Jn. 14:26). This Spirit unveils the values present in Jesus' earthly life,[26] helps us to appropriate these values as our own and in this way to put on the mind and heart of Christ.

Jesus Christ

The personal love, knowledge and following of Jesus Christ, inspired in us by the Holy Spirit of Christ and of the Father, is at the core of explicit Christian religious conversion, both radical and ongoing. Each Christian is called to make her or his own the words of Paul: "The life I now live in this body I live in faith in the Son of God who loved me and who sacrificed himself for my sake" (Gal. 2:20–21). The authentic Christian should be, above all, a person who is filled with a deep personal love of Jesus Christ the Savior, who now in glory beholds the Face of the Father and is "living forever to intercede for all who come to God through him" (Heb. 7:25).

In his *Foundations of Christian Faith* Karl Rahner remarks that "there must be a unique and quite personal relationship between Jesus Christ and each individual in his faith, his hope and his unique love."[27] Rahner insists that the vision of the Face of the Father which the glorified Jesus enjoys as man is not just an individual reward but that it is also a saving reality for all who are related to Christ.[28] As Pius XII stated in his encyclical *Mystici Corporis:*

> In the eternal glory of the Father, Christ sees and embraces all the members of His Church and He sees them far more clearly, embraces them far more lovingly, than does a mother the child of her bosom, far better than a man knows and loves himself.[29]

Saints like Ignatius of Loyola and Teresa of Avila received very special mystical graces in which they experienced the glorified Jesus as present to them in a very intimate way. Teresa, for example, describes a special gift in which an individual "is conscious that Jesus Christ our Lord is near," that Jesus is always "walking" with the person and is lovingly "looking at" the person.[30] Teresa says that this person is "greatly strengthened and gladdened by such good companionship."[31] This same kind of special grace is portrayed by the painter Ribalta in his famous *Christ Embracing Saint Bernard,* which hangs in the Prado museum in Madrid.

Yet, though some saints are gifted with a very special awareness of the presence to them of the loving Jesus, it is a matter of Christian faith that Jesus is present to anyone who lets him into his or her heart (Rev. 3:20) as Savior, Friend, Bridegroom. The calling of the Christotherapist, as of every Christian, is to turn toward Christ as Savior and Friend, to manifest a Spirit-inspired delight in the personal love of Jesus and to let the light of this love shine forth so that others may see it and be drawn themselves to taste the "infinite treasure of Christ" (Ep. 3:9).

Christ is also present to those who are open to him as Teacher of the Way and of the Truth which liberates and bestows abundant life. In the *Spiritual Exercises* Saint Ignatius wants the retreatant to encounter Christ not only as Friend and Lover but also as Revealer of those existential truths and values which lead to wholeness and holiness. Similarly, it is the task of the Christotherapist not only to manifest a deep personal love of Jesus Christ but also to help others personally appropriate those healing and life-giving meanings and values which Jesus incarnated in his own daily living and taught to his followers.

Christ communicates to us the truths that emancipate, and the values which enrich and transform human existence, in many different ways. Above all through his life, death and resurrection, Christ incarnates and reveals to us those existential meanings and values which constitute and promote wholeness and holiness.

A human being teaches most profoundly the truths and values which he or she most cherishes in the way that he or she lives and dies. For this reason Christ also teaches us in a very powerful way, through our encounters with Christians who communally and singly possess the mind and heart of Christ and radiate in their daily living those truths and values which he embraced, loved and lived. History bears witness that Christ has taught people the true way, and effected great conversions, simply by drawing individuals like Ignatius of Loyola to read about the lives of the saints.

Christ also communicates his liberating truths and transfiguring values through the Holy Scriptures and in sacramental encounters. Jesus' words and parables are powerful carriers of existentially transforming meanings and values. The simple expression, "love your enemies," can—in the power of the Holy Spirit—shake a person to the very foundations and effect a new creation, a new being in Christ (2 Cor. 5:17). Such parables as those of the prodigal son, and the shepherd who seeks out the lost sheep, are powerful vehicles of the Holy Spirit for unfolding those truths and values which Christ treasured in the inner sanctuary of his mind and heart.

In great symbolic actions such as washing the feet of his disciples at the Last Supper Christ teaches us how to live in a way that is truly God-like, and a complete reversal of the way the world deals with its own. James Gustafson remarks that the narrative of the foot-washing in John's Gospel depicts how God loves and serves us, and it also teaches the way that Christians ought to act toward others: "Christians ought to have an orientation toward others that issues in actions which meet the needs of men through humble loving service."[32] Using symbols like the "pearl of great price," "living water" and "light of the world," Christ teaches us about the incomprehensible riches of his own inner reality and the Kingdom of God.

In its descriptions of Christ's interpersonal encounters with others, Holy Scripture also provides us with the opportunity of a unique meeting with Christ as Teacher of the Way. By meditating on or contemplating Jesus' encounters with others, the seeker is herself or himself able to enjoy an intersubjective encounter with Christ. For example, a person who contemplates Christ as he catches Peter's eye just after Peter has denied the Lord for the third time (Lk. 22:59–62) can, with the aid of the Spirit, experience Christ looking at her or him; and this prayerful encounter can instruct the heart in ways which a great cascade of words could not.

Christ also teaches us, and empowers us to live as whole and holy Christians, through the great sacraments in which he himself is present, powerfully and transformatively at work. In *Christotherapy* I discussed the way Christ provides healing and growth through enlightenment in the diverse sacraments of the Christian Church.[33] I will not repeat myself here.

Christ also communicates life-giving meaning and values in the power of the Holy Spirit through the works of great painters, sculptors, musicians and other artists. Thomas Merton recounted that it was through the contemplation of Byzantine mosaics in the Church of Cosmas and Damian in Rome, and other Christian works of art, that he was drawn toward radical Christian conversion.[34] John Oesterreicher, in a beautiful paean to the spirituality of the greatest Western music, urges that such incomparable works as Bach's *St. Matthew Passion,* Mozart's *Requiem,* Handel's *Alleluia Chorus* only exist because of Christ. Oesterreicher even dares to refer to Christ as "the Core of Music."[35] I might add that Christ is not only the chief inspirer of perhaps the greatest music of the Western world but he is also epiphanized and encountered wherever and whenever this music is performed and inwardly assimilated, not only aesthetically but also spiritually.

In yet another way, Christ, as the Word of God through whom all things are created, communicates himself and the richness of existence in the splendors of nature. It was such an experience of Christ that led John of the Cross to sing:

My Beloved is the mountains,
The wooded valleys, lonely and sequestered,
The strange and distant islands,
The loud resounding rivers,
The loving breezes with their gentle whispers.[36]

The final role of Jesus Christ as Healer and Teacher is to lead the believing Christian to the Father, who is the ultimate Principle from whom all things come and the One to whom all things return. Jesus' prayer was centered on his beloved Father, and when he was asked to teach us to pray he told us to pray: "Our Father" (Lk. 11:2). It is Jesus' deepest mission to reveal the Father to us and to lead us to the Father in the Power of the Holy Spirit.

The Father

In John's account of the Last Supper, Jesus invites his disciples to rejoice because he is going to the Father (Jn. 14:28). To dwell in the heart of the Father, to see the unveiled Face of the Father is the crowning joy not only for Jesus in his humanity but also for all of his followers. Ignatian scholar Adolf Haas remarks that at the high point of Ignatius' mystical development and visions, it is the Person of the Father who plays the predominant role.[37] "The Father," for the mature Ignatius, "is in the Trinity somewhat like the central point of relationship, from which everything proceeds and to which everything is directed."[38]

Ignatius often cried out in the Spirit: "What a Father. . . ." [39] But who is the Father? In his lifetime Jesus told his disciples: "To have seen me is to have seen the Father" (Jn. 14:9). The supreme quality which Jesus manifested in all that he said and did during his earthly life was *love,* and it was this constant epiphany of love in the life of Jesus which led John to what is perhaps the most sublime statement about the Father in the New Testament: "God is love" (1 Jn. 4:16).

Juliana of Norwich recounts in the fifty-second chapter of her *Showings:* "And so I saw that God rejoices that he is our Father, and God rejoices that he is our Mother."[40] Juliana's emphasis on the motherhood of God is important because it offsets an anthropomorphic temptation to think that God is somehow intrinsically more male than female. Juliana's frequent reference to Jesus as "our tender Mother Jesus"[41] also frees us from the mistaken tendency to think that it is Jesus exclusively *as male* rather than *as a human being* who reveals the Father to us as the One who is Love. It is true that all forms of human love tell us something of the Love that is the First Person of the Blessed Trinity. But the biblical affirmation "God is love" moves beyond all descriptions of the First Person of the Trinity in either masculine or feminine terms.

The Christian mystics often use impersonal metaphors to describe the Trinity of Divine Persons. In one of his most exquisite poems, *Although by Night,* John of the Cross describes the Trinity as an "eternal stream" that "brims and flows," as a "fountainhead" with currents welling from its source whose waters quench the thirst of all creatures.[42] The Book of Revelation, too, in its magnificent fourth chapter, refuses to provide any anthropomorphic description of the One who sits on the throne but instead speaks of the "Throning One" as looking like "a diamond" and surrounded with flashes of lightning and flaming lamps (Rv. 4:1–6). Most certainly, our richest understanding of the First Person of the Trinity, who is Love, comes to us through human images of Love—perhaps especially the bridal imagery of Holy Scripture and of the mystics. But the use of impersonal images of water, light, fire and diamonds to describe the "Throning One," who is Love, helps us to realize that the Love who is our Father-Mother God surpasses all the images of perfect Love which the human heart can possibly devise, manifest or dream of.

> To the One who is sitting on the throne and to the Lamb, be all praise, honour, glory and power, for ever and ever (Rv. 5:13–14).

The Incarnation and Hidden Life

It is through knowing, loving and following Jesus Christ that every Christian is able to participate with Christ in his victorious conquest over the forces of evil and in his realization of the Kingdom of God. Saint Ignatius, at the beginning of the Second Week, proposes to the retreatant contemplations of the holy mysteries of the Annunciation, the Nativity, the Presentation of Jesus in the Temple, the Flight into Egypt and the Finding of the Child Jesus in the Temple. The basic petitionary prayer which Ignatius suggests to the retreatant for all of these contemplations is to "ask for an intimate knowledge of our Lord, who has become man for me, that I may love Him more and follow Him more closely."[43]

For Ignatius it is vital that the retreatant avoid grandiose, romantic misinterpretations of what it truly means to follow Christ the King, and learn instead the true mind and heart and way-of-being of the Lord, toward whom the retreatant turns in a commitment of total dedication and radical following. The contemplations of the Incarnation and other mysteries of the "hidden life" reveal Jesus as the one who, though rich as the Eternal Word, became poor for our sake (2 Cor. 8:9–10). He was born of humble parents in simple circumstances; he was subject to circumcision and all the other rites and customs of the time; he submitted himself in loving obedience and humble service to his parents and to his heavenly Father; he lived by far the greatest part of his life in obscurity in an area of the country viewed with contempt by the powerful and educated people of his time. In the mysteries of his birth and hidden life Jesus revealed the values which he cherished and which his followers are likewise called to embrace and exemplify in their lives: meekness and humbleness of heart, simplicity, quiet waiting for the call of God, listening to God wherever and whenever he speaks, total obedience, a love unswerving in its fidelity, rejoicing in the gifts of each day as they unfold.

The neurotic and the addict are able to turn confidently for help to such groups as *Alcoholics Anonymous* and *Emotions Anonymous* because in these groups they are met with compassion, understanding, and unconditional acceptance; at the same time they find in these groups a source of great strength and support. In a similar way the neurotic and the addict can find in Jesus of Bethlehem and Nazareth a source of great compassion and unconditional acceptance because Jesus experienced the weakness of human flesh in himself—except for sin (Heb. 4:15)—and because from the very beginning of his life he associated with the weak, the despised, and overlooked of the world. At the same time, the neurotic and the addict can find in Jesus a tower of strength, the greater Power who can restore them to wholeness and the joy of living. For Jesus, in his weakness and foolishness, is the very Power and Wisdom of God made flesh. "God's foolishness is wiser than human wisdom and God's weakness is stronger than human strength" (1 Cor. 1:25).

The Two Standards

In the meditation on the Kingdom, which stands at the threshold of the Second Week, Saint Ignatius invites the retreatant to turn toward Christ the King and to accept his summons to join in working for the realization of the Kingdom. In the contemplations of the Incarnation and of the Hidden Life the mystery of who Jesus really is and the existential truths and values which he incarnates and calls others to embrace are first revealed to the retreatant. In the meditation entitled the *Two Standards* Saint Ignatius presents the retreatant with a stark contrast between Satan and Christ (as they are at work in the world) and the strategies the two chiefs use to bring about their respective, antithetical goals. David Fleming correctly observes that the most important section of this meditation is the second part, which centers on Christ and his proposed means for achieving victory.[44] By focusing on Satan and his battle plans to start with, Ignatius accentuates and heightens by contrast the appeal and excellence of Christ and his methods. Even in the Second Week there is still a certain emphasis on turning from evil, through meditation on Satan and his wiles; but the chief focus in the meditation of the *Two Standards* and in remaining contemplations and meditations of the Second Week is on radical turning toward Christ.

The graphic descriptions Saint Ignatius gives of Satan and Christ are masterfully designed to dispose the retreatant for what I call existential diagnostic understanding and appreciative, discerning understanding. Satan is portrayed as ugly, "his appearance inspiring horror and terror";[45] he resides in Babylon, the city which symbolizes chaos and awful destruction; Satan is "seated on a great throne of fire and smoke."[46] Christ is described as strikingly handsome. "His appearance beautiful and attractive,"[47] he is standing on a plain near Jerusalem, the ideal city of peace where God dwells. Unlike Satan, who is seated on a throne of fire, enveloped in stinging, blinding smoke, Christ is standing in a lowly place. In standing, Christ radiates strength; yet, in standing in a lowly place he appears as approachable, as "meek and humble of heart" (Mt. 11:29). Ignatius' descriptions of Satan and of Christ are intended to help the retreatant understand existentially that to be in league with Satan is to be trapped in an alliance with the forces of evil and self-destruction, whereas to be in Christ's company is to be joined with the source of life and authentic self-realization.

In the first prayer of petition for the meditation on the *Two Standards,* Ignatius advises the retreatant to "ask for a knowledge of the deceits of the rebel chief and help to guard . . . against them; and also to ask for a knowledge of the true Commander, and the grace to imitate Him."[48] Ignatius then lays out for the retreatant the strategy of Satan—the great deceiver—which is to lay snares for human beings, to chain them with riches and the empty honors of the world, and by this to lead them into pride and all the other vices. In suggesting that Satan and his demons first tempt the unwary to want riches, Ignatius may be inspired by the Scriptural warning that "the love of money is the root of all evils" (1 Tm. 6:10). His reflections that a person who has riches tends to be honored and that basking in empty honors leads to pride and other vices are inspired by Scripture and are also easily verified in everyday experience.

In contrast to the strategy of Satan, Ignatius suggests that Christ's method is to attract those who would follow him "to the highest spiritual poverty" and sometimes to material poverty as well. Likewise, Christ tries to give those who are truly poor a willingness to accept "and even to desire the insults and contempt of the world"[49] so that they can become truly humble. This is no exhortation to masochism; it is the realization that, just as worldly acclaim and honors tend to beget pride and other vices, so the experience of "insults, hardships, persecutions . . . for Christ's sake" (2 Cor. 12:10) insulates the human spirit from pride, and brings to birth that humility of heart in which true strength and dignity reside.

There have been recurrent attempts among Christians and members of other religious traditions to work out lists of self-destructive thoughts, images, and behaviors, and of their positive, life-enhancing opposites. The apostle Paul, in his magnificent "hymn" to charity in the thirteenth chapter of his First Letter to the Corinthians, uses charity as the measuring rod in listing attitudes and behaviors which are intrinsically self-destructive and others which are constructive and life-producing. On the negative side Paul lists jealousy, boastfulness, conceit, rudeness, selfishness, resentfulness, taking offense, delighting in other people's sins. On the positive side he says the true fruits of charity are kindness, delight in the truth, patience, readiness "to excuse, to trust, to hope, and to endure whatever comes" (1 Cor. 13:4–7).

In the epistle to the Galatians, again writing in the context of Christian love, Paul contrasts attitudes and behaviors which destroy the loving unity of the Christian community with those which promote life in the Spirit and growth in the "works of love" (Ga. 5:14). On the side of self-indulgence, which is opposed to love and its works, Paul lists: snapping at one another, jealousy, bad temper, quarrels, envy, disagreements, indecency, drunkenness, sexual irresponsibility, factions, conceit, provocation. To these destructive ways of thinking, desiring and acting, Paul opposes those attitudes and behaviors which the Holy Spirit inspires: "love, joy, peace, patience, kindness, goodness, truthfulness, gentleness and self-control" (Ga. 5:22–23).

Like Jesus, Paul put great emphasis on the need for individuals to pay careful attention to their thoughts and desires. As I observed earlier, in his Second Letter to the Corinthians, Paul stresses the urgency of combatting destructive thoughts, of taking such thoughts prisoner and of bringing them into obedience to Jesus Christ (2 Cor. 10:3–6). On the positive side, the author of Colossians tells his readers to let their "thoughts be on heavenly things" where "Christ is, sitting at God's right hand" (Col. 3:1–2). There is also Paul's prayer for the Philippians that the peace of God will guard their hearts and thoughts; he closes that epistle with the beautiful exhortation:

> Finally, brothers, fill your minds with everything that is true, everything that is noble, everything that is good and pure, everything that we love and honour, and everything that can be thought virtuous or worthy of praise (Ph. 4:8–9).

Christian ascetics and spiritual masters from the apostolic period on followed the example of Paul in stressing the need to pay attention to one's thoughts and desires, to discriminate between death-bearing and life-creating ideas, images, and passions—to let go of the first and cherish the second.

An ancient treatise attributed to Saint Isaiah the Solitary is called *On Guarding the Intellect.*[50] Saint Isaiah urges his readers to guard their hearts, to seek "an exact knowledge about the nature of thoughts," to "recognize . . . evil thoughts for what they are,"[51] to "uproot these thoughts by means of spiritual knowledge"[52] and to see to it, with the help of prayer, that one's "thought is full of devotion and love of God."[53] Here we have a clear example of the holy practices of fasting and feasting of the mind and heart.

Evagrius Ponticus in his *Praktikos* wrote of eight kinds of "evil thoughts."[54] These evil or "passionate thoughts"[55] are as follows: gluttony, impurity, avarice, sadness, anger, acedia (sloth), vainglory and pride. Evagrius, and John Cassian[56] after him, offer graphic descriptions of each of these evil thoughts and their self-destructiveness. Evagrius also singles out, though not systematically, some positive attitudes and virtues which stand in opposition to these evil thoughts and ought to be cultivated in their place. For example, Evagrius suggests that it is proper to drive out thoughts of vainglory with humble thoughts.[57] In this way a person may realize a state of graced enlightenment, in which the vices are banished and virtue alone is loved. As Evagrius puts it: "Both the virtues and the vices make the mind blind. The one so that it may not see the vices; the other, in turn, so that it might not see the virtues."[58] Evagrius' list of eight evil thoughts is the forerunner of what we have come to know as the "seven capital sins." The difference is that sadness and vainglory are omitted from the "capital" sins while envy is added.[59]

Evagrius is a master in the art of existential clarification that disposes the person seeking healing and growth for diagnostic and appreciative understanding. For example, Evagrius shows how anger can become a constant irritant to a person, how it can overwhelm the soul at times of prayer, how it can become transformed into indignation which "stirs up alarming experiences by night" and can lead to bodily weakness and even at times to severe forms of illusion.[60]

But if Evagrius is a master of existential clarification that leads to diagnostic understanding and a consequent fasting of the mind and heart, he is equally brilliant at the form of existential clarification which is a catalyst for the appreciative understanding and feasting of the spirit. He suggests that holy readings, praying appropriate psalms and singing hymns[61] "invite the spirit to the constant memory of virtue."[62] For Evagrius Ponticus the person who "prays perfectly" is the one "who brings forth all the best of thoughts for God."[63] This is an echo of Paul's invitation to the Philippians to fill their minds with all that is good, worthwhile, and a rich expression of the feasting of the spirit.

In the tradition of Evagrius Ponticus, John Cassian and others, Dante's *Purgatory* contrasts the seven capital sins in their self-destructiveness with the seven virtues which the poet judges to be the opposites of the deadly sins. To the sin of pride Dante opposes the virtue of humility; to envy, charity; to wrath, meekness; to sloth, zeal; to avarice, poverty; to gluttony, abstinence; to lust, chastity. Dante tries to dispose his readers for the grace of diagnostic and appreciative understanding by contrasting the purgatorial sufferings of individuals who had sinned through pride and the other major vices with the interior riches of others who were exemplary in the virtues opposed to the deadly sins.

For those who are undergoing purgatorial cleansing, the particular form of punishment always fits the sin which is being cleansed. For example, the proud must crawl around in agonizing pain with their heads bowed to the dust "under the crushing weight of enormous slabs of rock."[64] The envious, who in this life "offended with their eyes, envying all the good they saw of others,"[65] have their eyes wired shut; and so it goes.

On the other hand, for the edification of the sinners who are being purified, Dante gives examples from the lives of individuals who practiced the virtues which the former sinned against. Usually he presents three instances of people who exemplified the virtue in question, and the first is always taken from the life of the Virgin Mary, the perfect Christian disciple. For instance, in opposition to prideful actions, Dante depicts Mary's humility at the moment of the Annunciation; and, opposed to the self-centeredness of the envious, Dante portrays Mary's concern for others at the feast of Cana, where the Virgin tells her Son that the wine is running out. Dante's aim is always to help the reader grasp vividly the self-destructiveness of the major vices, and experience the attractiveness and intrinsic excellence of the virtues.

It is enlightening to compare Dante's catalog of vices and their opposing virtues with Oscar Ichazo's list of what he calls the nine passions of the ego and the virtues which are their opposites.[66] Ichazo is the founder of the Arica Institute; he developed his list of nine passions and virtues in the light of his study of ancient, for the most part non-Christian, traditions, especially the Sufi school.[67] Ichazo's nine basic passions of the ego include six of what Christian tradition calls the seven capital sins. His table of passions omits lust but adds fear, deceit and excess. Like Dante, Ichazo opposes humility to pride. To gluttony, however, Ichazo opposes sobriety; to avarice, detachment; to anger, serenity; to envy, equanimity; to laziness, action. Finally, to the passions of fear, deceit and excess Ichazo opposes respectively the virtues of courage, truthfulness and innocence.

In Ichazo's view each person has a predominant passion which becomes a source of suffering for him or her. If, for example, deceit is the dominant passion, then the person "wants to be known for his accomplishments, positions of influence,"[68] and "finds it difficult to admit anything that might mar his public image, so he is often forced into deceit to protect his ego."[69] For healing to occur, the suffering person needs to recognize that the predominant passion, with its peculiar traps and fixations, is "a source of unhappiness, leading nowhere."[70] This corresponds to what I call diagnostic understanding. For the discovery of the true self to take place, in Ichazo's approach persons are "led by special exercises to experience the . . . virtues"[71] opposed to their predominant passions. For example, where deceit is the predominant passion, the appreciation of truthfulness will help the person realize his or her true self, and grasp that it is not necessary "to use deceit to maintain an outward image of importance."[72] This part of Ichazo's approach corresponds to what I call appreciative understanding.

Ichazo's system and philosophy of the human person are complex, and differ in many important ways from my own, but I bring his system into the discussion to show that the attempt to describe fundamental psychospiritual orientations in terms of their negative and positive polarities is transcultural and recurrent. It also shows how diagnostic and appreciative discernment are at work in an ancient (at least in inspiration), basically non-Christian framework.

Philosopher-anthropologist Gilbert Durand, in his lengthy study of the dynamics of the human imaginative process, proposes that one of the basic spontaneous functions of the imagination is to deal with threatening or overly dominant images by introducing polar opposite images into consciousness. For example, if images of inner worthlessness and inadequacy begin to dominate consciousness, then, "confronted with the feeling that inner uniqueness is collapsing, the imaginative system rushes to right the wrong by projecting opposite images which reassert goodness, individuality, and basic congruency with the world."[73] If a person is threatened from outside by dominant images which cause anxiety and fear, then the imagination spontaneously introduces within the person's psyche images which inspire a sense of confidence and security. This balancing operation of the imagina-

Temperaments of Hippocrates	Evil Thoughts of Evagrius Ponticus	Capital Sins	Virtues of Dante	Passions/Virtues of Oscar Ichazo	
Choleric	Anger	Anger	Meekness	Anger	Serenity
Melancholic	Sadness				
Phlegmatic	Acedia (sloth)	Sloth	Zeal	Laziness	Action
Sanguine					
	Avarice	Avarice	Poverty	Avarice	Detachment
	Gluttony	Gluttony	Abstinence	Gluttony	Sobriety
	Impurity	Lust	Chastity		
	Pride	Pride	Humility	Pride	Humility
	Vainglory				
		Envy	Charity	Envy	Equanimity
				Deceit	Truthfulness
				Fear	Courage
				Excess	Innocence

tion "may occur subconsciously, unconsciously or deliberately, depending on the level of the individual's reflected awareness of imagination and its operations."[74]

If Durand's view on the innate balancing function of imaginative activity is correct, then the attempts of Paul, Evagrius Ponticus, Dante, Oscar Ichazo and others to develop lists of destructive and correlative constructive forms of thinking, imagining, willing and acting are in harmony with (and perhaps partially rooted in and built upon) the spontaneous dynamics of imagination itself. This would mean too that the Ignatian meditation on the *Two Standards* with its vivid contrast between Satan and Christ and their aims and strategies, in fact enlists not only the forces of intelligence and will but also of primal imagination in the battle to bring the retreatant to Christ and his positive, life-giving values. Durand's study also substantiates the validity and fruitfulness of the fasting and feasting of imagination, mind and heart. For in Durand's view it is both possible and desirable to use the imagination in a reflective, conscious manner; and this occurs in the prayerful mind-fasting and spirit-feasting processes.

It is not difficult to see how the dynamics of the meditation on the *Two Standards* can be related to the healing of neurosis and addiction. In his *Decision Therapy* Dr. Harold Greenwald suggests that "all systems of decision-making [including those of the neurotic and the addict] deal in terms of what the payoffs are. How does this one compare with the other one?"[75] Comparison is at the core of the *Two Standards* meditation. For the neurotic and the addict in the process of radical conversion, it is best to transpose the meditation on the *Two Standards* into a meditation on the Standard of Sickness versus Health, the Standard of Negative Disintegration versus the Standard of Wholeness.

Key questions which face the neurotic and the addict are: What are the payoffs or advantages for staying sick? What are the payoffs or advantages for getting well? It may seem odd to think that there are any advantages to remaining sick. But for some people there is an apparent benefit in "wallowing in self-pity," in "nourishing a resentment," in "hating with a passion." In my transposition of the *Two Standards* meditation, the neurotic and addict are invited to compare and contrast the advantages and payoffs for clinging to an angry, fearful, sad, guilt-filled, shame-filled, envious, lustful, self-indulgent, avaricious, slothful, prideful, excessive or deceitful way of imagining, desiring, thinking, acting with the payoffs and advantages of turning toward a serene, courageous, joyful, guilt-free, self-accepting, caring, chaste, self-controlled, free, zealous, humble, innocent, honest way of living and being-in-the-world.

Obviously, because of their existential ignorance, their slavery to compulsion, their non-awareness, and their lack of freedom, neurotics and addicts at this stage of radical conversion should not focus so much on the objective immorality of their self-destructive ways of thinking, imagining, desiring and acting but rather on the suffering which inevitably flows from them. Focusing on the connection between their suffering and the attitudes and behavior which generate this suffering hopefully will aid the neurotic and the addict to deepen their diagnostic insights from the First Week of their radical conversion. This focus will help them to intensify their turning from the standards and strategies of the Kingdom of Illness and Negative Disintegration.

But above all, the key focus of the neurotic and the addict in their meditation on the *Two Standards* should be on the Standard of Health and Wholeness, especially the Standard of Health and Wholeness in Christ. At this point the Christotherapist should try in every way possible to help the neurotic and the addict to fix their attention on the excellence, the beauty, the worth, the attractiveness, the joy-producing quality of the values of the Kingdom of Wholeness—of the Standard of Christ.

Three Classes of Persons

The great meditations of the Second Week move toward the moment of Election, Decision, Choice. Fessard emphasizes that the meditations of the Second Week become progressively more specific and concrete as the retreatant moves from the inspiring encounter with Christ in the grand *Kingdom* meditation, to the demanding reflections on the contradictory goals and strategies of Satan and Christ in the *Two Standards* and then to the highly personal, demanding meditation on the *Three Classes of Persons.*[76] A principal aim of this meditation is to bring the retreatant to an inner state of radical detachment, so that he or she can make a proper, grace-inspired, God-initiated, God-consummated election.

In the meditation on *Three Classes of Persons* Saint Ignatius proposes a parable in which three different types of individuals have acquired a large amount of money, "not entirely as they should," and wish to "find peace in God" and rid "themselves of the burden arising from the attachment to the sum acquired."[77] Individuals of the first class "would like to rid themselves of the attachment they have to the sum acquired . . . but the hour of death comes and they have not made use of any means"[78] to realize true detachment. Men and women of the second class "want to rid themselves of the attachment, but they wish to do so in such a way that they retain what they have acquired." In effect these persons want God "to come to what they desire"[79] and so they fail to take the means necessary to reach true detachment. Those in the third class want to rid themselves of the attachment, but to do it in such a fashion that "they desire neither to retain nor to relinquish the sum acquired" but "seek only to will and not will as God our Lord inspires them."[80]

What we are dealing with in the meditation on the *Three Classes of Persons* is a purification and clarification of desires and attitudes: what Bertrand de Margerie refers to as a "therapeutic of human desires."[81] The first class undergoes no change in desire or attitude. The second class temporizes and wants to have it both ways. The third class alone is radically transformed in desire and attitude, and therefore truly detached and liberated. Although Ignatius speaks of attachment to a sum of money, the money really symbolizes inordinate attachment to any person, place, thing or object—internal or external.

The basic dynamics of the meditation on *Three Classes of Persons* can be used by the "normally abnormal" person as well as the seriously addicted or neurotic person and applied to past or present situations in his or her life. In reflecting on my own struggle with addiction to alcohol, I can see how, at different phases, I belonged to the first, then the second and finally—and hopefully lastingly—to the third class of persons.

For a long time, though I was (at least dimly) aware of a problem, I did nothing much about it. Then, as I became increasingly aware of my drinking problem and the pain it was causing me and others, I tried to improve other areas of my life in the hope that I could continue drinking moderately, while experiencing peace with myself, others and God. In this phase I gave up smoking—thank God—as a kind of barter with God, in the hope that somehow or other he would allow me to keep drinking—moderately, of course! Finally, under increasing internal and external pressures, I went to Guest House, stopped drinking and was able to find the necessary degree of physical, mental, psychic and spiritual detachment from the consumption of alcoholic beverages.

In my case, the interior detachment which characterizes Ignatius' third class of persons only came—and continued to develop—after I stopped drinking alcohol. But in his *Three Classes* meditation Ignatius is trying to help a basically healthy, converted person find interior detachment from subtle idolatrous tendencies, so that he or she will best be able to choose between two morally good alternatives, e.g., the alternative of marriage or entering a religious order. However, the attitude of basic detachment I needed *followed* my decision to stop drinking alcohol: the election I had to make was not between two morally good alternatives but between something which was clearly destructive and an alternative which, though painful, was life-giving and life-enhancing. It is clearly very important for the Christotherapist or the person who is adapting the dynamics of the *Three Classes* meditation to a neurotic or addictive problem to be very clear about the differences between the meditation as it functions in the *Spiritual Exercises* and as it is analogously applied outside retreat.

The Public Life of Jesus

The retreatant, after meditating on the *Two Standards* and the *Three Classes of Persons,* turns to contemplation of Jesus Christ as he reveals himself, his Standard, his commitment to the Father and his Kingdom in the events and teachings of his public life. Saint Ignatius suggests that the retreatant begin with a contemplation of Jesus' departure from Nazareth, his journey to the Jordan and his baptism by John. Later there are important contemplations on the theme of Jesus' temptations in the desert, the calling of the apostles, the Sermon on the Mount, the calming of the storm at sea, his preaching in the temple, the raising of Lazarus and the entry into Jerusalem on Palm Sunday.[82]

The contemplations of the Public Life are intended to bring the retreatant closer to making an election if an election is the focus of the retreat. The contemplations make concrete the principles articulated in the meditations on the *Kingdom,* the *Two Standards* and the *Three Classes of Persons.* Their aim is to help the retreatant grow more deeply in the realization of the Christ-self, come to an ever richer, more intimate knowledge and love of Jesus Christ, and become ever more fully conformed to Christ by putting on his mind and heart. By contemplating Christ in the mysteries of his public life the retreatant is called to imitate Christ by assimilating (with the aid of the Holy Spirit) Christ's "values, his totally unselfish and loving service of others, his passionate quest for his Father's will, his confidence in his Father, his hatred of hypocrisy and sin, his repeated recourse to prayer, his compassion for the weak."[83]

In the mysteries of his public life, Jesus is revealed as a whole and holy individual and this is the man whom the retreatant is called to imitate and to be conformed to.

Creatively applying some of Erik Erikson's categories[84] to Jesus in his public life, we see Jesus to be trusting rather than mistrustful in relationship to his Father, to other human beings and to the diverse summons of life as they unfold; yet, at the same time Jesus is not a naive optimist who is blind to the follies, the hypocrisy, the betrayals of others. Jesus is a realist in the best sense of the word; he trusts with unshaken confidence in the Father; he has a basic drive toward life and a hope for others; but Jesus has an intuitive knowledge which pierces to the very hearts of those whom he encounters (Jn. 6:64).

Jesus also manifests self-control and the ability to make firm decisions and adhere to them (Lk. 9:51); there is no sign in Jesus of self-doubt or indecisiveness. He constantly acknowledges the primacy of the Father and is obedient to the guidance of the Holy Spirit (Jn. 14:28; Lk. 4:1); yet, Jesus' acknowledgement of the Father's centrality in his life does not diminish his sense of individual uniqueness, responsibility and autonomy: "My Father goes on working, and so do I" (Jn. 5:17). Jesus speaks and acts with authority and he summons others to follow him unconditionally.

Jesus also constantly manifests initiative and creativity in his dealings with others; he has a purpose and he resolutely pursues it (Jn. 4:34). Nowhere does he reveal any sense of personal guilt or sinfulness; yet, he is not afraid or ashamed to undergo the baptism of John. Jesus' serenity of spirit flows from his inner awareness of his own spirit of goodness and innocence and the realization that the light within him will shine forth for those who have eyes to see it and hearts to receive it.

Jesus is also very industrious; he works until he is weary (Jn. 4:6) but he delights in the fruitfulness of his labors (Mt. 11:25). He knows, moreover, when it is time for him to go off alone to refresh himself (Mt. 14:23).

Although Jesus acknowledges the primacy of the Father he does not show the slightest trace of an inferiority complex or any lack of a sense of basic self-worth and value. He displays consummate competence in the ways he deals with others and he can quickly adapt to any kind of situation. Jesus does not reveal himself as a person lacking a sense of identity. He may ask others what they think of him, but this is not in order to learn about himself and his identity; it is to educate them (Mt. 16:13–18). Jesus shows that he possesses an utterly unique sense of being the Son of the Father, the beloved "Abba" (Mk. 14:36; Mt. 11:27) and this sense of sonship inspires in him a spirit of total fidelity to the Father. Jesus' sense of being the unique beloved of the Father enables him to love others in a way which is totally free from any neurotic search for self-fulfillment through the exploitation of others.

Certainly, Jesus is truly pained when he experiences rejection. It would be abnormal and a sign of insensitivity if he did not experience sorrow in the face of betrayal or abandonment. Yet there is no sign in the life of Jesus of neurotic isolation or escapist tendencies in the face of conflict. He values solitude and deliberately seeks it at times; but it is not the solitude of the escapist.

Constantly Jesus reveals himself as a person capable of extraordinary love, affection, and tenderness. Jesus is able to "relate" to all types of people; he is at ease with children and with the old and the sick. At the same time he delights in the companionship of youth and of men and women of his own age; Jesus is equally at home with women and with men, numbering both men and women among his most intimate friends.

Jesus' great capacity for love manifests itself in a powerful generativity, an ongoing service of others, a self-sacrificing care and concern which is proof that in this man "the kindness and love of God our saviour" (Tt. 3:4) have appeared. His indefatigable work for the good of others is the very antithesis of that stagnation which casts a pall over the lives of so many individuals. Jesus' daily life is maximally productive and yet it is a productivity which flows from profound inner security, strength, peace, self-assurance and not from any compulsion to fulfill unmet needs. Finally, when Jesus is confronted with the final reality of suffering and death, he manifests a spirit of acceptance which is the fruit of the deepest form of personality integration and wisdom (Mt. 16:21–23).

Jesus' Public Life and the Healing of Neurosis and Addiction

In submitting to the baptism of John, Jesus, though he is sinless and does not need any rite of purification, draws as close as he can to his sinful brothers and sisters so that the weakest and most despised among them can understand that in him they have a high priest who "can sympathize with those who are ignorant or uncertain because he too lives in the limitations of weakness" (Heb. 5:1–2). In a certain sense Jesus' humble descent into the waters of the Jordan provides a model for the neurotic and the addict who are initially called to humble themselves by acknowledging their powerlessness over their emotions and/or the object of their addiction. And just as the Father immediately sent his Spirit upon his son after he emerged from the Jordan and declared: "This is my son, my Beloved; my favor rests on him" (Mt. 3:17), so, after the neurotic and the addict acknowledge their weakness and powerlessness the Father reveals himself to them as the Greater Power that can restore them to sanity and wholeness; he is the One upon whom they can rely.

There is also a parallel between the battle which Jesus wages with Satan as he is tempted in the desert for forty days (Lk. 4:1–13) and the struggle of the neurotic and the addict as they attempt, with the help of the therapist or therapeutic group, to unmask and let go of the destructive strategies, standards and goals of the Kingdom of Sickness, and to discover and embrace the integrative, life-giving methods, attitudes and goals of the Kingdom of Health and Wholeness.

In reflecting on Jesus' summons to his disciples to leave all things and follow him, the neurotic and the addict can hear Jesus calling them to take courage and, little by little, to leave behind the attitudes and objects that enslave them; they hear a call to follow him by embracing his attitudes of trust, hope, purpose, and love that lead into the Promised Land of psychological and spiritual freedom and abundance of life.

In a very special way the neurotic and the addict, reflecting on Jesus' Sermon on the Mount, can begin to catch a glimpse of the rich psycho-spiritual happiness to which they are called and the "strategies for beatitude" which they can employ in moving toward citizenship in the Kingdom of Health and Wholeness in Christ. R. K. Harrison writes that

> [Jesus'] precepts in the Sermon on the Mount and elsewhere dealing with human motives and the deep working of the mind show by implication that he was acutely aware of the place emotional conflict, resentment, fear, anxiety, hatred, and the like had in the genesis of disease. So much is this the case that it has been said in recent years that the most assured finds of modern psychiatry constitute but one small part of the distilled wisdom contained in the Sermon on the Mount.[85]

In citing Harrison I don't mean to denigrate the discoveries of psychology and psychotherapy and their invaluable contribution to the field of mental health. But I do want to indicate that in the words and deeds of Jesus, in the parables and the beatitudes, there can be found a powerful therapeutic instrument which the Christotherapist can and should use to bring healing to the psychically and addictively wounded individual.

Three Kinds of Humility

The final reflection of the Second Week before consideration of the election is concerned with what Saint Ignatius called the *Three Kinds of Humility.* Briefly put, an individual possesses the first degree of humility who would prefer to die rather than to turn away from God in a radical, fundamental way.[86] A person is living the second kind of humility when he or she can say from the heart, "Not for all creation, nor to save my life, would I consent to commit a venial sin."[87] And a person possesses the third kind of humility when—all other things being equal—he or she would "choose poverty with Christ poor, rather than riches; insults with Christ loaded with them, rather than honors" and would desire "to be accounted as worthless and a fool for Christ, rather than to be esteemed as wise and prudent in this world."[88]

The motive of the third degree of humility is not a masochistic desire to suffer and be abused, but rather to be closely identified with Christ: "So Christ was treated before me."[89] The third degree of humility is the expression of the kind of love we see in Damien, the leper priest; in Saint Peter Claver, cleansing the wounds of the slaves; in the lives of countless women and men who have chosen to live in obscurity working with the imprisoned and the outcasts of society and who share in large measure in experiencing the contempt which "the world" heaps on the poor, the exploited, the deformed, the miserable. This third kind of humility is an expression of a "foolish" love which is "wiser" than any other form of loving; it is an expression of the most radical detachment, and at the same time of an attachment to God, to Christ, and to Christ in his least sisters and brothers, which is as "strong as Death" (Sg. 8:6) and which "no flood can quench, no torrents drown" (Sg. 8:7).

Saint Ignatius proposes for the retreatant prayerful reflections on the *Three Kinds of Humility* so that he or she can, with the help of God's grace, realize that spirit of detachment which will make an authentic election easier.

Clearly, in the healing of neurosis and of addiction the *Three Kinds of Humility* must be adapted a great deal. Basically, the neurotic and the addict in the throes of radical psychological conversion and/or conversion from addiction experience a growing desire to be free at all costs from the enslavement they experience, and to embrace the way of life, no matter how much pain it involves. The image of Christ poor, Christ humiliated, Christ despised can perhaps make it a bit easier to accept the deprivation, the "humiliation," the sufferings of withdrawal that accompany radical psychological conversion and conversion from addiction.

The Election, Decisions and Radical Conversions

For the retreatant engaged in the *Spiritual Exercises* with a view to making an election, in the Second Week Ignatius provides advice regarding the proper method, objects and "times" of an authentic election, and gives directions on how to bring about changes for the good in a state of life already chosen.[90] It is, of course, by analogy that I relate the election of the *Spiritual Exercises* to the decision or decisions which play a role in religious and moral conversion, psychological conversion, and conversion from addiction. It is important to keep in mind the significant differences (as well as similarities) between the role of election in the *Spiritual Exercises* and the role of decision(s) in the four conversion processes.

For a sinner who needs radical religious and moral conversion, a fundamental choice or decision *for* God and *against* idolatrous attachments is the core response to God's radical sanctifying activity, by which in an instant he effects a "new creation" (2 Cor. 5:17), removing the heart of stone and replacing it with a heart of flesh (Ezk. 11:19). The retreatant who makes his or her election generally is already in a state of ongoing religious and ongoing moral conversion, and the election is a deepening of the radical commitment to love and serve God which he or she already possesses (for instance, the decision to follow Christ by taking vows of celibacy, poverty and obedience).

For the neurotic who needs radical psychological conversion, it is almost always not one but many decisions which, together with other factors, gradually cause the shift from a radically neurotic way-of-being-and-acting to a state of ongoing psychological conversion. In contrast to the retreatant who prays to become more free from subtle forms of bias and attachment which impede the ideal exercise of a discerning freedom, the neurotic often begins in a state of almost complete enslavement to compulsions, and only gradually moves toward the point where he or she can exercise real freedom in regard to those compulsions.

I agree with Dr. Harold Greenwald that decisions play a vital role in healing of the neurotic condition. But I believe that a paralzying sense of worthlessness, the existence of repression, or the domination of unconscious destructive beliefs can block the neurotic sufferer's exercise of free choice—especially in the initial stages of healing. At the same time I accept the judgment of Drs. Barry and Ann Ulanov that "in the treatment of neuroses there comes a point where the patient's active willing choice of healing over illness determines the success or failure of the treatment."[91] Indeed, it is only at the point where the sufferer does make a choice—often a whole series of gradually more enlightened choices are involved—for healing over illness that the shift from radical to ongoing psychological conversion is clearly seen.

In the case of the addict who needs radical conversion from addiction, decision plays just as complex a role as in the healing of neurotic deformation. It is true that the Third Step of *Alcoholics Anonymous* proclaims: "[We] made a decision to turn our will and our lives over to the care of God as we understood Him."[92] It is also true that the decision of this Third Step is a decisive turning point in the healing process of the addict. But behind this "macro" decision, which often includes an effective and growing affective renunciation of the object of the addiction, there often exist many "micro" decisions which lead up to and make possible the decision of the Third Step.

In my discussion of the turning-from and turning-toward of

radical conversion from addiction, I used the First and Second of the famous *Twelve Steps* to depict concretely the psycho-spiritual shifts in attitude of the addict in the throes of radical conversion. Only in the Third Step is a decision actually spoken of, but I think it would be a mistake to conclude that no element of freedom is present in the stages when the addicts acknowledge their powerlessness over their object of addiction and come to believe that a Power greater than themselves can restore them to sanity.

Certainly, in the first stages of the healing of radical addiction there is most often a maximum of compulsion and a minimum of freedom. No doubt there are also powerful unconscious forces at work. In fact, Dr. Henry Tiebout, a great pioneer in the study of the psychological dimensions of alcoholic addiction, held that the act of surrender in which an alcoholic acknowledges from the deepest levels of the psyche that he or she is truly powerless over the addictive object and really needs help "is an unconscious event, not willed by the patient even if he should desire to do so."[93] Tiebout believed that surrender occurs when unconscious resistance and defiance and a grandiose conception of the self are rendered powerless by a concatenation of circumstances and the strong impact of reality. For Tiebout it is surrender which "initiates the switch from negative to positive,"[94] and the act of surrender is followed by a *state* of surrender in which the whole feeling structure of the individual shifts.

I agree with Dr. Tiebout that the phenomenon of surrender is not something which a person can deliberately plan or simply will into being. On the other hand, I am convinced, from my own experience, that the partly non-reflective event of surrender needs to be complemented, confirmed and developed through enlightened free decisions on the conscious level, in order that radical conversion from addiction may become a reality. Just as Drs. Barry and Ann Ulanov argue that there is a point in therapy when the neurotically suffering individual must freely choose health over sickness, so I believe that there is a point in the healing of radical addiction when the addict needs to choose freely to live out the results of his or her "surrender experience." Until this point is reached I would not speak of the addict as having passed from radical to ongoing conversion from addiction.

I believe that the Third Step is a powerful witness to, and expression of, the pivotal role of enlightened free decision in radical conversion. Indeed, in some cases of radical conversion from addiction there is one clear macro-decision which dramatically stands out as the turning point and core moment of that conversion. In many other cases, however, the occurrence of radical conversion from addiction is less dramatic and consists in an almost imperceptible growth in the exercise of enlightened free choices. In these cases it is often difficult to say at what point the person passed from radical to ongoing conversion from addiction.

In adapting the *Twelve Steps* to the stages of radical and ongoing conversion from addiction, I use the first three steps to depict radical conversion, and steps four through twelve to describe ongoing conversion from addiction. But I do not wish to imply any rigid classification here. Certainly a very strong ascetical dimension characterizes steps four through ten and for some persons it may be in carrying out one or more of these later steps that radical conversion from addiction really takes hold. Moreover, when I apply the term conversion to the healing of addiction I do so analogously, and this makes it difficult to say at what point radical conversion from addiction passes over into ongoing conversion from addiction.

But I can state that a person is only in a state of ongoing conversion from addiction when he or she (1) has truly surrendered at the unconscious as well as the conscious levels; (2) has effectively renounced the object of the addiction; (3) is in a state of growing affective detachment from the object of the addiction; (4) is positively attracted to the value of sobriety and the rich world of values connected with sobriety, and is actively embracing this new world of authentic values.

11

Confirming

The Third Week of the *Spiritual Exercises* focuses on Jesus Christ in the mysteries of his passion and death. The goal of the Third Week, according to a classical expression, is to "confirm the conformed."[1] Paul tells the Romans in his epistle to them:

> You have been taught that when we were baptized in Christ Jesus we were baptized in his death; in other words, when we were baptized we went into the tomb with him and joined him in death, so that as Christ was raised from the dead to the Father's glory, we too might live a new life (Rm. 6:3–4).

Paul is here describing the process of radical conversion in which an individual dies to sin and becomes a new creation in Christ. The first two Weeks of the *Spiritual Exercises* represent the twofold movement of radical conversion and help the retreatant to reenact in prayer the dynamics of radical reformation through Christ and conformation with Christ. The last two Weeks of the *Spiritual Exercises* represent the twofold movement of ongoing religious conversion and respectively aid the retreatant to confirm more totally his or her death to sin through contemplation of Christ in his suffering and dying and to be transformed more completely in the risen Christ through the prayerful beholding of him in the mysteries of his Easter victory.

The First Preface for the Eucharistic liturgies of the Lenten season proclaims: "As we recall the great events that gave us new life in Christ, you bring the image of your Son to perfection within us."[2] In the Third Week the retreatant contemplates Jesus in the "great events" of his passion and dying and in doing so confirms more totally the radical turning-from sin of the First Week by becoming ever more conformed to the image of Christ crucified. A chief goal of the Third Week is to gain the kind of "knowledge" Paul spoke of when he told the Corinthians: "During my stay with you, the only knowledge I claimed to have was about Jesus, and only about him as the crucified Christ" (1 Cor. 2:2–3). Just as in the First Week the retreatant sought to unmask sin for what it was and to reject it by meditating on a "sequence of sins," beginning with the sin of the angels and ending with personal sin, so in the Third Week the retreatant seeks to exclude every remnant of sin which remains by contemplating the sequence of sorrows which Jesus freely submits to in his passion.[3] The unfolding of the "process of sorrows" begins with the contemplation of Jesus at the Last Supper and culminates with the mystery of Jesus laid in the tomb.

But it is not enough to say that a chief goal of the Third Week is to gain "knowledge" of Jesus crucified unless one understands this "knowing" as a knowledge that is permeated, suffused, indeed, in a true sense, identified with love. The prayers of petition of the Third Week clearly reveal that growth in the personal love of Jesus is at the core of the Third Week experience. Ignatius states that "in the Passion it is proper to ask for sorrow with Christ in sorrow, anguish with Christ in anguish, tears and deep grief because of the great affliction Christ endures for me."[4] Ignatius stresses that the retreatant should ask for "compassion" because the Lord suffers for his or her sins.[5] Ignatius' words echo Paul's deep conviction expressed in the words: "I live in faith: faith in the Son of God who loved me and who sacrificed himself for my sake" (Gal. 2:20). The love of the Third Week is a suffering, compassionate love which focuses on Christ and the love of Christ and which impels the retreatant to ask "what I ought to do and suffer for Him."[6]

The whole of the *Spiritual Exercises* could be described as an apprenticeship in the practice of loving. In the First Week the retreatant is called to love himself or herself at least enough to turn from clearly self-destructive processes of sinning. This is the practice of Saint Bernard's first degree of love by which "man loves himself for his own sake."[7] The sinner is also summoned to love Christ at least because of what Christ has done for him or her. This is the practice of Saint Bernard's second degree of love whereby "man loves God for his own benefit."[8] In the Second Week of the *Spiritual Exercises* the retreatant is called to deepen his or her exercise of enlightened self-love[9] and also to begin to love Christ for himself as well as for what Christ has done for him or her. In the latter case the retreatant is beginning to practice

Saint Bernard's third degree of love in which "man loves God for God's sake."[10] In the Third Week the repentant sinner is called to grow yet more deeply in the love of Christ for his own sake and to seek to express this love in a desire to be one with Christ in his suffering and in his self-sacrificing service to others. There is a movement in the first three Weeks of the *Exercises* from the practice of an ascetical, purgative type of love of self through an illuminative type of loving which focuses on Christ as friend and companion toward a unitive, compassionate, suffering love of Christ for his own sake. It is fitting, then, that Saint Ignatius offers as the first contemplation of the Third Week the celebration of the Last Supper about which John initially writes:

> It was before the festival of the Passover, and Jesus knew that the hour had come for him to pass from this world to the Father. He had always loved those who were his in the world, but now he showed how perfect his love was (Jn. 13:1).

The Last Supper

In an election-centered retreat a principal goal of the Third Week is for the retreatant to seek confirmation through prayer of the decision which he or she has made at the end of the Second Week.[11] Every major life-decision carries with it a twofold ongoing dying to self. "To decide" means etymologically "to cut off." Thus, to decide to follow one pathway entails necessarily the exclusion of other pathways previously open to the person. This action of excluding is a true dying to self since the roads not taken obviously involved certain goods and life-possibilities, which are now closed off to the person. At the same time the positive choice one makes also bears with it an inevitable ongoing dying to self in different ways. If, for example, the retreatant makes the decision to accept a marriage proposal, then he or she has to be open to the many "daily dyings" to self which a truly authentic Christian marriage involves. For Christian marriage requires self-sacrifice; it demands a commitment for life which does not falter or turn back in the face of sickness, poverty, the difficulties of raising a family. Again, if, for example, the retreatant makes the decision to embrace "religious life," to take vows of perpetual chastity, poverty and obedience, this decision to follow Christ celibate, Christ poor, Christ obedient likewise entails an ongoing dying to the self.

Now it is not by accident that Saint Ignatius places the contemplation of the Last Supper at the very center of the *Spiritual Exercises* and immediately following the election. For Jesus himself, prior to the celebration of the last meal with his beloved apostles, had made certain decisions which made his passion and death a concrete inevitability. Contemporary Scripture scholarship confirms the view presented in the Gospels that Jesus through his words and deeds had set himself on a direct collision course with the key sources of power in the society of his day. Jesus was acutely aware of the direction his life was taking. He knew the fate of John the Baptist and of the prophets who preceded John and at the time of the Last Supper he seemed quite aware that the moment of confrontation was at hand and what its immediate outcome would no doubt be. There is good exegetical evidence that Jesus himself did say at his last meal with his disciples: "I tell you solemnly, I shall not drink any more wine until the day I drink the new wine in the kingdom of God" (Mk. 14:25).[12]

Gaston Fessard suggests that when Jesus at the supper took the bread, broke it and said, "This is my body" (Mt. 26:26), he was accepting the effects of the decisions of his public life and was freely offering himself in a sacrificial act of self-surrender. Fessard cites an ancient antiphon of Saint Ephrem on the Eucharist which reads in part:

> If He Himself had not slain Himself in the Mystery (the Eucharist)
>
> They (the murderers) would not have killed Him in reality.[13]

Fessard holds that in a profound sense Jesus' Eucharist offering caused his passion and death. I do not believe that it is right to take this in a fatalistic or masochistic sense. Rather, I think that the import of Fessard's insight is that Jesus, at the supper, confirmed his basic life-decisions, accepted their consequences and, like the Isaian suffering servant, offered himself for us all.

The retreatant, in imitation of the Master, in contemplating the mystery of the Eucharist and also in sharing in it, accepts the sufferings and dying to self which his or her election inevitably entails and unites the latter with the offering of the Lord. Here the decision of the retreatant is lifted up into a communal perspective and, just as Jesus said, "This is my body which will be given for you" (Lk. 22:19), so the retreatant says of his or her decision, "This is my body (my life) which will be given for you," and in this way in a self-transcending act fills up in his or her own flesh those things lacking to the passion of the Lord (Col. 1:24–25).[14]

Now, like the election of the retreatant, the neurotic's decision for psychic health over psychological deformation and the addict's choice of sobriety in place of compulsive enslavement also necessarily entail certain sufferings.

In the case of the neurotic, when the sufferer successfully engages in the struggle for decision and passes from radical to ongoing conversion the battle is not over. The "recovered and recovering" neurotic has to realize that, just because the health pattern is now in the ascendency, this does not mean that all neurotic tendencies are obliterated once and for all. Radical neurotic deformation, like radical addictive deformation, touches the whole person in his or her mind and "gut," feelings and imagination, self-image and self-concept, conscious and unconscious levels of psychic being. This means that even when the health pattern is clearly in the ascendency over the deformation pattern self-destructive tendencies and proclivities remain in varying degrees of dormancy in different areas of the total psyche and person. The neurotic, accordingly, in a state of ongoing psychological conversion must humbly acknowledge that his or her peculiar proclivities for malfunctioning remain, though in a diminished fashion. Dr. Angyal correctly observes that "recovery means no more than this: the strength of the neurotic pattern has been reduced, and he [the neurotic] has learned how to live in a wholesome fashion."[15] But the individual in ongoing conversion must keep in mind that his or her neurotic penchants come alive at once when the recoverer reverts to angry, self-centered, conceited, anxious, prideful forms of neurotic isolation.[16] The "recovered and recovering" neurotic, then, must constantly die to tendencies of the neurotic anti-self toward destructive self-pity, self-referential forms of imagining, phantasizing, thinking. There is a need for an ongoing practice of the processes of the fasting of the heart, mind and imagination. Further, the "recovered and recovering" neurotic is greatly aided in his or her attempt to confirm the rejection of the neurotic anti-self in radical conversion by uniting his or her sufferings to the Eucharistic offering of Jesus

Christ and by ratifying the death-sentence pronounced on the neurotic anti-self in the decision for health and wholeness which he or she has made. The contemplation of Christ in the mystery of his self-oblation and ongoing participation in Jesus' Eucharistic offering is a tremendous source of strength for the person in the stage of turning-from or ongoing psychological conversion.

In the case of the addict who has passed from the state of radical to ongoing conversion from addiction he or she must also realize that the struggle for sobriety and wholeness is not at an end once and for all. "The recovery of the addict . . . is a life-time adventure."[17] The "recovered and recovering" addict, like his or her neurotic counterpart, has to exercise eternal vigilance and to die daily to the addictive anti-self whenever and wherever its destructive tendencies and specific temptations manifest themselves. The addict, consequently, in the state of ongoing conversion from addiction needs to confirm his or her rejection of and turning-from the addictive anti-self in radical conversion through an ever deepening assimilation of the mind, heart, and imagination of the humble, self-sacrificing Christ.

One of the most effective ways for the neurotic and the addict in the stage of ongoing conversion to confirm and deepen their turning-from their respective neurotic, addictive anti-selves is to engage in the practice of steps four through ten of the *Twelve Steps* as they are utilized by *Alcoholics Anonymous, Emotions Anonymous* and other similar groups. This means that these "recovered and recovering" persons seek to: make searching and fearless moral inventories of themselves; admit to God, to themselves and to another human being, the exact nature of their wrongs; are entirely ready to have God remove all their defects of character; humbly ask God to remove shortcomings; make a list of all the people they have harmed through their neurotic and/or addictive behavior and become willing to make amends to all when this is possible and when to do so would not bring harm to these people or others; continue to take a personal inventory of defects and promptly admit them when they are recognized. The practice of these steps is an especially fruitful way for the neurotic and addict to unite their process of recovery to the sacrificial oblation of Jesus in the Eucharist and consequently to experience most powerfully the aid of the grace of Christ in dying daily to all that still opposes the total realization of true wholeness and selfhood in Christ.

The Passion and Death of Jesus

Subsequent to the contemplation of Jesus at the Last Supper, Saint Ignatius proposes to the retreatant contemplations of Jesus in his "sequence of sorrows," beginning with his agony in the garden and concluding with his death and burial. Among the suggested contemplations are Jesus' arrest in the garden, the diverse appearances of Jesus before Annas, Caiphas, Herod and Pilate, the mocking and crowning with thorns of Jesus, the denial of Peter, the condemnation of Jesus, the carrying of the cross, the crucifixion, death and burial. As in the case of the contemplations of the mysteries of Jesus in the earlier Weeks of the *Spiritual Exercises,* Ignatius suggests that the retreatant apply the total energies of his or her imagination, memory, feelings, mind and heart to the contemplation of each of the events in the process of sorrows.

There are special graces of healing and enlightenment, of growth in understanding and love connected with each of the mysteries which are subjects of contemplation for the Third Week. The divine dispensation and application, however, of these gifts of grace are in accord with the particular stages of conversion and special needs of the individual person who is focusing on the mystery of Jesus in his passion and death. Since the mysteries of Jesus' suffering and death are inexhaustibly rich in their life-giving meaning and value, I will look at a few dimensions of these mysteries which are of special relevance to the basic focus of this book.

David Stanley in his *Jesus in Gethsemane*[18] acknowledges as one possible interpretation of Jesus' agony that he did experience a momentary hesitation regarding the acceptance of death which he expressed in the offering of himself at the Last Supper. In this hypothesis Jesus' moment of hesitancy arose not from fear of physical suffering but from a searing realization of the immediate disastrous effects his death would have on his followers. The Shepherd would be stricken and this would mean "the dissolution of the little community of believers that alone had remained loyal to him."[19] I find a degree of plausibility in Stanley's theory only in a context where Jesus' prayer to the Father in his agony is viewed in its conditional nature, in its resolution and in the light of what Jesus did once he finished his prayer.

In Mark's account of Jesus' prayer there is a very forceful urgency in the words: "Take this cup away from me" (Mk. 14:36). But even in Mark Jesus' prayer ends with the words: "But let it be as you, not I, would have it" (Mk. 14:36–37). Jesus, realizing the immediate catastrophic effects his death will have on his followers and knowing that all things are possible to his Father, seeks an alternative to the "cup." But, Jesus makes the removal of the cup dependent on the will of the Father; and, even as he prays the Father confirms him in the offering which he made of himself at the Last Supper. Jesus then emerges from his prayerful struggle strengthened, confirmed and more resolute than ever to drink the cup to the very dregs. This is clear from Jesus' words to his disciples: "The hour has come. Now the Son of Man is to be betrayed into the hands of sinners. Get up! Let us go!" (Mk 14:41–42).

Jesus' struggle in the garden after he made his offering at the Last Supper shows just how deeply he became like us in everything except sin. Jesus' struggle in his prayer provides a source of strength for those who after making a very difficult decision are suddenly shaken to the depths of their being at the realization of certain awesome consequences which their decision necessarily entails. For even when a person has made a basically correct decision a momentary eclipse can occur which obscures the light of reason and heart underpinning the decision. In the period of this dark night the decider must struggle on in prayer and not lose heart. And, if the initial decision was, in fact, correct God will in the end confirm it. The final result will be that the decider, like Jesus, will emerge from his or her prayerful struggle more resolute than ever in a determination to carry out the decision, regardless of whatever difficult consequences it may entail.

Certainly, the neurotic and the addict who are in the initial stages of ongoing conversion from psychological and/or addictive deformations can take heart in contemplating Jesus in his agony. For at times even in more advanced stages of ongoing psychological conversion and conversion from addiction the "recovered and recovering" neurotic and addict can experience interior storms of intense agony and darkness where they wonder if their hard and tough decisions were really necessary and if there might not exist some less burdensome path to follow. These sufferers can learn from the example of Jesus to remain steadfast in their perseverance in prayer, to keep their focus clearly on the will of the Father for them and to trust that the Father will be with them and will guide them securely through their dark night of doubt and struggle.

Jesus' words, "Let us go,"uttered at the close of his solitary struggle in the garden, are words expressive of true freedom, firm determination and even a certain aggressiveness in the face of the hostile forces which threaten him. In John's account of the passion, when Judas, the chief priests, the Pharisees and guards enter the garden Jesus goes right up to them and asks: "Whom are you looking for?" (Jn. 18:5). Jesus in his first encounter with his arrestors displays a fearlessness which shows that he is in command and superior to his confronters, even though he permits them to arrest him. And throughout the events of his passion Jesus manifests an inward freedom and a type of self-presence which indicate that he goes to his death freely in trusting obedience to his Father and not blindly or fatalistically. Jesus in this way teaches all who will follow him that there is no need to fear those persons who can "kill the body but cannot kill the soul" (Mt. 10:28) and that holy courage and not cowardliness is the path to self-transcendence and victory. The apostle Paul showed himself to be the true disciple and imitator of Jesus when he wrote to the Romans:

> For I am certain of this: neither death nor life, no angel, no prince, nothing that exists, nothing still to come, not any power, or height or depth, nor any created thing, can ever come between us and the love of God made visible in Christ Jesus our Lord (Rm. 8:38–39).

Neurotics and addicts in the initial stage of ongoing conversion from their afflictions can learn much in prayerfully reflecting on Jesus' aggressive facing of his enemies in the garden. In the period prior to their radical conversion the neurotic and the addict generally became fearful in the face of difficulties, pain and temptations and all too quickly resorted to unconscious exaggerated use of defense mechanisms and often enough to the temporary oblivion provided by alcohol or other drugs. These tormented individuals thus verified in their fear-filled flights from reality the truth of Ignatius of Loyola's observation that "no wild animal on earth can be more fierce than the enemy of our human nature" when the person under attack "begins to be afraid and to lose courage."[20] Now, however, these same individuals in the stage of ongoing conversion can focus their entire attention on Jesus who in the garden confronts his enemies head on.

Strengthened by the example of Jesus and aided by his inward grace, recovered and yet recovering neurotics and addicts can take the offensive in their ongoing struggle to confirm more deeply the basic turning-from of their radical conversion. Now, instead of fleeing from the bright healing light of reality and from sufferings that purify, they can instead choose to face whatever challenges them with courage instead of fear. Now they can decide to bear and perhaps even embrace the discomfort and pain involved in taking responsibility for their past lives, in making amends to those they had harmed in some way and in resisting temptations to return to the pseudo comforts of their former way of existing in the world. In this way these converts to a life of sanity and freedom from compulsion continue to deepen the turning-from of their radical conversion. They also daily verify for themselves the truth of Ignatius of Loyola's keen observation that "the enemy becomes weak, loses courage, and turns to flight with his seductions as soon as one leading a spiritual life faces his temptations boldly, and does exactly the opposite of what he suggests."[21] The converts, then, keeping their eyes fixed on Jesus who "endured the cross, disregarding the shamefulness of it" (Heb. 12:2) will "not give up for want of courage" (Heb. 12:3–4) but will understand ever more deeply the words of the author of Hebrews: "In the fight against sin, you have not yet had to keep fighting to the point of death" (Heb. 12:4).

Earlier in this book I suggested that the metaphor of a "spiral" as well as the metaphor of "turning" is most useful to depict the diverse conversion processes in their inner unfolding. Erik Erikson warns those who choose to utilize his eight stage model, which begins with basic trust versus mistrust and culminates in ego-integrity versus despair, that it is dangerous to assume "that on each stage a goodness is achieved which is impervious to new inner conflicts"[22] and changes. He insists that "the personality is engaged with the hazards of existence continuously."[23] This means in the context of the ongoing conversions of the sinner, the neurotic and the addict that even when the processes involve forward and upward movements rather than backsliding and reversals that the recovered and recovering individuals will still have to face old difficulties and temptations in new, more subtle disguises and that creative, grace-inspired efforts will be needed to respond effectively to the new challenges. The metaphor of a spiral ascent is especially apt to describe these ongoing conversion struggles because in ascending a spiral a person covers the same ground but at successively higher levels and from a perspective that is at once familiar and yet new and alien to a degree. And a new perspective, though involving certain familiar elements, requires to a degree novel variations in response.

After his departure from the garden Jesus experiences a crescendo of challenges of a physical, psychic and spiritual nature. He is subjected again and again to various forms of physical torture, to savage verbal abuse and torment, to false accusations and judgments, to abandonment by his disciples, to constant challenges to the very meaningfulness of his life, mission and his dedication to the Father. In each case, however, Jesus confronts the situation at hand in an appropriate fashion and sets his face more resolutely toward Calvary.

Now the sinner in the state of ongoing religious and moral conversion is not above his Master (Mt. 10:24) and is called to imitate his Lord in the daily carrying of his or her cross (Lk. 9:23). Just as Jesus in his journey and climb toward Calvary had to deal again and again with attempts to deter him from his mission, so the repentant sinner in his or her daily carrying of the cross needs to fend off ever more subtle temptations to deviate from the ongoing ascent of the spiral of transcendence which leads inevitably toward life's summit where the final struggle with death must take place.

In similar fashion, the neurotic and the addict in the state of ongoing conversion need to follow their own particular way of the cross and the route up the spiral of transcendence which it entails. These recovered and yet recovering individuals need to develop with the help of God's grace "a kind of preconscious vigilance"[24] which will enable them to detect the subtle urgings of tempters—sometimes disguised as angels of light[25]—to sway them from their radical commitment to sanity and sobriety. They must learn to spot these self-destructive calls of the tempters at their very outset and nip them in the bud.[26]

There is no shame in experiencing old temptations in new garbs, as individuals in varying degrees of ongoing conversion seek to ascend the Mount of Calvary with Christ. For each human being has his or her own distinctive personality orientation and past history with particular proclivities toward certain weaknesses and temptations. We have seen this fact confirmed by such disparate thinkers as Hippocrates, Evagrius Ponticus, Oscar Ichazo and others. What is vitally important, however, is that each individual seek to develop that form of psychological and spiritual self-knowledge which will enable him or her to unmask the old temptation under its new guise and to deal with it in a victorious manner. Above all, the contemplation of Jesus in his sequence of sorrows, as he meets each challenge in a fruitful and self-transcending manner, will enable the disciple in ongoing conversion to move successfully along the spiral which will lead him or her inevitably to the Mount of Calvary and encounter with death which awaits every human being.

The Crucifixion and Detachment

Of all the events of the passion, the crucifixion and dying of Jesus most fully reveal the love, the "divine foolishness," the unsearchable mystery of God at work "in Christ . . . reconciling the world to himself" (2 Cor. 5:19). In my book *Christotherapy* I dwelt at length on the events of the passion of Jesus and especially on his crucifixion and dying.[27] I considered the root causes and forms of human suffering and evaluated them in the light of the saving event of the cross of Jesus Christ. I compared Elisabeth Kübler Ross' description of the five stages many cancer victims pass through, as they move toward death, with the Gospel accounts of Jesus' own struggle to come to grips with his own suffering and dying. I also drew a sharp contrast between Jesus, Buddha and Socrates in terms of their respective motives in dying, their manners of death and the effects their death had on others.

My present reflections on the crucifixion and dying of Jesus center on the phenomenon of detachment. I choose this focal point for a number of reasons. First, Ignatius of Loyola in the *Exercises* puts an emphasis on the fact that "the divinity hides itself"[28] during the final hours of Jesus—and this hiding implies a most radical summons to detachment on Jesus' part; second, detachment is at the very core of the deepening, the confirming of the turning-from of the ongoing conversions of the sinner, the neurotic and the addict; lastly, the prayer and reflections of mystics, such as Saint John of the Cross, manifest in a unique way a lived participation in the radical darkness and call to total detachment which Jesus experienced in his dying hours.

Prior to his crucifixion Jesus was stripped of his garments.

This external stripping is but a weak symbol of the far more radical "internal stripping" and emptying which Jesus experienced in his final hours. Saint Ignatius indicates that, though Jesus was God, the divinity he possessed hid itself and allowed "the most sacred humanity to suffer . . . cruelly."[29] Jesus was thus entirely bereft of the interior joy in the Holy Spirit which he experienced so often in his public life; likewise, Jesus suffered the betrayal of Judas, the denial of Peter, the flight of his disciples. Paul tells his Corinthians that the Lord Jesus, though rich, "became poor for your sake" (2 Cor. 8:9–10); and, never was Jesus' inner poverty of mind, psyche and spirit more total than on the cross. So great was Jesus' inner poverty and emptiness that he felt no consolation from the Father but later learned an obedience of total detachment by clinging to his Father in the darkness of naked trust. "Although he was Son, he learnt to obey through suffering" (Heb. 5:8).

Every disciple of Jesus is called to detachment and to ever deeper, more radical forms of detachment. Detachment, of course, is not an end in itself but rather a means for realizing authentic attachment. But the sting and agony of detachment is no less real in spite of this. "If any man comes to me without hating father, mother, wife, children, brothers, sisters, yes and his own life too, he cannot be my disciple" (Lk. 14:26–27). Further, every human being must sooner or later face the radical, total detachment of death itself. Karl Rahner has observed that every human being is called to radical poverty, celibacy and obedience in the moment of dying because the dying person must leave everyone and everything behind and trust in God alone.[30] But fortunately the dying disciple of Jesus is not totally alone because he or she possesses in Jesus a high priest who has himself tasted the radical detachment of dying and is therefore capable of compassion for human weakness (Heb. 4:15–16) and of strengthening those who trust in him.

In the case of the neurotic and the addict in the state of ongoing conversion from their afflictions there is a call to them to develop ever more liberating forms of detachment. Once again, the practice of detachment in the turning-from stage of ongoing conversion is only for the sake of realizing a deeper attachment to the authentic values of sanity, wholeness, sobriety, abundance of life. But, the focus for the moment is on the detachment phase of ongoing conversion and there is always a certain pain involved, even though the fruits of liberation are always experienced where authentic humanistic and Christian detachment is practiced.

There are, of course, degrees in the practice of detachment. A very elemental practice of detachment which can flow from the legitimate motivation of enlightened self-love is what I might term "Detachment from the Must." I use this latter expression to give a name to a method for achieving peace of mind and heart recommended by a contemporary therapist.[31] According to this method, an initial way to become free from emotional turmoil and unhappiness is to shift from a general attitude toward life of "I demand" to a general attitude of "I prefer." It almost inevitably follows that when a person makes an emotion-backed demand and the demand is not met, unhappiness and emotional upset result. But, "when a *preference* is not satisfied," no real emotional disturbance of any consequence results because "it was only a preference after all."[32]

This principle of "Detachment from the Must" is a very useful one, especially for individuals who are neurotically or addictively inclined, though it is also quite beneficial for the "normally abnormal" as well. If, for example, an individual is in a traffic jam it will make quite a difference if the person can say to himself or herself: "I would prefer to be elsewhere but I am not going to cling to an emotion-backed internal demand that I be elsewhere, even though I know I cannot be there." This principle makes good sense on a purely humanistic, psychological level. It is possible, however, to transpose this principle into a specifically Christian framework which frees it from any possible Stoic or fatalistic implications. In its transposed form the principle of "Detachment from the Must" becomes the principle of acceptance of an unpleasant, unavoidable or inescapable situation with the faith understanding that God can and will bring good from it in some way or other. The person still acknowledges, however, that from a purely human point of view he or she would prefer to be elsewhere. But at least the shift from an emotion-backed demand to a preference and a basic acceptance brings a certain peace of mind and heart which otherwise would be absent.

Saint Ignatius in his *First Principle and Foundation*[33] moves beyond the principle of "Detachment from the Must" to the well known "principle of indifference." Ignatius indicates that all human beings are created to praise, reverence and serve God and in this way to reach with God's grace the goal of salvation. Ignatius further points out that all things on the face of the earth are created to be of help to human beings in reaching salvation and that it is up to each person to make use of these created things insofar as they help in the attainment of salvation and to abstain from use of them to the extent that in certain circumstances their use would block the realization of the goal of salvation. Ignatius then proceeds to enunciate his famous principle of indifference:

> We must make ourselves indifferent to all created things, as far as we are allowed free choice and are not under any prohibition. Consequently, as far as we are concerned, we should not prefer health to sickness, riches to poverty, honor to dishonor, a long life to a short life. The same holds for all other things.
>
> Our one desire and choice should be what is more conducive to the end for which we are created.[34]

Here Ignatius basically articulates the view that the Christian should seek to cultivate an inner spirit of faith in divine providence which is so deep and profound that he or she simply says to the Lord: "God, here I am! I am coming to obey your will" (Heb. 10:7). The Ignatian principle of indifference expresses a type of inner detachment which goes beyond the detachment expressed in the principle of "Detachment from the Must."

But there is a yet more radical form of detachment which Ignatius proposes to those who wish to follow Christ in a more profound identification with him in the poverty, the abuses, the humiliations which he experienced, especially in his passion and crucifixion. Ignatius thus proposes to the retreatant in the Third Week "to consider that Christ suffers all this for my sins, and [to consider] what I ought to do and suffer for Him."[35] Here there is an echoing of the call to the *Third Kind of Humility* I discussed at the end of the Second Week. In embracing the *Third Kind of Humility* the retreatant makes the following resolution:

> Whenever the praise and glory of the Divine Majesty would be equally served, in order to imitate and be in reality more like Christ our Lord, I desire and choose poverty with Christ poor, rather than riches; insults with Christ loaded with them, rather than honors; I desire to be accounted as worthless and a fool for Christ, rather than to be esteemed as wise and prudent in this world. So Christ was treated before me.[36]

This *Third Kind of Humility* is only intelligible to those who are given the grace to understand how the lover desires to be with the Beloved and to share in the lot of the Beloved, above all when the Beloved is in difficult circumstances. This *Third Kind of Humility* is further rooted in an understanding that persecutions and abuse are the lot of all those who follow Christ in a radical manner (Jn. 15:20; Mt. 5:10). Finally, this *Third Kind of Humility* is rooted in the teachings of Paul that there is a certain way in which the disciples of Christ can fill up in their own flesh those things which are lacking to the passion of Christ (Col. 1:24–25).

Today we have countless examples of laywomen and men, of "religious" and priests who are living out the *Third Kind of Humility* in choosing to identify themselves with the poor and oppressed and to share in their lot and to experience the revilement, the abuse, the hatred and the persecution unto death which comes upon these poor of God.

In the case of recovered and recovering neurotics and addicts, they too have an opportunity to share at times in some small measure in the *Third Kind of Humility.* Society today widely misunderstands the situation of the psychotic, the neurotic, the addict. Society often chooses to ignore and even to express positive contempt and loathing for those suffering from the afflictions of psychological illness and addiction. It can then be a most excellent way of identifying with Christ humiliated for those who have experienced healing in these areas to acknowledge publicly, at times when it is appropriate, their status as recovered and recovering neurotics and/or addicts. In this way they can function as signs of hope for those who are fearful of the stigma and contempt which they fear might come upon them if they were to seek help for their emotional problems or addictive difficulties. In this way these wounded healers can also help to bring about a change in the attitudes of society in an area where there is still such wide misunderstanding and mistrust, despite the advances which have been made.

My final reason for focusing on the phenomenon of detachment in the context of the crucifixion and dying of the Lord is the central role which detachment plays in the upward spiral of Christian growth in prayer. For the lives and writings of the saints and mystics reveal that growth in the life of prayer involves ever deeper, more radical forms of purification and detachment.

There is, of course, the need for ongoing detachment from

sinful tendencies which remain even in the state of ongoing religious and moral conversion. As a person ascends in the prayerful spiral of transcendence the light shines ever more brightly and more subtle forms of sinfulness and imperfection are revealed. Such mystics as Saint John of the Cross also disclose the need for letting go at certain times of images and thoughts which are in themselves good and holy so that a deeper experience of the love of God dwelling quietly in the heart can be realized. It is for this reason that the anonymous mystical author of *The Book of Privy Counseling* writes concerning those who are at a certain stage of growth in prayer: "Let them fast awhile from their natural delight in knowing" since "knowledge is full of labor, but love, full of rest."[37] Growth in prayer then requires not only a fasting of the mind, heart and imagination from what is sinful but also a fasting for a time from forms of prayer which are no longer appropriate for certain stages in the ascent of the spiral of contemplative union with God.

No mystic, I believe, provides a more detailed account of the various turns in the upward spiral of detachment in prayer than Saint John of the Cross. Nor does any Christian mystic depict more graphically the awesome dark nights of radical detachment which certain individuals undergo, as they journey toward the heights of mystical marriage with Christ the Bridegroom. Most certainly, John of the Cross stresses that detachment is for the sake of greater attachment, that the passage through the various nights is for the sake of bridal union with God. Indeed, in his commentary on the first stanza of the *Spiritual Canticle* John puts these words on the lips of the lover God is drawing to himself: "My Spouse . . . You have not only drawn my soul away from all things, but . . . You have raised it up to Yourself while it was calling after You, now totally detached so as to be attached to You."[38] But the fact that detachment is for the sake of attachment does not diminish the terrible agony which the soul in the various nights of stripping and emptying experiences.

There is profound significance in the fact that John is called John *of the Cross.* John reveals in his poems and his commentaries and in his famous maxims that he experienced in his own prayer life a "most unique" sharing in the radical agony and inner stripping and detachment which Jesus experienced on the cross. In describing Jesus in his last moments on the cross John wrote:

> At the moment of His death He was . . . without any consolation or relief, since the Father left Him that way in innermost aridity. . . . This was the most extreme abandonment, sensitively, that He had suffered in His life. And by it He accomplished the most marvelous work of His whole life.[39]

John writes of Jesus' utter agony on the cross as one gifted with a certain ineffable personal taste of what Jesus had experienced. Likewise, John's experience in his own prayer and his knowledge of the mystical prayer of many holy persons enabled him to write to his beloved contemporaries:

> Oh! If we could but now fully understand how a soul cannot reach the thicket and wisdom of the riches of God, which are of many kinds, without entering the thicket of many kinds of suffering . . . ; and how a soul with an authentic desire for divine wisdom, wants suffering first in order to enter this wisdom by the thicket of the cross.[40]

The individual who reflects on the Ignatian contemplations of the Third Week, on the *Third Kind of Humility,* on the dark nights of detachment of John of the Cross must keep firmly in mind that neither for Ignatius of Loyola nor for John of the Cross is there any masochistic delight in suffering for its own sake. Without the original and personal sin of humankind there would be no world full of suffering as we experience it. Likewise, without the original and personal sin of humankind Jesus would never have been crucified. Suffering and death *as we experience them* are the fruit of sin. The suffering and death of Jesus, then, and the consequent *Third Kind of Humility* of Ignatius and the dark nights of John of the Cross are all part of the "foolishness of the cross" by means of which God defeats Satan, sin and its effects and brings the victory of the resurrection, of the Fourth Week, of the Mystical Marriage.

God the Father in the face of the sinfulness of humanity did not choose simply to remove sin and its effects from the world by a divine fiat or some miraculous manifestation of his omnipotence. Rather, he chose to show his respect for humankind and human freedom by sending his Son into the world as one of us. In his "divine foolishness" which is wiser than our wisdom the Father chose to bring good out of evil by permitting his son to confront sin and its effects head-on and in this way to defeat them by the self-transcending trust, hope, love and obedience of the cross. Even in the deepest interior agony and darkness of the cross Jesus continued to trust in the Father and in this way turned his agony, his suffering and his death into trophies of victory and stepping stones to glory. And the disciple is not above the Master. Each follower of Christ is called with Christ, through Christ and in Christ to face Satan, sin and its effects head-on. Each follower of Christ is called to pass through his or her own particular Golgotha, dark night or nights and to defeat sin and its effects by courageously confronting and transcending suffering and death through repentant and persevering faith, hope and love. There is consequently no masochism here. There is no Stoicism here. There is no fatalism here. There is no world-denial here. There is no denial of the terrible reality of sin and its effects in the world. But what there is here is faith, hope, love, courage, grace-inspired self-transcendence and incredible victory. What we have here in the cross of Jesus, in the *Third Kind of Humility,* in the deaths of the martyrs and the mystics is that wonderful divine foolishness and madness which is wiser than our wisdom and infinitely more sane than the so-called "sanity" of the world. As the Apostle Paul put it:

> Here are we preaching a crucified Christ; to the Jews an obstacle they cannot get over, to the pagans madness, but to those who have been called, whether they are Jews or Greeks, a Christ who is the power and wisdom of God. For God's foolishness is wiser than human wisdom, and God's weakness is stronger than human strength (1 Cor. 1:22–25).

12

Transforming

The Fourth Week of the *Spiritual Exercises* summons the retreatant to contemplate Jesus in the glorious mysteries of his resurrection, beginning with his various appearances after the resurrection and culminating with his ascension into heaven. At the end of the Fourth Week Saint Ignatius invites the retreatant to engage in a contemplation of God as he dwells in all things, is lovingly at work in all of creation and is constantly bestowing blessings and gifts in incredible abundance on his beloved human children.[1] The goals of this final contemplation of the retreat are an intensification in the love of God, a growing gratitude to God for all that he is and does and an ongoing, ever deepening desire to serve God with all the energies of one's mind, heart and spirit.

The basic prayer of petition of the Fourth Week is to ask "for the grace to be glad and rejoice intensely because of the great joy and the glory of Christ our Lord."[2] Contemplations of the Fourth Week are intended to deepen and intensify the turning-toward God and Christ which took place in radical conversion. And it is above all in rejoicing with Christ and for Christ because he is now in glory that the retreatant is empowered by the Holy Spirit to turn ever more fully toward Christ and to advance with ever-greater acceleration in the positive, upward spiral of ongoing conversion. And perhaps no text in Scripture expresses more powerfully and eloquently the dynamic, transformative power of the turning-toward phase of ongoing conversion than the words of Paul to the Corinthians: "All of us, gazing on the Lord's glory with unveiled faces, are being transformed from glory to glory into his very image, by the Lord who is the Spirit" (2 Cor. 3:18 N.A.B.).

There is a striking parallel between the type of movement which takes place as the First Week passes into the Second Week and the kind of shift which occurs as the Third Week gives place to the Fourth Week. In the First Week the meditations on sin and hell do not end in a cul-de-sac of absurdity but in grace-inspired contrition. And, through the divine initiative of Christ the King the reform of the First Week is transmuted into the dynamic conforming to the image of Christ of the Second Week. In similar fashion, the sorrow-filled contemplations of the Third Week do not terminate in the cold bitterness of despair but in an unshakeable trust in the Father. And through the divine initiative of the Father the confirmation of the Third Week, which consists in sorrowing with Christ and identification with him in his suffering and dying, is transformed into the joyous celebration with the risen Christ and the ongoing transfiguration into his image of the Fourth Week. For this reason, just as it is most appropriate to describe the Second Week as the "conforming of the reformed," so it is equally fitting to depict the Fourth Week in the classical terms of the "transforming of the confirmed."

The Appearances

The post-resurrection appearances of Jesus, as depicted in the New Testament, provide an inexhaustible source of life-giving truth and value for the person who contemplates them in faith. Three features which stand out in varying degrees in the evangelists' descriptions of the appearances are the divine initiative, a moment of privileged recognition and missioning.[3]

The role of divine initiative is manifest in all of Jesus' appearances to certain chosen followers. In Mark's Gospel it is first an angel who tells Mary Magdalene, Mary the mother of James, and Salome that Jesus has been raised up from the dead (Mk. 16:1–8). Then Jesus manifests himself to Mary Magdalene. In Matthew's account an angel likewise first informs some of the women who followed Jesus that he had been raised from the dead and then Jesus himself appears to them. Finally, Jesus manifests himself to the eleven disciples in Galilee (Mt. 28:1–20). In the accounts of Luke and of John there are more extended descriptions of various appearances and in all of them the divine initiative stands forth strikingly.

In religious conversion in both its radical and ongoing states it is always God who initiates, sustains and leads the process on toward ever richer developments. In the words of Paul: "It is God, for his own loving purpose, who puts both the will and the action into you" (Ph. 2:13). In the Fourth Week of the *Spiritual Exercises* Saint Ignatius stresses the initiative of Christ who after his death "sets free the souls of the just" and then "rising, appears in body and soul to His Blessed Mother"[4] and to others who followed him. Although the Scriptural accounts do not explicitly mention an appearance of Jesus to his mother, Ignatius takes it for granted, since Mary was with the holy women at the cross (Jn.19:25–27) and since she was also with the apostles and others "joined in continuous prayer" (Ac. 1:14) in the upper room at the time of Pentecost.

The Scriptural and Ignatian stress on the role of the divine initiative in the post-resurrection appearances is most significant because it is the basic experience of the Christian in ongoing as well as radical religious conversion that it is Jesus who "leads us in our faith and brings it to perfection" (Heb. 12:2). Indeed, the Christian, who in ongoing religious conversion ascends the spiral of transcendence at ever higher levels, experiences with growing intensity that it is Christ through the power of his Spirit who effects an ever more total turning-toward himself and an ever fuller transformation from glory to glory into his image (2 Cor. 3:18). Finally, it is the universal testimony of Christian mystics that, as they receive gifts of higher forms of prayer, they experience the growing dominance of God's action in drawing them to himself and that they yield to the initiative of the divine Lover with a freedom and love characterized by fruitful receptivity, dynamic passivity and an allowing of God to be ever more completely God for them.[5]

Two striking manifestations of divine initiative lie at the origins of the *Alcoholics Anonymous* movement and so also indirectly of those movements inspired by the *Twelve Steps* of *Alcoholics Anonymous.* Earlier, I described the conversion experience of Mr. Bill Wilson, principal founder of *Alcoholics Anonymous.* But Mr. Wilson was himself deeply touched and inspired, prior to his conversion, by the recovery from active alcoholism of Mr. Ebby Thatcher.[6] Mr. Thatcher, a friend of Bill Wilson's, told him outright that "God had done for him what he could not do for himself."[7] Now it was through the instrumentality of a group known as the *Oxford Group* that Thatcher received the gift of sobriety. And the *Oxford Group* was founded by Mr. Frank Buchman as a result of a vision which he had in 1908 of the suffering Christ.[8]

Mr. Bill Wilson in describing his own conversion speaks of experiencing a "sense of victory, followed by such a peace and serenity as I had never known."[9] Wilson also used the image of "being lifted up as though the great clean wind of a mountaintop blew through and through."[10] Clearly, the type of images Wilson uses in this description are those of resurrection, victory, power. These are "Fourth Week" types of images and they add a beautiful complement to the "Third Week" visionary experience of Frank Buchman. What stands out clearly, however, in the conversion experiences of both Buchman and Wilson is the divine initiative—the dominant presence of sheer gift and grace.

Certainly a feature which characterizes "recovered and still recovering" neurotics and addicts who faithfully practice the *Twelve Steps* is an ever deepening awareness of how God is dynamically at work in the events of their lives, in the persons they meet and in all their affairs. Indeed, inspired by the Eleventh Step, these individuals constantly strive to be ever more receptive to the initiative of God (as they understand him) in all aspects of their daily living. As they turn ever more fully toward the Kingdom of Wholeness, Sanity and Sobriety in Christ in their ascent of the spiral of transcendence, they seek "through prayer and meditation" to improve their "conscious contact with God . . . praying only for knowledge of His Will . . . and the power to carry that out."[11]

Besides divine initiative a moment of graced revelation/ recognition is also a particularly striking characteristic of various Scriptural accounts of Jesus' appearances after his resurrection. And in each instance of these privileged encounters with the risen Lord a transformation of inner attitude and feeling is effected in the chosen recipient of Christ's action.

It is in the accounts of Luke and John that the moments of revelation/recognition and their transformative effects are most in evidence. Luke, for example, tells the story of the two disciples of Jesus who had left Jerusalem and were on their way toward Emmaus. The disciples were "downcast" (Lk. 24:17) because their leader had been crucified. On the way Jesus joined them as a fellow journeyer but they did not recognize him. Jesus began to show them how the Scriptures foretold the suffering and ultimate triumph of the Christ: "Was it not ordained that the Christ should suffer and so enter into his glory?" (Lk. 24:26). The two disciples were clearly moved by what the stranger was telling them and they pressed him to stay with them that evening. Luke then recounts that while they were at table Jesus took "bread and said the blessing; then he broke it and handed it to them. And their eyes were opened and they recognized him, but he had vanished from their sight" (Lk. 24:30–32). Luke indicates the revelatory action of God both in his account of how Jesus explained the Scriptures to the two disciples and through the words "their eyes were opened." At the same time the evangelist states that "they recognized him." The immediate result is that the disciples recall how their hearts burned within them as Jesus had spoken to them on the road. They then instantly set out for Jerusalem to tell the Eleven that the Lord had risen. Where there was dejection there is now joy and enthusiasm. Where there was confusion and misunderstanding there is now enlightenment and faith.

Neurotics and addicts in a state of ongoing conversion often find that, like the disciples of Luke's Emmaus story, they too are gradually led by God to recognize and acknowledge a meaning in events and sufferings of the past which up to that point had seemed to be absurd and totally apart from any divine guidance. The facts of the past are not changed but they take on a new significance in the light of the resurrection-like experience of ongoing psychological conversion and/or conversion from addiction. Also, as a result of the gift of an enlightened understanding of the past, these recovered and still recovering individuals, like the disciples of the Emmaus story, undergo a profound change in their attitudes toward the past and lingering feelings of dejection and rejection are more and more replaced by feelings of joy, enthusiasm, acceptability, gratitude and love.

As I pointed out, John, like Luke, also provides examples of moments of revelation/recognition and the transformative effects which result in attitudes and feelings. Thus, for instance, John creatively recounts for us Jesus' appearance to Mary Magdalene. Mary is shown weeping outside the tomb where Jesus was laid. Jesus comes to Mary but she takes him for the gardener and asks him if he has taken the body away. Jesus simply replies with the word "Mary" (Jn. 20:16). At the moment Mary hears this revelatory word she recognizes Jesus, calls him "Master" and clings to him in love. Here again, there takes place a powerful transformation in attitude and feeling. Where there was sorrow and confusion there is now joy, faith, and a great love.

John recounts that Jesus appeared to his disciples a number of times (Jn. 21:14). In the evening of the day of resurrection John relates that Jesus stood among his disciples in the locked upper room, spoke the words "Peace be with you" (Jn. 20:20) and that the disciples who had been filled with fear experienced great joy. The apostle Thomas, however, was not present at this appearance of Jesus and he refused to accept the testimony of his fellow apostles and remained in doubt. But John recounts that a week later Jesus revealed himself to Thomas who was at that time with the other disciples. Jesus showed Thomas his wounds and invited Thomas to place his hand in the wounds. At the moment of this revelation Thomas recognized the Lord and his doubt was transformed into one of the greatest professions of faith in the whole of Scripture: "My Lord and my God" (Jn. 20:28). It is perhaps above all the confession of Thomas which leads Saint Ignatius to suggest to the retreatant that he or she contemplate

> the divinity, which seemed to hide itself during the passion, now appearing and manifesting itself so miraculously in the most holy Resurrection in its true and most sacred effects.[12]

John also recounts that Jesus appeared to Peter and the other disciples on the shore of Tiberias. John's account of Jesus' dialogue with Peter has special significance for anyone who has things in his or her past which he or she profoundly regrets. In John's account Jesus does not explicitly mention Peter's triple denial during the passion. But he does evoke from Peter a triple profession of love which culminates in the great intensity and burning intimacy of Peter's final response: "Lord, you know everything; you know I love you" (Jn. 21:17). Peter denied Jesus out of fear. But his grace-inspired threefold profession reveals in him the presence of that love which casts out fear (1 Jn. 4:18). Peter's faith-inspired recognition of Jesus as risen Lord and his profession of unqualified love filled his heart with a holy courage which enabled him later to embrace martyrdom for the sake of his Lord. Where there was once a fearful heart there is now a heart alive with holy fortitude. One clear message which this dialogue between Jesus and Peter is meant to teach the repentant sinner, the recovered and recovering neurotic and the addict is that God can and will bring good out of any negative situation or happening of the past for those who let him. This is why the Church in the resurrection liturgy of Holy Saturday can sing about Adam's sin as a "happy fault" since it resulted in the coming of such a great and glorious Redeemer. This is also why there comes a point in the ongoing conversions of the neurotic and addict when they can actually be grateful in a certain sense for their experiences of neurosis and addiction since God enabled them to become victors and sources of self-transcendence and service in and through these very sufferings. They often see that without these sufferings they might well have remained very mediocre, self-centered individuals at best. They also experience, to the extent that in ongoing conversion they must still struggle in one way or another with neurotic and/or addictive tendencies, difficulties, temptations, that, with God's help, they can utilize these battles as further opportunities for growth in virtue and self-transcendence.

Saint Ignatius believed, along with the whole Christian Church, that Christ continues to disclose himself to those who respond to his invitation to encounter him in the Word of Scripture and in other ways also. Ignatius accordingly invites the retreatant in the Fourth Week to contemplate Jesus in his appearances, to pray for the grace of recognizing him as risen Lord and above all to pray for "joy and happiness at the great joy and happiness of Christ our Lord."[13] Jesus had said to Thomas and the other apostles: "Happy are those who have not seen and yet believe" (Jn. 20:29). This, of course, is the condition of the retreatant and of all Christians who seek to grow in the knowledge and love of Jesus through a meeting with him in prayer and in other ways. And, although the retreatant encounters Jesus with the eyes of faith, he or she is still blessed with the same gifts of joy, peace, assurance, faith, hope and love which the first Christians received. As the First Letter of Peter expresses it: "You did not see him, yet you love him; and still without seeing him, you are already filled with a joy so glorious that it cannot be described" (1 P. 1:8). A self-transcending love which delights with Jesus and for Jesus because he is now in glory is surely one of the richest fruits of the prayerful event of revelation/recognition as it continues to take place in the lives of faithful Christians everywhere.[14]

One of the most important tasks of the recovered and still recovering individual (sinner, neurotic and addict) in the turning-toward stage of ongoing conversion is the recognition and appreciation of authentic values on all levels of existence. The task is in a sense sweet and light because the richness of appreciating authentic values for themselves is self-validating. There is a whole hierarchy of values, beginning with the vital values of basic physical health and wholeness and culminating in the highest levels of graced, mystical prayer. The recovered and recovering neurotic and addict as well as every Christian who is seeking to live a fuller more abundant human and divinized existence are called to feast appreciatively at the table of authentic human and divine values. Thus, Saint Ignatius suggests to the retreatant that he or she make use of natural values in the Fourth Week such as "the light and the pleasures of the season, for example, in summer of the refreshing coolness, in the winter of sun and fire" to create an atmosphere of joy. Ignatius also urges the retreatant "to call to mind and think on what causes pleasure, happiness, and spiritual joy."[15] Ignatius recognizes the worthwhileness of appreciative recognition and delighting in the most simple natural values as well as the most exalted spiritual values. Ignatius is here anticipating certain insights of Dr. Abraham Maslow who coined the expression "peak-experience" to describe moments in which individuals recognize and appreciate as worthwhile in themselves such values of Being as beauty, truth, goodness, aliveness, uniqueness, order.[16] Like Ignatius, Maslow seeks to help individuals who have some experience of such values, even though their experiences are weak, to focus attention, to notice, to name such experiences within themselves and to learn in the light of their own incipient peak-experiences "how to improve them, how to enrich them, how to enlarge them."[17]

It is the task of the Christotherapist to aid seekers to dispose themselves for the occurrence of moments of appreciative recognition of those natural and spiritual values which are especially relevant to the stages of development they have reached in their respective ongoing conversions. For example, the Christotherapist needs to help the recovered and recovering neurotic and addict to appreciate the basic values of fundamental psychic and physical health in the early stages of their respective ongoing conversions. The Christotherapist can then gradually lead the radically converted neurotic and addict to dispose themselves for the appreciative discernment of higher values of unique personhood, interpersonal communion, works of art, and spiritual values. This is not to say that in radical psychological conversion and conversion from addiction there is not already present an appreciative recognition of such values as the interpersonal and the spiritual. But at first the appreciation of these values is still newly awakened and there is need for an increased heightening of appreciative recognition of these values as radically converted neurotics and addicts are drawn to ever higher levels in the spiral of transcendence of ongoing conversion.

In similar fashion, the Christotherapist must be aware of the level in the ascent of the spiral of transcendence which the seeker in the stage of ongoing religious and moral conversion has reached. In the early stages of ongoing religious and moral conversion there is still a highly ascetical element involved and this means that the Christotherapist has to focus the attention of the seeker to an extent on those values which are especially relevant to basic ascetical practice, e.g. an appreciative reading of the lives of saints and converts. In later stages of ongoing religious and moral conversion where illuminative, unitive and mystical developments occur it is the task of the Christotherapist to facilitate openness on the part of the seeker to the ever richer Kingdom of values which God unveils.

It is very important for the Christotherapist to be aware of the particular developmental stage which the seeker is at. Thus, an individual who is seeking to come to grips with the intimacy stage of development will need to focus on a different set of natural and spiritual values than a person who is in the process of dealing with the generativity stage of development. At each of these stages there is a revelation/recognition dimension involved but God generally deals with the individual in terms of his or her natural stage of development. Or, as the Thomistic adage has it: Grace builds on nature.

A third striking feature of the appearances of Jesus after the resurrection is "missioning." An angel tells the women who come to the tomb that Jesus has been raised. He then tells the women to go and bring this good news to the disciples. When Jesus appears to the women he too sends them to his disciples with the good news that he will appear to them (Mt. 28:1–10). When Jesus, in John's account, appears to his disciples on the day of his resurrection he takes the initiative, reveals himself to them and then gives them the Holy Spirit and the mission to forgive sins in his name (Jn. 20:19–23).

Various Scripture scholars indicate that in John's Gospel the resurrection, the ascension and the sending of the Holy Spirit are all considered to be Easter events and to take place on the day of Jesus' resurrection. In John Jesus indicates that he must first ascend before the Holy Spirit can be given (Jn. 7:30). But Jesus confers the Holy Spirit on Easter and this implies that he is already ascended and with the Father.[18] In other Gospels a distinction is drawn between the events of the resurrection, the ascension and the sending of the Holy Spirit. Saint Ignatius offers contemplations of thirteen post-resurrection appearances, including, interestingly, the appearance of Jesus to Paul, and ends the series with the contemplation of the ascension. Scripture scholars offer a variety of explanations for the differences in the post-resurrection accounts of John and the other evangelists. These differences are not my concern here. I simply wish to underline that missioning, like divine initiative and revelation/recognition, is a dominant feature of the post-resurrection appearances. It is also a major feature of the Scriptural accounts of the ascension and of the sending of the Holy Spirit.

Jesus, the natural Son of God, through his incarnation becomes a true member of the human family. Through his life, death and resurrection Jesus redeems his human brothers and sisters and empowers them through the gift of the Holy Spirit to become adopted sons and daughters of the Father. After his ascension and the sending of the Holy Spirit, Jesus, while not losing his individuality, takes on a cosmic role and becomes Head of the Body which is the Church (Col. 1:18–20). Jesus is at one and the same time cosmic Lord and yet intimately identified with the very least member of the human family. Jesus so radically identifies himself with each member of the family of Adam that whatever is done to any of his least sisters and brothers is done to him (Mt. 25:31–46; Ac. 9:3–6). At the same time, Jesus is so one with those who through baptism become sharers in his death and resurrection and living members of his Body that he is able to send them forth in his name to bring the good news of salvation to all.

Saint Ignatius draws attention to the "office of consoler that Christ . . . exercises"[19] after his resurrection and this expresses most profoundly the chief activity of Jesus after his resurrection and up to and including his ascension to the Father and his sending of the Holy Spirit. Jesus first consoles his disciples by revealing himself to them and inspiring in them faith, hope, love, courage and interior blossoming of such fruits of the Spirit as peace, joy, assurance, gratitude. Jesus then sends out his disciples to console as he consoled, to "proclaim the good news to all creation" (Mk. 16:16), to teach (Mt. 28:20), to baptize (Mk. 16:16), to heal (Mk. 16:17–18), to forgive sins in his name (Jn.20:22–23), to exercise the office of good shepherd, leader and guide (Jn. 21:15–17; Mt. 18:18). Jesus tells his followers that they are to work without cease in seeking to bring the good news of salvation to every creature until the world ends and he returns to bring all the faithful to full participation in the glory of the resurrection and the face to face vision of the Father. Jesus then will also be subject to the Father so that he can be "all in all" (1 Cor. 15:28).

Each Christian in the upward spiraling of ongoing religious and moral conversion is called to turn ever more fully toward

Christ in prayer and also to turn toward Christ as he is present in the very least of his brothers and sisters who are created in the image and likeness of God. Each Christian is endowed with certain natural gifts and with specific charisms of the Holy Spirit to be used for the good of others. It is a task of the Christotherapist to aid the seeker to recognize appreciatively the particular natural gifts and spiritual charisms which he or she possesses. It is then the calling of the Christian to be constantly open to recognize and receive those individuals whom God sends to him or her for an experience of gifts of healing and growth which no one else at that particular moment in space and time is able to mediate to these individuals. In the life of each Christian there is a certain limited number of individuals he or she will be called upon to minister to and serve. One might almost speak of "the sacrament of the present person" to describe these unrepeatable, providentially arranged encounters. For in these meetings Christ is present both as the server and the served and they become privileged moments in which healing, growth and grace are communicated in visible and invisible manners. Each of these meetings with the "present person" is totally special and of immense significance, even though it may involve "nothing more" than the offer of a single word of comfort or a simple smile from the heart.

Jesus tells us that in the final analysis we will be judged in the light of how we ministered to those individuals whom God sent especially to us. And he sends certain ones to us each day and in every one of them Christ is present to be ministered to and served in some fashion. When, then, Jesus comes in glory to judge the living and the dead he will speak to us in the name of every individual he sent to us during our lives and with whom he identified himself. To some of us he will say either "I was hungry and you gave me food" or "I was hungry and you never gave me food." To others of us he will say either "I was thirsty and you gave me drink, I was a stranger and you made me welcome" or "I was thirsty and you never gave me anything to drink; I was a stranger and you never made me welcome." To still others of us he will say either "I was . . . naked and you clothed me, sick and you visited me, in prison and you came to see me" or "I was. . . . naked and you never clothed me, sick and in prison and you never visited me" (cf. Mt. 25:31–46). Such is the mystery of the drama of salvation and damnation. All hinges on the love of God and the love of neighbor and, of course, if we claim to love God but fail to love our neighbor and our enemies as well then we are liars and the truth of God does not dwell within us. As John of the Cross put it: "At the evening of life, you will be examined in love."[20]

The radically converted neurotic and addict, as they spiral upward in the turning-toward stage of ongoing conversion, are called, like all followers of Jesus Christ, to share with others the gifts of healing and wholeness which they have received. As Step Twelve of *Alcoholics Anonymous* puts it: "Having had a spiritual awakening as the result of these steps we tried to carry this message to alcoholics, and to practice these principles in all our affairs."[21] As I remarked above, each Christian is endowed with certain natural talents and is also offered special spiritual charisms for the good of others. In the case of the neurotic and the addict in the stage of ongoing psychological conversion and/or of conversion from addiction they are often uniquely qualified to minister to those who are still in need of radical healing of neurosis and/or addiction. Recovered and yet recovering neurotics and addicts are often gifted with a special sort of compassion, understanding and a capacity for "tough love" which makes them ideal ministers of healing for those who are still radically overpowered by a sense of worthlessness and/or enslaved by addiction to drugs, gambling or other forms of addiction. This is why it is proper to say that Step Twelve is the natural and ultimate flowering of the other eleven steps.

It is important to realize, however, that not all neurotics and addicts who are spiraling upward in ongoing conversion from their particular deformations are called to minister in a direct or primary fashion—except through prayer—to individuals in need of radical conversion from psychological or addictive sufferings. Each individual has his or her own unique combination of natural talents and spiritual charisms and these combinations can differ tremendously from person to person. This means that the type of ministry to others which recovered and recovering neurotics and addicts are called to offer can differ widely and need not be restricted to aiding sister or brother neurotics and addicts. It remains true, however, that when Jesus returns, many a converted neurotic and addict will hear Jesus speak such words as the following to him or to her: "I was filled with a sense of worthlessness and you gave me a sense of being lovable, worthwhile to myself and others"; "I was filled with anger, bitterness and resentment and you brought serenity, forgiveness and joying in the good of others into my life"; "I was a slave to alcohol and you helped me along the way to sobriety"; "I was addicted to gambling and you showed me the path to freedom."

The Contemplation to Attain Love of God

The meditation on the *First Principle and Foundation* has as a basic aim to prepare the retreatant for a proper entry into the prayer exercises of the Four Weeks. A twofold goal of the *Contemplation to Attain Love of God* is to place the retreatant in an optimal state of mind and heart for exiting from the intense prayer-experience of the *Spiritual Exercises* and to dispose the retreatant for carrying the fruits of the retreat into his or her daily living.

The *Contemplation* is a holistic prayer-experience because it engages the retreatant in the utilization of his or her memory, imagination, understanding and will and effects as well a deeper education and transformation of feelings.

In two introductory notes to the *Contemplation* Saint Ignatius reminds the retreatant that "love ought to manifest itself in deeds rather than in words"[22] and that "love consists in a mutual sharing of goods" in which "the lover gives and shares with the beloved what he possesses . . . and vice versa."[23] These notes of Ignatius express the same dynamic desire to serve and to share which characterize Step Twelve of the *Twelve Steps* of *Alcoholics Anonymous* and related groups.

Certain commentators on the *Spiritual Exercises* affirm that the *Contemplation* recapitulates and transforms into a higher unity the basic movements of the Four Weeks.[24] I agree with this interpretation of the *Contemplation.* I also think that a key reason for the telescoping in the *Contemplation* of central elements of the Four Weeks is to remind the retreatant that the experience of the retreat is a beginning, not an end; that the retreatant is called in his or her daily living to reenact in prayer and to manifest in actions the basic movements of the retreat, as he or she continues to ascend even higher in the upward spiral of ongoing conversion. This stress on repetition, which is so typically Ignatian, is also present in Step Twelve with its words about practicing "these principles in all our affairs."[25] There is a sense in which the recovered and yet recovering neurotic and addict also reexperience, though from the perspective of a radically converted, transformed consciousness, the different stages of psychological conversion and/or conversion from addiction, as they attend group meetings and also when they work with individuals who are at diverse stages in the healing process.

There are some commentators on the *Contemplation* who see it primarily as a particular method of prayer which Saint Ignatius recommends rather than as the culminating moment of the *Spiritual Exercises.*[26] I see it both as the final, crowning moment of the *Spiritual Exercises* and as a method of prayer which possesses certain affinities with the dynamics of the process of spirit-feasting as I have developed it.

In the process of spirit-feasting the core moments are (1) a prayer for existential appreciation of a particular life-enhancing truth or value; (2) a moment of existential recognition of the truth or value, as it is revealed; (3) an ongoing feasting of the understanding, heart, imagination and spirit in the unveiled, life-enriching truth or value. In the prayer of petition of the *Contemplation* Saint Ignatius suggests that the retreatant ask "for an intimate knowledge of the many blessings received, that filled with gratitude for all" he or she "may in all things love and serve the Divine Majesty."[27] Clearly, the Ignatian movement from a prayer for understanding to an experience of gratitude for a recognition of blessings received and a desire to demonstrate this gratitude through love and service offers a clear, if analogous, parallel, to the stages of the spirit-feasting process.

In the *Contemplation* Saint Ignatius proceeds to enumerate various blessings received by the retreatant through the development of four points which in some fashion recapitulate key gifts bestowed and truths and values revealed during the Four Weeks of the *Spiritual Exercises.*

In a first point, Ignatius asks the retreatant to "recall to mind the blessings of creation and redemption, and the specific favors"[28] he or she has received. This point recalls the gift of creation, which is so central to the meditation on the *First Principle and Foundation,* and the drama of liberation from sin and its effects, which is at the core of the First Week meditations. In a second point, Ignatius asks the retreatant to reflect on how God "dwells" and "makes a temple"[29] in him or her. This second point reminds the retreatant of the mystery of the Word-made-flesh in Jesus Christ and his dwelling among us which is central to the Second Week contemplations. In a third point, Ignatius asks the retreatant to consider how "God works and labors"[30] for him or her in creation. Of course, the supreme "labor" of God is the passion of the Eternal Word made flesh for us. As one writer puts it: " 'Works' (Spanish *trabaja*) has a nuance of pain . . . Ignatius is thinking of the Passion."[31] Finally, in a fourth point, Ignatius suggests to the retreatant that he or she consider "all blessings and gifts as descending from above."[32] Of course, the raising of Jesus from the dead and the Pentecostal sending of the Holy Spirit are the supreme gifts which descend from above. In this final point the retreatant is invited to lift his or her mind and heart to the things that are on high and this means above all to God himself who is the supreme Value and the ultimate Truth in whom all the brothers and sisters of Christ are called to delight eternally. The prayer of the Psalmist expresses very well the attitude of the retreatant at this point and also provides an excellent example of a most exalted form of spirit-feasting:

> Let me see you in the sanctuary; let me see how mighty and glorious you are . . .
> I will raise my hands to you in prayer.
> My soul will feast, and be satisfied and I will sing glad songs of praise to you.
>
> (Ps. 63:2, 4–5 T.E.V.)

The form of prayer and focus on blessings and existential truths and values of the *Contemplation* are also quite relevant to the development of the addict and neurotic who are spiraling upward in their ongoing conversion from addiction and/or psychological conversion.

It is most appropriate for the radically converted addict and neurotic to recall the type of bondage they suffered from and to grow daily in an existential appreciation of the new truths and values they have grown to savor as they enter more deeply into the Promised Land of Wholeness, Sobriety and Sanity. These individuals, like the retreatants of the Fourth Week, ought to pray daily for an appreciative recognition of the blessings they have received and for the gift of an ever-deepening sense of gratitude.

It is a frequent practice at certain meetings of *Alcoholics Anonymous* for individuals to tell the story of their lives insofar as it relates to their struggle with drinking. What is especially moving and powerful is to hear recovered and yet recovering alcoholics tell the story of their lives as active alcoholics and then as radically converted alcoholics in a state of ongoing conversion. They often describe in vivid detail the destructiveness for themselves and others of their period of active alcoholism. They then relate their basic experience of "conversion" or radical healing. And they conclude by extolling from the depths of their minds and hearts the values which the life of authentic sobriety continuously unveils to them. These self-manifestations, when carried out in a constructive fashion, result not only in a profound healing of memories through envisaging the past from a redeemed perspective but also in an intensified existential appreciation of life-enriching human and spiritual values. The important role of the telling of one's personal story as an effective agent in the healing processes of so many addicts and neurotics validates in a very concrete way contemporary emphases on the vital place of the story in the salvation history of humankind.[33]

After Saint Ignatius presents the first point of the *Contemplation* he suggests that the retreatant in gratitude to God for his many gifts make a total offering of himself or herself to the Divine Majesty in the prayer entitled *Take, Lord, and Receive:*

> Take, Lord, and receive all my liberty, my memory, my understanding, and my entire will, all that I have and possess. Thou hast given all to me. To Thee, O Lord, I return it all. All is Thine, dispose of it wholly according to Thy will. Give me Thy love and Thy grace, for this is sufficient for me.[34]

This prayer is meant to express a deep ratification on the part of the retreatant of his or her election and, at the profoundest level, a complete surrender of memory, imagination, intellect and will to the providential use and guidance of God. The retreatant entrusts all his or her powers of mind, heart, and imagination to the governance of God's love and grace which orders "all things for good" (Ws. 8:1).

One most excellent way for the retreatant and others to make this *Take and Receive* offering a vital reality in their daily living is to practice what I call "existential memory-enrichment" and ongoing feasting of the understanding, heart, will and imagination.

The memory is one of the richest powers God has bestowed on his human family. Saint Augustine somewhere speaks of the memory as a treasury. But a treasury can be empty or full; a treasury also can contain useless items, even dead men's bones, or it can overflow with incredible, priceless riches. Unfortunately, many individuals today make little use of the memory or fill it with worthless items and even at times with "mental garbage," to use a rather vivid expression of Dr. Hora.

But the individual who truly asks the Lord to take and receive his or her memory is called to fill the memory with authentic riches of mind, heart and imagination. I employ the adjective "existential" to describe this process because by using it individuals arrive at a new mode of *existing* in the world, a way of *existing* and being which involves dwelling in the inner castle of memory and daily adorning it with rich treasures to love and delight in. I have verified in many ways that the practice of the existential enrichment of memory proves to be a very powerful therapeutic agent and also a means of facilitating high-level psychological and spiritual maturation. The practice of this method also provides the individual with a rich inner treasury out of which the person can draw materials for the daily practice at ever higher levels in the ascent of the spiral of transcendence of the feasting of the understanding, heart, imagination and spirit.

Each individual is called to enrich the treasury of his or her memory in accord with the special psychological and spiritual needs and interests which he or she uniquely possesses. The Psalms, hymnic passages from the Hebrew and New Testaments, individual Scriptural sayings, poems of great aesthetic and spiritual power, canticles of the mystics and passages from the writings of the saints—all of these are potential materials for powerful existential memory-enrichment.

More specifically, individuals who are advancing in the way of prayer might seek to enrich their memories with poems and canticles of John of the Cross and other mystics. Individuals who are seeking to grow in the service of their neighbor and to find God in all things can profitably commit to memory such prayers as Francis of Assisi's *Lord, Make Me an Instrument of Your Peace* and the *Canticle of the Sun* and poems of Gerard Manley Hopkins such as *Pied Beauty, Hurrahing in Harvest, Spring and Fall, Inversnaid* and others. Neurotics and addicts should seek to enrich their memories with poetic and prose statements which are positive and directly oppose the particular demons they must struggle against. Where a person is battling with addiction Francis Thompson's *Hound of Heaven* can be a great help and comfort. Where a neurotic is struggling with the poison of envy, resentment or jealousy it can be very helpful to memorize Saint Paul's famous hymn to charity in 1 Cor. 13. Where a repentant sinner is fighting pride, memorizing Psalm 127 can prove a most effective antidote. "If Yahweh does not build the house, in vain the masons toil."

At times when I have proposed the process of existential memory-enrichment to individuals they have tended to ignore it as too obvious a thing to do to really be of much help. Others have no doubt simply avoided the practice because they felt their memories were too poor. But other individuals have let me know that they surprised themselves when they actually tried the method. I have received beautiful testimonies from persons who have discovered that the use of memory-enrichment provides a very rich source of healing and of growth. Even if a person has to struggle just to learn one line a day it can prove most beneficial. An individual recently wrote to me something like the following:

> When you suggested that I memorize some of the Psalms, I wanted to protest, "I have never been able to memorize." But, you know, I did—the first verses of Psalm 138—and I learned the secret! "I thank you, Yahweh, with all my heart . . ." comes to me at the oddest times during the day. I can see how making such thoughts a real part of you can make one's life really beautiful.

Existential memory-enrichment has many uses. I know a priest who has difficulties at times reading but who can now say the equivalent of his daily *Liturgy of the Hours* simply by drawing forth treasures from the house of his memory. I know individuals who have had completely new experiences when they got stuck in traffic jams or in doctors' offices or were undergoing painful physical examinations and instead of inwardly bemoaning their fate or even outwardly cursing they brought forth from the reservoir of their memory psalms, poems, hymns which were like a healing balm. There are times when even the very reflective person finds it too difficult to free himself or herself from situations just by thinking but memory can come to the rescue. The practice of memory-enrichment is profoundly useful for individuals who are struggling with deep problems of fear, depression, anger, guilt and other emotions. Existential memory-enrichment is a process which proves most helpful both in ordinary moments of boredom or mild anxiety and in more agonizing types of experiences.

In the *Take, Lord, and Receive* prayer the individual offers not only the memory but also the understanding and will to God.

And, as I remarked above, one of the best ways to make a reality of this offering in one's daily living is to practice the feasting of the imagination, understanding, heart and spirit. And the possible objects of spirit-feasting are endless. Individuals can spirit-feast on the smile of an infant, a sunny day, a symphony of Mozart, a painting of Rembrandt or the drawing of a loved child, a quasi-sacramental encounter with a person God has given to you for a brief moment or for a lifetime, a Eucharistic celebration, the mysteries of Christ revealed in Holy Scriptures, an inner experience of God's love and peace quietly pervading one's heart.

It is a very useful practice to dispose oneself prayerfully in advance for moments of revelation/recognition in which one can feast. For example, it is good to pray that God may let beauty, goodness or friendliness shine out in the face of a friend you are soon to meet again so that you can feast on these qualities and joyfully point them out to your friend. Again, it is life-enriching to put yourself in a prayerful disposition prior to visiting a museum or attending a concert so that the inner eyes of your heart will be open to the unveiling of beauty and to a consequent delighting in what is revealed to you. Dr. Maslow points out that we can educate ourselves to greater openness to peak-experiences. And, this education is all the more effective and fruitful when it is aided by the inward illumination of the Holy Spirit, whom we have called upon for assistance. It is also a most excellent practice for a person each evening before he or she retires to feast for some brief moments on the good happenings and gifts of the day that is just ending. In this way the fragrance of goodness and of grace fills the heart and one can then say:

> The joy that you give me is much greater than the joy of
> those who have plenty of grain and wine.
> As soon as I lie down, I go quietly to sleep; You alone, Lord,
> keep me perfectly safe.
>
> (Ps. 4:7–8 T.E.V.)

Spirit-feasting is very beneficial in aiding the recovered and recovering addict to lose interest in what negative, self-destructive "attractions" still remain by ever more powerfully centering his or her attention on those truths and values which are existentially valid and life-enriching. Some of the fruits of spirit-feasting in the addict in ongoing conversion are: a growing loss of interest in drinking or gambling or any other object of addiction and an ever intensifying thirst for tasting authentic human and spiritual values and for appreciative delighting in these values; a loss of the sense of isolation addiction produced and a growing experience of communion with others and an increasing capacity to be glad because others are glad; the loss of a self-pitying kind of existence and an increasing capacity for genuine concern for others and real caring; the loss of the sense of meaninglessness, disorder and chaos which so often dogs the addict and an ever deepening realization of the meaningfulness of existence and a growing sense of tranquility and peace; the loss of a sense of enslavement and an ever richer experience of true interior freedom; the loss of a consciousness intoxicated with mental garbage and the graced realization of a growing luminosity of consciousness and a sober intoxication with the things of God in Christ and the Holy Spirit.

The ongoing practice of spirit-feasting likewise entails for the recovered and recovering neurotic an ever diminishing interest in the self-destructive, negative phenomena which formerly mesmerized him or her and an ever deepening appreciative recognition of those truths and values which inspire and beget self-transcendence and an experience of abundant life. Some of the many fruits of spirit-feasting in the individual in ongoing psychological conversion are: a shift from hatred of self to a delight in the true self as good and lovable; a letting go of pseudo, false pride and a humble delighting in the truth of what one really is: an image and likeness of God and a brother or sister of Jesus Christ, the elder brother of us all; a loss of indifference toward others and a growth in empathy, compassion and warmth; a turning from endless self-seeking and self-referential thinking and acting and a deepening of self-transcending service to others. And the list could go on and on. But it is sufficient to realize that spirit-feasting tends to expel what is destructive and negative in the very process whereby it focuses on what is truly good, worthwhile, beautiful, divine.

Saint Ignatius introduces us to the *Spiritual Exercises* with the reminder in the first sentence of the *First Principle and Foundation* that the human being is created to praise God. In the fourth and final point of the *Contemplation* which concludes the *Spiritual Exercises* Ignatius focuses our attention not so much on the gifts of God as on God himself. Ignatius uses words reminiscent of the sentence of the epistle of James which states that "all that is good . . . everything that is perfect . . . comes down from the Father of all light" (Jm. 1:17). In the Fourth Week contemplations of the risen Christ Ignatius asks us to rejoice with Christ and for Christ because he is happy and in glory. In the last point of the *Contemplation* Ignatius again asks us to love God and delight in God because he is God, the absolute Fullness of Ecstatic Joy and Happiness. The highest form of spirit-feasting is to behold God in loving contemplation as Perfect Love, Perfect Truth, Perfect Beauty and to let the mind and heart express themselves in adoration, glorification and praise. The spirit-feaster who is lost in joying in God is like the spirit Dante describes in his *Paradise* "whose whole delight is to delight."[35]

Saint Augustine somewhere writes that when we are no longer pilgrims but enter into the "joy of the Lord," the glorious New Jerusalem, where we shall behold the Trinity face to face, then, "we shall repose and we shall see, we shall see and we shall love, we shall love and we shall praise . . . without end."[36] But even as pilgrims the author of the epistle to the Ephesians tells us that God the Father "chose us in Christ . . . to make us praise the glory of his grace" (Ep. 1:4, 6). Sister Elizabeth of the Trinity—Elizabeth of Dijon—was so overwhelmed by the sense of the vocation to praise God and the glory of his grace that toward the end of her life, as a result of God's special inspiration, she no longer called herself anything except "Praise of Glory" and in a postscript to a farewell letter she wrote to her sister she said: "This will be my name in heaven."[37] Saint Ignatius of Loyola and Sister Elizabeth of the Trinity shared in common a most profound devotion to the Holy Trinity. And they were both overwhelmed with the conviction that the deepest calling of the redeemed is to glorify and praise the Father, the Son and the Holy Spirit in all things. The richest form of prayer we can offer to God is the type of prayer expressed in such great hymns as the *Gloria* of the Eucharistic prayer, the *Te Deum* of the *Liturgy of the Hours* and the great hymns of praise of the Book of Revelation. All of these are ecstatic, self-transcending prayers of praising, honoring, adoring, thanking, glorifying God.

Psychologists who also understand from lived experience the deeper meaning of authentic Christian prayer tell us that there is great, grace-inspired power in prayers of praise, thanksgiving, honoring and adoring for making the person who utters these prayers not only holy but also ever more whole and radiant with abundant life. And this is as it must be. For the human heart is made for God and so the glorification, honoring, adoring and praising of God is the most perfect actualization of what it is to be fully human and alive in Christ. And perhaps nowhere is this profound existential truth more eloquently, simply and adequately expressed than in the Fourth Weekday Eucharistic Preface:

> Father ... we do well always and everywhere to give you thanks.
> You have no need of our praise,
> Yet our desire to thank you is itself your gift.
> Our prayer of thanksgiving adds nothing to your greatness,
> But makes us grow in your grace, through Jesus Christ our Lord.[38]

SECTION TWO

The Healing and Education of Feelings

2

THE PROCESS

13

Anxiety and Fear

Individuals who are seeking the healing of sinful, neurotic or addictive difficulties or who are in quest of ever higher levels of psychological and spiritual growth must always deal in some manner and degree with such basic human feelings as anxiety, fear, anger, sadness and guilt. These feelings are at the core of any truly developing person's experience of being and living. My goal in this and the remaining chapters of this book is to show in a very specific, concrete way how to apply the principles and methods of Christotherapy to the healing and education of these most fundamental human feelings.

Before zeroing in on the specific feelings of anxiety and fear I wish to sketch the sequence of stages involved in the healing and education of feeling responses in general. The reader will recognize in my sketch of stages a more differentiated development of my earlier outline of the stages of the processes of mind-fasting and spirit-feasting.

The Christotherapist in a diagnostic and appreciative approach to the healing and education of feelings should first assess whether the seeker is at ease and basically free in regard to the expression of his or her feelings. If the seeker is not free and comfortable in speaking about his or her feelings then it is the first task of the Christotherapist through existential loving to create a climate of acceptance, warmth, and "letting-be" in which the seeker can come to feel free and at ease with himself or herself and with the Christotherapist in expressing feelings.

The Christotherapist and the seeker of healing or deeper educational refinement in the feeling area need to be aware of seven possible stages in the healing and refining processes. I will present these stages from the perspective of the seeker.

Stages in the Healing and Education of Feelings

A first stage in the healing and refinement of feelings is the cultivation of an openness of the seeker to his or her feeling experiences. This requires attentiveness to even momentary flashes or intimations of the existence of certain feelings or subtle mood shifts. For often enough repressed feelings make brief but disguised appearances in such phenomena as facial constrictions, sharp denial that one has such and such a feeling, avoidance of certain areas of discussion or persons, rigidity and refusal to go beyond the superficial in conversation.

A second stage consists in identifying a certain feeling or mood, distinguishing it from other feelings, naming it and recognizing its recurrence.[1] To be able to have a feeling, to distinguish it from other feelings and moods is already to begin to enjoy a certain objectivity in reference to the feeling and to experience an initial control in regard to that feeling.

A third stage involves an owning and initial acceptance of a certain feeling as a real aspect of what I presently experience in myself. Very often this takes place when another person vividly acknowledges and owns a particular feeling and I am able to identify with the person in the feeling experience he or she is expressing. This experience of identification is a common phenomenon in such groups as *Emotions Anonymous* and *Recovery Incorporated.* I should also emphasize that feelings occur spontaneously and as such they are not to be viewed in a moral context. There is, for example, all the difference in the world between the spontaneous feeling of hatred and a hatred which is deliberately, freely and maliciously fostered. No spontaneous feeling is proof in itself of the moral state of the individual who has such a feeling.

A fourth stage consists in acknowledging to myself and, in appropriate circumstances, to another person or persons exactly how I feel, what mood I am experiencing. Human beings are social beings and they possess a spontaneous orientation, a natural desire to share themselves and how they feel with others. Moreover, often enough in the very process of manifesting oneself to another, a person gains deeper, more revelatory insight into his or her feelings. In *Christotherapy* I describe this as the healing law of revelation of the self to the self through self-manifestation.[2]

A fifth stage involves a prayerful focusing of attention on the objects which evoke one's specific feeling responses and a detecting in one's consciousness of the images, attitudes, fantasies, thoughts which mediate and to a greater or lesser degree determine one's feeling responses to given objects. At this stage the individual needs to develop the capacity to recognize the medium or lower "voices" in the "polyphony of consciousness," the "automatic" thoughts and images which occur in the background of one's consciousness.

At a sixth stage the individual needs to seek prayerfully a diagnostic or appreciative understanding of the existential quality of the objects of his or her feeling responses and of the images, fantasies, thoughts, attitudes which are mediating these feeling responses. The final goal of the individual at this stage is to arrive at an authentic discernment, a *correct* diagnosis or appreciation of the disvalue or value, the destructiveness or the constructiveness of the objects of his or her feeling responses and, very importantly, of the images, attitudes, ideas which mediate these feeling responses.

At a seventh and final stage the individual is called to make a free, positive decision to live in accord with the authentic diagnostic and appreciative discernment he or she has reached in stage six. The individual demonstrates the reality of this decision by ceasing to cultivate those objects, images, attitudes, ideas, fantasies which have clearly manifested themselves to be existentially invalid, death-bearing, self-destructive. The individual likewise actively lives out his or her decision by appreciatively cultivating those objects, images, attitudes, ideas which have revealed themselves as existentially valid, as life-giving, as sources of self-transcendence. As the individual engages in the ongoing practice of the authentic fasting and feasting of the mind and heart he or she experiences a fundamental healing and maturation in the area of basic feeling states and responses.

Anxiety

The term anxiety has its etymological roots in Greek and Latin words which involve the idea of strangling, compressing, stress. Anxiety is a general feeling state of psychic discomfort, tension, apprehension, uneasiness, unrest.

What causes anxiety? I do not believe there is only one cause. A baby, for example, experiences anxiety when it misses the person whom it loves and longs for[3] and on whom it depends for basic care and protection. A baby also experiences anxiety when he or she senses rejection[4] or a basic lack of love and acceptance. Individuals also commonly experience anxiety in periods of developmental crisis and personality disintegration.

There are normal, healthy forms of anxiety and there are neurotic types of anxiety. Anxiety, for example, is normal and healthy for a baby who temporarily misses his or her protector. But neurotic anxiety arises when a baby is subjected to repeated experiences of long-lasting periods of abandonment by the protector. Neurotic anxiety also occurs in the individual who experiences radical rejection or mere extrinsic valuation.

There is some evidence to suggest that the baby in its early stages of development first manifests a type of startle in the face of a threat; at a further stage of development anxiety is felt; still later there is a feeling response of fear when the baby develops to the point where it can perceive threats from specific objects in its environment.[5] If this analysis is correct, then anxiety is a more primal feeling experience than fear.

Fear

Anxiety *tends* to consist in a generalized feeling state without a clearly defined object whereas fear is a feeling always related to a very specific threatening object, either real or imagined. Fear, like anxiety, can be normal or neurotic. The fear response is normal when it is proportionate to the particular object that is threatening, e.g. intense fear is a normal response to an attack by a vicious animal. Fear is neurotic, however, when there is a radical disproportion between the fear-response and the threatening object. I do not include here, however, the fear-responses of children which are products of their lively, developing imaginations. Fear is also neurotic when it manifests itself in phobias of various types. These latter are explainable in terms of traumatic events, neurotic anxiety and other causes.

Neurotic fear can have its roots in neurotic anxiety. The rejected individual, for example, experiences a sense of impotence in the face of threats to his or her basic personhood and worth. The rejected person is also lacking in a basic sense of trust in existence. He or she thus stands alone and is caught as a result in a double bind. He or she experiences a sense of inner worthlessness and powerlessness in the face of various threats, and at the same time feels no trust in other human beings and in reality itself as a source of protection.

Educating the Feeling of Fear

Just as a person can grow throughout his or her life in an ongoing refinement of aesthetic feelings, so an individual can move from a level of primitive fear responses to highly mature, spiritualized fear responses. Kazimierz Dabrowski, for example, describes a primitive form of fear which arises as a reaction to threats of natural disasters, physical pain, sudden death.[6] But Dabrowski also depicts higher level types of fear which are altruistic and even cosmic.[7] It is then desirable to seek both for oneself and others an authentic education and maturation of feeling responses of fear.

Images and symbols are powerful instruments for the education of feelings and, unfortunately, for the miseducation of feelings as well. The images and symbols of Holy Scripture, of Dante's *Divine Comedy,* of Ignatius' *Spiritual Exercises* and similar writings are especially fruitful sources for the authentic education and transformation of feeling responses, including the feeling of fear.

Jesus' parable of the Rich Fool (Lk. 12:16–20) who spent his time figuring out how to increase his holdings instead of preparing to meet his Lord effects an education of fear on the purgative level of the meditator on the parable. Likewise, Dante's vivid symbolic portrayal of the sufferings of the damned and Ignatius' First Week meditations on sin and hell can aid the meditator to experience a salutary education of the feeling of fear in the face of the self-destructive effects of sin. The meditator, however, on Jesus' parable and on Dante's and Ignatius' vivid descriptions of sin and hell is aware of the presence of God's creative and redemptive love and so his or her fear is transformed from a cringing servile fear into a filial fear which reverences God's Lordship and worships him "in reverence and fear" (Heb. 12:29).

The education and refinement of fear involves a certain hierarchy of levels of maturation. At one level a person's astonishment that he or she is not afraid where fear should be present serves as a catalyst in the education of fear.[8] Here Jesus' advice can prove instructive: "Do not be afraid of those who kill the body but cannot kill the soul; fear him rather who can destroy both body and soul in hell" (Mt. 10:28). At another level one's experience of disquietude at the fact that one is more fearful about one's own state of health than about the health of a person one loves can provide a stimulus for maturation in the quality of one's fear.[9] One can begin perhaps to imitate Paul the Apostle in his care for others: "There is my daily preoccupation: my anxiety for all the churches. When any man has had scruples, I have had scruples with him" (2 Cor. 11:28–29). In Paul, as in his Master Jesus, there is revealed a deep empathy and sensitivity to the fear and anxieties of others. At this level of the education of fear "the primary element in fear is altruistic concern, care for others, for those who are weak, easily frightened and taken advantage of by others."[10] There are also, at a very high level of emotional maturation, the fears and anxieties of the mystics as they confront the mysteries of contingency and death at their deepest levels and experience those purifications of mind and heart which lead to the highest forms of union with God in prayer possible in this life. In describing various levels in the education of fear I have not attempted to be exhaustive but rather simply to focus attention on some important stages in this ongoing process in the education of the feeling of fear.

The education of the feeling of fear and of other feelings as well does not take place within a vacuum, but occurs as a dynamic element within developmental and/or conversional processes going on within the person. Erik Erikson, Daniel Levinson, Gail Sheehy and others all indicate that there is a series of crisis-stages which occur in the individual who is growing chronologically and psychologically. At these times there is often an intensification of feelings of anxiety, fear, anger, frustration, sadness, depression and other emotions. Likewise, Kazimierz Dabrowski offers evidence that as an individual moves beyond a primitive stage of personality integration on the way toward the highest level of personality integration he or she passes through various stages of positive disintegration in which lower levels disintegrate to make way for the higher. As individuals pass through various stages of positive disintegration they can experience intense feelings of anxiety, fear, shame, guilt and other emotions. Dabrowski insists, however, that these intense feeling experiences are not necessarily pathological but rather inner dynamisms which move the individual toward the highest ideal of personality integration. Dabrowski points out that as the individual moves closer toward this highest level he or she affirms and befriends those "fears and anxieties which are altruistic, existential, or even cosmic."[11] The individual also purifies states of fear and anxiety "of everything that is not empathic, social, or existential."[12]

Clearly, the authentic education of fear and of other emotions requires in the educator a knowledge of the roles particular emotions play in the various stages of personality development. The Christotherapist must recognize that not all intense experiences in individuals of anxiety, fear, depression, and frustration are neurotic. They can just as well be heralds of a breakthrough toward a new and higher level of personality integration. But the correct discernment of the meaning of the particular fear, anxiety or other emotion which a person is experiencing is not an easy task. It requires a highly refined development of the capacities for existential, diagnostic and appreciative discernment.

Besides the educational encouragement of healthy feelings of anxiety and fear there is also the process of healing neurotic forms of anxiety and fear. In most contemporary works which treat of the emotions of anxiety and fear the focus is almost exclusively on the pathological expressions of these emotions. But I felt it important to show that the feelings of anxiety and fear can be positive and life-enhancing as well as destructive and that individuals are called to educate themselves and others in wholesome and holy forms of anxiety and fear.

As I indicated already, there are a variety of causes of neurotic anxiety and fear. My outline of the seven stages for the healing and education of feelings provides a fundamental method for attempting to uncover and deal with the various forms of anxiety and fear as well as other emotions. But I must limit myself here to presenting one basic concrete example of precisely how the Christotherapist can guide a person suffering from a key form of neurotic anxiety and certain specific fears through the four stages of the psychological conversion process. I hope that counselors, spiritual directors and others, drawing upon their own knowledge and experience, will be able to make creative applications of my general principles in specific problem areas I have not touched upon.

An Example

Jack, about thirty-five years old, comes to Betty, a Christotherapist, seeking help because he is in extreme emotional distress. In early conversations Jack explains that his mother and father never got along and are now separated. Jack further recounts that his mother paid very little attention to him as he was growing up, except to criticize him constantly for not doing better in whatever he happened to be doing either at home or at school. Jack frankly admits that he never felt really loved by his mother and that he in turn found it difficult to express affection toward her, even though he desperately wanted her love. Jack describes his father as a weak man, dominated by his mother. Jack's father did show affection toward him but was very insecure himself and suffered from hypochondriasis and phobias of various types.

Jack reveals in therapy that he feels like a failure, even when he succeeds in various endeavors. No matter how much he achieves, he still feels a deep gnawing sense of inner worthlessness. What is worse, Jack often experiences an intense anxiety that at times verges on panic. He becomes very tense in crowds and at times, while riding the subway, he has experienced such agonizing fear that it was all he could do to keep himself from screaming out to the conductor: "Stop the train! I've got to get off!" Jack is also constantly afraid, like his father, that he is going to get some dreadful disease. He hates to be around sick people and avoids them whenever he can. In general Jack manifests himself to his Christotherapist as a person whose life is full of worry, fearfulness, phobic tendencies and anxiety.

Within a few sessions it is manifest to Betty that Jack is one of the rejected ones who is in need of "psychic birth." Betty accordingly seeks to beget in Jack a sense of self-worth and self-confidence through the ongoing practice of holistic existential loving. Betty notes that Jack is more fortunate than many other rejected individuals because he discerns rather early in the process of therapy that he was rejected by his mother. In many cases the rejected individual has repressed the fact of rejection and it takes some time in therapy before the reality of rejection is recognized and acknowledged.

Betty, early in therapy, points out to Jack that he has taken a very important first step in the movement away from the neurotic hell of anxiety and fear in which he dwells in making the decision to seek help and in acknowledging openly his sense of powerlessness in dealing with his anxiety and phobias and of how unmanageable his life has become. Neurosis is a "*negating of possibilities, it is the shrinking up of one's world.*"[13] For this reason many neurotics are fearful of taking any action. Yet, the failure to seek help is itself a kind of decision which entombs the sufferer more deeply in his or her neurotic hell. Betty tells Jack about the First Step of *Emotions Anonymous* in which powerlessness over one's emotions and unmanageability in one's life are acknowledged, and she congratulates Jack for, in effect, taking this first step. Betty also tells Jack about Maurice Nesbitt, a man like Jack who had to struggle mightily with fear, and who in his book *Where No Fear Was* wrote:

> In the first place, one has got to admit that one is afraid. This is a humiliating confession to make, and one makes it very reluctantly. But in a matter so important as this, honesty is the best policy.[14]

Betty, up to this point, has employed a number of psychological means to help Jack begin to turn away from his radical neurotic condition, e.g. existential loving, encouragement in his "first step," providing him with an example of another neurotic sufferer with whom he could identify. But Jack is a believing Christian and he tells Betty that he came to her because he hoped that she, as a Christotherapist, could show him how to use Christian principles and prayer in his quest for psychological healing. Betty, in response, at once tells Jack that she has been praying for him since he first called and made an appointment to see her. She also indicates that if he would feel comfortable with the procedure, she would pray with him briefly at the beginning and end of their sessions. Jack is delighted with this procedure. Betty did not begin their first session with a prayer because she wanted to find out what Jack's views about God and prayer were. Betty knew from her training that it is a mistake to presume from the outset of a therapeutic encounter that the seeker will be open to making prayer an explicit factor in the session.

Betty next seeks to help Jack come to a gut-level diagnostic understanding that his inner sense of worthlessness and his basically negative self-image and self-concept are a lie rooted largely in his experience of rejection. Betty counters this lie with the truth that Jack is a child of God, created in the image and likeness of God. Betty stresses that "God is love" (1 Jn 4:8) and that God loves and delights in each of his creatures who are in his image and likeness. Little by little Betty teaches Jack how to spot the self-destructive thoughts of "how inferior I am," "how unlovable I am," which occur intermittently in the background of his consciousness. Betty helps Jack to see the lie in these thoughts and to let go of them. In their place Betty suggests that Jack put images of himself as a beloved child of God, as a brother of Jesus Christ, as a friend whom Betty and others like and appreciate. Betty is here using both psychological and spiritual means to help Jack let go of those negative beliefs and images which belong to the lie that is Jack's anti-self and to cultivate those truths which reveal to Jack his true self as a lovable child of God, created in God's own image.

Jack's problem, however, is not limited to the struggle to come to a realization of his intrinsic worth and acceptability as a person. He is beset with intense fears and debilitating phobias. Certainly, as Jack gradually comes to a felt-realization and appreciation of his value as a person, he will experience an increase in self-confidence and a diminishment in the intensity of his felt anxiety, and also of his fears and phobias. But the psychic-birthing process is for the most part lengthy and it is necessary for the Christotherapist to provide immediate aid to Jack in dealing with his fears and phobias.

Jack has already taken a major first step in the process of a radical turning-from his fears and phobias in acknowledging his sense of powerlessness in their regard. Betty needs to help Jack come to the existential insight that his excessive fears in certain areas are largely due to the fact that when he was very young he could not feel total trust and security in the presence of a parent he sensed did not love him. For this reason, even when ordinary dangers threatened him, he felt an exaggerated fear since he lacked trust in his maternal protector. Moreover, because his father was a neurotically fearful individual, Jack also tended to make his own the intense fear responses of his father. Dr. Albert Ellis would say that Jack's neurotic responses flowed from the irrational idea "that if something seems dangerous or fearsome, you must preoccupy yourself with and make yourself anxious about it."[15] Betty needs to help Jack locate this idea as one of the automatic thoughts or images which recur in the background of his consciousness so that Jack can see it for what it is—irrational and untrue—and begin little by little to let go of it.

But Betty also needs to help Jack begin to make a radical turn toward a Higher Power which can bestow on him a sense of trust in life and courage in living. Because Betty knows that she can tap the reservoir of faith which Jack possesses she begins to encourage him to focus his attention on God as a Loving Protector who is always present to him and providentially at work in his life. Betty encourages Jack to pray over and even commit to memory Psalm 91 in which God promises that he will protect those who trust in him:

> I rescue all who cling to me,
> I protect whoever knows my name,
> I answer everyone who invokes me,
> I am with them when they are in trouble.
>
> (Ps. 91:14–15)

Betty also recommends other Psalms to Jack as especially helpful for the healing of fear, such as Psalm 23, the *Good Shepherd,* and Psalm 27 *In God's Company There Is No Fear.*[16] Betty also encourages Jack by pointing out to him that in his turning to God for help in his struggle with fear and by entrusting himself to the providential care of God, he has, in effect, carried out the Second and Third Steps of *Emotions Anonymous* in which neurotics come to believe that a Power greater than themselves can restore them to sanity and make a decision to hand their will and their lives over to God. This knowledge is most beneficial to Jack because it helps him to realize that he is following a path which has aided countless human beings to move toward mastery over their fears.

As a further aid to Jack in helping him to deepen the turning-toward stage of his radical psychological conversion Betty suggests that Jack meditatively read the book by Hannah Hurnard entitled *Hinds' Feet on High Places.*[17] This book is an allegory in which a character named "Much Afraid," who is a member of the "Family of Fearings" and dwells in the village of "Much Trembling," is helped by the Chief Shepherd to escape from the valley and to finally reach the "High Places where 'perfect love casteth out fear.' "[18] Betty knows that this book is a potential source of a powerful bibliotherapeutic experience for Jack because the author of this book, like Jack, had to struggle with fear, and the book expresses in allegorical form the author's own passage through the various stages of the healing of fear. Hannah Hurnard herself acknowledges in a preface to *Mountains of Spices,* a sequel to *Hinds' Feet on High Places:*

> I was born with a fearful nature—a real slave of the Fearing Clan! But I have since made the glorious discovery that no one has such a perfect opportunity to practice and develop

> faith as do those who must learn constantly to turn fear into faith.[19]

The Bible, of course, is the supreme bibliotherapeutic source. Maurice Nesbitt acknowledges that he found healing "by the simple expedient of re-reading the Biblical record and adapting the material imaginatively"[20] to his own condition. But the books of Hannah Hurnard are themselves steeped in the imagery of Holy Scripture and alive with the healing hope and inspiration which Christ, the Chief Shepherd, gives to all who open themselves to him and his transforming touch. I should point out that the person Jack in my case presentation is a well educated individual. Obviously the Christotherapist must adapt the use of bibliotherapy to the mentality and cultural stage of development of the seeker.

In the clinical example I am presenting, Jack is suffering from certain severe phobias as well as from an excessive sense of fearfulness in facing up to the challenges of life. I have found working with various individuals suffering from phobias that Viktor Frankl's "paradoxical intention"[21] is a very powerful psychological technique for either eliminating or significantly alleviating phobic difficulties. Accordingly, I have integrated the technique of paradoxical intention into my spiritual-psychological synthesis.

Viktor Frankl, as early as 1929, made use of the technique of paradoxical intention.[22] Succinctly expressed, the core of paradoxical intention, as applied to phobias, consists in intending or wishing for, "if only for a second,"[23] the very thing one fears. Frankl observed that in persons suffering from phobias a certain chain of psychic events took place which resulted in a kind of vicious circle. Specifically, Frankl noted that if a person had a certain experience, e.g. sweating profusely in meeting one's boss, the individual in some cases became fearful that he or she would manifest this embarrassing somatic phenomenon again in similar circumstances. But the fear of recurrence tended to bring about the very thing one feared. "A self-sustaining vicious circle is established: A symptom evokes a phobia; the phobia provokes the symptom; and the recurrence of the symptom reinforces the phobia."[24] Frankl discovered, however, that if he encouraged the phobic individual to intend deliberately the occurrence of the very symptom he or she feared, then this exercise of "paradoxical intention" tended to break the vicious circle and the symptom often disappeared.

In the clinical example I have been presenting, Jack suffers from a severe case of hypochondriasis. He is constantly fearful that he will come down with some dread disease. Betty, accordingly, seeks to help Jack learn the technique of paradoxical intention. She teaches him that when, for example, he begins to experience a fear that he will get cancer, he should internally say to himself: "I hope to get cancer and the sooner the better. And for good measure I hope I come down with several other serious diseases as well." Jack should repeat this process of paradoxical intending whenever he begins to experience the appearance in his consciousness of the old fear. There is a very high probability that Jack will experience the complete disappearance of his phobia or at least a significant mitigation of the intensity of his phobia and a growing capacity to cope with it in an adequate fashion.[25] I myself have utilized paradoxical intention in a good number of different cases of phobia and it has produced excellent results. In fact, I dealt with a case similar to Jack's in my example, and within one week the phobia regarding the contracting of some fearful illness had disappeared. Also, it is especially appropriate for the Christotherapist to utilize a method like paradoxical intention because the latter is a psychological procedure which effects a certain self-transcendence[26] in which the sufferer actually laughs at the phobia and grows in an inner sense of self-detachment and freedom.[27]

Betty continues to aid Jack in the turning-toward stage of his radical conversion from neurotic anxiety and fear. She encourages him to deepen himself daily, with the help of the Holy Spirit, in his commitment to Christ, and to learn to deal successfully with temptation he is sure to encounter. Accordingly, like "Much Afraid" in *Hinds' Feet on High Places,* and, like the person who commits himself or herself to the following of Christ the King in the Ignatian meditation on the Kingdom, Jack entrusts himself ever more fully to the Chief Shepherd. Likewise, with Betty's help Jack learns to unmask the strategies and temptations of "the Fearing Clan," e.g., neurotic attitudes and behavior and to discern appreciatively the attitudes and methods of the Good Shepherd.

A principal temptation the fear-neurotic experiences in varying degrees in both radical and ongoing psychological conversion is cowardice. Jack, then, needs to cultivate faith and holy courage. And, "courage consists not of the absence of fear and anxiety but of the capacity to move ahead even though one is afraid."[28] What Jack must do is fix his eyes on Jesus Christ and contemplate him in such mysteries as his calming of the storm at sea (Lk. 8:22–25) and his raising of the fear-filled, doubting Peter from the waters (Mt.14:28–32). Jack should also keep constantly in his heart the words which Jesus spoke to Jairus, the synagogue official, when he was told that his daughter was dead: "Fear is useless; what is needed is trust" (Mk. 5:37 N.A.B).

A second temptation the "Much Afraid" type of person is subject to is an overwhelming fear of suffering. In Hurnard's *Hinds' Feet on High Places* the Chief Shepherd assigns two guides to help "Much Afraid" in her ascent to the "High Places." These two guides are named Sorrow and Suffering.[29] The Shepherd tells "Much Afraid" that she must trust these guides and learn to befriend them. She will learn valuable lessons from them and in the end their names will be changed into Joy and Peace.[30] Jack must also keep in mind, as a source of courage, that "there are such things as treasures of darkness. The darkness, thank God, passes. But what one learns in the darkness one possesses forever."[31]

Dr. Abraham Low also provides some very helpful assistance to neurotics who basically fear the pain and discomfort of their neurotic symptoms. First, Low points out that neurotic symptoms, e.g. a panicky feeling, are "distressing and annoying but not at all dangerous."[32] Low also suggests that neurotics deliberately cultivate "THE WILL TO BEAR DISCOMFORT"[33] since he holds that what the neurotic primarily fears is the discomfort present in the symptoms.[34] I believe that by *combining* the cultivation of the truth that neurotic symptoms are distressing but not dangerous with the practice of the will to discomfort, the neurotic can often "break the back," so to speak, of the neurotic symptomatology. This is so because, as in the case of paradoxical intention, the very basis of the fear is undermined and at times completely removed. The methods of Low are strictly psychological, but I believe that at a more profound level they can be rooted in a growing spiritual detachment in the face of suffering. I am not here urging a form of Stoicism, but rather a radical detachment rooted in an unswerving trust in God's providence in all things.

A third temptation the fear-neurotic suffers is the tendency to give way easily in the face of neurotically threatening situations. Here the sufferer would do well to keep in mind some advice Saint Ignatius gives regarding dealing with a temptation of the devil. Ignatius points out that if a person faces the temptations of the evil one boldly "the enemy becomes weak, loses courage, and turns to flight."[35] On the other hand, if the tempted individual begins to "be afraid and to lose courage in temptations, no wild animal on earth can be more fierce than the enemy of our human nature."[36] The same is true as regards neurotic fear. If a person refuses to face the object of his or her fear, the dominance of the fear becomes greater and greater and it becomes successively more difficult to overcome it. In the case of the fear-neurotic there is often the tendency to use a drug or some other escape mechanism in the face of fear. But then the last state of the person is much worse than his or her original condition.

A fourth difficulty to which the fear-neurotic is subject is the temptation not to persevere in the struggle to overcome and to move from radical to an ever richer state of ongoing psychological conversion. In this case it is most important for the fear-neurotic and, indeed, for every neurotic, to begin each day by entrusting himself or herself to the care of the Good Shepherd during that day and by resolving to persevere at least for that day in the struggle with fear. A key maxim of *Alcoholics Anonymous* is "A day at a time," and this motto is equally applicable in the case of the neurotic. Jesus himself taught this very attitude when he said: "Do not worry about tomorrow; tomorrow will take care of itself" (Mt. 6:34). Indeed, the lives of countless individuals offer indisputable proof that persevering "a day at a time" blossoms often enough into a lifetime of authentic perseverance.

In my present discussion of anxiety and fear, and elsewhere throughout this book, I have referred to *Emotions Anonymous* and to *Recovery Incorporated.* Each of these self-help groups has proven to be a very rich source of aid, comfort and healing in varying degrees to thousands of suffering persons.[37] In fact, it is quite appropriate in certain circumstances for a Christotherapist actively to suggest to a seeker that he or she attend one or other of these groups as a complementary aid to the therapy he or she is receiving. I have found, for example, that a person suffering from phobic difficulties can often derive significant help by participating in *Recovery Incorporated.*

There are significant differences between the principles and methods of *Emotions Anonymous* and *Recovery Incorporated.*

There is not, for example, the spiritual stress in the latter which is so characteristic of the former. But there are also some important similarities in the approaches of the two groups. In both, for example, there is a climate of basic support and encouragement. Likewise, in both, individuals are encouraged to give personal examples of how they suffered in the past from some particular neurotic difficulty; how they previously handled their neurotic problem in a destructive way; how they are now learning to handle their problem in a constructive, healing way through the use of the principles and methods of the group to which they now belong.

The personal testimonies of individuals within *Emotions Anonymous* and *Recovery Incorporated* are very powerful therapeutically when they are presented in an appropriate fashion. They promote self-expression and the freedom from repression which this often facilitates. They often give certain listeners to these stories insight into their own self-destructive attitudes and strategies for dealing with their neurotic pain. They force individuals who have been unconsciously or nonreflectively engaged in various forms of denial or rationalization regarding their real state to face themselves in a new way. They release tensions in individuals who identify deeply with what they hear and are led as a result to express their own feelings in an open way. They give each member a sense that he or she is not alone in his or her particular form of neurotic suffering. They evoke individual and group support for persons who are beginning to deal with their problems in a constructive fashion. They provide hope for beginners who see that others had problems as bad as or worse than their own, and yet managed with varying degrees of success to overcome these difficulties. They provide an opportunity for individuals who are at various stages of ongoing conversion to offer the support of example and of positive care and concern for those fledglings who are in need of radical psychological conversion.

As I indicated earlier, in the case of the healing of neurotic deformation the shift from radical to ongoing psychological conversion involves more often than not a gradual rather than a sudden transition. In the case of Jack, then, which I have been presenting in the past few pages, there comes a point where through the experience of the existential loving of Betty and others and through his continuing practice of mind-fasting, spirit-feasting and other methods, he arrives at a point where the psychological health pattern is in clear ascendency over the sickness pattern in his life. Jack is now in a state of ongoing psychological conversion.

Saint Ignatius of Loyola offers two sets of "Rules for the Discernment of Spirits." He indicates that the first set of rules is more suited to the First Week of the *Spiritual Exercises* and that the second set is more appropriate for the Second Week.[38] Saint Ignatius does not offer special rules for the last two Weeks of the *Spiritual Exercises* but presumes that the rules he has already elaborated will suffice for the last two weeks as well. Analogously, the basic set of existential methods I have already articulated, e.g., the methods of diagnostic and appreciative discernment, are equally applicable in the turning-from and turning-toward stages of ongoing psychological conversion. But there are further nuances involved in the application of these methods in the stages of ongoing psychological conversion and I would like to indicate some of these as they apply in the case of Jack which I have been presenting.

Jack, accordingly, although he is now in a state where he is more psychologically healthy than ill, must still deepen his rejection of neurotic attitudes and behaviors, which still tend to manifest themselves at times in greater or lesser degrees of intensity. Jack is now, however, less dependent on his Christotherapist and growing in his capacity for a certain self-therapy.

Among the qualities which Jack needs to cultivate in the turning-from stage of this ongoing psychological conversion is the virtue of humility. Jack needs to keep clearly in mind that he is recovered and *yet recovering*. It will be helpful for Jack to cultivate what Dr. Low calls a sense of "averageness."[39] The person who appreciatively develops a sense of "averageness" avoids the pitfalls of the sentimentalist illusions of grandiosity and exceptionality.[40] It is, of course, legitimate and, indeed, important for a person to "endorse"[41] himself or herself for dealing well with a neurotic difficulty. To endorse oneself is to acknowledge to oneself that one has had a victory in a struggle with some neurotic symptom. But this act of self-endorsement should be an act of self-endorsement *in Christ;* an acknowledgement of a success realized with the help of the greater Power. Thus it does not mean that the person yields to illusions of grandiosity. Both the recovered and yet recovering addict and neurotic must beware of developing a false sense of pride or security. For the result is too often a relapse. Consequently, it is important for Jack to contemplate Jesus in the humble actions of his daily life, to seek to imitate Jesus who was "gentle and humble in heart" (Mt. 11:29) and who, though "his state was divine, yet . . . did not cling to his equality with God but emptied himself to assume the condition of a slave" (Ph. 2:6–7).

Another quality which Jack must learn to appreciate and cultivate is *patient perseverance.* This is needed when periods of darkness and discouragement come. Even in ongoing psychological conversion certain symptoms can reappear and in intense form. Jack may experience, for example, an outbreak of certain phobic tendencies which he thought were gone forever. He will be tempted to give in to discouragement and/or to engage in some self-destructive form of escape from the pain of the symptoms. At this time Jack must hold his ground and might recall the advice of Saint Ignatius who says that "in time of desolation we should never make any change, but remain firm and constant in the resolution and decision which guided us the day before the desolation."[42]

A further quality which Jack should prayerfully seek to develop is compassion. No one truly understands a particular suffering of another better than a person who has gone through the same thing. Jack should daily make the prayer of Saint Francis of Assisi his own and seek to practice what he prays: "Lord, make me an instrument of your peace."

Jack's Christotherapist, Betty, can also help him to grow in self-knowledge by suggesting to him that he prayerfully read such works as Dante's *Purgatory,* Hurnard's central chapters in *Hinds' Feet on High Places* where "Much Afraid" passes successfully through many tribulations, and, above all, the passion accounts in the Gospels. Betty should also suggest that Jack prayerfully memorize certain passages from these works, for in times of struggle and desolation these passages, like an oasis in the desert, will prove a source of refreshment and strength to move ahead patiently and with courage.

In ongoing psychological conversion, of course, the deepening movement of turning-from is always accompanied by an intensified turning-toward. And, in the measure God grants, the twofold movements are repeated at successively higher levels in the ongoing ascent of the spiral of transcendence.

As Jack advances in the turning-toward stage of his ongoing psychological conversion, he grows in an ever richer felt sense of God's love for him and he experiences more deeply the fruits of the psychic birth Betty and others have brought about in him. He is filled with gratitude to Betty for mediating to him an experience of how much Christ loves and values him. He experiences his own inner worth, lovableness and value as a person, and he becomes increasingly more trustful toward himself, others and God. Anxiety and fear diminish in him as holy trust and courage increase.

In the First Epistle of John the author writes that "in love there can be no fear, but fear is driven out by perfect love . . . and anyone who is afraid is still imperfect in love" (1 Jn.4:18). The author of the epistle is speaking, of course, of the type of fear which is the result of sin and of the type of love which is the gift of God poured into our hearts by the Holy Spirit who is given to us (Rm. 5:5). It is important, consequently, not to misuse this text by identifying the type of fear which is described with neurotic fear or the type of love which is spoken of with merely human love. These distinctions are vital because it is possible for a person who experiences a deep sense of worthlessness and great neurotic fears, due to human rejection, to possess nonetheless the gift of God's love in his or her heart—and in rich measure. This is so because psychological conversion and religious conversion are not identical realities.

In the case of Jack's psychological conversion, however, Betty uses throughout the process both psychological and spiritual means. And Jack, in turn, utilizes throughout both psychological and spiritual means in his quest to pass from his initial inner neurotic hell to ever higher levels in the upward spiral of ongoing psychological conversion. Consequently, in his recovery process Jack experiences not only a radical psychological conversion, but also, at the same time, growth in ongoing religious and moral conversion. For this reason, the text of the First Epistle of John I just quoted is applicable to Jack in a special way, since his inner growth in the love of God has enabled him to become ever more free from fears due to his own sins as well as from his neurotic anxieties and fears.

To further his own continuous growth in the upward spiraling of ongoing psychological, religious and moral conversion it can be very helpful for Jack to read prayerfully such works as Dante's *Paradise*, Part Two of *Hinds' Feet on High Places* entitled "Joy cometh in the morning"[43] and the *Spiritual Canticle* of Saint John of the Cross, with the accompanying commentary. Saint John is commenting, of course, on the Song of Songs in the light of his own inner mystical experiences. As Jack turns ever more fully toward the Lord and toward others in self-transcending forms of love and service he will be able to say with the Bride in the *Spiritual Canticle:*

Now I occupy my soul
And all my energy in His service.
I no longer tend the herd,
Nor have I any other work
Now that my every act is love.[44]

In the case of Jack, I have been offering an example of the ideal case in which an individual moves from a need for radical psychological conversion to a high level in the upward spiraling of ongoing psychological conversion. I believe that such profound healings do occur. But I also believe in many cases they do not. Why? Some individuals, of course, are not healed of their radical psychological woundedness because no one comes to their aid. God in his providence generally works through the instrumentality of human beings. Consequently, if people who are suffering from a famine are not supplied with food, they die. Similarly, if individuals suffering from radical love-deprivation do not encounter anyone who will bestow on them the gift of "psychic birth," they generally remain prisoners of their deep sense of worthlessness. These unloved persons, however, belong to God who loves them, and they are encompassed by his providence in a fashion which transcends our narrow understanding of God's ways. Again, there are individuals who are so severely crippled psychologically that their deformation seems almost as "irreversible as the loss of . . . physical limbs."[45] Yet, even in these cases, at times "the spirit can grow in the midst of, in spite of, and through the instrumentality of" the very illnesses they suffer from.[46] There can be developed "the willingness to act even without feeling,"[47] and there can blossom "the tentative and 'careful' acts of love and goodness"[48] and a "growth in the sense of the need for God's help."[49] Further, there are others who do pass from a state of radical to ongoing psychological conversion and continue to suffer very intensely at times, and this, despite the fact that these individuals are at a high level of religious and moral conversion. I can only suggest that perhaps these individuals are undergoing a purgatorial type of suffering which is the equivalent of the dark nights which the mystics pass through. In yet other cases, there are individuals who pass from radical to ongoing psychological conversion and become very effective instruments in the healing of others but still suffer from recurrences of intense phobic or other types of difficulties. Perhaps, like the Apostle Paul, these individuals are permitted to continue experiencing a certain "thorn in the flesh" lest they should become proud as a result of the healing which God works through them. They are constantly reminded through their suffering that God shows his power in choosing the weak to overcome the strong. Ultimately, of course, God alone knows the meaning of the sufferings each individual undergoes. It is his will that each of us should seek to be free from psychological deformations. But it is also his will that when we have done all we can do we should accept what we and others cannot change, in patience and serenity, and we should unite our sufferings with those of Christ to do what we can "to make up all that has still to be undergone by Christ for the sake of his body, the Church" (Col. 1:24–25).

14

Anger

What is anger? It is universally agreed that anger is one of the most basic human emotional responses. There is also agreement that anger, unlike fear, disposes an individual more to fight than to flee when threatened or frustrated in some manner. In an uninhibited expression of anger "the blood 'boils,' the face becomes hot, the muscles tense."[1] The greater the anger, the greater the flow of energy in the person and the greater the need for some kind of physical expression or action.[2] One theorist suggests that in the individual's emotional development rage is the earlier, more simple forerunner of anger. In this view rage is a primitive emotion which arises in the face of a perceived, immediately threatening danger of some kind and results in attack.[3] Anger requires a higher level of cognitive development in the individual than does rage, though like rage, it is often provoked, at least in part, by an assault of some sort and can result in strong, aggressive actions.

I have been offering a descriptive sketch of anger in its basic motivations, physical expressions and possible effects. I would like to look now at anger in terms of its basic causes and from a less descriptive point of view. I have found Dr. Aaron Beck's explanation of the process that evokes the emotional response of anger more illuminating than most.[4]

Beck, first of all, criticizes some of the classic attempts to provide an explanation of the causes of anger. For Beck it is inadequate to state simply that anger is an emotional response to an attack of some sort. Some individuals experience an overriding anxiety and become paralyzed rather than angry in the face of an attack.[5] Again, Beck finds that it is not sufficient simply to describe anger as an emotional response to the frustration of a drive or wish of some kind. There are many cases in which an individual will experience the frustration of some drive or wish without becoming angry, e.g., if a husband comes home to find dinner unprepared he will experience the frustration of his desire for a good meal but if at the same time he discovers that his wife is ill he will not experience anger, even though he has been frustrated in his desire for food.[6]

In Beck's theory the kinds of situations which usually lead to anger are: "(1) direct and intentional attack; (2) direct, unintentional attack; (3) violation of laws, standards, social mores."[7] For Beck the common factor which is involved in arousing a response of anger in a person is "the individual's appraisal of an assault on his domain, including his values, moral code, and protective rules."[8] But this common factor is not sufficient by itself to cause an angry response. Further conditions required are that the individual must "take the infringement seriously and label it negatively";[9] that the individual must not be primarily anxiously fearful in the face of the assault, since this would eliminate the possibility of the response of anger; and, finally, that "the individual must focus primarily on the wrongfulness of the offense and the offender rather than on any injury he may have sustained."[10]

There is one element in Beck's analysis of anger which deserves particular attention. This is Beck's point that for anger to occur "the individual must focus primarily on the wrongfulness of the offense and the offender rather than on any injury he may have sustained." I believe that Beck has hit upon a core element which is present in all forms of anger: normal and neurotic. Dr. Robert Solomon in his brief but brilliant analysis of anger in his book *The Passions* puts this same view in even sharper focus when he writes: "The key to anger is its judgment of *indictment* and *accusation.* Anger is a judgment of personal *offense.*"[11] John Bowlby in his classic work *Separation* provides two striking examples of how very young children reacted with anger penetrated with indictment when they were separated from their parents either because of sickness or an unavoidable storm. In the one case, Laura, a two year old child who had to be in the hospital for an operation later looked reproachfully at her mother and said: "Where *was* you, Mummy? Where *was* you?"[12] In another case, a little girl was separated from her father during a tornado, and when she saw him again she hit him with anger. Bowlby remarks that

> both these little girls seemed to be acting on the assumption that parents should not be absent when their child is fright-

ened and wants them there, and were hopeful that a forceful reminder would ensure that they would not err again.[13]

In the cases I have just described we see the element of indictment present at a very young age in the anger of normal young children. Now if indictment is a core element in the anger of normal individuals it is not surprising that it is present in perhaps an even sharper form in individuals who have experienced rejection. Dr. Evoy in discussing anger in rejected individuals points out that a prominent characteristic of the anger of rejected individuals was "imputability."[14] "Intense anger seemed to carry at least the connotation of injustice. . . . At least implicitly, the rejected felt that the person who caused their anger ought not to have acted that way."[15] I have focused somewhat intensively on the indictment element present in anger because in both the education and healing of anger it will be crucially important for individuals to come to grips with the indictment element in their anger and to deal with it in an authentic fashion.

Anger, since it always involves indictment, "requires a responsible agent as its object."[16] Evoy remarks that "when real rage was occasioned in the rejected by nonhuman elements, the frustrating situations or things invariably appeared to have been reductively personal. These enraged rejected at least inferred that some person was at fault."[17] Anger is usually directed at another, but it can be directed at oneself. When I am not watching my step, for example, and I stumble against a stone in my path, I may react by kicking the stone in anger but my anger is, in fact, self-directed, an indictment of myself for my carelessness.

Anger, like fear, can be either normal or neurotic. Anger is neurotic when it has its roots in the anxiety of rejected or extrinsically valued individuals. Anger is also neurotic when it is repressed. Likewise, anger is neurotic or flowing from immaturity when there is a radical disproportion between the anger-reaction and the situation/person evoking the reaction. I use the adjective "normal" in the present context to describe all forms of anger which are not neurotic. As I use it, then, the adjective normal does not imply any moral judgment about the quality of the anger or the level of development the anger represents. Thus, for example, in my terminology both a sinful display of anger and an exercise of righteous anger are "normal."

It is possible to educate the feeling response of anger just as it is possible to do so in the case of fear. In Dabrowski's theory at the very lowest level of development anger seems often to arise "without clear reason."[18] Anger in its most primitive forms is brutal and frequently results in aggressive acts. "It is aroused by obstacles in the realization of such needs as self-preservation, sex, ownership of property, power."[19] Anger at this lowest level of development tends to be intense and to lack control. The dominant presence of this form of anger in an adult reveals great psychic immaturity and/or neurosis.

At a somewhat higher level of psychological development a greater self-control in the expression of anger appears and it is less brutal. Parents can aid children to move toward this higher level by concretely demonstrating qualities of self-control in the face of provocation. They can teach their children to care for animals, to learn that animals naturally react aggressively to bad treatment and that it does not make any sense to get angry at an animal when it reacts to bad treatment. Parents could easily show their children through examples drawn from Holy Scripture how Jesus manifested a sensitivity toward animal life in his teaching about the shepherd who looks for the lost sheep (Mt. 18:12) and in his remark about how the providence of the Father extends even to a sparrow (Mt. 10:29). These examples will help children to learn to care for all living things and to control their anger in dealing with animals. Above all, parents should always seek to exercise a holy, enlightened anger toward their children when it is called for and they should show their children from Holy Scripture how much care and love Jesus had for children (Mt. 19:14). The example of the parents and of Jesus will prove most effective in teaching children to care for their peers and to exercise a proper self-control in expressing anger toward their peers.

At a yet higher level of development anger does not get out of control and its outward expressions are less frequent. But there is an anger toward oneself that easily arises.[20] This type of anger manifests itself especially in developmental crises when a person sees the gap that exists between his or her present state and the ideals that beckon one onward. Here the education of anger requires an attitude of authentic realism which excludes yielding to excessive, perfectionistic demands but which also acknowledges the need for ongoing growth. Here meditating on Jesus' education of his disciples proves helpful. Jesus did show anger at the slowness of his disciples to understand (Mk. 8:17–18; Mt. 16:22–23). But he also challenged his disciples to think over clearly the implications of what following him really meant before they made hasty commitments: "Can you drink the cup that I am going to drink?" (Mt 20:22). At the same time Jesus was quick to forgive his disciples and others who failed. In Jesus' dealings with his disciples it is clear that he at times became angry with them and expected them to be angry with themselves at their folly and stupidity and lack of growth. But Jesus also forgave them and he consequently expected them to be forgiving toward themselves, just as they would be toward others.

In Dabrowski's model the individual who reaches the highest level of personality integration manifests a powerful love toward others. In this type of person there is also a profound empathy present and "deep understanding of other psychological types and of their developmental level (yet without an approval of their negative aspects)."[21] There is a desire to promote friendship and to create conditions in which the need for anger is eliminated. But even at this highest level of integration "anger may arise in confrontation with moral, ethical, and social evil as in Christ's confrontation with the money changers in the Temple."[22]

It is characteristic of the individual who, with the aid of the Holy Spirit, has realized a high level of personality integration that he or she will be capable of righteous anger, but will equally possess a highly developed capacity for sympathy, compassion and forgiveness. The authentic, righteous anger of the person at this high level of development will be generally directed toward those who abuse, violate, exploit, torture others—either individuals or groups. In regard to slights, harms or injuries done to himself or herself the individual who is living at this very high level of self-transcendence will be more inclined to turn the other cheek (Mt. 5:39), to walk the extra mile (Mt. 5:41), to excuse because of ignorance (Lk. 23:34), to forgive (Ac. 7:59), rather than to lash out in anger. Of course, if the enlightened persecuted or misused individual sees that an expression of righteous anger would serve as an effective instrument in bringing about healing in those who are dealing with him or her in some unjust fashion, then the enlightened one will act accordingly.

Because today there is such massive abuse, mistreatment, enslavement, exploitation of both individuals and groups, it is important to consider what qualities individuals should possess as valid existential prerequisites for arriving at a just indictment of exploiters and abusers and for expressing and acting upon the righteous anger they feel in an authentic, healing and life-giving manner.[23]

First of all, because anger flows from indictment it is vital that individuals who seek to exercise righteous anger in the name of the injured and exploited should be free from radical neurotic deformation and addiction. These latter deformations blind individuals in their capacity to see reality as it really is. Also, individuals suffering from these radical deformations are inclined to manipulate and exploit the very individuals whom they are supposedly aiding through their so-called "righteous anger" and the aggressive acts that often flow from it. I presuppose, then, in a person who is going to exercise righteous anger in the name of others either freedom from neurotic or addictive qualities, or at least a high level of ongoing psychological conversion and conversion from addiction.

Secondly, because the capacity for deep selfless love is a necessary companion virtue in a person who feels called to exercise righteous anger in the name of others, it is crucial that the person seeking to reach a valid indictment should possess the inward gift of God's love, poured forth into his or her heart by the Holy Spirit. It is the individual who is ascending ever higher in the upward spiral of ongoing religious conversion who will be most free from biases and self-seeking and will thus be most capable of judging righteously and acting upon this judgment in an authentic fashion.

Now, as I indicated earlier, moral conversion is a first fruit of true religious conversion. And, since anger is rooted in judgments of indictment and accusation, if an individual is to avoid successfully the subjective distortions and individual bias in his or her judgments, it is essential that he or she be ruled by authentic values and not fundamentally by fears, desires and selfish concerns. Ongoing moral conversion, then, like ongoing religious conversion, is a prerequisite if a person is to exercise truly righteous anger in a constructive, creative fashion.

Besides the presence in a person of the invisible gift of the Holy Spirit, who is at work in all persons of good will, the presence in a person of explicit belief in Jesus Christ will prove most helpful in aiding an individual to judge righteously and to act upon righteous anger in an effective, constructive manner.

Jesus Christ in his life and teachings incarnated and gave witness to a specific view of the meaning and role of anger in human living. Jesus, for example, did not hold that injustices of an individual or collective nature are unreal, merely appearances, and that consequently it is unenlightened to respond to injustice with indictment, righteous anger and action. Again, Jesus did not take a Stoic view in the presence of the sufferings unjustly imposed on others. Jesus was quite capable of experiencing and expressing righteous anger and he lashed out in very stinging words against the hypocrisy of those who "used" religion and its prescriptions against the poor, the deprived, the sick (Mt. 15:1–9; Mk. 3:1–6).

Jesus clearly distinguished, as did his followers, between a just and an unjust, a righteous and an unrighteous, a holy and a sinful anger. Jesus was not thinking here of the spontaneous feelings of anger which arise apart from any control or exercise of freedom on the part of the individual who experiences an immediate surge of anger in the face of some attack or injustice. But Jesus did recognize that individuals could reflect on their anger and its motives and that in the light of this reflection they could then exercise a certain freedom in regard to their anger by acknowledging that in certain cases their anger was misguided and by exercising self-control in regard to the way they acted upon their anger. In this context Jesus warned that an individual who was angry with his brother without just cause was in danger of judgment (Mt. 5:21–22). Paul the Apostle also expressed anger in sharp words when he felt it was the righteous thing to do. But the author of Ephesians also instructs his readers that when they exercise their anger they should do so in a way that is not sinful (Ep. 4:26–27). Finally, Christ and his disciples clearly taught that it was a sin to hate anyone. Again, it is important to distinguish between a hatred that is spontaneously experienced and a hatred that is deliberately, freely fostered and nourished. Only the latter is a sin.

Christ clearly taught that it is ultimately only God who knows the inner core and heart of the human person. God alone is the final Judge of the conscience of the human being. The rest of us can always make mistakes in our judgments. Judges and juries make tragic mistakes despite their best efforts. Innocent people have been condemned to death and executed and only later did the terrible mistake come to light. For this reason each human being must humbly acknowledge the fallibility of his or her judgments regarding the actions and motivations of others. This does not mean that we must abstain from indictments, from righteous anger and from acting upon righteous judgment and anger. It does mean that we must do so knowing that in any individual case we could be mistaken. It also means that we must never play

God in regard to our knowledge of any human heart. We must leave the final judgment to God alone.

Finally, there is a need for a certain intellectual conversion in those who seek to reach valid indictments, especially when these individuals are dealing with indictments, righteous anger and consequent actions in the sophisticated arena of the political, social spheres. Here the social activist needs to be very faithful to the exigencies of the human mind and heart toward true attentiveness, understanding, reasonableness and responsibility. Today there is reason for much righteous anger in the face of massive racial discrimination, exploitation of the poor, and a multitude of other injustices. But to be a truly effective servant of the tortured, the economically deprived, those treated unjustly in any area, it is vital to be free from radical psychological deformation and addiction, to be in an ongoing state of religious and moral conversion, to be a true listener to the Gospel of Jesus Christ, to be a person deeply endowed with a capacity for selfless love, for compassion, for forgiveness as well as for feeling, expressing and acting upon righteous anger in the name of Jesus Christ who is one with all who suffer.

Unfortunately, besides normal anger in its positive dimensions and stages, there is also neurotic anger in its diverse forms. I would like now to consider concretely the healing of neurotic anger in the framework of the four basic stages of psychological conversion. But I will not limit myself, as I did in the previous chapter, to an extended treatment of just one concrete case.

Perhaps the most severe form of neurotic anger has its roots in the neurotic anxiety of individuals who experienced rejection or extrinsic valuation in their early years. In some of these cases the anger is repressed. In other cases, individuals tend to live lives dominated by angry moods and by frequent angry outbursts toward others. These individuals are constantly indicting others internally and striking out at others in sharp verbal abuse and, at times, in actual physical attacks.

The healing of individuals who suffer from a neurotic anger—repressed or expressed—which has its roots in rejection, requires on the part of the Christotherapist the practice of holistic existential loving and working through together with the sufferer the seven stages in the healing of feelings which I have described in the previous chapter.

Individuals who have repressed their anger either because of rejection or because they were taught that it was evil to express anger provide unconsciously a variety of clues to the presence in them of repressed anger. Trembling, unexplained sweating[24] and "tenseness in the body (particularly in hand, arm, and facial muscles)"[25] are frequently signs of repressed anger in a person. Likewise, irritability, annoyance, talk of being harassed, often signal the presence in a person of repressed anger.

Initially, it is up to the Christotherapist to create a climate of warmth and acceptance in which the sufferer who manifests likely symptoms of repressed anger can begin to relax and to communicate with an increasing sense of freedom and openness about how he or she feels. In cases where the sufferer has experienced severe rejection and where the repression of anger is very deep, the Christotherapist may have to bring the person to a basic sense of self-worth and a change in self-image and concept before the sufferer will experience the surfacing of the repressed anger in his or her consciousness and become capable of naming it, owning it and getting insight into it. In these cases an observation of Carl Rogers applies: "The change in self precedes, rather than follows, the recovery of denied or repressed materials."[26]

The type of case I have just described is, in my opinion, the exception rather than the rule. Dr. Baars, for example, has recently suggested that "the number of repressive neurotics seems to be on the decline since people repress their emotions less and less."[27] I maintain that in most cases an individual's repressed anger is "in the twilight of what is conscious but not objectified."[28] The individual experiences the anger but is not able to identify it, to distinguish it from other feelings and to name it for what it is. In these latter cases it is the task of the Christotherapist to aid the sufferer to bring the anger out of its twilight zone by helping the person to advert to those images, thoughts and forms of self-talk occurring in the background of consciousness which are the source of the anger which is conscious but not objectified, experienced but not understood. Once this initial task is accomplished, then the Christotherapist can aid the person to move gradually through the other stages involved in the healing of feelings such as anger.

Apart from the group of individuals who are victims of repressed anger, there is a much wider group of individuals who dwell in the hell of a neurotic anger that is constantly felt and openly expressed in ways that are both self-destructive and injurious to others. The neurotic anger of these individuals is often rooted in rejection and/or in existential miseducation regarding the dynamics of anger and its proper expression.

The type of person I have just described is usually *driven* to seek help from a therapist because he or she cannot bear any longer the pain and friction which result from living in a constant state of angry entanglements with others as well as with oneself. In cases of this sort a very important first step is for the sufferer to admit to himself or herself and to the therapist that he or she is powerless over the emotion of anger and that the constant experience and expression of anger has made his or her life unmanageable and quite miserable. Often enough, this acknowledgement is implicit in the very decision of the person to see the therapist. But it is very important therapeutically for the sufferer to acknowledge his or her experience of powerlessness explicitly. Through this humble admission the sufferer initiates the process of turning away from the radical neurotic hell of anger in which he or she has been living.

As I have stressed earlier a key element in anger is indictment. It is then vitally important for a person whose life is basically dominated by anger to seek to get at the indictments which underlie the anger and to evaluate them. But to reach the state where this is possible the angry person must identify, name, own and in a sense take responsibility for the anger he or she is experiencing. Once a person has passed through these stages then he or she is in a position to seek prayerfully an understanding of the nature of the indictments which underlie the anger.

Oscar Ichazo and others, as I indicated in an earlier chapter, hold that every individual tends to have a dominant passion and that this passion with its particular fixation and traps leads a person into unhappiness and needs to be balanced with its opposing virtue. Now, as far as anger is concerned, as far back as Hippocrates certain types of people were identified as choleric by nature. I am inclined to believe that for a variety of reasons, normal, as well as abnormal, individuals do tend to develop certain dominant emotional orientations, e.g. a melancholic temperament, a sanguine temperament, etc. Of course, where rejection and/or existential miseducation enter into the picture, natural temperamental orientations will be subject to distortions, deformations in varying degrees of intensity. Consequently, I believe that it is fair to assume that where neurotically distorted anger is present in individuals it is generally rooted in many false indictments and in unwarranted "leaps to judgment" before sufficient evidence for making a good judgment is available. I am not implying that a person who has experienced rejection can have no valid reasons for indicting the person or persons who rejected him or her in a righteous anger, although, even in the case of rejection, the rejecting persons were often rejected themselves and so are more deserving of compassion than of indictment from an objective point of view. I do hold, however, that a rejected person who is constantly indicting everyone from God to the next-door neighbor for whatever ills befall him or her is more wrong than right in the indictments he or she makes. And I think that any person whose life is dominated by anger even in everyday situations will come to learn through the practice of existential diagnosis, carried out in a climate of love and acceptance, that most of his or her angry indictments of self or others are unenlightened, unnecessary, unjustified, ill-advised and a source of more misery than good. The occurrence of this diagnostic discernment, facilitated by the aid of the Holy Spirit, will enable the anger-prone neurotic to unmask the false indictments and errors underpinning his or her anger and to turn from them in an ongoing fasting of the mind, imagination and heart.

Now in the immediately preceding pages I have been focusing on the two types of neurotics whose key problem emotion is anger, namely, the "repressive"-anger neurotic and what I might term the "expressive"-anger neurotic. In discussing the appropriate therapy for the repressive-anger neurotic I stressed the basic importance initially of facilitating in the sufferer the surfacing of the repressed anger. On the contrary, in commenting on the proper therapy for the expressive-anger neurotic I indicated the need to help the sufferer come to the existential diagnostic insight that false, unenlightened, ill-advised indictments underlie the major portion of his or her angry outbursts.

There is not, I believe, any contradiction involved in the different emphasis in my approach to the healing respectively of the repressive and the expressive anger neurotic. Where anger is radically repressed there is no capacity for the expression of anger, even where such an expression is appropriate and, in fact, required from an objective point of view. Accordingly, in this case the first task of the Christotherapist—along with existential loving—is to work at bringing the repressed anger to consciousness in the sufferer and then to help the sufferer to identify the anger, distinguish it from other feelings, name it and own it. On the contrary, where a person comes to a therapist complaining that he or she is almost constantly in an angry mood and is continuously lashing out at others in bitter, angry indictments and accusations, it is the task of the therapist—along with existential loving—to help the person to engage in ongoing diagnostic discernment regarding the legitimacy of his or her indictments and accusations. As the therapy progresses the expressive-anger neurotic will come to a diagnostic discernment that most of his or her indictments are unjustified and unnecessary.

Currently, there are two schools of thought in psychology with quite divergent emphases regarding the appropriate way to proceed in the healing of anger. One of these schools places great emphasis on the dangers of repression, on the vital need for self-expression, on the importance in the case of anger of expressing one's anger, of letting one's anger out, of "ventilating" it. The other school stresses the need to control one's anger, to eliminate angry feelings and expressions as much as possible from one's life.

Dr. Conrad Baars, to some extent at least, falls into the first school in terms of the strong emphasis he places on the fact that feeling anger is not bad or evil in itself; that as individuals who have unconsciously repressed their anger begin to experience it they should tell themselves "over and over again that it is all right to feel angry," and they should thank God for letting them experience his goodness in their feeling anger.[29] Baars, who spent two years in the Nazi concentration camp of Buchenwald, also states quite bluntly that "next to my faith in God, it was my constant anger at the Nazis for having deprived me of my liberty and their inhuman treatment of their prisoners that stimulated my determination to survive and to deny them the satisfaction of seeing me die."[30]

Drs. Albert Ellis, Paul Hauck,[31] Abraham Low, Thomas Hora and others tend to fall in varying degrees into the second school of thought regarding anger. Dr. Ellis, in fact, states in unequivocal language that it is possible to sum up the essence of emotional disturbance in one word: "blaming."[32] And Dr. Ellis goes on to list as his third major irrational idea the following: "the idea that when people act obnoxiously and unfairly, you should blame them and damn them, and see them as bad, wicked or rotten individuals."[33] Among the reasons Ellis lists for the irrationality of this third idea is the fact that people are not as free as we think they are in most of the things they do. And this means for Ellis that blaming and the anger which flows from it are basically unhelpful and destructive phenomena.

Dr. Baars is quite critical of the basic approach of *Recovery Incorporated* and of its founder, Dr. Abraham Low. Dr. Baars states that "the practical effect of the *Recovery* concept is to promote, rather than eliminate, the process of neurotic repression through will-training."[34] I am quite sure that Dr. Baars would be equally critical of the approaches of Drs. Albert Ellis, Paul Hauck and Thomas Hora in regard to their methods of dealing with anger. But, I rather suspect that if Low were living today he would probably be quite critical of Baars' basic approach to the healing of neurotic anger.

From my point of view it is possible to gain certain valid insights from both of the opposing camps which I have just described. I believe the way to do this is to distinguish clearly between the different emphases involved in the treatment respectively of the repressive-anger neurotic and the expressive-anger neurotic. The approach of Baars and of others who share in his basic orientation to some degree is very helpful in dealing with the repressive-anger neurotic. The approach of Low, Hauck and others of a similar nature is quite useful for dealing with the expressive-anger neurotic. I believe that my own seven stage approach to the healing of feelings incorporates the key valid insights of both approaches and is sufficiently flexible to allow for a diversity of emphasis in dealing with specific cases.

Earlier I stated that it is vital for the expressive-anger neurotic, in the turning-from stage of his or her radical psychological conversion, to engage in an ongoing diagnostic discernment in which there is a gradual unmasking of the falsity of the indictments which underpin the majority of his or her angry accusations and outbursts. I think that attendance at meetings of *Recovery Incorporated* and/or *Emotions Anonymous* can often hasten the occurrence of ongoing authentic diagnostic discernment. I also think that it can often prove useful to read certain passages from Low's *Mental Health Through Will Training*[35] where Low shows through concrete examples how individuals who are what I call expressive-anger neurotics easily fall into the trap of rash judgment and then suffer all kinds of miserable consequences. Most importantly, however, Low also shows often enough step by step just how the individuals were led to make the false indictments and consequently how they can avoid making such mistakes in the future. I suggest for a start that the interested reader study Low's presentation of the case of a woman named Mona and her angry day, beginning at the butcher shop and ending at home.[36] As Low's presentation unfolds the reader will see that Low is not seeking to bring Mona to suppress her anger; rather his aim is to help her come to the diagnostic insight that her angry indictments at the butcher shop were unjustified and resulted in a whole day of further unnecessary and unjustified anger and pain.

As further psychological helps for the individual who is in the turning-from stage of radical conversion I suggest that he or she reflectively think over some of the following ideas: (1) If an individual is inclined through habit and/or temperament to make hasty indictments and angry accusations, the reasonable and responsible thing for this person to do would be to seek to cultivate the habit—particularly in minor matters—of giving the other persons the benefit of the doubt; (2) angry indictments and accusations tend often enough to evoke in others an equally angry reaction, and this tends to establish a vicious cycle of mounting anger on both sides in which no one wins and everyone is a loser; (3) when a parent is constantly indicting his or her children and expressing anger toward them this often causes the children to become fearful and repressive of their own emotions, or else they learn the bad habit of acting just like their parent; there is also the danger that the children will become sullen, moody and hostile; often enough the children will tend to take out their anger on others when they are afraid to respond to their parent; this is also the case in adult relationships where the husband or wife who is rebuked by his or her boss will remain silent in the presence of the superior but then explode angrily at his or her spouse or children at home; (4) living in a state of constant anger is harmful to the physical as well as the spiritual and psychological health of the person.[37]

As spiritual helps for the expressive-anger neurotic who is in the turning-from stage of radical conversion, I suggest the following meditations and readings: (1) Jesus taught:

> Do not judge and you will not be judged; because the judgments you give are the judgments you will get, and the amount you measure out is the amount you will be given. Why do you observe the splinter in your brother's eye and never notice the plank in your own? . . . Hypocrite! Take the plank out of your own eye first, and then you will see clearly enough to take the splinter out of your brother's eye (Mt. 7:1–5).

(2) Jesus' disciple James taught: "Be *quick to listen* but *slow* to speak and slow to rouse your temper; God's righteousness is never served by man's anger; so do away with all the impurities and bad habits that are still left in you" (Jm. 1:19–21). Clearly James means that God is never served by a person's unrighteous anger; (3) Jesus in his parable of the unmerciful servant (Mt. 18:23–35) teaches that if we are willing to be judged mercifully by others we should be equally ready to judge and deal with others in a merciful fashion. As you recall, in the parable a merciful king cancelled the entire debt his servant owed him, instead of sending the servant to prison. But this very servant went out and had a fellow servant thrown into jail because of a very small debt that he owed. The other servants told the king about this and he called the unmerciful servant to him and said: "I cancelled all that debt of yours when you appealed to me. Were you not bound, then, to have pity on your fellow servant just as I had pity on you?" (Mt. 18:33). Matthew concludes the parable by adding: "And in his anger the master handed him over to the torturers till he should pay all his debt" (Mt. 18:34–35). These meditations I have proposed should at least appeal to the enlightened self-interest of the meditator and to that legitimate love of self which Saint Bernard lists as the first degree of love.

In the turning-toward stage of the radical psychological conversion of the expressive-anger neurotic a major breakthrough occurs when the expressive-anger neurotic comes to believe that a Power greater than himself or herself is available as a major source of aid in the healing process. For the non-believer the greater Power is often understood as a group such as *Emotions Anonymous.* The Christian believer also finds great help in groups such as *Emotions Anonymous, Recovery Incorporated,* or similar groups. But the Christian believer often comes with God's help to find in Christ the greater Power who can restore him or her to wholeness. For the expressive-anger neurotic it is important to contemplate Christ as the teacher who says: "Learn from me, for I am gentle and humble in heart, and you will find rest for your souls" (Mt. 11:29–30).

It is most important, I believe, for the person who is an expressive-anger neurotic to imitate Christ and his followers in those qualities and virtues which directly or indirectly oppose a judgmental, accusatory, hostile, aggressive way of thinking, phantasizing, imagining, desiring, acting. As spiritual aids in developing an ongoing appreciative discernment of those Christly values which are opposed to self-destructive forms of angry indictment and expression, I suggest the following texts and readings for meditative and contemplative consideration: (1) In the fifth chapter of Matthew Jesus says, "Happy the gentle; they shall have the earth for their heritage" (Mt. 5:4); again Jesus teaches: "Happy the merciful: they shall have mercy shown them" (Mt. 5:7) and, "Happy the peacemakers: they shall be called sons of God" (Mt. 5:9). It is important to realize the beatitudes are formulas for realizing true happiness and that Jesus lived them daily, and in formulating them, he was only expressing what he himself knew to be true from his own deepest experience. (2) Jesus constantly revealed himself as a gentle person who was again and again moved with compassion: "And when he saw the crowds he felt sorry for them because they were harassed and dejected, like sheep without a shepherd" (Mt. 9:36–37) and Jesus urged his followers to "be compassionate as your Father is compassionate" (Lk. 6:36); even in the case of the adulterous woman Jesus said: " 'Has no one condemned you?' 'No one, sir' she replied. 'Neither do I condemn you,' said Jesus; 'go away and don't sin any more' " (Jn. 8:10). An appreciative cultivation of compassion is one of the most powerful ways to expel an angry, accusatory spirit. (3) If it is true that love drives out fear, it is also true that it expels a hostile, condemnatory spirit, for Paul says of love that it is "always patient and kind . . . it is never rude or selfish; it does not take offence, and is not resentful . . . it is always ready to excuse" (1 Co. 13:4–7). The appreciative discernment of the existentially valid, beneficial qualities of loving and the incarnating of these values in one's life is the most effective way of all to expel self-destructive forms of anger from one's heart. (4) In cantos fifteen through seventeen of his *Purgatory* Dante portrays wrath and how it is cleansed through the virtue of meekness toward friends and enemies alike; the reflective, prayerful reading of these cantos of Dante fills the heart with a spirit of meekness, mercifulness and love.

In discussing the turning-toward stage in the radical conversion of the expressive-anger neurotic I have not mentioned the role of the Christotherapist. But it is similar to the role the Christotherapist played in the lengthy case study I presented in the chapter on *Anxiety and Fear.* Here too, where the expressive-anger neurosis is rooted in rejection, it is necessary for the Christotherapist to engage in the ongoing practice of existential loving and to help the sufferer to come to a proper appreciation and love of himself or herself and of others. Likewise, it is up to the

Christotherapist to embody personally and to clarify for the sufferer the virtues which are opposed to the self-destructive forms of anger. Hopefully, through the beneficent experience of loving acceptance and the practice of the feasting of the heart, mind, imagination and spirit on the existentially valid, life-giving qualities of gentleness, mercy, compassion, meekness and love, the expressive-anger neurotic will hand his or her life ever more fully over to the care and guidance of God and will be conformed ever more deeply with the image of Jesus Christ in the power of the Holy Spirit. In this way the expressive-anger neurotic will pass from the stage of radical to ongoing psychological conversion.

I have focused attention mainly on the radical conversion of the expressive- rather than of the repressive-anger neurotic for a number of reasons. In my own experience I have encountered more of the former than of the latter type of anger neurotic. Secondly, once the Christotherapist aids the repressive-anger neurotic to make the unconscious anger conscious, then slowly this type of neurotic, too, will have to learn to distinguish between existentially valid and invalid forms of anger and to express the former and to let go of the latter. Of course, this process will be slow,[38] mistakes will be made and the practice of diagnostic discernment will develop much more slowly than in the case of the expressive-anger neurotic.[39] Finally, I believe that psychologists, psychiatrists and charismatic healers have already done a great deal of writing on the healing of repressed anger and I do not wish simply to repeat their efforts.[40]

The expressive-anger neurotic who is now in the turning-from stage of ongoing psychological conversion needs to confirm, through the practice of diagnostic discernment and the consequent fasting of the mind and heart from destructive forms of anger, the basic turning-from of radical conversion.

There are a number of psychological and spiritual means which the expressive-anger neurotic can utilize in his or her deepening in ongoing conversion of the turning-from of radical conversion.

Here I will list a few of the psychological means which the recovered and yet recovering expressive-anger neurotic might utilize as he or she moves at different levels in the turning-from stage in the upward spiral of ongoing conversion. (1) Dr. Low stresses the need for the individual seeking the goal of recovery to be constantly on the alert for spotting various methods of sabotage of the recovery process, e.g. the common tendency to ignore or discredit improvements which have taken place;[41] overlooking certain symptoms which trigger emotional disturbance;[42] failure to notice the process in which the person begins to work himself or herself up into an angry outbreak;[43] not adverting to the irrational thinking which leads up to angry indictments against the God one feels abandoned by, or against other human beings, or against oneself.[44] (2) The practice of steps eight and nine of the *Twelve Steps* is a very effective means for deepening the turning-from of ongoing conversion; in these steps the recovered and yet recovering expressive-anger neurotic makes a list of all the people he or she has hurt in the past through angry indictments and outbursts and then attempts to make amends to all of these individuals to the extent possible. (3) The cultivation of key psychic dynamisms which Dabrowski lists as shapers of development is helpful; by cultivating the "subject-object in oneself" dynamism the individual learns to become a critical observer of his or her inner mental life.[45] By seeking to engage the dynamism of "autopsychotherapy" the individual seeks to work out "self-designed psychotherapy methods [and] preventive measures."[46]

Among the spiritual means for realizing with God's help the goal of turning ever more deeply from destructive forms of anger, the most important is contemplating Christ in his passion. The Scriptural accounts of Christ in his passion depict him as "the lamb of God" (Jn. 1:29), as the one who "like a sheep that is led to the slaughter-house, like a lamb that is dumb in front of its shearers . . . never opened his mouth" (Ac. 8:32). Jesus in his passion displays compassion (Lk. 22:26–34) and forgiveness of his enemies (Lk. 23:34). It is important for the expressive-anger neurotic to contemplate Jesus in his passion because Jesus shows them that even when one is unjustly treated, ultimately forgiveness is more important than blame and indictment, that serenity and calm in the face of one's accusers is a much more powerful response in most cases than anger. Jesus teaches that a display of love is the most powerful weapon of all against unjust treatment of oneself. Jesus' disciple Paul learned this lesson very well since he wrote to the Romans:

> Never repay evil with evil but let everyone see that you are interested only in the highest ideals. Do all you can to live at peace with everyone. Never try to get revenge; leave that, my friends, to God's anger. As Scripture says: Vengeance is mine—I will pay them back, the Lord promises. But there is

> more. If your enemy is hungry, you should give him food, and if he is thirsty, let him drink. Thus you heap hot coals on his head. Resist evil and conquer it with good (Rm. 12:17–21).

Another important spiritual means for the use of the recovered and recovering expressive-anger neurotic is the practice of steps four through seven of the *Twelve Steps* in which the individual engages in a searching and fearless moral inventory, admits to God, to himself or herself, and to another how he or she has hurt others through unjust angry indictments and outbursts, becomes eager to have God remove his or her defects of character in the area of anger, and prays humbly that God will remove them. It is important to recall that the person who is in ongoing psychological conversion has reached a point in the healing of his or her expressive-anger where he or she has realized a certain degree of freedom and responsible choice regarding anger and its expression. As another means of spiritual help the individual who is in ongoing recovery might find it helpful to read Hannah Hurnard's *Mountains of Spices*[47] since Hurnard there deals in her allegory with "characters" such as Gloomy and Spiteful, Umbrage and Resentment—all relatives of Anger.

As the recovered and recovering expressive-anger neurotic engages in the turning-toward state of ongoing psychological conversion, he or she should above all focus on Christ as the embodier of serenity, gentleness, peace. Dante, as I have indicated, suggests that the person whose dominant sin is anger should seek to cultivate the virtue of meekness. Oscar Ichazo, on the other hand, teaches that the individual whose predominant passion is anger should endeavor to cherish the virtue of serenity. Jesus in his life constantly incarnated and preached to others the beautiful existential qualities of meekness, serenity and peace. Jesus manifested his great serenity, for example, when in the midst of the storm at sea, as his apostles cowered in fear, he awoke and calmed the storm (Lk. 8:22–25) with a simple word of rebuke. He remained calm and at peace throughout the whole situation. Jesus was also basically a man of peace and he pronounced as truly blessed those who imitated him as a peace-maker (Mt. 5:9). Jesus radiated a spirit of compassion, mercy and joyfulness. Jesus' joyfulness burst forth in his song of praise to his Father: "I bless you, Father, Lord of heaven and of earth, for hiding these things from the learned and clever and revealing them to mere children" (Mt. 11:25). Also, the chief characteristics of Jesus' resurrection appearances are a spirit of peace, joy, forgiveness, reassurance, love.

As regards the turning-from and turning-toward of the ongoing psychological conversion of the repressive-anger neurotic, there will, of course, be the need to overcome the temptation to remain silent out of fear when the rights of others and one's own rights are violated. In these cases it will be necessary for the repressive-anger neurotic to assert himself or herself in the name of justice. But even here, as the repressive-anger neurotic ascends higher and higher in the upward spiral of ongoing psychological conversion, he or she will experience a growth in freedom from repression and there will be less and less need to assert oneself when one's own rights are violated. But, where it is a case of the violation of the rights of others, this is another matter. When Jesus was arrested in the garden, he did not fight back, but he did speak up for the disciples and say: "If I am the one you are looking for, let these others go" (Jn. 18:8–9).

There is a difference, finally, between an important Buddhist view of anger and the Christian view. Anger in a certain Buddhist perspective is "an ego-centered attitude which makes the mind restless";[48] anger is, together with cupidity-attachment, arrogance, lack of intrinsic awareness, indecision and opinionatedness, one of the six basic "emotionally tainted mental events."[49] For this reason "anger does not allow one to settle on the pleasures of this life and produces immeasurable frustrations in the next life."[50] "In short, anger does not offer one the slightest chance to be happy."[51] I believe that this view of anger is shared *in one degree or another* by Hora,[52] by Grover B., the founder of *Neurotics Anonymous*[53] and by many others. I myself find much that is attractive in this negative view of anger; for, if we lived in a world *without* sin there would be no such thing as anger. Further, I agree with a growing number of scientists that anger is for the most part more of a liability than an asset[54] to the human race. I also believe that much of the anger people experience is more harmful than helpful.

It remains part of Christian belief, however, that there is such a thing as righteous, healthy, holy anger. And this is most true where an individual is confronted with the exploitation of the helpless, the poor, the deprived. Jesus showed anger at the exploitation of others and Paul also indicates that God will visit his vengeance on those who mistreat and abuse others. It remains true, however, that it is God's will that we should seek to be at peace with all human beings as much as we can and that only the person whose heart is filled with compassion, mercy, forgiveness and love can have any certainty that the anger he or she shows in defense of others is truly righteous and not a subtle form of sinful or neurotic self-seeking.

15

Sadness and Depression

Sadness in its most primitive form is perhaps more accurately named distress. The latter is the type of feeling a person spontaneously experiences when she or he is faced with some present internal or external evil such as illness or physical mistreatment. Sadness in the more proper sense is less primitive than distress because it involves "elements of reflection."[1]

To be sad is to be afflicted with grief, unhappiness, a pain that is more than merely physical. Thomas Aquinas suggests that sadness is felt in the face of a present evil but that the present evil always involves the absence of some good.[2] For example, the sadness a person feels about a friend who has cancer is also a sadness about the friend's lack of health. Dr. Robert Solomon argues that sadness, sorrow and grief all involve a judgment of some kind of loss. He speaks of a "small loss in sadness, large loss in sorrow, traumatic loss in grief."[3] I agree with Solomon and others who hold that there are degrees of intensity of "sadness" and that the element of loss is always involved. I believe that in depression, which is a most intense form of sadness, the element of loss is especially in evidence. I am prescinding here from those forms of depression which are organic or biochemical in origin.

There are healthy and unhealthy forms of sadness. It is healthy to be sad when a friend is suffering. It is unhealthy to be sad when a disliked person escapes some suffering which he or she did not deserve. There is need for a healing and refining of feelings of sadness just as there is in other feeling areas. It is one of the tasks of the Christotherapist to aid individuals in the healing and education of feelings of sadness.

In Dabrowski's framework, at the most primitive level of personality integration, an individual experiences displeasure or disappointment at the failure to effect external forms of success. Dabrowski describes this type of feeling of disillusionment as a short-lived, pseudo-sadness.[4] At a higher level an individual feels sadness over imperfections, distance from one's ideals, lack of sufficient creativity; sadness is also experienced in being separated from loved ones, in the breaking up of deep relationships. At a yet more developed level, sadness results from viewing the pain and suffering of others and one's inability to help others distinguish what is truly important from the non-essential.[5] At the highest level sadness "results from deep solitude of thought in relation to transcendence and the absolute, in relation to one's own death and the death of others."[6]

The meditations and contemplations of the *Spiritual Exercises* provide the Christotherapist with a dynamic set of clues for aiding the seeker in the progressive education and refinement of his or her feelings of sadness. In the First Week of the *Spiritual Exercises* Ignatius encourages the retreatant to pray for a type of purgative sadness over the destructiveness of sin, especially in one's own life. In the Second Week the retreatant is invited to contemplate the call of Christ the King and he or she can experience in prayer a certain sadness in realizing how great the gap is between the call and his or her response. In the Third Week the retreatant prays for the gift of sorrowing with Christ in his suffering and dying. Finally, in the Fourth Week sadness is transformed into joy with the contemplation of the risen and glorified Christ. The retreatant, however, cannot remain indefinitely with his or her eyes fixed on the heavens where Christ has ascended into glory. The retreatant must go forth from the blissfulness of the Fourth Week to labor for the spread of the Kingdom and this can lead to moments of deep sadness, as the former retreatant encounters again and again the mysteries of suffering, apparent failure, and dying in the lives of those for whom he or she labors. It is also possible to experience a type of mystical sadness which in Dabrowski's words "results from deep solitude of thought in relation to transcendence and the absolute." The Christotherapist is called to provide the seeker with those materials for meditation and contemplation which can lead him or her toward ever deeper refinement in feelings of authentic sadness.

Depression

Depression is a very complex reality. There is accumulating evidence that various depressive states have biological, that is, metabolic, genetic or biochemical causes. The Christotherapist should be aware of this fact and should be very careful regarding the diagnostic process. I believe that many individuals have undergone much needless suffering due to the fact that a therapist failed to make a correct diagnosis.

I am going to be relatively brief in my discussion of the nature of depression and of the process involved in the healing of depression. I am going to limit my considerations to those depressive states which are psychological, not biological in origin and which are at most severely neurotic but not psychotic.

I hold that severe neurotic depression is often rooted in rejection or being valued for what one can achieve rather than for oneself; it also generally involves negative, destructive, beliefs about oneself, the world and the future.[7] This cluster or set of negative images, thoughts, attitudes, beliefs is often not recognized *as such* and in large measure exists in the twilight zone of consciousness.

As in the case of anger, I also find the approach of Dr. Aaron Beck to depression most enlightening. Dr. Beck's book entitled *Depression: Clinical, Experimental and Theoretical Aspects*[8] is widely recognized as a major contribution to psychiatric literature. He also synthesizes his approach to depression in his more recent *Cognitive Therapy and the Emotional Disorders.*[9] In Beck's analysis it is a sense of loss, either imagined or real, that lies at the core of depression. As he puts it, the depressed person "*regards himself as lacking some element or attribute that he considers essential for his happiness.*"[10] Such lacking or lost elements can be as diverse as attractiveness to others, competence in attaining goals, tangible possessions, status, good health or even a longed-for goal finally achieved which involved unrealistic or exaggerated expectations. In the last instance there is an experience of disillusionment and letdown.

Beck does not deny that such emotions as anger and anxiety can accompany depression. But he does not see these emotions as constitutive of the core of depression itself. Sadness is for Beck the key emotion connected with depression. Beck notes that the same external circumstances can bring about sadness in one person, anxiety in another and anger in a third. He writes:

> If we know the meanings attached to the event, we can generally predict which emotion will be aroused. Paramount meanings are determined by the person's habitual patterns of conceptualizing particular kinds of life situations and also by his psychological state at the time the situation occurs. If

> his main concern is with danger, he feels anxious; if he is preoccupied with loss, he feels sad; if he focuses on the unacceptable behavior of the offender, he feels angry.[11]

Where Beck uses the expression "anxious" I would speak of fear, since I prefer to use the word fear when a definite object is clearly involved.

Dr. Hora analyzes depression in a fashion which parallels rather closely the view of Beck. In regard to the dynamics of depression Hora writes: "What is involved in depression? There are two things: First, there must be an attachment to some thing, some place, some one, or some idea. And then there is a loss of that which we are attached to."[12] In a similar vein Dr. Willard Gaylin observes in his recent book *Feelings:* "It becomes obvious, then, that whatever we overvalue in terms of our pride system will be a potential source of depression if its existence is threatened."[13] Hora's and Gaylin's comments confirm Beck's theory that depression is rooted in the loss, either imagined or real, of something the person considers "essential for his happiness."

I must emphasize here that there is a normal, healthy sadness and sorrowing which a person experiences in the face of a traumatic event such as the loss of a loved one. My concern here is not with this normal, healthy sorrowing and grieving but with what is unhealthy. It is true, of course, that even grieving over the loss of a loved one can become unhealthy and neurotic. But there is a normal grieving process which must be allowed to take its course where the loss of a loved one is concerned.

In coming to grips with depression Christotherapy is holistic and utilizes certain insights of sound psychology together with Christian revelational principles of healing.

As I already indicated, I believe that rejected or extrinsically valued individuals are especially prone to depression. The first aim of Christotherapy, accordingly, in dealing with the depressed person is to love and affirm the person in a holistic manner. The Christotherapist says to the depressed person with heart, mind and feeling: "I am glad that you exist!" The Christotherapist in an open and prayerful spirit seeks to discern the good qualities in the depressed person and to behold in him or her an individual created in the image and likeness of God and loved "even unto death" by Jesus Christ. Moreover, in every way possible the Christotherapist seeks to awaken in the depressed person a sense of his or her worth and value as a human being, as a child of God and as a brother or sister of Christ.

The Christotherapist seeks to create a climate of love and acceptance in which the depressed person can begin to be open to a healing and growth through enlightenment in which destructive beliefs and assumptions are unmasked, seen for what they really are and let go of and in which integrative, life-enhancing meanings and values are discovered, appreciated and loved. Once the individual begins to verify for herself or himself that her or his sadness is flowing from these previously unobserved destructive attitudes, then the person can begin to let go of them. This process of "letting go" involves a fasting of the mind, of the heart and of the imagination. This fasting is not repressive because it is conscious, freely engaged in and flows from enlightenment. In like manner the person is aided to discover life-giving values and meanings and to nourish and delight in them in an ongoing fashion. In the healing of depression, accordingly, there is needed a basic cognitive, evaluative, imaginative restructuring in which "devils" of negativity are driven out and "angels of light" are invited into the sanctuary of the spirit.

I should mention here that apart from the practice on the part of the depressed person of mind-fasting and spirit-feasting there is a need for the individual to make use of such means as physical exercise, good eating, recreation, rest, working with one's hands, and seeking out new projects for creative activity. Indeed, in the initial stages of the healing process the practice of existential loving on the part of the Christotherapist and the engagement on the part of the depressed person in the types of activities I have just mentioned may constitute the most essential elements in the therapy. These elements will gradually facilitate in the depressed person a growing capacity to engage in the prayerful processes of the fasting and feasting of the mind, heart and imagination.

In the context of the healing of depression, radical psychological conversion involves a fundamental letting go of those attitudes, beliefs, assumptions which distortedly elevate some element into an absolute prerequisite for happiness or even for continuing to exist and a turning-toward and embracing in the mind, heart and imagination of those truths about oneself, the world, the future and God which are life-encouraging, life-enhancing, life-fulfilling.

I do not wish to imply that the severely depressed person is generally culpably responsible for being in a depressed state. The depression, as I already stated, can be due to a profound existential ignorance of the heart and mind resulting from severe rejection and the distorted mind-sets, heart-sets and image-sets which are inevitable accompanying factors. I must also emphasize, however, that there does come a point in the healing of depression where the exercise of true freedom becomes a possibility and indeed, a moral imperative. As Drs. Ann and Barry Ulanov put it: "In the treatment of neurosis there comes a point where the patient's active willing choice of health over illness determines the success or failure of the treatment."[14] They add that

> this moment in a neurotic's cure is or will become a moral one, supported by value rather than compelled by necessity. This is a most delicate, and dangerous, time in the treatment, for the neurotic no longer at this point suffers extremes. His symptoms no longer compel a choice for treatment over indulgence.[15]

Now, besides radical psychological conversion from depression there is also ongoing conversion. It is not enough for a radical shift from sickness to health to have taken place. There is need for an ongoing conversion in which negative, self-centered depressive tendencies are relentlessly opposed and above all in which authentic meanings and values are cultivated. There is an ongoing deepening of the turning-from and the turning-toward effected in radical conversion. Individuals with depressive tendencies need to be constantly vigilant in fasting from those thoughts, desires, images of a self-pitying, self-referential nature and above all they need to engage in an ongoing feasting of the spirit in which life-enriching meanings and values are cherished, appreciated and ever more deeply loved. As Hora expresses it: "*Only attachment can bring freedom from attachment*. . . . The trouble is that we are reaching out for the wrong kind of attachment. So we can only be healed by attaching ourselves to that which is existentially valid."[16]

But Christotherapy also seeks to integrate the Christ dimension into the process of the healing of depression. It remains to offer some brief suggestions about the way in which it is possible to relate the mystery of Christ to the healing of depression in terms of the elements in the *Spiritual Exercises.* As we have already seen, in the First Week of the *Spiritual Exercises* the retreatant meditates on sin and the hell which flows from sin and these meditations lead to a renewed turning away from the sin, expressed in deepening contrition and an acceptance of one's acceptance by Christ. Now, the depressed person at the beginning of treatment finds herself or himself in a this-worldly hell in which the pain of loss is deeply felt and self-respect is almost dead. The active presence of the loving Therapist, Jesus Christ, and of the Christotherapist, as the instrument of Christ, begins little by little to awaken self-acceptance and valid self-love in the depressed person. In this climate of love and acceptance through existential diagnosis the individual is helped gradually to uncover the excessive attachments in certain mind-sets and heart-sets, to verify at a "gut-level" that the pain of loss is flowing from these destructive attitudes, etc., and to begin to let go of these destructive assumptions about life and happiness. Here there is initiated the basic turning-from of radical psychological conversion.

In the Second Week of the *Exercises* there are a series of contemplations of Christ in the mysteries of his birth, public life and calling of disciples which inspire in the retreatant a renewed turning toward Christ in a more intimate loving and following of him wherever he may lead. Now the Christotherapist directs the attention of the depressed person toward those positive, life-giving human values revealed in Christ and in the "good news" of his Kingdom. The sufferer is gently reminded that if she or he makes the quest for the Kingdom of God first of all her or his priorities, everything else will be taken care of (Mt. 6:33). In this way the process of existential appreciation is initiated in which through the cultivation in prayer of truths and values revealed in Christ there takes place the turning-toward new life of radical psychological conversion. This is manifested in an increasing series of grace-inspired free choices in which the individual turns away from what is destructive and embraces what is life-giving. But radical psychological conversion is not the end. Ongoing contemplation of Christ in his passion and growing concern for others who suffer enable the individual who is at once recovered and recovering to die more deeply to any forms of self-pity and self-referential thinking which tend to reawaken depressive tendencies.

Finally, an ongoing beholding of the glorious features of the risen Christ and a commitment to his mission to be women and men for others deepen the turning-toward or radical option for life and for joy over depression which took place in radical psychological conversion.

APPENDIX

16

Guilt[1]

The issue of guilt is central both to psychotherapy and to religion. Sigmund Freud provided perhaps the key impetus for the psychological study of the origin and nature of guilt. The hypothesis of Freud regarding the meaning of guilt is an extremely complex and nuanced one, as Dr. Edward V. Stein in his brilliant *Guilt: Theory and Therapy*[2] has shown. As a means of presenting the briefest outline of Freud's theory, I can do no better than to cite a summary statement offered by Dr. Stein:

> For Freud the problem of guilt is to be understood in terms of the personality, driven by instinctual forces of love and hate from the id, seeking to find satisfaction and release of these drives by means of the ego (rational control system and organizing center). The ego must relate the inner needs not only to an external real environment of satisfying resources but also to a complex and vague "social reality," a system of values mediated to him through his parents or other emotionally significant surrogates. This "value environment" becomes *dynamic* for him through the process of identification and introjection by which he internalizes as his superego the parental ideals. Freud made clear his belief that the child adopts the parental *superego* more than parental *behavior* as his superego content. This internal memory constellation, ego ideal, or parent image is the focal medium through which self-evaluation, self-love, self-hatred, and punishment are channeled. Through it the instinctual forces of the id are fed back as feeling states to the ego. Guilt is ego anxiety over punishment or loss of love from the superego.[3]

There have been many partially or totally negative responses to Freud's hypothesis regarding the origin and nature of guilt. One of the most sharply negative responses has been that of Dr.

O. Hobart Mowrer.[4] Again, if I may cite Stein: "Mowrer believes neurosis is the result of a *real guilt anxiety* which results from the subject's failure to learn to abide by moral cues. He thus suffers from conscience-pain which is justified according to Mowrer and which he needs to respond to by way of a behavior change in the direction of more moral behavior."[5] Mowrer suggests that in Freud's view it is the duty of the psychoanalyst "to align himself with and to speak for the instincts, in opposition to the moral or pseudomoral forces within the personality which have instituted the repression."[6]

Dr. Stein retorts, however, to Mowrer in the following manner:

> How Mowrer, if he ever read *Civilization and Its Discontents,* can write, "Freud . . . did not take guilt seriously" is incredible. Mowrer writes, "Psychoanalysis is not messianic but demonic." Yet is there not something also demonic about ignoring the distinctions Freud established between real and neurotic guilt, ignoring the *fact* that Freud admitted the relevance (though he did not emphasize the importance) of real guilt, and then, by denying the distinction, turn the clock of history back by confusing the two?[7]

Two extreme hypotheses regarding the origin and nature of guilt are: (1) All guilt is neurotic guilt. (2) All guilt is real and the result of infringement of authentic moral demands. A common approach today is to opt for the view that there is a neurotic guilt that is destructive and results from a tyrannical, ill-formed superego but that there is also a real, valid guilt that results from the violation of a properly informed conscience. Dr. John W. Glaser outlines the basics of this synthesizing approach in an article entitled "Conscience and Super-Ego."[8]

Dr. Glaser sets up a series of contrasting characteristics which exist between the superego and genuine conscience.[9] Thus, for example, the superego "commands that an act be performed for approval, in order to make oneself lovable, accepted";[10] conscience, on the other hand, "invites to action, to love";[11] the superego is introverted and static; the authentic conscience is extroverted and dynamic, sensitive in a developmental way to values outside the self. The superego is authority-figure-oriented; conscience is value-oriented; the superego is past-oriented; the conscience is future-oriented; the superego begets an urge to be punished and thereby to earn reconciliation; conscience makes good past injuries but looks to the future and constructive building; the superego involves a possibly great disproportion between the guilt that is experienced and the value in question; in conscience there is an experience of guilt which is proportionate to the significance of the value in question. Glaser enunciates still further contrasts between the superego and conscience but the above characteristics serve to highlight the basic differences Glaser discerns. Basically Glaser sees the superego as a principle of prepersonal censorship and control. The superego does have an important function to perform in Glaser's view but it must be integrated into mature conscience if psychic stability and authentic growth are to be realized.

Two further hypotheses of note regarding the nature and origin of guilt are those of Dr. Herbert Fingarette and Dr. Thomas Hora.

Dr. Fingarette in his *The Self in Transformation*[12] stresses that guilt accrues to evil wishes as well as to evil deeds and that these wishes can be unconscious as well as conscious. In Fingarette's view:

> Guilt accrues according to the moral character of a wish or an act and . . . this is not limited to acts or wishes for which we have assumed responsibility. Responsibility comes relatively late in life; guilt appears very early in life. Thus we can be guilty where we are not responsible. . . . In this sense, at least, we are born into sin. For we are involved with evil and guilt before we are able to assume that responsibility for our self which might, at least ideally, keep us from having the wishes which constitute morally the fact of the spirit's corruption.[13]

Dr. Fingarette further notes that:

> . . . it is easy to see that our argument is consistent not only with psychoanalytic doctrine but also with a large segment of traditional morality as found embedded in religious views. It is common in Christian thought to argue that we are born sinners, but not to argue that we are responsible beings when we are children. And it is central to Buddhist thought that it is moral corruption and spiritual illusion into which we are born, but that responsibility and illumination are the eventu-

al means of achieving purity and sanity. . . . It must be added that the guilt of a responsible person has a different quality, or at least a different significance, from that of a non-responsible person.[14]

Dr. Thomas Hora in his *Existential Metapsychiatry*[15] takes the position, analogous to that of some schools of Hindu thought, that sin is, in fact, ignorance and that guilt too is rooted in error about the authentic way of thinking and valuing in the world. As Hora puts it: "To be a sinner is not really a sin, it is just one aspect of the human condition where man is born in ignorance and educated to increased ignorance."[16] Hora further writes, "It is interesting to consider that we have two choices. We can either plead guilty or admit to ignorance."[17] Finally, Hora adds, "The only way that guilt can be healed is by facing up to the truth of ignorance. Whatever wrong we did or thought we did can only be avoided in the future if we become enlightened on the issue involved."[18] Hora's view is in harmony with that of Fingarette at least to the extent that he acknowledges that guilt can be connected with unconscious wishes for which we are not sinfully responsible. But Hora parts company with Stein, Mowrer, Glaser, Fingarette and myself when he apparently denies that a person can freely (sinfully) violate authentic normative conscience and hence experience real, valid guilt.

What then are the parameters within which the Catholic Christian psychotherapist is able to envisage the issue of guilt? The Catholic Christian perspective excludes, in my opinion, the hypothesis which reduces *all* guilt to neurotic guilt and the hypothesis which explains *all* guilt in terms of nonculpable ignorance or error. The Catholic Christian perspective, however, is open to the possibility that guilt can be neurotic as opposed to real at times and that some forms of guilt can be rooted in a non-morally-culpable ignorance or error, often unconsciously operative.

Guilt and Christotherapy

As far as the theory of the nature of guilt is concerned, I hold that (1) guilt can be either neurotic or real and that (2) guilt, whether it is neurotic or real, can be rooted in desires, wishes, valuations, ideations, assumptions, beliefs, imaginings, phantasies which are either consciously or unconsciously operative.

In dealing with a person suffering from guilt, I stress first, as a Christotherapist, the importance of existential loving, of a holistic acceptance of the person who is tormented by guilt. In this respect I can in large measure appropriate as my own Dr. Stein's wise observation:

> The single most critical factor in relating to the guilt-laden person is *acceptance.* For real or neurotic reasons, or *both,* he cannot accept himself. . . . Probably the most commonly approved canon of therapy is the acceptance of the patient as *he is.* . . . This acceptance means an openness to the person, whatever he presents. It means recognition of his feeling and sensitivity to its meaning for him, whether this is a profound depression, an anguished neurotic self-laceration, or a realistic assessment of values violated or unfulfilled. Theologically and psychiatrically this is a *sine qua non* of a therapeutic relationship.[19]

Of course, as Dr. Stein also observes,[20] loving acceptance of the person is not identical with approval of all that the suffering person wishes, desires, phantasizes, and does.

Secondly, in working with a guilt-burdened person I stress the need for existential discerning and clarification on the Christotherapist's part in the healing of the person and on the need for an ongoing engagement in the prayerful processes of mind-fasting and spirit-feasting on the part of the sufferer.

More specifically, in regard to the healing of guilt, I would like to make six observations.

First, Dr. Fingarette is correct that a certain guilt accrues to immoral wishes, desires, and phantasies, even when these are unconsciously operative and not deliberately entertained. Examples of such desires might be incest, and sado-masochism. This is, I believe, in accord with the view of Dr. Hora that there are certain forms of wishing, cherishing, desiring, believing, thinking, phantasizing, imagining, etc. that are intrinsically destructive, disintegrative and disease-producing. Shame and guilt can then be experienced by a person to the extent that immoral wishes, desires and phantasies are operating, even though unconsciously and hence apart from real moral culpability.

I should stress here that I hold a non-rigid view on the degree of separation between the unconscious and conscious dimensions of the human person. This view, as I stated earlier, is perhaps best articulated in a comment of Dr. Wilhelm Stekel:

> Our thinking is a polyphony. There are always several thoughts working simultaneously, one of which is the bearer of the leading voice. The other thoughts represent the medium and low voices. . . . In this framework the whole material with which we deal in psychoanalysis is capable of becoming conscious. It is to be found predominantly in the lower voices. To quote Klages, the thing in question . . . is not so much a thing that is not thought as one that is not recognized.[21]

For me, then, the process of rendering the unconscious conscious is most often a matter of helping the suffering person to recognize through an existential diagnostic insight tinged with emotion the lower voices or thoughts which are present in consciousness but not recognized. Thus, for example, in the case of the person who is experiencing guilt as a result of an unconsciously operative immoral wish, the aim would be to make this wish conscious through engagement respectively on the part of the Christotherapist and sufferer in existential discerning and clarification and in the process of mind-fasting.

Second, Dr. Fingarette rightly insists that the primary task of the therapist is not to alleviate guilt feelings at any cost but rather to get at the wish, etc., which is the source of the guilt feelings and to help the sufferer to eliminate the wish or to transform it into something moral and authentically human. As Fingarette expresses it:

> We can perhaps get a better perspective on the matter if we note that the objective of psychoanalytic therapy, and of morality, is to remove both the wish *and* its attendant guilt. This is accomplished in the final analysis *by removing the evil wish.* Removal of the wish brings with it the removal of the guilt. The relationship between the wish and the guilt is left essentially unchanged. They appear together and disappear together.[22]

Third, Mowrer, Drakeford and others are correct that real moral guilt which is unacknowledged can manifest itself in symptoms "of varying degrees of severity, from vague discomfort to complete immobilization."[23] What the guilt-plagued person needs here is an existential, diagnostic insight into the true meaning of the symptoms, an acknowledging to himself or herself, to another and to God of the real nature of the guilt and an engagement in some sort of penance or responsible restitution where another has been injured. In this regard it is interesting that Carl Jung[24] urged his devout Catholic patients to make use of the sacrament of reconciliation and of the other sacraments as well.

Fourth, Drs. Glaser, Baars and Terruwe rightly argue that very early miseducation can lead a person to believe that a certain desire is evil when in fact it is innocuous or positively good. Dr. Anna Terruwe gives the example of the boy who experiences a sexual urge and is told that the very experience of sexual feeling is evil and immoral.[25] This type of miseducation can produce severe neurotic guilt feelings and repressive activity. Unfortunately, however, the opposite situation can also prevail. A widespread contemporary view is that anything on the sexual level is permitted "as long as nobody gets hurt." This kind of approach can actually lead to the repression of real and authentic guilt and the person can be far worse off at the end of therapy than he or she was at the beginning.

Fifth, Dr. Hora makes a valid point in insisting that non-culpable ignorance and error are often at the roots of guilt. In this case it is not so much confession as enlightenment that is needed.

Sixth, Dr. Kazimierz Dabrowski is correct that guilt in a person is very often not a matter of pathology but the sign of a call to growth in the individual:

> The sense of guilt . . . usually arises when one is dissatisfied with one's deeds, if they prove to be contradictory to the level of personality that the individual considers he should have reached.[26]

I conclude in asserting that often enough the person who comes to the therapist for help is suffering from a combination of neurotic guilt and real guilt. And, if this is the case, only the therapist who has an adequate understanding of the dynamics of both forms of guilt and their interrelationship and has a consciousness alive with authentic values and meanings will be able to help the suffering person instead of harming him or her and making the last state of the sufferer worse than the first. This is why the spiritual-psychological, synthetic approach of Christotherapy is so helpful for aiding individuals in dealing with guilt.

Notes

Chapter One

1. John Dunne, *The Way of All the Earth* (New York: Macmillan Company, 1972), p. ix.

2. Bernard Tyrrell, *Christotherapy: Healing Through Enlightenment* (New York: Seabury, 1975).

3. Thomas Hora, *Existential Metapsychiatry* (New York: Seabury Press, 1977).

4. Bernard Tyrrell, *Christotherapy,* p. 137.

5. In my use of the terms *counseling* and *psychotherapy* I tend to follow the usage of Gerald Corey in his *Theory and Practice of Counseling and Psychotherapy* (Monterey, California: Brooks/Cole Publishing Company, 1977). Corey often uses the terms counseling and psychotherapy interchangeably, and so do I. But Corey also suggests that counseling tends to aim "at the resolution of particular life crises," whereas psychotherapy "is much more concerned with personality-structure changes" (p. 9). I see the principles of Christotherapy as useful both for dealing with *ad hoc* crisis situations and for more long term psychological transformation.

6. Regis Duffy, "Book Review of Christotherapy," in *The American Ecclesiastical Review,* 169 (October, 1975), pp. 568–569.

7. Cf. Bernard Tyrrell, "On the Possibility and Desirability of a Christian Psychotherapy," *Lonergan Workshop,* Vol. I, edited by Fred Lawrence (Missoula, Montana: Scholars Press, 1978), pp. 143–185.

8. Individuals can also undergo an "intellectual conversion." Cf. Bernard Lonergan, *Method in Theology* (New York: Herder & Herder, 1972), p. 238.

9. Louis J. Puhl, S.J., *The Spiritual Exercises of St. Ignatius* (Chicago: Loyola University Press, 1951).

10. Gaston Fessard, *La Dialectique des Exercises spirituels de saint Ignace de Loyola.* Two volumes. (Paris: Aubier, 1956 and 1966).

11. In using the paradoxical expression "recovered and recovering," I am seeking to describe the state of a person who has passed from radical psychological conversion to ongoing psychological conversion, and from radical active addiction to ongoing conversion from addiction. In a true sense the individual has recovered since the health pattern is now dominant; but there is still an ongoing recovery taking place and this lasts a lifetime.

12. Carl Jung, "The Process of Individuation: *Exercitia Spiritualia* of St. Ignatius of Loyola" in *Modern Psychology,* Vols. 3 and 4, Notes on

Lectures given at the Eidgenössishe Technische Hochschule, Zurich, in the summer semester, 1940.

13. Carl Jung, *Aion.* Vol. 9, Part 2 of *The Collected Works of C.G. Jung*, Bollingen Series XX (New York: Princeton University Press, 1973).

14. Louis J. Puhl, *The Spiritual Exercises of St. Ignatius,* p. 12.

15. Carl Jung, *Aion,* p. 165, No. 253.

16. Bernard Tyrrell, *Christotherapy,* pp. 26–28.

17. Maurice Nesbitt, *Where No Fear Was* (London: Epworth Press, 1966); Seabury Press just reprinted this book.

18. The Guest House I attended is located near Rochester, Minnesota. The address is Guest House, RFD 4, Box 954, Rochester, Minnesota 55901.

19. Anonymous Authors, *Alcoholics Anonymous*, 2nd Edition (New York: Alcoholics Anonymous World Services, Inc., 1955).

20. Dennis and Matthew Linn, *Healing of Memories* (New York: Paulist Press, 1974).

21. Msgr. David E. Rosage, *Discovering Pathways to Prayer* (Locust Valley, New York: Living Flame Press, 1975).

22. For a good discussion of the controversial "baptism in the Spirit" see Donal Dorr, *Remove the Heart of Stone* (New York: Paulist Press, 1978).

23. Cardinal Leo Joseph Suenens, "Spiritual Ecumenism: Our Common Hope," *New Covenant,* Vol. 8, No. 7, January 1979, p. 5.

24. Andras Angyal, *Neurosis and Treatment: A Holistic Theory* (New York: Viking Press, 1973).

25. Augustine, *Great Books of the Western World,* Vol. 18 (Chicago: Encyclopaedia Britannica, 1952), p. 60.

26. Ibid.

27. Ibid., p. 61.

28. Ibid.

29. Thomas Aquinas, *Basic Writings of Saint Thomas Aquinas,* Vol. 2, edited by Anton C. Pegis (New York: Random House, 1945), *Summa Theologica* I–II, Q. 113, art. 6, response.

30. Ibid., art. 8, response.

31. Ibid., art. 5, reply to objection 3.

32. Hans Küng, "Christian Conversion," *Conversion,* edited by Walter Conn, p. 275.

33. Bernard Lonergan, *Method in Theology* (New York: Seabury Press, 1972), p. 240.

34. Bernard Lonergan, "Theology in Its New Context," *Conversion,* edited by Walter Conn, p. 20.

35. Karl Rahner, "Conversion," *Conversion,* edited by Walter Conn, p. 205.

36. Ladislas Orsy, *Blessed Are Those Who Have Questions* (Denville, New Jersey: Dimension Books, Inc., 1976), p. 46.

37. Ibid.

38. Ibid.

39. Ibid.

40. The theologians Robert Doran and Donald Gelpi write respectively of "psychic conversion" and "affective conversion." Cf. Robert Doran, *Subject and Psyche: Ricoeur, Jung and the Search for Foundations* (Washington, D.C.: University Press of America, 1977), esp. pp. 240ff.; Donald Gelpi, *Experiencing God* (New York: Paulist Press, 1978), esp. pp. 179ff.

41. Andras Angyal, *Neurosis and Treatment: A Holistic Theory;* cf. esp. pp. 220–260.

42. Ibid., p. 260.

43. Kazimierz Dabrowski, *Psychoneurosis Is Not an Illness* (London: Gryf Publications Ltd., 1972).

44. In the book *Alcoholics Anonymous,* the co-founder of A.A. describes the healing of his addiction in terms of a conversion experience. Cf. *Alcoholics Anonymous,* p. 14. Dr. Harry M. Tiebout in 1951 wrote an article entitled "Conversion as a Psychological Phenomena [sic] in the Treatment of the Alcoholic," *Pastoral Psychology,* Vol. 2, April 1951, pp. 28–34. More recently, C. Roy Woodruff in his book *Alcoholism and Christian Experience* has discussed at length categories of conversion in the area of the healing of alcoholism (Philadelphia: Westminster Press, 1968).

45. The *Twelve Steps* are listed on pp. 5–9 of *Twelve Steps and Twelve Traditions* (New York: Alcoholics Anonymous World Services, Inc., 1952). The author of this work is anonymous.

46. Literature available from *Emotions Anonymous,* P.O. Box 4245, St. Paul, Minnesota 55104.

47. For a view that supports my position, see Michael Stock, " 'Meaning' in Mental and Emotional Suffering," *The Bulletin of the National Guild of Catholic Psychiatrists,* Vol. 23, 1977, pp. 49–53.

48. Puhl, op. cit. Cf. Puhl's introduction to his edition of the *Spiritual Exercises* for comments on textual manuscripts, etc.

Chapter Two

1. Cf. Bernard Lonergan, *A Second Collection,* edited by William F. J. Ryan, S.J. and Bernard Tyrrell, S. J.(London: Darton, Longman and Todd, 1974), pp. 258–259.

2. Dante Alighieri, *The Purgatorio,* a translation by John Ciardi (New York: New American Library, 1961), p. 173.

3. Bernard Lonergan, *Method in Theology* (New York: Herder and Herder, 1972), p. 55. The final precept "Be Loving" or "Be in Love" has appeared in some of Lonergan's recent lectures.

4. Roberto Assagioli, *Psychosynthesis* (New York: Viking Press, 1971).

5. Ibid., p. 19.

6. Thomas Hora, *Dialogues in Metapsychiatry* (New York: Seabury Press, 1977), p. 72.

7. Ibid., p. 209.

8. Ibid.

9. Thomas Hora, a taped telephone interview of Dr. Hora with the participants of the *Winter Conference on Metapsychiatry,* Laguna Beach, California on March 3, 1979. The tape is available from Dr. Jan Linthorst, 2854 North Santiago Blvd., Suite 103, Orange, California 92667.

10. Thomas Hora, *Dialogues in Metapsychiatry,* p. 68.

11. Andras Angyal, *Foundations for a Science of Personality* (New York: Viking Press, 1972), p. 123.

12. Cf. Shirley C. Samuels, *Enhancing Self-Concept in Early Childhood* (New York: Human Sciences Press, 1977), p. 24.

13. Cf. Bernard Longeran, *Method in Theology,* esp. pp. 6–13.

14. Roberto Assagioli, *Psychosynthesis,* p. 17.

15. Bartholomew M. Kiely, *Psychology and Moral Theology* (Gregorian University Press, 1980), pp. 86–96.

16. Cf. Bernard Lonergan, *Method in Theology,* pp. 33–34. Lonergan speaks of "the twilight of what is conscious but not objectified," p. 34.

17. Wilhelm Stekel, *Compulsion and Doubt* (New York: Grosset and Dunlap, 1962), p. 229.

18. Aaron Beck, *Cognitive Theory and the Emotional Disorders* (New York: International Universities Press, 1976), esp. pp. 29–38.

19. Cf. Raymond Hostie, *Religion and the Psychology of Jung* (New York: Sheed and Ward, 1957), p. 72.

20. Robert Solomon, *The Passions: The Myth and Nature of Human Emotion* (Garden City, New York: Anchor Press/Doubleday, 1976), pp. 392–410.

21. Cf. Bartholomew Kiely, *Psychology and Moral Theology,* p. 88.

22. Cf. the incisive critique of Jung by Robert Doran, "Jungian Psychology and Christian Spirituality: III," *Review for Religious,* Vol. 38, No. 6, November 1979, pp. 857–866.

Chapter Three

1. Cf. Bernard Boelen, *Personal Maturity* (New York: Seabury Press, 1978). The ideas in this first paragraph are taken largely from pp. 13–30.

2. David Ausubel, M.D., *Ego Development and the Personality Disorders* (New York: Grune and Stratton, 1952), pp. 48–64.

3. Conrad W. Baars, M.D., *Born Only Once* (Chicago: Franciscan Herald Press, 1975), p. 12.

4. Abraham H. Maslow, *Motivation and Personality* (New York: Harper and Row, 1970), esp. pp. 35–46.

5. Rene Spitz, "Anaclitic Depression," *The Psychoanalytic Study of the Child,* 2 (New York: International Universities Press, 1947), pp. 313–342.

6. Cf. Jean Piaget, *The Construction of Reality in the Child,* trans. by Margaret Cook (New York: Ballantine Books, 1971).

7. Cf. Jim Fowler and Sam Keen, *Life Maps,* edited by Jerome Berryman (Waco, Texas: Word, Inc., with Winston Press, 1978).

8. Erik Erikson, *Childhood and Society,* (New York: W. W. Norton 1963), pp. 247–274.

9. Lawrence Kohlberg, "Education for Justice: A Modern Statement of the Platonic View," *Moral Education* (Cambridge, Massachusetts: Harvard University Press, 1970).

10. Bernard Boelen, *Personal Maturity.*

11. Kazimierz Dabrowski with Michael M. Piechowski, *Theory of Levels of Emotional Development,* Vol. I: *Multilevelness and Positive Disintegration* (Oceanside, New York: Dabor Science Publications, 1977), pp. 30–36.

12. Ibid., pp. 37–56.

13. Ibid., p. 15.

14. Bernard Lonergan, *A Second Collection,* edited by William F. J. Ryan, S.J. and Bernard J. Tyrrell, S.J. (London: Darton, Longman and Todd, 1974), p. 221.

15. Ibid.

16. Carroll E. Izard, *Human Emotions* (New York: Plenum Press, 1977), p. 97.

17. Ibid., pp. 87; 286.

18. Ibid., pp. 237–238.

19. Ibid., p. 239.

20. Ibid.

21. Ibid., p. 250.

22. Ibid., pp. 364–365.

23. Ibid., pp. 241–242.

24. Ibid., pp. 297; 390.

25. Ibid., pp. 444–445.

26. Erikson, pp. 273–274.

27. David Ausubel, *Theory and Problems of Child Development* (New York: Grune and Stratton, 1958), p. 320.

28. Bernard Lonergan, *Method in Theology* (New York: Herder and Herder, 1972), p. 65.

29. Abraham Low, M.D., *Mental Health Through Will-Training* (Boston: Christopher Publishing House, 1968), p. 115.

30. Ibid., p. 178.

31. Authors Anonymous, *Emotions Anonymous,* (St. Paul, Minnesota: Emotions Anonymous International, 1978), pp. 31–33.

32. Bernard Lonergan, *Method in Theology,* pp. 31–32.

33. Jerome Murphy-O'Connor, *Becoming Human Together* (Wilmington, Delaware: Michael Glazier, Inc., 1977), pp. 177–178.

34. Ibid., p. 178.

35. John Powell, *Fully Human, Fully Alive* (Niles, Illinois: Argus Communications, 1976).

36. Bernard Lonergan, "Christology Today: Methodological Reflections," a talk presented at the *Colloque de Christologie,* Laval University, Quebec City, March 22, 1975, p. 27.

37. Cf. Viktor Frankl, *The Unconscious God* (New York: Simon and Schuster, 1975), and *The Unheard Cry for Meaning* (New York: Simon and Schuster, 1978).

38. Frankl, *The Unheard Cry for Meaning,* p. 35.

39. Ibid.

40. Maslow, *Motivation and Personality,* p. 134.

41. Bernard Lonergan, *Insight* (New York: Philosophical Library, 1957), pp. 476–477.

42. Bernard Lonergan, "Mission and the Spirit," *Experience of the Spirit,* edited by Bassett and Huizing (New York: Seabury Press, 1974), pp. 74–75.

43. Ibid., pp. 73–74.

44. Lonergan, *Insight,* pp. 476–477.

45. Dabrowski, *Theory of Levels of Emotional Development* I, pp. 39–40.

46. Daniel Levinson, *The Seasons of a Man's Life* (New York: Ballantine Books, 1978).

47. Gail Sheehy, *Passages* (New York: Bantam, 1977).

Chapter Four

1. William Glasser, *Reality Therapy* (New York: Harper and Row, 1965), esp. pp. 5–41. Glasser prefers to substitute the term "irresponsible" for mental illness and its various subcategories (p. 15).

2. Anna M. Terruwe, M.D. and Conrad Baars, M.D., *Loving and Curing the Neurotic* (New Rochelle: Arlington House, 1972), esp. pp. 55–180.

3. John Evoy, *The Rejected: Psychological Consequences of Parental Rejection* (University Park: Pennsylvania State University Press, 1981).

4. Ibid., p. 14.

5. Conrad Baars, *Born Only Once* (Chicago: Franciscan Herald Press, 1975), pp. 5–8.

6. Andras Angyal, *Neurosis and Treatment: A Holistic Theory* (New York: Viking Press, 1973), p. 80.

7. Ibid.

8. Erik Erikson, *Childhood and Society* (New York: W. W. Norton, 1963), p. 248.

9. Kayla F. Bernheim and Richard R. J. Lewine, *Schizophrenia* (New York: W. W. Norton, 1979), pp. 121–122. These authors do not hold that lack of loving acceptance is the basic cause of schizophrenia.

10. Cf. Bernard Tyrrell, *Christotherapy* (New York: Seabury Press, 1975), pp. 32–33.

11. Evoy, *The Rejected,* pp. 18–21.

12. Ibid., pp. 18–21; 125–127.

13. Ibid., p. 18.

14. Ibid., p. 20.

15. Ibid., p. 104.

16. Ibid., p. 105.

17. Ibid., p. 66.

18. Ibid., pp. 116; 126.

19. Ibid., pp. 89; 71.

20. Andras Angyal, *Neurosis and Treatment: A Holistic Theory,* p. 85.

21. Ibid.

22. Ibid.

23. Ibid., p. 224.

24. Bernard Lonergan, *Insight* (London: Darton, Longmans, 1957), p. 476.

25. Albert Ellis, *Reason and Emotion in Psychotherapy* (New York: Lyle Stuart, 1971), p. 61. The quote is in italics in the text.

26. Evoy, *The Rejected,* p. 123.

27. James Gill, "Psychiatry, Psychology and Spirituality Today," *Chicago Studies* (Vol. 15, Spring, 1976, No. 1), pp. 35–36.

28. Cf. Bernard Lonergan, *A Second Collection* (London: Darton, Longman and Todd, 1974), p. 271. Lonergan is here offering his interpretation of the view of psychiatrist Herbert Fingarette.

29. Cf. John W. Drakeford, *Integrity Therapy* (Nashville: Broadman Press, 1967), pp. 7–13.

30. Viktor Frankl, *The Unconscious God* (New York: Simon and Schuster, 1975), p. 117.

31. Ibid., p. 131.

32. Ibid., p. 48.

33. Viktor Frankl, *The Unheard Cry for Meaning* (New York: Simon and Schuster, 1978), pp. 22–23.

34. Ibid., pp. 19–29.

35. Angyal, *Neurosis and Treatment: A Holistic Theory,* p. 140.

36. Ibid., pp. 157, 161.

37. Phil Brown, *Toward a Marxist Society* (New York: Harper Colophon Books, 1974).

38. Thomas Szasz, *The Myth of Mental Illness* (New York: Hoeber-Harper, 1965).

39. R. D. Laing, *The Politics of Experience* (New York: Ballantine Books, 1967).

40. Karl Rahner, *Foundations of Christian Faith* (New York: Crossroad Books, 1978), p. 115.

41. Murphy-O'Connor, *Becoming Human Together* (Wilmington: Michael Glazier, Inc., 1977), p. 141.

42. Karen Horney, *The Neurotic Personality of Our Time* (New York: W. W. Norton, 1964).

43. Frankl, *The Unheard Cry for Meaning,* pp. 23–25.

44. Horney, *The Neurotic Personality of Our Time,* pp. 288–289.

45. Ibid.

46. Ibid., p. 290.

47. Frankl, *The Unheard Cry for Meaning,* pp. 71–73; 95–96.

48. Bernard Lonergan, *Collection* (New York: Herder and Herder, 1967), pp. 245–246.

49. Thomas Hora, *In Quest of Wholeness,* edited by Dr. Jan Linthorst in 1972 (available from Dr. Linthorst at 2854 North Santiago Blvd., Suite 103, Orange, Calif. 92667), p. 1.

50. George Mann, *Recovery of Reality* (New York: Harper and Row, 1979).

51. Ibid., pp. 32–40.

52. Ibid., pp. 59–64.

53. William Glasser, *Positive Addiction* (New York: Harper and Row, 1976).

54. James Royce, *Alcohol Problems and Alcoholism* (New York: Free Press—a division of Macmillan Publishing Company, 1981), p. 292.

55. Stanton Peele with Archie Brodsky, *Love and Addiction* (New York: Taplinger Publishing Company, 1975).

56. Ibid., p. 61. The quote is in italics in the text.

57. Cf. George Hagmaier and Robert Gleason, *Counseling the Catholic* (New York: Sheed and Ward, 1959), p. 78.

58. Cf. Bernard Tyrrell, " 'The Sexual Celibate' and Masturbation," *Review for Religious,* 35, No. 3 (May 1976): 399–408.

59. Cited by George Anderson, "Compulsive Gambling: Talking to the Experts," *America,* Vol. 140 (February 3, 1979), p. 69.

60. Peele, *Love and Addiction,* pp. 71–113; 171–197.

Chapter Five

1. Viktor Frankl, *The Unheard Cry for Meaning* (New York: Simon and Schuster, 1978), p. 29.

2. Roberto Assagioli, *Psychosynthesis* (New York: Viking Press, 1971).

3. Mary Baker Eddy, *Science and Health* (Boston: First Church of Christ Scientists, 1875).

4. Roberto Assagioli, *Psychosynthesis*, p. 192.

5. Ibid.

6. Ibid., p. 193.

7. Roberto Assagioli, "What Is Psychosynthesis?" *Synthesis*, I. No. 1, 1974, Workbook, p. 71.

8. Ibid.

9. Ibid.

10. Roberto Assagioli, *Psychosynthesis*, p. 195.

11. John A. Sanford, *The Kingdom Within* (Philadelphia: J. B. Lippincott Company, 1970).

12. John A. Sanford, *Dreams and Healing* (New York: Paulist Press, 1978).

13. John A. Sanford, *Healing and Wholeness* (New York: Paulist Press, 1977).

14. Ibid., p. 156.

15. Ibid.

16. Ibid., p. 134.

17. Ibid.

18. John A. Sanford, *The Kingdom Within*, p. 216.

19. Ibid., p. 217. The citation is in italics in the text.

20. Ibid., p. 214.

21. Sanford's psychological-spiritual approach is unique and multifaceted, as are the other approaches to a psychological-spiritual synthesis I describe in this chapter. Unfortunately, I can only point out a few of the more salient characteristics of each approach.

22. Alphonse Calabrese and William Proctor, *The Christian Love Treatment* (Garden City: Doubleday and Company, Inc., 1976).

23. Ibid., pp. 62–63.

24. Ibid., p. 77.

25. Ibid., p. 67.

26. Ibid., p. 51.

27. Ibid., p. 145.

28. Ibid., p. 68.

29. Ibid., pp. 115ff.

30. Dennis and Matthew Linn, *Healing of Memories* (New York: Paulist Press, 1974).

31. Dennis and Matthew Linn, *Healing Life's Hurts* (New York: Paulist Press, 1978).

32. Elisabeth Kübler-Ross, *On Death and Dying* (New York: Macmillan Company, 1971).

33. Dennis and Matthew Linn, *Healing Life's Hurts*, esp. pp. 85–101.

34. Lawrence Crabb, Jr., *Basic Principles of Biblical Counseling* (Grand Rapids: Zondervan Press, 1976).

35. Lawrence Crabb, Jr., *Effective Biblical Counseling* (Grand Rapids: Zondervan Press, 1977).

36. Ibid., p. 190. For a critique of Crabb see Gary R. Collins, edited and with a contribution by H. Newton Malony, *Psychology and Theology* (Nashville: Abingdon, 1981), esp. pp. 30–33.

37. Ibid.

38. Bernard Tyrrell, *Christotherapy* (New York: Seabury Press, 1975), p. xiv.

39. Thomas Hora, *Existential Metapsychiatry* (New York: Seabury Press, 1977), p. 1.

40. Thomas Hora, "The Problem of Negative Counter-Transference," *American Journal of Psychotherapy,* 5, 1951, pp. 560–567.

41. Thomas Hora, "The Dissocial Superego," *American Journal of Psychotherapy,* 6, 1952, pp. 513–519.

42. Thomas Hora, "Masochistic Use of Anxiety," *American Journal of Psychotherapy,* 7, 1953, pp. 449–453.

43. Thomas Hora, *Existential Metapsychiatry.*

44. Thomas Hora, *Dialogues in Metapsychiatry* (New York: Seabury Press, 1977).

45. Ibid., p. 11.

46. Ibid., p. 9.

47. Ibid., p. 221.

48. Ibid., p. 209.

49. Ibid.

50. Ibid.

51. Ibid., p. 75.

52. Ibid., p. 17.

53. Ibid., p. 177.

54. Ibid., p. 12.

55. Ibid., p. 209.

56. Ibid.

57. Ibid., p. 72.

58. Ibid., p. 6.

59. Ibid., p. 11.

60. Ibid., p. 179.

61. Ibid., p. 209.

62. Ibid.

63. Ibid.

64. Ibid.

65. Ibid., p. 211.

66. Ibid.

67. Ibid.

68. Thomas Hora, *Existential Metapsychiatry,* p. 106.

69. Ibid.

70. Ibid.

71. John B. Cobb, Jr., *The Structure of Christian Existence* (Philadelphia: Westminster Press, 1967); cf. pp. 62–65.

72. Ibid., p. 63.

73. Ibid., p. 64.

74. Ibid., p. 65.

75. E. Mansell Pattison, "Social and Psychological Aspects of Religion in Psychotherapy," *Insight* (Fall, 1966), esp. pp. 29–31.

76. Paul Vitz, *Psychology as Religion* (Grand Rapids: William B. Eerdmans Publishing Co., 1977).

77. I am referring to the Pelagian heresy which denied the complete inability of the human being to attain by his or her own natural effort the supernatural gift of grace lost through original sin. Cf. *The Teachings of the Catholic Church,* prepared by Josef Neuner and Heinrich Roos and edited by Karl Rahner (Staten Island: Alba House, 1967), esp. pp. 131–141.

78. I agree with Bernard Lonergan that it is necessary to hold the real distinction between grace and nature as operative principles if one is to do theology in a proper way. Theological abuse of the terms natural and supernatural has occurred. But this does not justify the elimination of the distinction between nature and grace but requires a proper understanding of this distinction. Cf. Bernard Lonergan, *A Second Collection,* edited by William F. J. Ryan and Bernard J. Tyrrell (London: Darton, Longman and Todd, 1974), esp. pp. 117–133. Cf. also Bernard Tyrrell, "The New Context of the Philosophy of God in Lonergan and Rahner," *Language, Truth and Meaning,* edited by Philip McShane (Notre Dame: University of Notre Dame Press, 1972), pp. 284–305.

79. John Powell, *He Touched Me* (Niles, Illinois: Argus Communications, 1974); cf. pp. 40–48.

80. Ibid., p. 42.

81. Roberto Assagioli, *Psychosynthesis,* p. 203.

82. Bernard Tyrrell, *Christotherapy,* pp. 27–28.

83. Roberto Assagioli, *The Act of Will* (Baltimore: Penguin Books, 1973), p. 20. See asterisk at the bottom of the page.

84. Bernard Lonergan, *Method in Theology* (New York: Herder and Herder, 1972), pp. 340–343.

Chapter Six

1. Louis J. Puhl, S.J., *The Spiritual Exercises of St. Ignatius* (Chicago: Loyola University Press, 1951), p. 142, No. 317.4.

2. Allen E. Wiesen, *Positive Therapy* (Chicago: Nelson Hall, 1977), p. 41.

3. Where religious elements of a destructive nature are deeply em-

bedded in the neurotic patterns of individuals there is need for great caution in using spiritual means. Prayer for the person, of course, is always an essential element in the Christotherapeutic practice.

4. Sandra Schneiders, *Spiritual Direction.* (Chicago: Published by the National Sisters Vocation Conference, 1977), p. 33.

5. Adrian van Kaam, *Dynamics of Spiritual Self-Direction* (Denville, New Jersey: Dimension Books, 1976), p. 373.

6. William Connolly, "Noticing Key Interior Facts in the Early Stages of Spiritual Direction," *Review for Religious,* Vol. 35, 1976, p. 115.

7. Thomas Merton, *Spiritual Direction and Meditation* (Collegeville: The Liturgical Press, 1960), p. 8.

8. John English, *Spiritual Freedom* (Guelph: Loyola House, 1974), p. 18.

9. Thomas Merton, *Spiritual Direction and Meditation,* p. 8.

10. William Kraft, "Psychology and Religious Life," *Review for Religious,* Vol. 35, No. 6, 1975, p. 894.

11. Friedrich Wulf, "Spiritual Direction," *Sacramentum Mundi,* Vol. 6, p. 165.

12. John English, *Spiritual Freedom,* p. 15.

13. John Wright, "A Discussion of Spiritual Direction," *Studies in the Spirituality of Jesuits,* 4:2 (March, 1972); cf. pp. 41–51.

14. William Peters, "Spiritual Direction and Prayer," *Communio,* Vol. 3, 1976, p. 358.

15. John Wright, "A Discussion of Spiritual Direction," pp. 41–49.

16. James Gill, "Psychiatry, Psychology and Spirituality Today," *Chicago Studies,* Vol. 15, Spring, 1976, No. 1; cf. pp. 36–37.

17. Damien Isabell, *The Spiritual Director* (Chicago: Franciscan Herald Press, 1976), p. 14.

18. Ibid., p. 18.

19. Gerald Corey, *Theory and Practice of Counseling and Psychotherapy* (Monterey, California: Brooks/Cole Publishing Company, 1977), p. 9.

20. Adrian van Kaam, *Dynamics of Spiritual Self-Direction,* p. 373.

21. Robert Rossi, "The Distinction Between Psychological and Religious Counseling," *Review for Religious,* Vol. 37, No. 4 (July, 1978), p. 550.

22. Adrian van Kaam, *Dynamics of Spiritual Self-Direction,* p. 373.

23. Sandra Schneiders, *Spiritual Direction,* p. 32.

24. Ibid.

25. I take the expression "Tremendous Lover" from the title of Eugene Boylan's book *This Tremendous Lover* (Westminster, Md.: Newman, 1974).

26. Albert Ellis, *Reason and Emotion in Psychotherapy* (New York: Lyle Stuart, 1971), p. 63. The quotation is in italics in the text.

27. William Kraft, "Psychiatrists, Psychologists and Religious," *Review for Religious,* 37, No. 2 (March, 1978), p. 164.

28. Carl Jung, "Psychotherapy and a Philosophy of Life," *The Collected Works,* XVI (London: Routledge and Kegan Paul, 1954), p. 79.

Chapter Seven

1. Cf. Christina Maslach, "Burned-Out," *Human Behavior,* September, 1976, pp. 16–22.

2. Cf. Alfred C. Kammer, *Studies in the Spirituality of Jesuits* (published by the American Assistancy Seminar on Jesuit Spirituality), X, No. 1, January, 1978.

3. Thomas Hora, *In Quest of Wholeness,* edited by Jan Linthorst (2854 North Santiago Blvd., Suite 103, Orange, Calif. 92667).

4. Alexander Pope, *An Essay on Criticism,* III.lxvi.

5. Bernard Lonergan, an unpublished response to a *Questionnaire on Jesuit Philosophical Studies,* 1976, p. 13. Available in the Lonergan Center at Regis College, Toronto, Ontario, Canada.

6. Cf. Bernard Lonergan, *Method in Theology* (New York: Herder and Herder, 1972), pp. 238–240.

7. Bernard Lonergan, *De Constitutione Christi* (Rome: Gregorian University, 1961), p. 17.

8. Cf. Bernard Lonergan, *The Way to Nicea* (Philadelphia: Westminster Press, 1976), pp. 88; 90; 128–133; 135–137.

9. Bernard Lonergan, *Insight* (New York: Philosophical Library, 1957).

10. Bernard Lonergan, *Method in Theology,* pp. 41–47.

11. Albert Ellis, *Reason and Emotion in Psychotherapy* (New York: Lyle Stuart, 1971), p. 80. The quotation is in italics in the text.

12. Eli Chesen, *Religion May Be Hazardous to Your Health* (New York: Peter H. Wyden, 1972).

13. Adrian van Kaam, *The Dynamics of Spiritual Self-Direction* (Denville, New Jersey: Dimension Books, 1976), p. 379.

14. Ibid., p. 381.

15. Kenneth Leech, *Soul Friend* (London: Sheldon Press, 1977), p. 89.

16. Kazimierz Dabrowski, *Personality Shaping Through Positive Disintegration* (Boston: Little, Brown and Co., 1967), p. 58.

Chapter Eight

1. *The Cloud of Unknowing,* edited with an introduction by William Johnston (Garden City: Doubleday Image Book, 1973), p. 88.

2. Paul D. Morris, *Love Therapy* (Wheaton, Illinois: Tyndale House Publishing, 1974).

3. Everett L. Shostrom and Dan Montgomery, *Healing Love* (New York: Bantam Books, Inc., 1979).

4. Donald J. Tyrell, *When Love Is Lost* (Waco, Texas: Word Book Publisher, 1972).

5. Alphonse Calabrese and William Proctor, *The Christian Love Treatment* (Garden City: Doubleday, 1976).

6. Damien Isabell, *The Spiritual Director* (Chicago: Franciscan Herald Press, 1976), p. 55.

7. Josef Pieper, *About Love,* translated by Richard and Clara Winston (Chicago: Franciscan Herald Press, 1974), p. 19.

8. Ibid., p. 117.

9. John of the Cross, *The Collected Works of St. John of the Cross,* translated by Kieran Kavanaugh and Otilio Rodriguez (Washington D.C., ICS publications, Institute of Carmelite Studies, 1973), No. 24, p. 703.

10. In my book *Christotherapy,* I distinguished between "existential diagnosis" and "existential discernment." Cf. pp. 10–13. In the present book I try to bring my work more into harmony with classical usage by using existential discernment as a general category and then subdividing it into a diagnostic and appreciative phase.

11. Cf. Paul W. Pruyser, *The Minister as Diagnostician* (Philadelphia: Westminster Press, 1976), p. 37.

12. Bernard Tyrrell, *Christotherapy,* p. 80.

13. Louis J. Puhl, S.J., *The Spiritual Exercises* (Chicago: Loyola University Press, 1951), p. 142, no. 316.3.

14. Cf. Thomas Merton, *The Way of Chuang Tzu* (New York: New Directions Publishing Corporation, 1965), p. 53. Merton speaks of "fasting of the heart" but Hora and others refer to it as "mind-fasting."

15. In *Christotherapy* I offer certain biblical texts for a Christian grounding of my notions of "mind-fasting" and"spirit-feasting." Cf. esp. pp. 78–83; 99–105.

16. Cf. Thomas Hora, "Tao, Zen and Existential Psychotherapy," *Psychologia,* 1959, 2, p. 239.

17. Bernard Tyrrell, *Christotherapy,* p. 81.

18. Lawrence Crabb, *Effective Biblical Counseling* (Grand Rapids: Zondervan Corporation, 1977), esp. pp. 146–160.

19. Ibid., p. 158.

20. Ibid., p. 159.

21. Thomas Aquinas, *On the Truth of the Catholic Faith: Summa Contra Gentiles Book Three: Providence, Part 2,* translated by Vernon J. Bourke (Garden City: Image Book, a division of Doubleday, 1956), p. 143, no. 2.

22. Roberto Assagioli, *Psychosynthesis* (New York: Viking Press, 1971), pp. 22–24.

23. Ibid., pp. 24ff.

24. Ibid., p. 22. The quotation is in italics in the text.

25. Ibid., pp. 72–73. For Assagioli a conscious complex is a "conglomeration of psychological . . . 'elements' which have developed a strong emotional charge."

26. Ibid., p. 23.

27. Ibid.

28. Roberto Assagioli, *The Act of Will* (Baltimore: Penguin Books, 1973), pp. 215–217.

29. Ibid., p. 216. The original statement is in italics.

30. Assagioli, *Psychosynthesis,* pp. 24ff.

31. Ibid., p. 24.

32. Ibid., pp. 24–25.

33. Ibid., p. 202.

34. Ibid., p. 203.

35. As a philosopher I am within the Aristotelian-Thomist-Lonerganian tradition. I hold that the soul is the form of the body and that together they constitute the human essence. This essence is actuated by the act of existence. When I use "spirit" in the present statement I am referring to the soul as transformed by sanctifying grace. In my psycho-spiritual terms it is the natural self transformed by the Christ-self.

36. Cf. Robert Doran, *Subject and Psyche: Ricoeur, Jung, and the Search for Foundations* (Washington, D.C.: University Press of America, 1977).

37. Ann Faraday, *The Dream Game* (New York: Harper and Row, 1974); cf. pp. 67–69 and pp. 112–118.

38. Ibid., p. 115.

39. Ibid., p. 68.

40. Ibid., p. 115.

41. Ibid., p. 68.

42. Robert M. Doran, *Subject and Psyche: Ricoeur, Jung and the Search for Foundations,* p. 215.

43. An unpublished article by Fredrick E. Crowe, entitled "Dreams and the Ignatian Preludes to Prayer." Crowe is at Regis College, Toronto.

44. John A. Sanford, *Dreams and Healing* (New York: Paulist Press, 1978).

45. Morton T. Kelsey, *Dreams,* (New York: Paulist Press, 1978).

46. Thomas Hora, "Tao, Zen and Existential Psychotherapy," *Psychologia* 2 (1959), p. 240.

47. Dennis and Matthew Linn, *Healing Life's Hurts* (New York: Paulist Press, 1978), pp. 143–145.

Chapter Nine

1. Gaston Fessard, *La Dialectique des Exercises spirituels de saint Ignace de Loyola,* vol. I (Paris: Aubier, 1956), p. 40. Fessard cites the original Latin formulas, pp. 40–41. The translation is my own.

2. Anonymous Authors, *Alcoholics Anonymous* (New York: Alcoholics Anonymous World Services, Inc., 1955), p. 14.

3. Ibid.

4. There was no influence of the *Spiritual Exercises* on Bill Wilson in his formulation of the *Twelve Steps.* But in late 1941 a Jesuit priest, Father Edward Dowling, met Mr. Wilson and pointed out to him certain parallels which he found between the *Twelve Steps* and the *Spiritual Exercises.* Unfortunately, there does not appear to be any extant material indicating what parallels Dowling saw between the *Spiritual Exercises* and the *Twelve Steps.* I only learned of the history of the connection between Wilson and Dowling in June 1981 through the book *Not-God: A History of Alcoholics Anonymous* by Ernest Kurtz (Center City, Minnesota: Hazelden Educational Services, 1979), esp. pp. 98–100.

5. Louis J. Puhl, S.J., *The Spiritual Exercises of St. Ignatius* (Chicago: Loyola University Press, 1951), p. 2, no. 4.

6. Ibid., p. 26, no. 48. For a discussion of the meaning of petitionary prayer see Bernard J. Tyrrell, *Christotherapy* (New York: Seabury Press, 1975), pp. 99–102.

7. Ibid.

8. Ibid., p. 29, no. 55.

9. Ibid., p. 31, no. 63.

10. Ibid.

11. Ibid.

12. Ibid., p. 32, no. 65.

13. Gaston Fessard, Vol. I, p. 40. The translation is my own.

14. Gerald P. Kirk, "The Organic Structure of the *Spiritual Exercises* according to Père Gaston Fessard," *The Modern Humanist,* Vol. XVI, Winter 1961, pp. 3–4.

15. Cited and translated by Gerald P. Kirk, ibid., p. 2.

16. Louis J. Puhl, p. 28, no. 54.

17. Louis J. Puhl, p. 3, no. 7.

18. Dante Alighieri, *The Divine Comedy,* I, *Hell,* translated by Dorothy L. Sayers (Baltimore: Penguin Books, 1964), Canto I, p. 74, lines 112ff.

19. Louis J. Puhl, p. 1, no. 2. I should add that directors of those making the *Exercises* should adapt the classical meditations of Ignatius in accord with the psychological, social, cultural and personal background and needs of the retreatant.

20. Ibid., p. 32, no. 66.

21. Ibid., p. 31, no. 63.

22. Andras Angyal, *Neurosis and Treatment: A Holistic Theory* (New York: Viking Press, 1973), p. 266.

23. David A. Stewart, *Thirst for Freedom* (Center City, Minnesota: Hazelden, 1960), p. 110.

24. Ibid., p. 112.

25. Angyal, p. 225.

26. Harry M. Tiebout, M.D., *The Act of Surrender in the Therapeutic Process* (New York: National Council of Alcoholism, Inc.), p. 9.

27. Cited in the *Penguin Book of Religious Verse,* edited by R. S. Thomas (Baltimore: Penguin Books, 1963), p. 37.

28. Angyal, p. 224.

29. Ibid., p. 265.

30. Ibid., p. 84.

31. Cf. my article, "Christotherapy and the Healing of Communal Consciousness," *The Thomist,* XL, 4, October, 1976, pp. 626–629.

32. Roberto Assagioli, *Psychosynthesis* (New York: Viking Press, Inc., 1971), p. 23.

33. Puhl, p. 33, no. 68.

34. Dante, *The Inferno,* translated by John Ciardi (New York: Mentor Book, 1961), p. 103, lines 3–5.

35. Ibid., p. 107, ft. 3.

36. *The Works of Bernard of Clairvaux,* Vol. 5 (Washington, D.C.: Cistercian Publications, Consortium Press, 1974), p. 115.

37. Ibid.

38. Dante, *The Inferno,* translated by John Ciardi, p. 174, line 3.

39. Ibid., p. 236, lines 48–50.

40. Puhl, p. 28, no. 53.

41. Ibid., p. 30, no. 61.

Chapter Ten

1. David Stanley, S.J., "Contemplation of the Gospels," *Theological Studies,* 29, 1968, pp. 420–421.

2. Thomas Green, *When the Well Runs Dry* (Notre Dame: Ave Maria Press, 1979), p. 40.

3. David Stanley, "Contemplation of the Gospels," p. 421.

4. Gaston Fessard, *La Dialectique des Exercises spirituels de saint Ignace de Loyola,* Vol. I, (Paris: Aubier, 1956), pp. 40–41.

5. Louis J. Puhl, *The Spiritual Exercises of St. Ignatius* (Chicago: Loyola University Press, 1951) p. 7, no. 18.

6. John J. English, *Spiritual Freedom* (Guelph, Ontario: Loyola House, 1974), p. 123.

7. Louis J. Puhl, p. 44, no. 95.

8. *Roman Missal: The Sacramentary* (New York: Catholic Book Publishing Company, 1974), preface 51, p. 475.

9. Edouard Pousset, *Life in Faith and Freedom,* translated and edited by Eugene L. Donahue, S.J. (St. Louis: The Institute of Jesuit Sources, 1980); cf. pp. 91–93.

10. Cited by Archibald M. Hunter, *Interpreting the Parables,* (Philadelphia: The Westminster Press, 1963), p. 49.

11. Cited in the *Penguin Book of Religious Verse,* edited by R.S. Thomas (Baltimore: Penguin Books, 1963), p. 37.

12. Andras Angyal, *Neurosis and Treatment: A Holistic Theory* (New York: Viking Press, 1973), p. 227.

13. Ibid.

14. Ibid.

15. Allen E. Wiesen, *Positive Therapy* (Chicago: Nelson Hall, 1977), esp. chapter one, entitled "Negative Therapy," pp. 1–13.

16. Colin Wilson, *New Pathways in Psychology* (New York: Taplinger Publishing Company, 1972), pp. 189–195.

17. Ibid., p. 190.

18. Ibid.

19. Ignatius of Loyola, *Spiritual Diary,* cited by Adolf Haas in "The Mysticism of St. Ignatius According to His *Spiritual Diary,*" in *Ignatius of Loyola: His Personality and Spiritual Heritage,* edited by Friedrich Wulf, S.J. (St. Louis: Institute of Jesuit Sources, 1977), pp. 164–199.

20. Cf. Gilles Cusson, S.J., *Pédagogie de l'expérience spirituelle personnelle* (Montréal: Les Editions Bellarmin, 1968), pp. 77ff., esp. ft. 4, pp. 77–78.

21. Louis J. Puhl, p. 51, no. 109.

22. Cf. especially Bernard Lonergan, "Consciousness and the Trinity," an unpublished talk delivered at the North American College, Rome, in the Spring of 1963. The talk is available in the Lonergan archives at Regis College in Toronto, Ontario, Canada.

23. Bernard Lonergan, *De Deo Trino, II, Pars Systematica* (Rome: Gregorian University Press, 1964), pp. 225–235.

24. Cf. Peter Bier, "Meaning in Our Relation to the Trinity," *Trinification of the World,* edited by Thomas A. Dunne and Jean-Marc Laporte (Toronto: Regis College Press, 1978), p. 10.

25. *Roman Missal: Lectionary for Mass* (New York: Catholic Book Publishing Company, 1970), p. 135.

26. David M. Stanley, S.J., *Jesus in Gethsemane* (New York: Paulist Press, 1980), p. 14.

27. Karl Rahner, *Foundations of Christian Faith* (New York: Seabury Press, 1978), p. 307.

28. Ibid., p. 308.

29. Pius XII, *The Mystical Body of Christ* (London: Catholic Truth Society, 1943), pp. 46–47.

30. Teresa of Avila, *Interior Castle* (New York: Doubleday Image Book, 1961), pp. 179–180.

31. Ibid., p. 180.

32. James M. Gustafson, "The Relation of the Gospels to the Moral Life," *Jesus and Mary's Hope,* Vol. II, edited by Donald Miller and D. Y. Hadidian (Pittsburgh: Pittsburgh Theological Seminary, 1971), p. 113.

33. Bernard Tyrrell, *Christotherapy* (New York: Seabury Press, 1975), pp. 188–203.

34. Thomas Merton, *The Seven Storey Mountain* (New York: Harcourt Brace and Company, 1948), pp. 108–113.

35. John M. Oesterreicher, *Walls Are Crumbling* (New York: Devin-Adair Company, 1952), p. 120.

36. Gerald Brenan, *St. John of the Cross* (Cambridge: Cambridge University Press, 1976), p. 213.

37. Adolf Haas, "The Mysticism of St. Ignatius According to His Spiritual Diary," p. 183.

38. Ibid.

39. Ibid., p. 184.

40. Juliana of Norwich, *Showings,* translated with an introduction by Edmund Colledge, O.S.A. and James Walsh, S.J. (New York: Paulist Press, 1978), p. 279.

41. Ibid., p. 298.

42. Gerald Brenan, *St. John of the Cross,* pp. 165–166.

43. Louis J. Puhl, p. 49, no. 104.

44. David Fleming, *A Contemporary Reading of the Spiritual Exercises* (St. Louis: Institute of Jesuit Sources, 1976), p. 41.

45. Louis J. Puhl, p. 60, no. 140.

46. Ibid.

47. Ibid., p. 61, no. 144.

48. Ibid., p. 60, no. 139.

49. David Fleming, p. 42.

50. Cf. *The Philokalia,* translated and edited by G.E.H. Palmer, Philip Sherrard and Kallistos Ware, Vol. I (London: Faber and Faber, 1979), pp. 20ff.

51. Ibid., p. 24.

52. Ibid., p. 25.

53. Ibid., p. 27.

54. Evagrius Ponticus, *The Praktikos,* translated with an introduction and notes by John Eudes Bamberger O.C.S.O. (Spencer, Mass: Cistercian Publications, 1970), pp. 16ff.

55. Ibid., p. 20.

56. Cf. *The Philokalia,* pp. 72–108.

57. *The Praktikos,* p. 32.

58. Ibid., p. 33.

59. Cf. Chart in this book, p. 180.

60. Evagrius Ponticus, *The Praktikos,* p. 18.

61. Ibid., p. 20.

62. Ibid., p. 35.

63. Ibid., p. 76.

64. Dante, *The Purgatorio,* translated by John Ciardi (New York: Mentor, 1961), p. 112.

65. Ibid., p. 139.

66. Cf. Chart in this book, p. 180.

67. Cf. John C. Lilly and Joseph E. Hart, "The Arica Training," *Transpersonal Psychologies,* edited by Charles T. Tart (New York: Harper and Row, 1977), pp. 331–339.

68. Ibid., p. 337.

69. Ibid.

70. Ibid., p. 335.

71. Ibid., p. 337.

72. Ibid., p. 338.

73. Cf. Matthias Neuman, O.S.B., "Toward an Integrated Theory of Imagination," *International Philosophical Quarterly,* Vol. XVIII, no. 3, September, 1978, p. 262. This and the following quotation are Neuman's summary of Durand's position.

74. Ibid.

75. Harold Greenwald, *Decision Theory* (New York: Peter H. Wyden, 1973), p. 18.

76. The original Ignatian title is *Three Classes of Men.* Cf. Louis J. Puhl, p. 64, no. 149.

77. Ibid., p. 64, no. 150.

78. Ibid., no. 153.

79. Ibid., no. 154.

80. Ibid., no. 155.

81. Bertrand de Margerie, S.J., *Theological Retreat* (Chicago: Franciscan Herald Press, 1976), p. 130.

82. Saint Ignatius also suggests other possible mysteries for meditations, such as the conversion of Magdalene, the Transfiguration, etc.

83. Edward Yarnold, "The Basics of the Spiritual Exercises," *The Way: Supplement 16* (Summer, 1972), p. 13.

84. Cf. Erik Erikson, *Childhood and Society* (New York: Norton and Company, 1963), pp. 247–274.

85. R. K. Harrison, "Healing, Health," *The Interpreter's Dictionary of the Bible,* Vol. II, edited by George Arthur Buttrick (New York: Abingdon Press, 1962), p. 547.

86. Louis J. Puhl, S.J., p. 69, no. 165.

87. Ibid., no. 166.

88. Ibid., no. 167.

89. Ibid.

90. Ibid., pp. 71–78, nos. 169–189.

91. Ann and Barry Ulanov, *Religion and the Unconscious* (Philadelphia: Westminster Press, 1975), p. 198.

92. Anonymous Authors, *Twelve Steps and Twelve Traditions* (New York: Alcoholics Anonymous World Services, 1971), p. 35.

93. Harry M. Tiebout, M.D., *The Act of Surrender in the Therapeutic Process* (New York: National Council on Alcoholism), p. 3.

94. Ibid., p. 14.

Chapter Eleven

1. Gaston Fessard, *La Dialectique des Exercises spirituels de saint Ignace de Loyola* (Paris: Aubier, 1956), I, p. 40.

2. *The Sacramentary* (New York: Catholic Book Publishing Company, 1974), p. 389.

3. Cf. Fessard, p. 118.

4. Louis J. Puhl, S.J., *The Spiritual Exercises of Saint Ignatius* (Chicago: Loyola University Press, 1951), p. 84, no. 203.

5. Ibid., p. 81, no. 193.

6. Ibid., p. 82, no. 197.

7. Bernard of Clairvaux, *The Works of Bernard of Clairvaux* (Washington, D.C.: Cistercian Publications, Consortium Press, 1974), Vol. 5, p. 115. The citation is capitalized in the text.

8. Ibid., p. 117. The citation is capitalized in the text.

9. Cf. Joseph A. Bracken, S.J., "The Double 'Principle and Foundation' in the *Spiritual Exercises*," *Woodstock Letters*, Vol. 98 (1969), pp. 320–322; 331."

10. Bernard of Clairvaux, p. 118. The citation is capitalized in the text.

11. I do not wish to imply that the election always occurs in the case of an individual making the *Exercises* at a point between the Second and Third Weeks. I am simply describing the election as it ideally occurs in the classical movement of the *Exercises.*

12. Walter Kasper, *Jesus the Christ* (New York: Paulist Press, 1976), pp. 117–118.

13. Gaston Fessard, p. 114, ft. 1. The translation is my own.

14. I am indebted to Fessard for the basic example of the analogy between the offering of Christ and that of the retreatant. Cf. pp. 114–115.

15. Andras Angyal, *Neurosis and Treatment: A Holistic Theory* (New York: Viking Press, 1973), p. 260.

16. Ibid.

17. David Stewart, *Thirst for Freedom* (Center City, Minnesota: Hazelden, 1960), p. 38.

18. David Stanley, *Jesus in Gethsemane* (New York: Paulist Press, 1979); cf. pp. 274–275.

19. Ibid., p. 139.

20. Louis J. Puhl, p. 145, no. 325, 12.

21. Ibid.

22. Erik Erikson, *Childhood and Society* (New York: Norton and Company, 1963), p. 274.

23. Ibid.

24. Andras Angyal, p. 254.

25. Louis J. Puhl, p. 148, no. 332.4.

26. Andras Angyal, p. 254.

27. Bernard Tyrrell, *Christotherapy* (New York: Seabury Press, 1975), pp. 107–134.

28. Louis J. Puhl, p. 82, no. 196.

29. Ibid.

30. Karl Rahner, "On the Evangelical Counsels," *Theological Investigations,* Vol. VIII (New York: Herder and Herder, 1971), pp. 155–156, ft. 26.

31. Ken Keyes, Jr., *Handbook to Higher Consciousness* (Berkeley: Living Love Center, 1975).

32. Ibid., p. 21.

33. Louis J. Puhl, p. 12, no. 23.

34. Ibid.

35. Ibid., p. 82, no. 197.

36. Ibid., p. 69, no. 167.

37. *The Cloud of Unknowing,* translated by William Johnston (New York: Doubleday and Company, Inc., 1973), pp. 187–188. For an excellent contemporary expression of imageless prayer see M. Basil Pennington, O.C.S.O., *Centering Prayer* (Garden City: Doubleday and Company, 1980).

38. John of the Cross, *The Collected Works of St. John of the Cross,* translated by Kieran Kavanaugh and Otilio Rodriguez (Washington, D.C.: Institute of Carmelite Studies, 1973), p. 423.

39. Ibid., p. 124.

40. Ibid., p. 549.

Chapter Twelve

1. Cf. Louis J. Puhl, *The Spiritual Exercises of St. Ignatius* (Chicago: Loyola University Press, 1951), pp. 101–103, nos. 230–237.

2. Ibid., p. 95, no. 221.

3. Cf. Xavier Léon-Dufour, *Resurrection and the Message of Easter* (New York: Holt, Rinehart and Winston, 1974), pp. 244; 255–261.

4. Louis J. Puhl, p. 95, no. 219.

5. Cf. Bernard J. Tyrrell, S.J., *Christotherapy* (New York: Seabury Press, 1975), pp. 19–24.

6. Cf. John Burns, *The Answer to Addiction* (New York: Harper and Row, 1975), pp. 174; 176–177.

7. Anonymous Authors, *Alcoholics Anonymous* (New York: Alcoholics Anonymous World Services, Inc., 1955), p. 11.

8. Cf. John Burns, *The Answer to Addiction,* pp. 173, 176–178.

9. Anonymous Authors, *Alcoholics Anonymous,* p. 14.

10. Ibid.

11. Anonymous Authors, *Twelve Steps and Twelve Traditions* (New York: Alcoholics Anonymous World Services, 1971), p. 98.

12. Louis J. Puhl, pp. 95–96, no. 223.

13. Ibid., p. 97, no. 229. Note IV.

14. For a discussion of the relationship between encounters of the apostolic witnesses with the Risen Jesus and the faith-encounters of contemporary Christians with Jesus read Walter Kasper, *Jesus the Christ* (New York: Paulist Press, 1976), pp. 136–140.

15. Louis J. Puhl, pp. 97–98, no. 229, Note IV.

16. Abraham Maslow, *Religious Values and Peak-Experiences* (New York: The Viking Press, 1970), pp. 91–94.

17. Ibid., p. 89.

18. Bruce Vawter, "The Gospel According to John," *The Jerome Biblical Commentary,* edited by Raymond Brown, S.S., Joseph Fitzmyer, S.J. and Roland Murphy, O. Carm. (New Jersey: Prentice-Hall, 1968), p. 464.

19. Louis J. Puhl, p. 96, no. 224.

20. John of the Cross, *The Collected Works of John of the Cross,* translated by Kieran Kavanaugh, O.C.D. and Otilio Rodriguez, O.C.D. (Washington, D.C.: Institute of Carmelite Studies, 1973), p. 672, no. 57.

21. Anonymous Authors, *Twelve Steps and Twelve Traditions,* p. 109. The quotation is in italics in the text.

22. Louis J. Puhl, p. 101, no. 230.1.

23. Ibid., p. 101, no. 231.2.

24. Cf. Michael Buckley, S.J., "The Contemplation to Attain Love," *The Way: Supplement 24,* Spring 1975, pp. 92–104 and Edouard Pousset, S.J., *Life in Faith and Freedom,* translated and edited by Eugene L. Donahue, S.J. (St. Louis: Institute of Jesuit Sources, 1980), pp. 195–199. I am indebted to Gaston Fessard, Michael Buckley and Edouard Pousset for a number of important insights into the meaning and role of the *Contemplation to Attain the Love of God* in the *Spiritual Exercises.*

25. Anonymous authors, *Twelve Steps and Twelve Transitions,* p. 109. The quotation is in italics in the text.

26. Cf. Michael Buckley, S.J., "The Contemplation to Attain Love, pp. 92–93, esp. ft. 9.

27. Louis J. Puhl, p. 101, no. 233.

28. Ibid., p. 101, no. 234.

29. Ibid., p. 102, no. 235.

30. Ibid., p. 103, no. 236.

31. Edouard Pousset, S.J., *Life in Faith and Freedom,* p. 198.

32. Louis J. Puhl, S.J., p. 103, no. 237.

33. Cf. John Navone, S.J., and Thomas Cooper, *Tellers of the Word* (New York: Le Jacq Publishing, 1981). This book of Navone and Cooper is the best systematic work on the theology of story.

34. Louis J. Puhl, S.J., p. 102, no. 234. First Point.

35. Dante, *The Paradiso,* translated with notes by John Ciardi (New York: New American Library, 1970), p. 106, line 24.

36. Cf. Dietrich von Hildebrand, *Liturgy and Personality* (New York: Longmans, Green and Co., 1943), p. 15.

37. Cf. Marie Michel Philipon, O.P., *The Spiritual Doctrine of Sister Elizabeth of the Trinity* (Westminster, Maryland: Newman Bookshop, 1947), p. 86.

38. *The Sacramentary* (New York: Catholic Book Publishing, 1974), p. 453.

Chapter Thirteen

1. Bernard Lonergan, "Religious Studies and Theology," a lecture presented as The Donald Mathers Memorial Lecture at Queens University, Kingston, Canada, 1976, p. 7.

2. Bernard Tyrrell, *Christotherapy* (New York: Seabury Press, 1975), pp. 196–197.

3. Sigmund Freud, "Inhibitions, Symptoms and Anxiety," *The Complete Psychological Works of Sigmund Freud,* Vol. 20 (London: Hogarth Press, [n.d.], pp. 136–137.

4. John Evoy, *The Rejected: Psychological Consequences of Parental Rejection* (University Park: Pennsylvania State University Press, 1981), p. 131.

5. Cf. Rollo May, *The Meaning of Anxiety* (New York: W. W. Norton and Company, Inc., 1977), pp. 220–221.

6. Kazimierz Dabrowski with Michael M. Piechowski, *Theory of Levels of Emotional Development,* Vol. I, *Multilevelness and Positive Disintegration* (Oceanside, New York: Dabor Science Publications, 1977), p. 86.

7. Ibid., p. 89.

8. Ibid., p. 87.

9. Ibid.

10. Ibid., p. 90.

11. Ibid., p. 89.

12. Ibid.

13. Rollo May, *The Meaning of Anxiety,* p. 381.

14. Maurice Nesbitt, *Where No Fear Was* (London: Epworth Press, 1966), p. 20.

15. Albert Ellis and Robert Harper, *A New Guide to Rational Living* (Englewood Cliffs, N.J.: Prentice-Hall, Inc., 1975), p. 145.

16. These are titles given to these Psalms in the Jerusalem Bible.

17. Hannah Hurnard, *Hinds' Feet on High Places* (Wheaton, Illinois: Tyndale House Publishers, Inc., 1975).

18. Ibid., p. 11.

19. Hannah Hurnard, *Mountains of Spices,* (Old Tappan, New Jersey: Fleming H. Revell Company, 1973), p. 6.

20. Maurice Nesbitt, *Where No Fear Was,* p. ix.

21. Viktor Frankl, *The Unheard Cry for Meaning* (New York: Simon and Schuster, 1978), esp. pp. 114–150.

22. Ibid., p. 114.

23. Viktor Frankl, *Psychotherapy and Existentialism* (New York: Simon and Schuster, 1967), p. 146.

24. Viktor Frankl, *The Unheard Cry for Meaning,* p. 115.

25. For evidence that the use of paradoxical intention does not worsen the psychic state of the patient or simply cause symptom substitution, cf. *The Unheard Cry for Meaning,* p. 124.

26. Viktor Frankl, *Psychotherapy and Existentialism,* pp. 45–46.

27. Ibid., pp. 146–147.

28. Rollo May, *The Meaning of Anxiety,* p. 377. The statement in the original is in italics.

29. Hannah Hurnard, *Hinds' Feet on High Places,* pp. 54–58.

30. Ibid., p. 204.

31. Leslie Weatherhead, *Prescriptions for Anxiety,* (Nashville:Abingdon Press, 1956), p. 31. The second sentence which I quote is in italics in the original.

32. Abraham Low, *Mental Health Through Will Training* (Boston: Christopher Publishing House, 1968), p. 312. The original statement is in italics.

33. Ibid., pp. 141–145.

34. Ibid., p. 142.

35. Louis J. Puhl, *The Spiritual Exercises of St. Ignatius* (Chicago: Loyola University Press, 1951), p. 145, no. 325.12.

36. Ibid.

37. I do not intend to imply that I necessarily accept all the views expressed by the founders of these two movements in their various writings.

38. Louis J. Puhl, *The Spiritual Exercises of St. Ignatius,* cf. p. 141, no. 313; p. 147, no. 328.

39. Abraham Low, *Mental Health through Will Training,* pp. 82 ff.

40. Ibid.

41. Abraham Low, *Selections,* Vol. I (Chicago: Recovery Inc., 1966), p. 37.

42. Louis J. Puhl, *The Spiritual Exercises of St. Ignatius,* pp. 142–143, no. 381.5.

43. Hannah Hurnard, *Hinds' Feet on High Places,* p. 189.

44. John of the Cross, *The Collected Works of St. John of the Cross,* translated by Kieran Kavanaugh, O.C.D. and Otilio Rodriguez, O.C.D. (Washington, D.C.: Institute of Carmelite Studies, 1973), p. 520.

45. Michael Stock, " 'Meaning' in Mental and Emotional Suffering," *Bulletin of the National Guild of Catholic Psychiatrists,* Vol. 23, 1977, p. 50.

46. Ibid., p. 52.

47. Ibid., p. 53.
48. Ibid.
49. Ibid.

Chapter Fourteen

1. Carroll E. Izard, *Human Emotions* (New York: Plenum Press, 1977), p. 331.
2. Ibid.
3. Silvano Arieti, "Cognition and Feeling," *Feelings and Emotions*, edited by Magda Arnold (New York: Academic Press, 1970), p. 136.
4. Aaron Beck, *Cognitive Therapy and the Emotional Disorders* (New York: International Universities Press, Inc., 1976).
5. Ibid., p. 65.
6. Ibid.
7. Ibid., p. 71.
8. Ibid.
9. Ibid.
10. Ibid., p. 72.
11. Robert C. Solomon, *The Passions* (Garden City, New York: Anchor Press, 1976), p. 287.
12. John Bowlby, *Attachment and Loss II: Separation* (Harmondsworth, Middlesex: Penguin Books, Ltd., 1975), p. 286.
13. Ibid.
14. John Evoy, *The Rejected: Psychological Consequences of Parental Rejection* (University Park: The Pennsylvania State University Press, 1981), p. 170.
15. Ibid., p. 171.
16. Robert Solomon, *The Passions,* p. 288.
17. John Evoy, *The Rejected,* p. 170.
18. Kazimierz Dabrowski with Michael M. Piechowski, *Theory of Levels of Emotional Development: Vol. I—Multilevelness and Positive Disintegration* (Oceanside, New York: Dabor Science Publications, 1977), p. 133.
19. Ibid.
20. Ibid., p. 134.
21. Ibid., p. 135.
22. Ibid.
23. Cf. Bernard Tyrrell, "The Role of Conversion in the Avoidance of 'Burnout,' " *Lonergan Workshop Papers,* 1978. This paper will be published in a forthcoming volume of the *Lonergan Workshop Papers.*
24. John Evoy, *The Rejected,* p. 169.
25. Linda Amadeo and James J. Gill, "Managing Anger, Hostility and Aggression," *Human Development,* Vol. I, No. 3, Fall, 1980, p. 39.

26. Carl R. Rogers, *Client-Centered Therapy* (Boston: Houghton Mifflin Company, 1965), p. 148.

27. Conrad W. Baars, *Feeling and Healing Your Emotions* (Plainfield, New Jersey: Logos International, 1979), p. 116.

28. Bernard Lonergan, *Method in Theology* (New York: Herder and Herder, 1972), p. 34.

29. Conrad Baars, *Feeling and Healing Your Emotions,* p. 183.

30. Ibid., p. 149.

31. Paul Hauck, *Overcoming Frustration and Anger* (Philadelphia: Westminster Press, 1974).

32. Albert Ellis and Robert A. Harper, *A New Guide to Rational Living* (Englewood Cliffs, N.J.: Prentice-Hall, Inc., 1975), p. 113.

33. Ibid. The original statement is in italics.

34. Conrad Baars, *Feeling and Healing Your Emotions,* p. 229.

35. Abraham Low, *Mental Health Through Will Training* (Boston: Christopher Publishing House, 1968).

36. Ibid., pp. 152–156.

37. Paul Hauck, *Overcoming Frustration and Anger,* p. 30.

38. Conrad Baars, *Feeling and Healing Your Emotions,* p. 181.

39. Ibid., pp. 184–185.

40. Besides Conrad Baars' work just cited cf. Dennis and Matthew Linn, *Healing Life's Hurts* (New York: Paulist Press, 1977), esp. pp. 102–117. I highly recommend the article by the editors of *Human Development* entitled "Anger, Hostility, and Aggression," Vol. I, No. 2, Summer, 1980, pp. 36–42 and the article by Linda Amadeo and James Gill, "Managing Anger, Hostility, and Aggression," as cited above.

41. Abraham Low, *Mental Health Through Will Training,* pp. 252ff.

42. Ibid., pp. 284–290.

43. Ibid., pp. 291ff.

44. Ibid., pp. 296–303, esp. p. 298.

45. Kazimierz Dabrowski with Michael M. Piechowski, *Theory of Levels of Emotional Development: Vol. I—Multilevelness and Positive Disintegration,* p. 49.

46. Ibid., p. 51.

47. Hannah Hurnard, *Mountains of Spices* (Old Tappan, New Jersey: Fleming H. Revell Company, 1973).

48. Herbert V. Guenther and Leslie S. Kawamura, *Mind in Buddhist Psychology* (Emeryville, California: Dharma Publishing, 1975), p. 64.

49. Ibid.

50. Ibid., p. 67.

51. Ibid.

52. Thomas Hora, *Existential Metapsychiatry* (New York: Seabury Press, 1977), cf. pp. 64–65, 48, 103ff.

53. Neurotics Anonymous, *The Laws of Mental and Emotional Illness* (Washington, D.C: Neurotics Anonymous, 1965–1979), cf. pp. 59ff. *Neurotics Anonymous* is not to be confused with *Emotions Anonymous.* The two groups are completely separate.

54. Cf. Carroll E. Izard, *Human Emotions,* p. 333.

Chapter Fifteen

1. Kazimierz Dabrowski with Michael M. Piechowski, *Theories of Levels of Emotional Development: Vol. I—Multilevelness and Positive Disintegration* (Oceanside, New York: Dabor Science Publications, 1977), p. 130.

2. Thomas Aquinas, *The Summa Theologica,* translated by Fathers of the English Dominican Province and revised by Daniel J. Sullivan in *Great Books of the Western World,* Vol. 19, edited by Robert Maynard Hutchins (Chicago: Encyclopaedia Britannica, Inc., 1952), Part I of Second Part, Q. 36, a. 1, p. 781.

3. Robert C. Solomon, *The Passions* (Garden City, New York: Anchor Press/Doubleday, 1976), p. 357.

4. Kazimierz Dabrowski, p. 130.

5. Ibid., pp. 130–131. It is difficult to state clearly when sadness passes into depression. Some would say that it is principally a matter of the intensity and duration of the sadness. I might also note that just as Dabrowski sees some forms of sadness as signs of the occurrence of a positive disintegration and as providing an impetus for growth so Dr. Roberto Assagioli holds that as a result of a spiritual awakening a person can sometimes experience a type of depression in the aftermath. This can lead to despair or it can be utilized as a means of growth. It can become a means of growth if it is made clear to the sufferer that "the exalted state he has experienced could not, by its very nature, last forever and that reaction was inevitable. . . . The recognition that this descent or 'fall' is a natural happening affords emotional and mental relief and encourages the subject to undertake the arduous task confronting him on the path to Self-realization": *Psychosynthesis* (New York: Viking Press, 1971), p. 49. The Christotherapist needs to be able to distinguish clearly between forms of sadness and depression which are phases in spiritual crises and those which are expressions of deep neurotic deformation. The Christotherapist uses a different combination of spiritual and psychological means in dealing respectively with spiritual desolations and neurotic depression.

6. Ibid., p. 131.

7. Aaron Beck, *Cognitive Therapy and the Emotional Disorders* (New York: International Universities Press, Inc., 1976), pp. 105–106.

8. Aaron Beck, *Depression: Causes and Treatment* (Philadelphia: University of Pennsylvania Press, 1972).

9. Aaron Beck, *Cognitive Therapy and the Emotional Disorders.*
10. Ibid., p. 105.
11. Ibid., p. 74.
12. Thomas Hora, *Existential Metapsychiatry* (New York: Seabury Press, 1977), p. 207.
13. Willard Gaylin, *Feelings* (New York: Harper and Row, 1979), p. 106.
14. Ann and Barry Ulanov, *Religion and the Unconscious* (Philadelphia: Westminster Press, 1975), p. 198.
15. Ibid., p. 199.
16. Thomas Hora, p. 209.

Chapter Sixteen

1. My chapter on guilt is placed within the Appendix because it is largely a stylistically revised version of a section of an article entitled "Christotherapy: A Concrete Instance of a Christian Psychotherapy," which appeared in *The Bulletin of the National Guild of Catholic Psychiatrists,* 23, 1977, pp. 54–73. Cf. esp. pp. 66–73.
2. Edward Stein, *Guilt: Theory and Therapy* (Philadelphia: Westminster Press, 1968).
3. Ibid., p. 37.
4. O. Hobart Mowrer, *The Crisis in Psychiatry and Religion* (New York: Van Nostrand Reinhold Company, 1961), esp. pp. 142–155.
5. Stein, *Guilt: Theory and Therapy,* p. 142.
6. Mowrer, *The Crisis in Psychiatry and Religion,* p. 20.
7. Stein, *Guilt, Theory and Therapy,* p. 143.
8. John Glaser, "Conscience and Superego," *Psyche and Spirit,* edited by John Heaney (New York: Paulist Press, 1973), pp. 33–55.
9. Ibid., pp. 41–42.
10. Ibid., p. 41.
11. Ibid.
12. Herbert Fingarette, *The Self in Transformation* (New York: Harper and Row, 1963).
13. Ibid., p. 168.
14. Ibid., p. 169.
15. Thomas Hora, *Existential Metapsychiatry* (New York: Seabury Press, 1977).
16. Ibid., p. 103.
17. Ibid., p. 104.
18. Ibid., p. 105.
19. Stein, *Guilt: Theory and Therapy,* p. 162.
20. Ibid., p. 163.
21. William Stekel, *Compulsion and Doubt* (New York: Grosset and Dunlap, 1962), p. 229.

22. Fingarette, *The Self in Transformation,* p. 150.

23. John Drakeford, *Integrity Therapy* (Nashville: Broadman Press, 1967), pp. 9–10.

24. Carl Jung, *The Collected Works,* 16, Bollinger Series XX (Princeton: Princeton University Press, 1959), p. 16.

25. Anna Terruwe, *Psychopathic Personality and Neurosis* (New York: P. J. Kenedy, 1958), p. 96.

26. Kazimierz Dabrowski, *Personality Shaping Through Positive Disintegration* (Boston: Little, Brown, 1967), p. 27.

Name Index

Subject Index